D1590841

Cavalry on the Roads to Gettysburg

Kilpatrick at Hanover and Hunterstown

By

George A. Rummel III

WHITE MANE BOOKS

This White Mane Books publication
was printed by
Beidel Printing House, Inc.
63 West Burd Street
Shippensburg, PA 17257-0152 USA

In respect for the scholarship contained herein, the acid-free paper used in this book meets the guidelines for permanence and durability of the Committee on Production Guidelines for Book Longevity of the Council on Library Resources.

For a complete list of available publications
please write
White Mane Books
Division of White Mane Publishing Company, Inc.
P.O. Box 152
Shippensburg, PA 17257-0152 USA

Library of Congress Cataloging-in-Publication Data

Rummel, George A., 1951-
    Cavalry on the roads to Gettysburg : Kilpatrick at Hanover and Hunterstown / by
George A. Rummel III.
        p. cm.
    Includes bibliographical references (p.) and index.
    ISBN 1-572-49174-4 (alk. paper)
    1. Hanover (York County, Pa.), Battle of, 1863. 2. Hunterstown (Pa.)--History,
Military--19th century. 3. Kilpatrick, Judson, 1836-1881. 4. United
States--History--Civil War, 1861-1865--Cavalry operations. 5. United States. Army of
the Potomac. 6. Generals--United States--History--19th century. I. Title.

E475.51 .R86 2000
973.7'34 21--dc21
                                                                99-045935

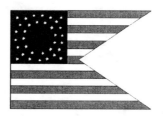

Contents

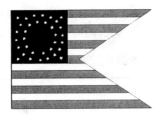

Illustrations

Abbreviations

Anthony	=	William Anthony, *Anthony's History of the Battle of Hanover (York County, Pennsylvania) Tuesday, June 30, 1863* (Hanover, Pa.: William Anthony, 1945)
Boudrye	=	Louis N. Boudrye, *Historic Records of the Fifth New York Cavalry, First Ira Harris Guard* (Albany: S. R. Gray, 1865)
GAR III	=	George A. Rummel III
LC	=	Library of Congress
NA	=	National Archives
USAMHI	=	U.S. Army Military History Institute

Preface

June 1863 was a momentous period of adjustment for the newly re-organized Cavalry Corps of the Army of the Potomac. Only recently, Alfred Pleasonton had taken the reins of the battered corps and was in the process of instituting several changes that would impact the lives of many individuals. For three weeks in June the mounted branch of the Army of the Potomac had fought a series of cavalry actions against a formidable, if not superior, opponent in the form of J. E. B. Stuart's cavalrymen in the Army of Northern Virginia. After two long years of war, the Union horsemen finally held their own during fierce contests at such places as Brandy Station, Upperville, Middleburg, and Aldie. The fortunes of the Yankee cavalry had finally begun to turn in their favor.

Additionally, at the end of June, the fates of three novice brigadier generals were tied very closely to that of the overall destiny of the Cavalry Corps. The three new brigadiers, Kilpatrick, Farnsworth and Custer, served with the utmost distinction in their division. Although Elon Farnsworth's life was cut short after only five days in command of his new brigade, Judson Kilpatrick, and particularly George Custer, continued their careers throughout the war and provided an impetus for the Union horsemen previously unknown in the Cavalry Corps.

As the Army of the Potomac began to march north to fulfill their destiny at Gettysburg, General Kilpatrick's division was given the task of screening the center of the advancing force. That assignment placed the newest division in the Cavalry Corps on a direct path of confrontation with General Stuart and his men. On June 30, 1863, those two forces of cavalry encountered each other, somewhat unexpectedly, in the small town of Hanover, Pennsylvania. The ensuing furious fighting in the streets of the town proved, once again, that the Union cavalry could contend on an equal basis with their battle-hardened opponents. Showing that their tenacious stance at Hanover was not an accident, the 3rd Division repeated their performance a few days later at Hunterstown.

The new brigadier generals demonstrated that they were capable of performing their unprecedented assignments. They positively reinforced Alfred Pleasonton's decision of placing them, three relatively inexperienced cavalry officers, in command of a division and two brigades.

George A. Rummel III
Bridgeport, West Virginia
April 1999

Acknowledgments

For well over twenty-five years, the cavalry actions at the small Pennsylvania communities of Hanover and Hunterstown have held a special fascination for me. Undoubtedly, that attraction, in no small part, is related to my overall interest in the Cavalry Corps of the Army of the Potomac during the Gettysburg Campaign. Over the course of those many years I had the opportunity to accumulate a substantial amount of information from a multitude of sources, much of it concerning the fighting at both Hanover and Hunterstown. I would like to take this opportunity to mention many of the research collections and offer my sincere thanks, although somewhat belatedly, to the members of their staffs. Some of them include:

Adams County Historical Society, Gettysburg, Pa.;
Adams County Public Library, Gettysburg, Pa.;
Gettysburg National Military Park, Gettysburg, Pa.;
Hanover Public Library, Hanover, Pa.;
Library of Congress, Washington, D.C.;
National Archives, Washington, D.C.;
Virginia Historical Society, Richmond, Va.;
U.S. Army Military History Institute, Carlisle Barracks, Pa.
   (Archives, Library and Photographic branches);
U.S. Military Academy, West Point, N.Y.
   (Archives and Library branches);

I would like to express my deep appreciation to Harold E. Collier of White Mane Publishing for accepting this book for publication. I, also, wish to thank my editor at Beidel Printing House, Beverly Kuhn, for her knowledgeable assistance in correcting the many shortcomings submitted with the first copy of the manuscript.

And finally, I would like to thank my wife, Patricia A. Rummel for her support in this latest project. As usual, she endured another round of reading, and rereading, my manuscript and offered her own invaluable insights and suggestions about ways to improve it. I truly appreciate her reasoned comments, as well as her devotion to seeing this adventure through from beginning to end.

Chapter 1:

Hanover and Hunterstown

HE last few days of the month of June 1863, along with the opening days of July, proved to be anything but routine and normal particularly for the loyal citizens living near the Mason-Dixon Line. The cities, towns, and numerous country hamlets on both sides of the dividing line between the counties of south-central Pennsylvania and north-central Maryland would soon host some very unexpected and extremely unwished-for guests. Very shortly the peace and serenity, that the region had known throughout the first two years of the Civil War, would be supplanted by the sights, sounds, and associated horrors of men engaged in mortal combat in the very midst of some of the area's most tranquil communities.

During the Civil War's crucial summer months of 1863, destiny cruelly dictated that thousands and thousands of soldiers from two tremendously powerful armies—the United States' Army of the Potomac and the Confederacy's Army of Northern Virginia—would clash numerous times throughout a brief three week period. Both armies soon would cross the Potomac River from their most recent engagements and encampments in the battle-devastated portions of northern Virginia. After crossing the river, one major battle and dozens of lesser known skirmishes and engagements, usually totally unanticipated by both factions, broke out amid the bucolic and pastoral surroundings in the northern portions of central Maryland, as well as in a number of southern Pennsylvania localities.

After two very long and at times incredibly frustrating years of devastating warfare, the Confederate leadership in Richmond determined to try, again, to shift the war out of the ravaged arena of the state of Virginia and into the relatively unscathed Northern border states. The allure of the North's resources was a tremendous temptation not easily ignored by President Jefferson Davis' fledgling government or by General Robert Edward Lee's mighty Army of Northern Virginia. Davis, a graduate of the U.S. Military Academy (U.S.M.A.) at West Point in the Class of 1828 and Lee, likewise an alumnus of U.S.M.A. in the subsequent Class of 1829, both agreed the time was right to carry the war northward. The previous year had seen the Southern army maneuver into the western and central sections of Maryland, where they fought a score of relatively minor skirmishes and one significant battle with the Army of the Potomac near Sharpsburg. The Army of Northern Virginia's success was considerably less than what they anticipated. The Southerners gained no long-term accomplishments for their ultimate cause but the outcome now, they hoped, would prove more beneficial.

Now in the very middle of 1863 the moderately sized south-central Pennsylvania farming and industrial community of Gettysburg was about to take center stage and become world famous and forever remembered as the site of a major three-day battle between the armies of the North and the South. Gettysburg was only one of the many towns and villages affected by the Confederacy's current decision to move the two-year-old dispute north of the Mason-Dixon Line. Shortly, in conjunction with the three days of fighting about to take place on the main stage at Gettysburg, two other relatively minor, but highly significant, contests would unfold in the neighboring Pennsylvania villages of Hanover and Hunterstown. Practically ignored in the overall history of the campaign, the engagements fought just two days apart at those two normally quiet communities found the forces of both the United States and the Confederate States represented on the field of combat entirely by a considerable portion of their mounted troops—both artillery and cavalry.

Hanover, a small and usually serene and peaceful borough of roughly 1,650 residents, was just a short six miles north of the Mason-Dixon Line and in the far western section of York County, very close to the Adams County boundary. Initially named McAllistertown after Richard McAllister, one of the earliest settlers in the region, the town was originally established in 1763. Due to an increasing number of German settlers, McAllistertown was eventually renamed during the late eighteenth century in honor of the German town of Hannover. In 1860, the Pennsylvania community of Hanover included some 600 private homes or other inhabitable buildings within the actual town limits.[1]

As York County's second largest community, Hanover embraced a productive mixture of both agricultural and manufacturing interests. Besides the scores of individual farms in the surrounding area, most of the remainder of the town's adult population worked in some nineteen wagon and carriage manufacturing shops, seventeen blacksmith shops, or twelve cigar-producing factories. In addition there was a multitude of skilled iron workers, experienced clock assemblers, and accomplished weavers located throughout the industrious borough. Because of their unique status the citizens could, quite reasonably, expect a visit by an extremely hungry and seriously under-equipped Confederate Army. If the rapidly advancing Southern troops deemed to push that far north and east during their current invasion, the residents of the York County region would get their first unwished-for glimpse of the vaunted Army of Northern Virginia soldiers.

Chiefly, Hanover prospered because of its central location but most of all because of its rail connection to the industrial city of York in the east, the largest city in the county. A relatively new rail line also directly connected the town of Hanover to Gettysburg in the west. The Hanover, Hanover Junction and Gettysburg Railroad, running between Gettysburg and Hanover, had been completed, finally, some five years earlier in 1858.[2]

The same railroad ran to Hanover Junction in the east, where it connected with the much larger Northern Central Railroad that was the direct line to York. Besides the Hanover, Hanover Junction and Gettysburg Railroad running through the northern portions of Hanover, another rail line, the Littlestown Railroad, also directly connected the smaller Adams County community of Littlestown with Hanover. That seven-mile-long railroad had been in full operation between the two towns since November 1856.[3]

Along with their agricultural and industrial concerns, the inhabitants of Hanover were also well represented in their spiritual needs and concerns. The people had four churches with moderately sized congregations located inside the town's borders. Many of the residents, mostly of the Protestant faith, worshipped at the Emmanuel Reformed Church, St. Matthew's Lutheran Church, the United Brethren Church, or the Methodist Church. Many of those places of worship, as well as the town's public halls and other large meeting places would become extremely familiar to the scores of cavalrymen, both North and South, who fought and received serious wounds during the fighting in the streets and alleys of Hanover on June 30.[4]

Like many of the surrounding communities, Hanover had a number of improved roads radiating from near its center to other important towns and cities in the immediate vicinity. Hanover counted five main thoroughfares that directly connected it to other major towns. The York Road led to the city of York, located almost nineteen miles to the northeast. Another road, the Baltimore Pike, stretched to the largest city in Maryland over forty miles to the southeast. A third primary route, the Frederick Road, ran almost forty miles to that city in the southwest. The Carlisle Road extended roughly thirty miles toward the northwest to Carlisle. Finally, the Abbottstown Road connected that small town, ten miles to the north, with Hanover.

Most of the roads leading from Hanover consisted of hard-packed dirt. The one turnpike, the Baltimore Pike, was a macadamized road, paved with a compacted layer of gravel and small broken stones. In addition, all wagon and horse traffic from the community of Hanover could easily access additional secondary roads leading to Westminster, sixteen miles to the south, Harrisburg, thirty-six miles to the north or Gettysburg, fourteen miles to the west.

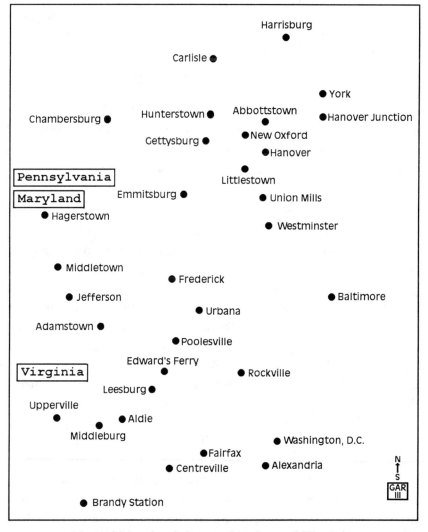

Map of Maryland, Pennsylvania, and Virginia
(GAR III)

For many days during the last weeks of June, the general population in the counties of south-central Pennsylvania had received frequent multiple warnings and dozens of other false alarms about the impending arrival of a swiftly advancing Confederate Army. However, now at the very end of June the rumors quickly changed to fact. Hundreds of refugee civilians from points as far away as Virginia and as near as Frederick County, Maryland and Chambersburg, Pennsylvania began to pass through the streets of Hanover in a valiant effort to outdistance the rapidly moving Rebel soldiers. Those displaced persons who journeyed through the town only tended to intensify the confusion and anxiety prevalent among the citizenry of Hanover. Everyone in the town knew what they had to do in the event of a full-scale Confederate invasion and they immediately directed all their efforts toward accomplishing that objective. Few, if any, of the residents really anticipated the complete magnitude of the events that would shortly develop, virtually, in their own backyards.[5]

The Hanover townsfolk learned from the seemingly endless stream of fleeing civilians that Lieutenant General Richard Stoddert Ewell (U.S.M.A., Class of 1840) and his troops had passed through Chambersburg to the west on the 23rd of the month. He and his battle-hardened soldiers were followed closely by the divisions of lieutenant generals James Longstreet (U.S.M.A., Class of 1842) and Ambrose Powell Hill (U.S.M.A., Class of 1847) on June 27. More disturbing news, as well as dozens of unsubstantiated rumors, continued to filter through the streets of Hanover. The hearsay concerned the passage of some additional Confederate infantry units through the city of York, supposedly heading for the Susquehanna River, on June 28. Other Southern units marched through Gettysburg to the west of Hanover. In addition, reports about thousands of Confederate cavalrymen sighted near Hanover continued to circulate around town. Obviously, many of the rumors were about to be proven factual this time.[6]

In frightened anticipation of the enemy's contemplated advance upon their peaceful community, many of the town's most affluent and prosperous citizens had already evacuated themselves and their families to safer havens. They transferred a great portion of their treasured personal property, including furniture and clothing, to the perceived safety of the Susquehanna River's eastern shore. Other members of the community unable, or unwilling, to move away from their homes and businesses simply buried, or otherwise secreted, their most precious possessions, money, and other worthwhile commodities being sought by the Southern forces. The majority of the citizens, both in the town and the surrounding countryside, also began moving most of their horses, cows, and other livestock toward the perceived safety of the Susquehanna.

The residents of Hanover recalled with dread that, less than a year earlier, they had come very close to another visit from the advancing Confederate Army during the Antietam Campaign in the autumn of 1862. At that time, the town's newspaper, the *Hanover Spectator,* in its Friday edition of September 12, 1862, reported that:

> The invasion of Maryland was on every tongue. The meagre accounts of the newspapers only sharpened the appetite for more news. On Sunday, the excitement reached its culmination. What before were nothing more than vague rumors assumed a condition of stern reality. A crisis was upon us. From early dawn, refugees from Frederick and Carroll Counties, Maryland, came pouring into town, some on horseback, others in carriages and wagons, each and all declaring that the enemy had crossed the Potomac and that Stonewall Jackson was in Frederick.[7]

Already during the midmorning of June 27, a small detachment of a Confederate cavalry force, led by thirty-year-old Lieutenant Colonel Elijah Viers White, had marched into Hanover and entered the town's Center Square, much to the surprise and consternation of many of the remaining local inhabitants.

Colonel White's mounted troopers were members of the 35th Battalion Virginia Cavalry from Brigadier General William Edmondson "Grumble" Jones' (U.S.M.A., Class of 1848) brigade of Major General James Ewell Brown Stuart's (U.S.M.A., Class of 1854) cavalry division. Those Southern horsemen happened to pass through the York County community on their way to Hanover Junction, the major rail center to the east of Hanover. There they hoped to wreak havoc with the railroad. The Confederates specifically wanted to destroy any bridges and railroad equipment. Additionally, they wanted to cut any telegraph wires found in the immediate vicinity. The tiny village of Hanover Junction was where the Hanover, Hanover Junction and Gettysburg Railroad intersected the main trunk line of the Northern Central Railroad.[8]

Lieutenant Colonel Elijah V. White,
35th Battalion Virginia Cavalry
(LC)

During their current foray through the Maryland and southern Pennsylvania countryside, Lieutenant Colonel White's mounted force had already paid a short surprise visit to Gettysburg in the west. They marched through the streets of that place a few hours earlier on that Saturday before their arrival in the center of Hanover. While in the town of Hanover, the Rebel cavalry troopers found little of any use to them due to the general evacuation or concealment of all the citizen's valuable property and equally valuable livestock. The gray-clad cavalrymen departed the town within a very short time without causing any major physical depredation or other damage to the town's buildings or its frightened residents. Finally, after two long years of bitter fighting, the Civil War had arrived at Hanover's front door.

Located about fifteen miles to the northwest of Hanover, Hunterstown, originally settled in the mid-eighteenth century by an Irish immigrant named David Hunter, was one of the oldest communities in Adams County.[9] During the remainder of the eighteenth century, Hunterstown was, at the very least, as prosperous and important as other surrounding communities in the immediate area, to include Gettysburg. The village of Hunterstown actually came very close to becoming the county seat of the newly designated Adams County in 1800, which had been formed from a portion of York County on January 22, 1800. Gettysburg won the distinction of becoming the county seat, mainly because of the town's leading citizen and founder, James Gettys. Mostly through Gettys' singular efforts, his town received the designation as the county seat principally because of his guarantee to raise the money needed to erect the necessary county buildings.[10]

By the summer of 1863 the tiny village of Hunterstown, numbering a little over a hundred homes and farms, was just like many other small farming communities in Pennsylvania. The center of the town boasted just one small hotel, a couple of general merchandise stores, a one-room schoolhouse, and a number of private homes, clustered together. Like the towns of Gettysburg and Hanover, the small community of Hunterstown served as the hub for a number of roads radiating to other points in the surrounding countryside. The roads principally connected Hunterstown to Gettysburg in the southwest, to Harrisburg in the northeast, and to York in the east. Unlike Gettysburg and Hanover there was no railroad line through Hunterstown. The closest rail connection was the Hanover, Hanover Junction and Gettysburg Railroad located to the south of the village near the York Pike in the direction of Gettysburg. In direct contrast to Gettysburg and Hanover, the town of Hunterstown had reached its zenith fifty years earlier and was now definitely on the decline during the mid-nineteenth century.

During the early evening hours of June 29, much as a similar visit to Hanover two days previously, a small detachment of Southern cavalry entered the quiet streets of Hunterstown. Those horsemen belonged to the late Brigadier General Thomas Reade Rootes Cobb's Georgia Legion of Brigadier General Wade Hampton's cavalry brigade. An officer identified only as Captain Crawford commanded the squadron, composed of roughly eighty-five officers and enlisted men from companies A and H.[11]

Detached from the main body of General Stuart's cavalry column, then located near Westminster, Maryland, the captain and his men were one of the many foraging expeditions dispatched to gather any available horses and supplies for the Southern cavalry force. Captain Crawford and his detail had orders to check the homes and surrounding farms in the Hunterstown area. In addition they were to gather any available intelligence of any military importance or of the presence of any of the enemy's forces.[12]

It is not extremely clear how successful or unsuccessful the little known Captain Crawford's foraging party was in obtaining any supplies or in reporting any information of military importance. Like the community of Hanover, the few hundred residents living around Hunterstown, had ample warning of the Confederate soldiers' approach and, most likely, concealed their valuables and animals as best they could. The nervous inhabitants were as ready for any invasion of their town as they could ever hope to be. They did not expect, and rightfully so, any actual fighting to take place so close to them. Their community could not be classified, in any reasonable manner, as being of any particular military importance to either the North or the South. Nonetheless, like their neighbors in the communities of Hanover and Gettysburg, the citizens of Hunterstown received an particularly unwelcome surprise when a fierce fight, luckily short in duration, suddenly erupted in the middle of their neighborhood.

Notes to Chapter One

1. 1860 U.S. Census for the Borough of Hanover, York County, Pennsylvania. National Archives, Washington, D.C.; Chamber of Commerce, Publisher, *Encounter at Hanover: Prelude to Gettysburg* (Hanover, Pa.: Hanover Chamber of Commerce, 1963), pp. 3-4.
2. Chamber of Commerce, *Encounter at Hanover*, p. 5.
3. Ibid., p. 6.
4. Ibid., p. 5.
5. William Anthony, *Anthony's History of the Battle of Hanover (York County, Pennsylvania) Tuesday, June 30, 1863* (Hanover, Pa.: William Anthony, 1945), p. 58.
6. John W. Schildt, *Roads to Gettysburg* (Parsons, W.Va.: McClain Printing Company, 1978), pp. 223-39; Chamber of Commerce, *Encounter at Hanover*, pp. 14-15.
7. *Hanover Spectator*, September 12, 1862.
8. Anthony, *Battle of Hanover*, p. 52.
9. Samuel P. Bates, *A History of Cumberland, Franklin and Adams Counties* (Chicago: Warner Beers & Co., 1886), p. 337.
10. William A. Frassanito, *The Gettysburg Bicentennial Album* (Gettysburg: The Gettysburg Bicentennial Committee, 1987), p. 6.
11. *Philadelphia Record*, September 15, 1901; Ezra J. Warner, *Confederate Generals in Gray: Lives of the Confederate Commanders* (Baton Rouge: Louisiana State University Press, 1959), p. 56. Thomas Cobb was the original colonel of the force that bore his surname as their unit designation. He received a mortal wound during the Battle of Fredericksburg and died December 13, 1862.
12. Wilbur S. Nye, "The Affair at Hunterstown," *Civil War Times Illustrated* (February 1971): 22-34.

Chapter 2:

__Revamp the Cavalry Corps__

HORTLY after the large-scale cavalry battle fought at Brandy Station, Virginia on June 9, 1863, then Brigadier General Alfred Pleasonton (U.S.M.A., Class of 1844) began to wage a vigorous and energetic campaign for permission to modify the size, general appearance, and specific duties of his command—the Cavalry Corps of the Army of the Potomac. For several months previously and mainly at the expense of his immediate commanding officer, Major General George Stoneman (U.S.M.A., Class of 1846), Pleasonton had lobbied army headquarters for authority to remodel the much maligned and abused horse corps. The surprising results of the hotly contested engagement with the Rebel cavalry at Brandy Station, although not a definitive victory for either side, greatly bolstered General Pleasonton's already immoderately inflated reputation. That, along with his typically exaggerated assertions of apparently minor accomplishments, hopefully proved to his superiors that he could handle the complexities of a much higher-level command assignment.

Pleasonton, also, believed on a purely personal and somewhat pretentious note, that his rank should correspond, naturally, with any increased leadership responsibilities that might happen to occur. Therefore, the lowly brigadier thought that he should, without any further delay, receive a commission as a major general of volunteers. He zealously campaigned for the comparable rank with that of the infantry corps commanders serving in the Army of the Potomac. Pleasonton reasoned that he deserved an immediate promotion for his courageous actions in the Maryland Campaign of 1862. During that campaign he led a cavalry division consisting of twelve regiments.[1] Additionally, his self-proclaimed heroic actions in the Battle of Chancellorsville during the previous month of May only added to his arsenal of justifications for a promotion. He unabashedly sought his immediate advancement through an intensive lobbying campaign of his superiors and friends in key positions. Ultimately he accomplished his objective.[2]

Alfred Pleasonton, acting as the temporary commander of the Army of the Potomac's mounted corps since May 22, had replaced General Stoneman as the cavalry chief. Like Pleasonton, Stoneman was a career cavalryman from one of the Regular Army's five ante-bellum mounted regiments.[3] George Stoneman held the rank of captain in the cavalry branch, the identical rank as Pleasonton, at the very beginning of the Civil War. That point rankled Pleasonton since he had graduated from West Point two full years ahead of Stoneman. Promotions were extremely slow in the peace-time Regular Army.

Both Pleasonton and Stoneman received their promotions to the rank of captain on the same date, March 3, 1855. That date saw the authorization of two additional mounted regiments, thus increasing the number of officers needed to staff them. However, after that promotion, Stoneman accepted his Regular Army commission to major on May 9, 1861, almost a full year before Pleasonton received his appointment to the same rank. Trivial as it was, that fact was one of the many truly insignificant reasons why Alfred Pleasonton did not particularly care for George Stoneman. Because of such reasoning he would willingly take every opportunity to discredit Stoneman in the eyes of their superiors in the Army of the Potomac and in the offices of the War Department in Washington, D.C.[4]

During the Chancellorsville Campaign in 1863, Stoneman became a major liability to Major General Joseph Hooker (U.S.M.A., Class of 1837), the most recently chosen commander

Brigadier General Alfred Pleasonton
(GAR III)

Major General George Stoneman
(GAR III)

of the Army of the Potomac. In large part, the lack of faith with Stoneman was due to the failure of his independent cavalry raid in the rear of the Southern army while General Hooker and his army engaged the main body of the Army of Northern Virginia at Chancellorsville.

"Stoneman's Raid," as the failed foray became known, did cause some alarm and apprehension in the Confederate capital city of Richmond. Sadly, the Union horsemen accomplished very little else of positive note during the raid. Overall, their actions only served to deprive General Hooker of some much needed cavalry support during the actual fighting at the Battle of Chancellorsville.

During the Chancellorsville engagement, General Pleasonton received a temporary demotion from division to brigade command. The primary reason for Pleasonton's newest woes was because of the most current friction between Stoneman and himself. Pleasonton recently submitted some highly accusatory and blatantly erroneous reports against his superior. General Pleasonton did not deploy with his divisional command when George Stoneman and the rest of the Cavalry Corps started on their raid toward Richmond. Instead, Pleasonton took personal command of Colonel Thomas Casmir Devin's 2nd Brigade of the 1st Division and remained with the main body of the Army of the Potomac near the village of Chancellorsville in a supporting role. Colonel Devin's small brigade of volunteer cavalry regiments included the 6th New York, the 8th Pennsylvania, the 17th Pennsylvania, and Troop L of the 1st Michigan.[5]

While Colonel Devin, the steadfast commanding officer of the 6th Regiment, New York Volunteer Cavalry, directed the brigade under the direct supervision of Pleasonton, the regiment remained under the immediate command of Lieutenant Colonel Duncan McVicar. Unfortunately, the thirty-five-year-old McVicar died on April 30 while leading his regiment in a minor engagement against a hostile force of cavalry near Spotsylvania Court House. During the same period, Major Pennock Huey commanded the 8th Regiment, Pennsylvania Volunteer Cavalry. Shortly, Huey would jump two grades and receive a promotion to the rank of colonel and be given the command of a full brigade of cavalry. Colonel Josiah Holcomb Kellogg (U.S.M.A., Class of 1860) commanded the 17th Regiment, Pennsylvania Volunteer Cavalry. Kellogg held the rank of captain in the Regular Army's 1st Cavalry Regiment. Unlike many of his fast-moving and promotion-conscious classmates, he remained as the colonel of the 17th Pennsylvania Cavalry until his resignation from the army in December 1864.

General Stoneman thought that he had placed his troublesome subordinate, Alfred Pleasonton, in a position in which he could garner no personal glory for someone else's actions, as Pleasonton customarily did. Stoneman erred greatly in his assessment of the situation, which eventually rebounded on him and assisted greatly in his ultimate demise as the Cavalry Corps commander. Instead of playing a calculated minor screening role with Hooker's army Pleasonton had the opportunity, at least in his mind and in the minds of his willing accomplices, to perform a major role in saving the Army of the Potomac from complete and utter defeat at Chancellorsville.[6]

Alfred Pleasonton gathered new laurels and additional supporters in the War Department because of his perceived personally heroic actions during the Battle of Chancellorsville. Conversely, George Stoneman became a scapegoat because of his bungled operation during the raid to Richmond. With a few well-placed additional inflammatory accusations and some personal aspersions from Pleasonton, General Stoneman became a symbol for the failure of the Union cavalry through the first two years of the war.

Soon after returning from the failed raid that had taken his cavalrymen deep into the enemy's territory, General Stoneman reluctantly traveled to Washington on a medical leave of absence. He could no longer avoid treatment of his hemorrhoids, or the commonly referred to ailment known as piles, an extremely unfortunate occurrence for any cavalryman, whether a private or a major general. Partly because of his medical condition and partly because of Alfred Pleasonton, he never again returned to lead his cavalry command in the Army of the Potomac. However, because he was a career soldier and still had a number of valuable skills, Stoneman soon received a new assignment. He accepted the command of the new Cavalry Bureau in Washington, on July 28, 1863. The previously mentioned combination of ill health and his subordinate's well-placed sniping enabled General Hooker to nominate Pleasonton as Stoneman's successor as the temporary Cavalry Corps commander in the Army of the Potomac.

Originally established by the War Department, the Cavalry Bureau looked after the unique and special requirements of the cavalry arm. General Stoneman's new command was responsible for organizing and equipping all cavalry regiments serving in the U.S. Army. The bureau was responsible for supplying forage for horses in the field. They erected and maintained wooden stables for newly acquired horses, located primarily in the Washington area. Additionally, the bureau trained and supplied hundreds of blacksmiths, farriers, and veterinary surgeons to properly care for the horses and the requirements related to the particular needs of the cavalry. Stoneman remained in Washington, D.C. as the head of the Cavalry Bureau until 1864. In February of that year he assumed operational command of the XXIII Corps, an infantry command, in the Department of Ohio. Eventually, George Stoneman was able to return to the cavalry branch, leading the Cavalry Corps of the Army of the Ohio in Georgia until inauspiciously captured in July 1864.[7]

On at least one occasion Brigadier General Pleasonton had the opportunity to converse, face-to-face, with Major General Hooker. He probably spoke to him on June 10, immediately after his limited success in the cavalry action at Brandy Station. Pleasonton informed Hooker about his ambitious plan for the consolidation, along with much tighter control, of the Army of

the Potomac's Cavalry Corps. Obviously, his subordinate's rec-
ommendations profoundly impressed Hooker because he quickly
implemented many of them without much discussion from other
commanders or from the War Department in Washington.

The next day, on June 11, Pleasonton received a succinct
message from Hooker's general headquarters referencing his
proposed reorganization plan. The communiqué sent from General Hooker's chief of staff, Major General Daniel Butterfield,
stated: "If you consider it essential for the efficiency of your
corps and the good of the service, make the change." Additional
correspondence received from Lieutenant Colonel Charles
Greene Sawtelle (U.S.M.A., Class of 1854), Chief Quartermaster of the Cavalry Corps, echoed Butterfield's statement: ". . . I
have seen the general [Hooker], and he approves of your ar-
rangement of dividing the corps into two parts."[8]

Before the day was over, Pleasonton, acting with uncharacteristic speed, the same quickness that appeared to elude him in
many future field operations, took the two communications from
army headquarters as a consensus of his superior's true opinion
and backing of his plan. He immediately issued the following
general order to his troops:

> General Orders} Headquarters, Cavalry Corps,
> Numbers 18.   }   June 11, 1863.
>
> The following arrangement of the Cavalry
> Corps will take effect as soon as practicable:
>
> I. The First Division will be composed of the
> cavalry now belonging to Pleasonton's divi-
> sion and Buford's reserve brigade, and will be
> formed into three brigades, to be named the
> First, Second, and Third. This division to be
> commanded by Brigadier General John Buford.
>
> II. The Second Division will consist of the
> cavalry of the present Second and Third Divi-
> sions, to be formed into three brigades, to be
> named First, Second, and Third. This division
> will be commanded by Brigadier General D.
> McM. Gregg.

III. Division commanders will form their brigades as soon as possible, and report the regiments and companies belonging to each to these headquarters, without delay.

IV. The Horse Artillery Brigade will furnish the batteries to each division, to be under the orders of the division commanders until further orders.

By command of Brig.-General Pleasonton:

[A. J. Alexander,]
Assistant Adjutant-General.[9]

Brigadier General Pleasonton wasted very little time instituting additional changes for his newly acquired cavalry command. Always the consummate military planner, Pleasonton was not completely happy with his predecessor's previous divisional organization of the Cavalry Corps. He reorganized his new corps by establishing the following regimental and command assignments on June 14:[10]

Army of the Potomac Cavalry Corps
Reorganization Plan

Old Cavalry Corps	New Cavalry Corps
Brig. Gen. Alfred Pleasonton	*Brig. Gen. Alfred Pleasonton*
1st Division	1st Division
Brig. Gen. John Buford	*Brig. Gen. John Buford*
1st Brigade	1st Brigade
Col. William Gamble	*Col. William Gamble*
8th Illinois Cavalry	8th Illinois Cavalry
3rd Indiana Cavalry	12th Illinois Cavalry
8th New York Cavalry	3rd Indiana Cavalry
	8th New York Cavalry
2nd Brigade	2nd Brigade
Col. Thomas C. Devin	*Col. Thomas C. Devin*
6th New York Cavalry	6th New York Cavalry
9th New York Cavalry	9th New York Cavalry
17th Pennsylvania Cavalry	17th Pennsylvania Cavalry
3rd (West) Virginia Cavalry	3rd (West) Virginia Cavalry

Reserve Brigade

Maj. Charles J. Whiting

6th Pennsylvania Cavalry
1st United States Cavalry
2nd United States Cavalry
5th United States Cavalry
6th United States Cavalry

2nd Division

Col. Alfred N. A. Duffié

1st Brigade

Col. Louis P. di Cesnola

1st Massachusetts Cavalry
6th Ohio Cavalry
1st Rhode Island Cavalry

2nd Brigade

Col. J. Irvin Gregg

3rd Pennsylvania Cavalry
4th Pennsylvania Cavalry
16th Pennsylvania Cavalry

3rd Brigade

Maj. Samuel H. Starr

6th Pennsylvania Cavalry
1st United States Cavalry
2nd United States Cavalry
5th United States Cavalry
6th United States Cavalry

2nd Division

Brig. Gen. David McM. Gregg

1st Brigade

Col. John B. McIntosh

1st Maryland Cavalry
1st New Jersey Cavalry
1st Pennsylvania Cavalry
3rd Pennsylvania Cavalry

2nd Brigade

Brig. Gen. Judson Kilpatrick

1st Massachusetts Cavalry
2nd New York Cavalry
4th New York Cavalry
6th Ohio Cavalry
1st Rhode Island Cavalry

3rd Brigade

Col. J. Irvin Gregg

1st Maine Cavalry
10th New York Cavalry
4th Pennsylvania Cavalry
16th Pennsylvania Cavalry

3rd Division

Brig. Gen. David McM. Gregg

1st Brigade

Brig. Gen. Judson Kilpatrick

1st Maine Cavalry
2nd New York Cavalry
10th New York Cavalry

2nd Brigade

Col. Percy Wyndham

1st Maryland Cavalry
1st New Jersey Cavalry
1st Pennsylvania Cavalry

Lieutenant Colonel
C. Ross Smith,
Chief of Ordnance,
Cavalry Corps
(GAR III)

Lieutenant Colonel
Charles G. Sawtelle,
Chief Quartermaster,
Cavalry Corps
(NA)

Furthermore, on June 13, as an additional measure of his new status, Brigadier General Pleasonton appointed many new officers to his rapidly expanding personal staff. Wanting his own men in the positions of responsibility within the corps, he introduced the first of many personnel changes to his newly re-organized corps with the official assignments of specifically chosen staff officers. Those staff members were men whom he could trust and who demonstrated similar interests, aspirations, and ambitions during their terms of military service. Many of the selected officers had already served on his brigade and division staffs in various capacities. The permanent appointments to his staff, extracted from General Order No. 19, Headquarters, Cavalry Corps, dated June 13, 1863, included:[11]

Col. George Alexander Hamilton Blake (1st U.S.) – Commissary of Musters
Lt. Col. Andrew Jonathan Alexander (3rd U.S.) – Chief of Staff
Lt. Col. Albert Smith Austin (U.S.V.) – Commissary of Subsistence
Lt. Col. Charles Greene Sawtelle (U.S.V.) – Chief Quartermaster
Lt. Col. Charles Ross Smith (6th Penna.) – Chief of Ordnance
Maj. William H. Crocker (U.S.V.) – Inspector General
Surg. George Laurie Pancoast (U.S.V.) – Medical Director
Asst. Surg. George McCulloch McGill (U.S.V.) – Medical Inspector
Capt. Andrew Jacob Cohen (U.S.V.) – Assistant Adjutant General
Capt. Thomas Drummond (5th U.S.) – Provost Marshal
Capt. Elon John Farnsworth (8th Ill.) – Additional Aide-de-Camp
Capt. John Green (2nd U.S.) – Additional Aide-de-Camp
Capt. Frederick Cushman Newhall (6th Pa.) – Assistant Inspector General
Capt. Vincent E. Von Koerber (1st Md.) – Topographical Engineer
1st Lt. George Armstrong Custer (5th U.S.) – Additional Aide-de-Camp
1st Lt. Daniel W. Littlefield (7th Mich.) – Additional Aide-de-Camp
1st Lt. Curwen Boyd McLellan (6th U.S.) – Additional Aide-de-Camp
1st Lt. Enos Blossom Parsons (8th N.Y.) – Additional Aide-de-Camp
1st Lt. David Richardson (6th N.Y.) – Act. Assistant Commissary Subsistence
1st Lt. John W. Spangler (6th U.S.) – Acting Assistant Quartermaster
1st Lt. Woodbury M. Taylor (8th Ill.) – Chief Ambulance Officer
1st Lt. Clifford Thomson (1st N.Y.) – Additional Aide-de-Camp
1st Lt. George H. Thompson (1st R.I.) – Additional Aide-de-Camp
1st Lt. Leicester Walker (5th U.S.) – Additional Aide-de-Camp
1st Lt. George W. Yates (4th Mich. Inf.) – Additional Aide-de-Camp

**Colonel George A. H. Blake,
Commissary of Musters,
Cavalry Corps
(USAMHI)**

In a somewhat unusual situation Colonel George Alexander Hamilton Blake, a Regular Army colonel and an assigned commander of one of the six regular cavalry regiments, was now subordinate in rank to General Pleasonton. Alfred Pleasonton was a Regular Army major but, in addition, was a brigadier general and was soon to be a major general of volunteers. Colonel Blake, a twenty-seven-year veteran of the army, was the most recently appointed senior officer of the 1st U.S. Cavalry. He replaced Colonel Benjamin Lloyd Beall on February 15, 1862, who retired, mainly because of ill health, after almost twenty-six years on active duty with the Regular Army's dragoon and cavalry regiments.

Colonel Blake only briefly served in the field with the 1st U.S. Cavalry during the Civil War, instead relinquishing the field command of the regiment to a succession of junior officers. Throughout most of the Gettysburg Campaign, Captain Richard Stanton Chandler Lord (U.S.M.A., Class of 1856) commanded the 1st U.S. Cavalry Regiment until wounded on July 9 near Boonsboro, Maryland.[12]

After Alfred Pleasonton had received his commanding general's tacit permission to reorganize his new command, he did so by consolidating the three small divisions into two larger ones. Pleasonton then continued with the next step in his very specific agenda. He desperately needed to procure additionally qualified officers to command the divisions, brigades and regiments in the mounted corps. To accomplish that lofty goal, some of the current commanders would be forced to accept reassignments or be otherwise relieved of their present commands.

One of General Pleasonton's previous requests for an individual's advancement paid off almost immediately after he accepted command of the Cavalry Corps. In a brief note dated June 14, 1863, to Secretary of War Edwin McMasters Stanton, Pleasonton expressed his gratitude to the secretary for Colonel Hugh Judson Kilpatrick's (U.S.M.A., Class of May 1861) promotion to the rank of brigadier general of volunteers on the previous day.[13]

Judson Kilpatrick, he dropped his first name in favor of his middle name, was the brash and somewhat flamboyant colonel of the 2nd Regiment, New York Volunteer Cavalry. He had held that commission since December 1862. A native of New Jersey, he was born on January 14, 1836, on the Kilpatrick family farm in Deckertown. His physical description in 1863 showed that he was approximately five feet, seven inches tall and weighed barely 140 pounds.[14]

Kilpatrick graduated seventeenth in a class of forty-five from the U.S. Military Academy in May 1861, in one of the five-year classes originally instituted by then Secretary of War Jefferson Davis in 1855. The young Kilpatrick received his commission as a second lieutenant in the 1st U.S. Artillery. His early claim to fame seems to have been because of his recognition as the first Regular Army officer wounded in the war at the Battle of Big Bethel, Virginia in June 1861. Though not serious, the shrapnel from a projectile fired by an enemy artillery battery struck Kilpatrick in a very embarrassing place—his left buttock.[15]

With his brazen self-promotion, the recently promoted brigadier general had an almost identical attitude to that of his new corps commander. Like Pleasonton, Kilpatrick had a tendency to exaggerate his true activities in various field operations and skirmishes against the enemy. He spent a great deal of his time promoting his own individual accomplishments and virtues, both orally and in writing, while failing to actually achieve many of them.

While assigned as the lieutenant colonel of the 2nd New York Cavalry, some of Kilpatrick's more questionable practices landed him in the Old Capitol Prison in Washington, D.C. for almost three months. His arrest stemmed from a number of offenses, but primarily for the alleged selling of government property. The U.S. government eventually dropped the charges in January 1863 and he immediately received a promotion to the vacant colonelcy of the 2nd New York regiment upon his release.[16] Evidently, for the time being, Judson Kilpatrick's lies and misdeeds counted for very little and his reward seemed to be a prestigious promotion to brigadier general. There appeared to be a direct correlation with deceit and false allegations just as with Pleasonton and his promotion.[17]

Up to the present time, while leading a brigade of cavalry in the rigors of field service, Kilpatrick had exhibited a tendency to send others where he himself would not dare go. Kilpatrick lacked the finesse and tactical abilities of many of his peers, preferring instead to commit his troopers to seemingly senseless slaughter on many battlefields. Usually in any combat situation, a brigade commander was not expected to be at the head of his troops and Kilpatrick seems to have taken that quite literally. Although only rarely found in the forefront of any of his attacking regiments Kilpatrick did exhibit brief glimpses of audacious personal behavior on the battlefield.

Many of Judson Kilpatrick's contemporaries did not hesitate to lead their men forward into the maelstrom of battle. Colonel Benjamin Franklin "Grimes" Davis (U.S.M.A., Class of 1854) was killed at the Battle of Brandy Station on June 9 while leading his men. Colonels Wyndham and di Cesnola, two other cavalry brigade commanders, received serious wounds at Brandy Station and Aldie. In a few days, two of Kilpatrick's own brigadiers from his newly assigned division would lead elements of their own brigades during the third day's fighting at Gettysburg and one would lose his life because of Kilpatrick's preposterous orders.[18]

After the reorganization of the Cavalry Corps, General Pleasonton exhibited no discernible plans to replace two of his most combat experienced and highly respected division commanders. Thus far, both brigadier generals, John Buford (U.S.M.A., Class of 1848) and David McMurtrie Gregg (U.S.M.A., Class of 1855), had served admirably throughout the war. They had more than proven their capabilities in previous engagements with the enemy and would continue to do so in the forthcoming Gettysburg Campaign. Both were career cavalrymen with lengthy terms of service in the mounted branch. Additionally, Buford and Gregg were graduates of West Point, a definite advantage in Pleasonton's increasingly tainted point of view.[19]

The other current division commander from Stoneman's old regime, Colonel Alfred Napoleon Alexander Duffié, did not fare as well as his peers during General Pleasonton's reorganization. Unfortunately Duffié lost his division command slot in the process, mainly because of Pleasonton's prejudices. Pleasonton considered all non-native-born Americans both officers and enlisted men, who served in the army during this time of crisis, to be no more than mercenaries. In his fanaticism to cleanse the corps of such individuals, he personally targeted at least four senior, foreign-born, division and brigade commanders for removal from their commands within his newly reformed corps. The new major general commanding the Cavalry Corps actively sought the removal of Colonel Alfred Duffié, who was born in France, Colonel Louis di Cesnola, a native of Italy, Major General Julius Stahel, whose birthplace was in Hungary, and Colonel Percy Wyndham, a recent immigrant from England, from their individual division and brigade commands.[20]

In a letter to John Farnsworth, a friend and former comrade-in-arms, Alfred Pleasonton wrote: "I have no faith in foreigners saving our Government, I conscientiously believe that Americans only should rule in this matter & settle this rebellion—& that in every instance foreigners have injured our cause. . . ."[21] Unfortunately, Colonel Alfred Duffié fit directly into that category as defined by Pleasonton's missive, having been born in Paris. As an added indictment against him, he resigned his commission in the French Army at the onset of the American Civil War. He schemed to seek his fame and fortune in a land where severe fighting might erupt at any moment.[22]

Colonel Duffié, a graduate of the French Military Academy of St. Cyr at Versailles in the Class of 1854, served with distinction and honor in various cavalry actions throughout the continents of Africa and Europe. He arrived in the United States in the autumn of 1859. Duffié was on an extended leave of absence from his command, a leave granted in order to recuperate from wounds received in battle.[23]

On August 9, 1861, Duffié applied for, and ultimately accepted, a volunteer commission as a captain in Company A of the 2nd Regiment, New York Volunteer Cavalry. In less than a week, he advanced another grade to the rank of major after the commissioned officers held an election to select the regiment's senior field officers. That was the same regiment that carried Judson Kilpatrick as its lieutenant colonel while Alfred Duffié served as one of the three original majors.[24]

In July 1862, the twenty-eight-year-old Duffié resigned his commission as a major in the 2nd New York and received an appointment as the colonel of the 1st Regiment, Rhode Island Volunteer Cavalry. His appointment did not meet with the approval of many of the regiment's junior officers but he eventually won their loyalty. He continued to serve with additional valor and distinction in the various cavalry campaigns of the Army of the Potomac. Because of his distinguished service in the action at Kelly's Ford, Virginia, in March 1863, General Hooker recommended him for promotion to brigadier general of volunteers. The promotion carried a date of rank of June 23, 1863, but the commission did not arrive until after his forthcoming debacle at Aldie, Virginia. Upon receiving the notification of his new promotion, a very bewildered and totally perplexed Duffié, in a letter written about his peculiar circumstance, stated: "When I do well, they take no notice of me. When I go make one bad business, make one fool of myself, they promote me. . . ."[25]

On June 17, in what could be construed only as an act of extreme misfortune and bad luck, Colonel Duffié and his regiment, the 1st Rhode Island, embarked on an extremely dangerous reconnaissance toward Middleburg, Virginia. Recently demoted from division command, Duffié returned to regimental command because of an inferred lackluster performance at the Battle of Brandy Station a week earlier.

During the early morning hours of June 17, Pleasonton's Cavalry Corps headquarters issued the following order to General David Gregg, commanding the 2nd Division: ". . . One regiment of your command will be sent through Thoroughfare Gap as far as Middleburg to-night, scouting the country well in that vicinity. . . . The officer going to Middleburg will report anything that occurs." On the surface, at least, General Pleasonton was not culpable for selecting Colonel Duffié and the 1st Rhode Island Cavalry for the dangerous mission. In the absence of supporting evidence, whether he unofficially suggested which regiment to send to Middleburg continues to remain a mystery.[26]

Colonel Alfred N. A. Duffié
Commander, 2nd Division
(LC)

General Gregg immediately forwarded General Pleasonton's order to his division's 2nd Brigade commander, Judson Kilpatrick. General Kilpatrick selected the small regiment of Rhode Islanders for the reconnaissance. In his written order Kilpatrick directed that Colonel Duffié would:

> . . . proceed with your regiment from Manassas Junction, by way of Thoroughfare Gap, to Middleburg. On your arrival at that place, you will at once communicate with the headquarters of the Second Cavalry Brigade [Kilpatrick's], and camp for the night. From

Middleburg you will proceed to Union; thence
by the way of Snickersville to Percyville [Pur-
cellville]; from Percyville [Purcellville] to
Wheatland; than passing through Waterford to
Noland's Ferry, where you will join your
brigade.[27]

The reconnaissance mission to the small settlement of Middleburg seemed to lack any direct or otherwise useful purpose,
other than to send the Frenchman's small regiment of Rhode Islanders into the very midst of General Stuart's Confederate
stronghold. Judson Kilpatrick and the remainder of his brigade
remained well out of range to support the 1st Rhode Island in
any capacity. Although he could not have known the exact locations of all J. E. B. Stuart's brigades and regiments, General
Pleasonton should have known that Middleburg was a place
where the Confederate cavalry congregated in force. Undoubtedly, the Union cavalry's commanding general never
should have sent one little regiment, without the proper backup
and support, into a stronghold of the Confederacy's cavalry.

That lone Union cavalry regiment, numbering no more than
275 commissioned officers and enlisted men, to nobody's surprise, subsequently became engaged in a bitter and one-sided
contest with a brigade of cavalry, consisting of roughly four
times the number of men, in the streets of Middleburg. Some of
the enemy's cavalry belonged to Brigadier General Beverly Hol-
combe Robertson (U.S.M.A., Class of 1849). General Robertson's brigade consisted of only two regiments, the 4th and 5th
North Carolina Cavalry, respectively commanded by Colonel
Dennis Dozier Ferebee and Colonel Peter Gustavus Evans.
Ironically, Colonel Evans would receive a mortal wound just
four days later in another fierce engagement with the Union
cavalry forces at Middleburg.[28]

Around five o'clock in the afternoon, Colonel Duffié realized that he was in a very dangerous and extremely untenable
position. He dispatched Captain Frank Allen, the commander of
Troop G, with two enlisted men from Troop M, privates Calvin

Claflin and Charles O. Green, to seek assistance from the Union cavalry forces located at Aldie some five miles to the east. Allen's tiny detail was the second one sent by Duffié. He previously dispatched another group of three men to brigade headquarters earlier in the afternoon but their status was unknown to him. Duffié originally wanted to send a full troop with Captain Allen, but the junior officer determined that he needed only two men to accomplish his perilous mission.[29]

After taking a circuitous route to evade the enemy's numerous patrols in the area Captain Allen and his two men arrived roughly four hours later at Brigadier General Kilpatrick's headquarters of the 2nd Brigade, 2nd Division situated at Aldie. For whatever the reason, Kilpatrick chose not to act on Duffié's urgent request for aid. Instead he stated to Captain Allen "that his brigade was so worn out that he could not send any reenforcement to Middleburg . . . ." Instead, the brigade commander forwarded the message to General Gregg, his division commander. General Gregg, in turn, routed the request to General Pleasonton's headquarters.[30]

Perhaps Judson Kilpatrick was fully aware of his commanding general's intention to let Alfred Duffié's command fend for itself at Middleburg. Perhaps Judson Kilpatrick also harbored some personal resentment toward the foreign-born colonel or bore some type of petty grudge against him from their time together in the 2nd New York Cavalry. In any event, it was unconscionable that General Kilpatrick would abandon a former comrade and subordinate from the Harris Light Cavalry to his ill-timed fate. Conversely, in defense of General Kilpatrick, it should be noted that Colonel Duffié's request for assistance did arrive well after darkness had enveloped the area. With few exceptions, the night-time hours were not at all conducive to any type of mounted rescue operations in the face of the enemy, especially in their territory.

Eventually, upon receipt of Colonel Duffié's critical message for assistance, General Pleasonton also refused to send any reinforcements to the beleaguered Rhode Islanders, which at that time was already too late. Pleasonton chose callously to abandon them and their colonel to the overwhelming Confederate forces. At roughly ten o'clock that night, Colonel Duffié, having heard nothing from Captain Allen or his brigade commander, determined that both his first and second pleas for assistance had not reached Kilpatrick, so he sent another junior officer, this time with a twenty-man detail, toward the brigade headquarters at Aldie. In his official report of the affair Duffié stated that he "heard nothing from either party, and believe that both have been captured."[31]

The outcome for the regiment from New England was quite predictable given the circumstances. The much larger cavalry brigade under the command of General Robertson decimated Colonel Duffié's tiny command. Instead of retreating upon learning that Confederate troops were to the south and east, the Rhode Island men had quickly barricaded the streets of the town, but to no avail. The Southerners' first charge forced the Union cavalrymen from the streets of the town.

After hiding in the woods for the rest of the night, the colonel was barely able to escape with four other officers and twenty-seven enlisted men. Meanwhile, twenty-eight-year-old Lieutenant Colonel John Leverett Thompson eluded the pursuing Rebels with an additional eighteen men from his command. The 1st Rhode Island suffered roughly 225 casualties with over 200 of those losses being listed as captured by the enemy.

Early in the morning hours of June 19, Colonel Duffié and the remnants of the once proud 1st Regiment, Rhode Island Volunteer Cavalry, wearily trudged into Fairfax Court House after having reentered the safety of the Union lines near Centreville. A few other lucky members of the 1st Rhode Island eventually trickled back into the Union fortifications. Those fortunate survivors of the regiment immediately traveled to the security of Washington to recuperate and refit after their harrowing ordeal.[32]

Pleasonton publicly feigned his extreme displeasure (while probably being secretly elated with Duffié's ultimate fate) with the results of the Frenchman's mission and wrote in his official report that:

> . . . I have heard nothing from Duffie. Some of his men are in, and they say Duffie gave the order for his men to scatter and get back the best way they could. . . . I cannot understand Duffie's conduct, and must await further advices.[33]

Additionally, as if losing his regiment was not enough, Pleasonton disparaged Colonel Duffié even further as "totally unfitted to command a Regiment," even though he had carried out the exact orders issued to him by his superiors. The new Cavalry Corps commander also unsuccessfully sought the immediate court-martial of his subordinate for disobedience to orders. General Pleasonton believed that Colonel Duffié had allowed General Stuart and his cavalrymen "to obtain such a position as to be able to kill, wound, & capture a large number of his men & officers."[34]

Shortly after his embarrassing rout at Middleburg and subsequent return to the Cavalry Corps' headquarters at Fairfax Court House, Colonel Alfred Duffié was completely taken unaware and thoroughly surprised with a promotion, much to his delight and General Pleasonton's chagrin, to the rank of brigadier general of volunteers.

In a letter to Pleasonton, dated June 24, Brigadier General Seth Williams (U.S.M.A., Class of 1842), Hooker's assistant adjutant general, informed him that: "Colonel Duffie has been made a brigadier-general, and it is the present intention of the general to assign him to duty with General Stahel. His regiment, as soon as in readiness, will return to you."[35] After receiving word of his promotion Duffié immediately reported to Washington. Because of the pending changes in the cavalry commands, Duffié never did join Stahel but received an unwelcome reassignment to the out-of-the-way Department of West Virginia.

General Pleasonton had finally dominated in Duffié's removal from his command—one foreigner out of his command.[36]

Coincidentally, at the same time Alfred Duffié was experiencing Pleasonton's personal prejudices, through no discernible or deviously hatched plot on General Pleasonton's part, another of the general's foreign-born nemeses found himself removed from Pleasonton's immediate realm of concern. The unintentional target, Colonel Luigi (Louis) Palma di Cesnola, an Italian-born count, was the former commander of the 1st Brigade, 2nd Division before Pleasonton's corps reorganization. Relieved of his brigade command, Colonel di Cesnola returned to the command slot of the 4th Regiment, New York Volunteer Cavalry, a position he held since September 1862.

Count di Cesnola had graduated from the Royal Military Academy in Turin, Italy and received an immediate assignment to the Sardinian Army's cavalry branch. He served with valor and distinction in a variety of European battles in the Crimean War before arriving in the United States in 1860. In September 1861 he mustered in as a major and in February 1862 as the lieutenant colonel in the 11th Regiment, New York Volunteer Cavalry. He resigned from that regiment in June 1862 to accept the commission as colonel of the 4th Regiment, New York Volunteer Cavalry.[37]

In February 1863, the U.S. Army summarily dismissed him for allegedly stealing a half dozen Remington pistols and shipping them to his wife in New York City. The charge, initially brought by a jealous and vindictive subordinate, turned out to be an unpleasant mistake. A recruiting detachment of his men currently on duty in the city was to receive the shipment of pistols. The army fully exonerated him and reinstated him to the command of his regiment. Even though the government cleared him of all the charges, the colonel felt his reputation unduly tarnished and briefly contemplated resigning his commission.[38]

Only recently, Colonel di Cesnola found himself, once again, placed under arrest for allowing his horsemen to ride their horses through the camp site of some neighboring infantry-men. The penalty dispensed by Cavalry Corps headquarters seemed quite severe for such a minor breach of discipline, which had been the total fault of a subordinate. At the time of the altercation with the Confederate cavalry at Aldie on June 17, Colonel di Cesnola still remained, technically, under arrest for the supposed crime committed by his men but he, nonethe-less, led his regiment into battle without any side-arms. Upon learning of this extreme act of heroism and leadership, General Kilpatrick sent an aide-de-camp to General Pleasonton's head-quarters with a request to release Colonel di Cesnola from ar-rest. Under the circumstances a reluctant Pleasonton had no alternative but immediately to grant the request.

Colonel Luigi di Cesnola,
Commander,
1st Brigade, 2nd Division
(NA)

The next mounted charge made by the men of the 4th New York Cavalry found their colonel leading them again, but this time he carried his pistol and his saber. During that charge, Colonel di Cesnola was severely wounded, shot three times—once each in the hand, arm and head. His mortally wounded horse also fell on top of him, trapping him underneath. He quickly became a prisoner of the Southern cavalry. As a tribute to his gallantry in the action at Aldie, Colonel Luigi di Cesnola received the Medal of Honor. Colonel di Cesnola remained a prisoner of war until March 1864 when a prisoner exchange allowed his release. Accordingly, while still a guest of the Confederacy, he mercifully found himself essentially eliminated from receiving the full brunt of Pleasonton's bigotry—two foreigners out of the way.[39]

The third unfortunate and high-ranking foreigner under General Pleasonton's direct command was Sir Percy Wyndham of the 1st Regiment, New Jersey Volunteer Cavalry, most recently the commander of the Cavalry Corps' 2nd Brigade of the 3rd Division. Wyndham was a British subject and a true soldier of fortune. He was undeniably a mercenary who had already spent the last thirteen years of his life flitting from one hot-spot to another in Europe. He offered his services to whichever side happened to appeal to him. He received a recommendation for the senior position in the 1st New Jersey by no less an individual than Major General George Brinton McClellan (U.S.M.A., Class of 1846), commander of the Army of the Potomac at that time. Colonel Sir Percy Wyndham was twenty-eight years old when he received the coveted commission as colonel of the 1st New Jersey Cavalry.

Sir Percy originally arrived in the United States in October 1861 after taking a one year leave of absence, which eventually stretched for almost five years, from his most recent command in the Italian Army. At the Battle of Brandy Station on June 9, Colonel Wyndham received a comparatively slight wound in the leg while directing his men in a rear guard action against the enemy's pressing cavalry. The wound, not thought serious at first, eventually forced the colonel to withdraw from the battle-field after some time had passed because of the loss of blood.[40] Wyndham neither felt the true force of the changes nor the actual resentment of his new corps commander since he was away on convalescence leave at the time of Pleasonton's ethnic purification of the senior officers in the Cavalry Corps.[41]

Colonel Sir Percy Wyndham,
Commander,
2nd Brigade, 3rd Division
(LC)

Although he lost the command of his brigade soon after General Pleasonton's reorganization, the Englishman briefly returned to lead his regiment again in September 1863. For whatever reason, though he thoroughly despised foreigners, Pleasonton seems to have fostered a greater flexibility toward

Sir Percy than toward any of the others. It is quite possible, and even likely, that Pleasonton found Wyndham more palatable because of his Anglo-Saxon background, much the same way that McClellan had done earlier in the war.

When his successor as brigade commander, Colonel John Baillie McIntosh, became seriously incapacitated in a fall from his horse in September, Colonel Wyndham actually commanded his old brigade again. Less than a month later, Wyndham was arbitrarily relieved of all his command duties and responsibilities. He received orders to report immediately to the Adjutant General's Office in Washington for further assignment.

No discernible reason can be ascertained as to why Percy Wyndham was unexpectedly and unceremoniously dropped as the commanding officer of the New Jersey cavalry regiment. It was highly unlikely that General Pleasonton had much, if anything, to do with his removal. Quite possibly Colonel Wyndham had made some enemies, both in the Washington political circles and the military hierarchy, while on medical leave and it was through their influence that he lost his field command.

Colonel Wyndham never returned to the Army of the Potomac except for a brief time at the end of June 1864 when he, quite unexpectedly, appeared at the encampment of the 1st New Jersey Cavalry and attempted to retake control of the regiment. The lieutenant colonel commanding the regiment, John Wood Kester, arrested Wyndham and ordered him escorted back to Washington, D.C. Eventually released from arrest he mustered out of the volunteer service in July 1864—three foreigners out of Pleasonton's command with only one remaining.[42]

Of course, during that same period and for his own personal advancement in rank, General Pleasonton also continued touting his own merits, capabilities, and philosophies to any one of importance, either military or civilian, who would listen. Unfortunately some of the reasoning behind Alfred Pleasonton's campaign for his own promotion was based largely upon his substantial ego, dubious political connections, and his own deep-seeded prejudices about foreign-born officers serving in important positions within the Union Army. His tirade against foreigners in the officer corps of the U.S. Army was a theme with which many other officers whole-heartedly sympathized and one with which they unconditionally concurred.

Now Alfred Pleasonton set his sights on the last remaining foreigner along his path to greater glory and advancement, Major General Julius H. Stahel, a native of Hungary. Unlike his campaigns to be rid of the subordinate Duffié and di Cesnola, Pleasonton harbored a deep personal dislike for Stahel. Pleasonton unabashedly coveted Stahel's cavalry command. However there was one minor problem confronting Pleasonton. The Hungarian immigrant outranked him as a major general by almost three months! Alfred Pleasonton's date of rank as a major general was June 22, 1863, while Julius Stahel's date of rank was March 17, 1863.

General Stahel's troopers were assigned to the Department of Washington and served on duty in northern Virginia, patrolling a large area from the Potomac River in the north to the Occoquan River south of Alexandria. They acted independently from the major Union force stationed in the area, the Army of the Potomac, and Pleasonton's cavalry command. The new commander of the Cavalry Corps wanted that changed. So now Major General Pleasonton aimed directly to discredit his final high-ranking foreign-born foe—Major General Stahel.

Julius H. Stahel was born in Szeged, Hungary on November 5, 1825, and served briefly in the Austrian army. He enlisted as a private and rose to the rank of lieutenant. Shortly after his discharge, he emigrated to the United States in 1859 and worked as a journalist in New York City until the beginning of the Civil War. He assisted in raising the 8th Regiment, New York Volunteer Infantry in 1861 and served first as its lieutenant colonel in April 1861 and then as its colonel in August 1861. He either had an aptitude for commanding troops or friends in government, both of which seem hard to accept, because he received a promotion to the rank of brigadier general in November 1861. In March 1863, Julius Stahel received his promotion to major general of volunteers and, after his insufferable reassignment from the eastern theater, won the Medal of Honor at the Battle of Piedmont, Virginia on June 5, 1864.

Meanwhile, during his unquestionably blatant and flagrant campaign for an additional star, but apparently unaware of the actions already taken on his behalf by Major General Hooker, Brigadier General Pleasonton solicited the enthusiastic assistance of one of his junior staff officers and willing protégé—Elon John Farnsworth. The youthful Captain Farnsworth obviously shared some of his commander's long term ambitions and goals, as well as some of his prejudicial thoughts and ideas about foreign-born officers.

Brigadier General John F. Farnsworth,
Former Cavalry Brigade Commander
(NA)

The young captain's uncle happened to be Pleasonton's old friend and confidant, John Franklin Farnsworth, a forty-three-year-old lawyer and a two-term member of the United States Congress before the war. The elder Farnsworth originally organized the 8th Regiment, Illinois Volunteer Cavalry in 1861, becoming its first colonel. He gallantly served in Pleasonton's division of cavalry in 1862 and received his promotion to brigadier general of volunteers in November 1862. In March 1863 he resigned his commission to take his seat, again, as a Republican in the U.S. House of Representatives. It was in his capacity as a congressman, and as a close friend of President Abraham Lincoln, that both Pleasonton and Farnsworth's own nephew sought his assistance in Pleasonton's campaign for advancement and, ultimately, the young Farnsworth's advancement, too.

In a lengthy letter to his uncle, one that glorified and praised the virtues of his superior, the younger Farnsworth stated that:

> Pleasonton is still not a Major General. While Pleasonton has fought thru 3 severe battles, all this time Stahel has four or five thousand cavalry in and about Washington just doing nothing at all. Trains passing between here and Fairfax C. H. are burned by Bushwhackers, our dispatches intercepted and yet Stahel does nothing. Now if you can do anything to get the cavalry consolidated and Stahel left out, for Gods sake do it.
>
> You hardly know or can imagine the bitter feeling that exists among the officers of the cavalry towards Stahel and those who are trying to set him and other Dutchmen up, Duffié has failed on two occasions. . . . Now try and talk all this [Brig. Gen. Pleasonton's promotion] into the President and you can do an immense good.[43]

In another letter written to Congressman Farnsworth on the very same day, one that closely mirrored the same malicious and slanderous thoughts as his subaltern, Alfred Pleasonton expressed some of his straightforward feelings toward Major General Julius Stahel:

We have done some hard and splendid fighting, and although we have always been victorious against superior forces, it is at the
sacrifice of many good men – my force is also
becoming small. Now my good friend, you
know what this means – it is riding a good
horse to death, and making sacrifices.

Our cavalry business is badly managed and
will lead us into trouble unless speedily cor-
rected. We have too many detachments independent of each other scattered over this
country. We need reinforcements, including
Stahel's div., which heretofore has been scattered about frittering away on trifling objects
– Remember Stahel ranks me and if put over
me, I shall retire – as I have no faith in foreigners saving our Government or country –
Stahel has not shown himself a cavalry man
and it is ruining cavalry to place it under him.
Stahel's force is watching empty air down
about Warrenton. Tell the President from me
that I will sacrifice my life to support his Government and save the country, but that I will
not fight under the orders of a Dutchman, that
I conscientiously believe that Americans only
should rule in this matter and settle this
rebellion.

I should have been made a Major General –
My commission should date from Antietam or
South Mountain to give me the proper rank to
command a corps. Give me 15,000 cavalry, let
me place my own officers over it. . . .Do assist
us until we can get a head of the rebs.[44]

Finally, Pleasonton's headstrong tenacity and behind-the-
scene political lobbying paid off for both him and three of his
youthful subordinates. Unbeknownst to Pleasonton, General
Hooker on June 18 had endorsed a recommendation for his cavalry chief's promotion and forwarded it to Washington for
prompt action. A short four days later word arrived at Hooker's
headquarters stating that the former dragoon had received his
coveted promotion as a major general in the volunteer service.
As an additional reward he would no longer be just the temporary commander of the Army of the Potomac's Cavalry Corps.

Major General Pleasonton's plan for the new and revamped Cavalry Corps was now almost complete. June 1863 had thus far proved to be a very productive month for Alfred Pleasonton, his benefactors, and his disciples. Positive performances for Pleasonton's command in the many battles with Stuart's cavalry had greatly helped to bolster his claims. Although he had more than his share of detractors in the Army of the Potomac and in Washington, many other individuals admired him primarily because of his organizational capabilities. During the early stages of his career he had spent a considerable amount of his time as a regimental adjutant in the dragoons.

After Major General Butterfield received a severe wound at the Battle of Gettysburg, Pleasonton split the duties as General Meade's chief of staff with Major General Gouverneur Kemble Warren (U.S.M.A., Class of 1850). Alfred Pleasonton had served as the adjutant of the 2nd Dragoons from July 1854 to March 1855 and as an acting assistant adjutant general from November 1855 to July 1860 with a few short breaks in between for other assignments. His organizational skills made him well suited for the chief of staff position.

Rumors circulated around the campfires of the Army of the Potomac that Alfred Pleasonton, ultimately, would become Meade's permanent chief of staff and that General Stoneman would return to command the Cavalry Corps. Both rumors were unfounded and completely false. Major General Andrew Atkinson Humphreys (U.S.M.A., Class of 1841) ultimately became General Meade's new chief of staff. George Meade did not want Hooker's man, Butterfield, to remain on his staff. Butterfield's wounding provided the necessary means to get rid of him. Major General Alfred Pleasonton, much to his relief, received permission to return to the top position of the army's mounted corps.

Eventually, the lackluster performance by Pleasonton forced his replacement in 1864 as the Cavalry Corps commander by Major General Philip Henry Sheridan (U.S.M.A., Class of 1853). Pleasonton found himself being handled much the same way that he had treated Julius Stahel a year earlier. To make room for the popular Sheridan the army exiled Pleasonton to the Department of Missouri in 1864 where he commanded the cavalry of that department.

At the close of the Civil War hostilities and in the downsizing of the military, Pleasonton, a major general of volunteers, retained only his Regular Army rank of major. In 1866, the reorganization of the U.S. Army allowed him but one opportunity for a promotion from his rank of four years earlier. The military establishment offered the insignificant rank, as he saw it, of a mere lieutenant colonel in the 20th U.S. Infantry. He presumably wanted to remain in the cavalry service with the 2nd Cavalry, but that was obviously not what his superiors intended for him. Pleasonton, it seems, had burned too many bridges behind him as he climbed to the top. He was now on his way down and nobody was there to stop his fall.[45]

After the war, many of Pleasonton's wartime subordinates now outranked him. Two such officers included Thomas John Wood (U.S.M.A., Class of 1845) and Innis Newton Palmer (U.S.M.A., Class of 1846), the new colonel and lieutenant colonel, respectively, of the 2nd U.S. Cavalry. Wood had actually commanded the 2nd Cavalry since November 1861, though detached from the regiment and serving in the volunteer service as were most of the Regular Army's senior commissioned officers. Pleasonton's class had been ahead of both Wood and Palmer at West Point and he ranked both in the volunteer service. The treatment he received was unacceptable to the profoundly proud and pompous cavalryman and he therefore refused the appointment to the infantry.[46]

Now in June 1863, as another year of the war was beginning, Major General Alfred Pleasonton had two additional concerns waiting for him to address. Both of the remaining issues were partially completed and both would come to fruition on June 28 in the city of Frederick, Maryland.

Major General Alfred Pleasonton and Staff,
Warrenton, Virginia – October, 1863
(LC)

Seated on ground, left to right: 1st Lt. Woodbury M. Taylor, Ambulance Officer, 8th Illinois Cavalry; 1st Lt. Enos B. Parsons, A.A.D.C., 8th New York Cavalry; Capt. Frederick C. Newhall, A.A.I.G., 6th Pennsylvania Cavalry; 1st Lt. Clifford Thomson, A.A.D.C., 1st New York Cavalry; Surg. George L. Pancoast, Medical Director, U.S. Volunteers; Capt. Benjamin Tucker Hutchins, A.A.D.C., 6th United States Cavalry.

Seated on chairs, left to right: Lt. Col. Albert S. Austin, Commissary of Subsistence, U.S. Volunteers; Col. George Alexander Hamilton Blake, Commissary of Musters, 1st United States Cavalry; Major General Alfred Pleasonton, Corps Commander; Lt. Col. Charles Ross Smith, Chief of Staff, 6th Pennsylvania Cavalry; Capt. Henry B. Hays, 6th United States Cavalry.

Standing, left to right: 1st Lt. Ira W. Trask, A.A.D.C., 8th Illinois Cavalry; 1st Lt. George W. Yates, A.A.D.C., 4th Michigan Infantry; 1st Lt. James Franklin Wade, A.A.D.C., 6th United States Cavalry; 1st Lt. Henry Baker, A.A.D.C., 6th United States Cavalry; 1st Lt. Leicester Walker, A.A.D.C., 5th United States Cavalry; Capt. Charles C. Suydam, A.A.G., 5th New York Cavalry; 1st Lt. Daniel W. Littlefield, A.A.D.C., 7th Michigan Cavalry; Unidentified; 1st Lt. Curwen B. McLellan, A.A.D.C., 6th United States Cavalry; Capt. Vincent E. Von Koerber, Topographical Engineer, 1st Maryland Cavalry; 1st Lt. Gerrard Irvine Whitehead, A.A.D.C., 6th Pennsylvania Cavalry.

Notes to Chapter Two

1. Edward J. Stackpole, *From Cedar Mountain to Antietam, August-September, 1862* (Harrisburg: The Stackpole Company, 1959), p. 306.
2. Pleasonton's military promotions included: Cadet at the U.S. Military Academy – September 1, 1840 to July 1, 1844; Brevet 2nd Lieutenant, 1st Dragoons – July 1, 1844; 2nd Lieutenant, 2nd Dragoons – November 3, 1845; Brevet 1st Lieutenant – May 9, 1846; 1st Lieutenant, 2nd Dragoons – September 30, 1849; Captain, 2nd Dragoons – March 3, 1855; Major, 2nd Cavalry – February 15, 1862; Brigadier General, U.S. Volunteers – July 16, 1862; Brevet Lieutenant Colonel – September 17, 1862; Major General, U.S. Volunteers – June 22, 1863; Brevet Colonel – July 2, 1863; Brevet Brigadier General, U.S. Army – March 13, 1865; Brevet Major General, U.S. Army – March 13, 1865; Mustered out of Volunteer Service – January 15, 1866; Lieutenant Colonel, 20th Infantry – July 28, 1866; Declined and resigned – January 1, 1868; Re-appointed, by Act of Congress, Major, U.S. Army – October 23, 1888, and placed on the Retired List.
3. The five prewar mounted regiments were the 1st and 2nd Dragoons, the Regiment of Mounted Rifles, and the 1st and 2nd Cavalry. Another cavalry regiment, the 3rd Cavalry, was organized in June 1861. On August 3, 1861, the six regiments of mounted troops consolidated into a single corps known as cavalry with the numerical designation 1 through 6 according to each regiment's seniority. The 1st Dragoons became the 1st Cavalry, the 2nd Dragoons became the 2nd Cavalry, the Mounted Rifles were renamed the 3rd Cavalry, the 1st Cavalry became the 4th Cavalry, the 2nd Cavalry became the 5th Cavalry, while the 3rd Cavalry, as the newest regiment, was re-designated as the 6th Cavalry.
4. George Stoneman's military promotions included: Cadet at the U.S. Military Academy – July 1, 1842 to July 1, 1846; Brevet 2nd Lieutenant, 1st Dragoons – July 1, 1846; 2nd Lieutenant, 1st Dragoons – July 12, 1847; 1st Lieutenant, 1st Dragoons – July 25, 1854; Captain, 2nd Cavalry – March 3, 1855; Major, 1st Cavalry – May 9, 1861; Brigadier General, U.S. Volunteers – August 13, 1861; Major General, U.S. Volunteers – November 29, 1862; Brevet Colonel – December 13, 1862; Lieutenant Colonel, 3rd Cavalry – March 30, 1864; Brevet Brigadier General, U.S. Army – March 13, 1865; Brevet Major General, U.S. Army – March 13, 1865; Colonel, 21st Infantry – July 28, 1866; Retired – August 16, 1871.
5. Frederick H. Dyer, *A Compendium of the War of the Rebellion,* 3 vols. (New York: Yoseloff, 1959), 1:323-325; Henry P. Moyer, *History of the Seventeenth Regiment Pennsylvania Cavalry* (Lebanon, Pa.: Sowers Printing Company, 1911), p. 40.
6. Pennock Huey, *A True History of the Charge of the Eighth Pennsylvania Cavalry at Chancellorsville* (Philadelphia: Porter & Coates, 1885), pp. 30-59. A major controversy over General Pleasonton's exact participation and true involvement in the Battle of Chancellorsville was still going strong when Pennock Huey's book was printed after the war. Some of the actual participants' accounts differed greatly from General Pleasonton's

Notes to Chapter Two (*continued*)

recollections of the events. Pleasonton convinced his superiors, particularly Hooker, that he had single-handedly saved the Army of the Potomac, through his sheer brilliance and audacity, from an utter rout before General Lee's advancing forces.

7. *War of the Rebellion: A Compilation of the Official Records of the Union and Confederate Armies* (Washington, D.C., 1880 - 1901), Series 1, Volume 27, Part 3, p. 11. (Hereafter cited as OR – 3.)

8. OR – 3, p. 57. Pleasonton's headquarters received both messages on June 11, 1863, at 10:30 A.M. Charles Sawtelle began his career in the Civil War as Regimental Quartermaster of the 6th U.S. Infantry. He rose rapidly in the ranks, his entire career being spent in the Quartermaster Department. In 1897 he retired from active duty as the Quartermaster General of the U.S. Army.

9. Ibid., p. 64.

10. Dyer, *A Compendium of the War*, 1:324.

11. OR – 3, pp. 97-98.

12. Pension File of George A. H. Blake, 1st U.S. Cavalry Regiment. Records of the Record and Pension Office, Record Group 15, National Archives, Washington, D.C. Colonel Blake additionally served for a brief time as a brigade commander in the Cavalry Reserve of the Army of the Potomac during a four month period in 1862.

13. OR – 3, p. 105.

14. Mary Elizabeth Sergent, *They Lie Forgotten* (Middletown, N.Y.: The Prior King Press, 1986), pp. 150-51.

15. Alfred Davenport, *Camp and Field: Life of the Fifth New York Volunteer Infantry* (New York: Dick & Fitzgerald, 1879), p. 58.

16. Deposition File of H. Judson Kilpatrick, U.S. Army. Record Group 94, National Archives, Washington, D.C.

17. Kilpatrick's military promotions included: Cadet at the U.S. Military Academy – July 1, 1856 to May 6, 1861; 2nd Lieutenant, 1st Artillery – May 6, 1861; Captain, 5th New York Volunteer Infantry – May 9, 1861; 1st Lieutenant, 1st Artillery – May 14, 1861; Resigned Volunteer Commission – August 14, 1861; Lieutenant Colonel, 2nd New York Volunteer Cavalry – September 25, 1861; Lieutenant Colonel, Staff – Additional Aide-de-Camp – January 29 to March 21, 1862; Colonel, 2nd New York Volunteer Cavalry – December 6, 1862; Brigadier-General, U.S. Volunteers – June 13, 1863; Brevet Major – June 17, 1863; Brevet Lieutenant-Colonel – July 3, 1863; Brevet Colonel – May 13, 1864; Captain, 1st U.S. Artillery – November 30, 1864; Brevet Brigadier-General, U.S. Army – March 13, 1865; Brevet Major-General, U.S. Army – March 13, 1865; Major-General, U.S. Volunteers – June 18, 1865; Resigned Army Commission – December 1, 1865; Resigned Volunteer Commission – January 1, 1866.

Notes to Chapter Two (*continued*)

18. Edward G. Longacre, *The Cavalry at Gettysburg: A Tactical Study of Mounted Operations during the Civil War's Pivotal Campaign 9 June-14 July 1863* (Cranbury, N.J.: Associated University Press, 1986), pp. 67, 78, 108.

19. David Gregg's military promotions included: Cadet at the U.S. Military Academy – July 1, 1851 to July 1, 1855; Brevet Second Lieutenant of Dragoons, July 1, 1855; Second Lieutenant, 1st Dragoons – September 4, 1855; First Lieutenant, 1st Dragoons – March 21, 1861; Captain, 6th Cavalry – May 14, 1861; Colonel, 8th Pennsylvania Cavalry Volunteers – January 24, 1862; Brigadier-General, U.S. Volunteers – November 29, 1862; Brevet Major-General, U.S. Volunteers – August 1, 1864; Resigned – February 3, 1865.
John Buford's nineteen years of military promotions included: Cadet at the U.S. Military Academy – July 1, 1844 to July 1, 1848; Brevet 2nd Lieutenant, 1st Dragoons – July 1, 1848; 2nd Lieutenant, 2nd Dragoons – February 17, 1849; 1st Lieutenant, 2nd Dragoons – July 9, 1853; Captain, 2nd Dragoons – March 9, 1859; Major, Staff, Assistant Inspector General – November 12, 1861; Brigadier General, U.S. Volunteers – July 27, 1862; Major General, U.S. Volunteers – December 16, 1863.

20. Another of General Pleasonton's brigade commanders, Colonel William Gamble, was born in Ireland. Gamble took over Colonel Davis' brigade after the latter's death. He seems to have been spared Pleasonton's wrath against foreigners probably because he had emigrated to the United States in 1838. Before the beginning of the war, Gamble also served in the 1st Dragoons as an enlisted man, eventually being promoted to sergeant-major of the regiment.

21. Alfred Pleasonton to John F. Farnsworth, June 23, 1863; Alfred Pleasonton Papers, Library of Congress, Washington, D.C. (Hereafter cited as Pleasonton MSS.) This letter was marked "Private" and was obviously for Congressman Farnsworth's eyes only. It was that type of attitude that would come back and haunt an increasingly bitter and cynical Alfred Pleasonton after the war.

22. Ezra J. Warner, *Generals in Blue: Lives of the Union Commanders* (Baton Rouge: Louisiana State University Press, 1964), p. 131. Alfred Duffié took a leave of absence from the French Army when he came to the United States in 1859. He married a woman from New York and was still on official leave when the Civil War began.

23. George N. Bliss, *Duffié and the Monument to His Memory* (Providence: privately printed, 1890), pp. 1-3.

24. Frederick Phisterer, *New York in the War of the Rebellion, 1861-1865*, 5 vols. (Albany: J. B. Lyon Company, 1912), 1:765, 769, 770.

25. George N. Bliss, *The First Rhode Island Cavalry at Middleburg, Va., June 17, 1863* (Providence: privately printed, 1911), p. 27.

26. OR – 3, p. 171.

Notes to Chapter Two (*continued*)

27. *War of the Rebellion: A Compilation of the Official Records of the Union and Confederate Armies* (Washington, D.C., 1880 - 1901), Series 1, Volume 27, Part 1, p. 962. (Hereafter cited as OR – 1.)
28. Robert K. Krick, *Lee's Colonels: A Biographical Register of the Field Officers of the Army of Northern Virginia* (Dayton, Ohio: Morningside House, Inc., 1992), p. 132.
29. Charles O. Green, *An Incident in the Battle of Middleburg, Va., June 17, 1863* (Providence: privately printed, 1911), pp. 9-10. Captain Allen was also assigned to the temporary command of Troop M at this time in the war.
30. OR – 1, p. 965.
31. Ibid., p. 963.
32. Ibid., p. 964. The 1st Rhode Island Cavalry did not officially and completely rejoin the Army of the Potomac's Cavalry Corps until the fall of 1863, although two troops were ready to return for duty in the field by the end of July 1863.
33. Ibid., pp. 909-10.
34. Alfred Pleasonton to the Adjutant General, Army of the Potomac, June 29, 1863, Cavalry Corps Headquarters; Letters Sent, February 1863 – April 1865; E-1439; Record Group 393; National Archives, Washington, D.C.
35. OR – 3, p. 288.
36. Warner, *Generals in Blue*, pp. 131-32. Alfred Duffié continued to serve inauspiciously in the Department of West Virginia until captured by Confederate partisans in October 1864. He was exchanged some four months later and was eventually mustered out of the volunteer service in August 1865.
37. Phisterer, *New York in the War of the Rebellion*, 1:813.
38. Louis P. di Cesnola Congressional Medal of Honor File; Box 170, B168US1863; Record Group 94; National Archives, Washington, D.C.
39. Ibid.
40. Henry R. Pyne, *The History of the First New Jersey Cavalry: Sixteenth Regiment, New Jersey Volunteers* (Trenton: J. A. Beecher, 1871), p. 152; OR – 1, p. 966.
41. William S. Stryker, comp., *Record of Officers and Men of New Jersey in the Civil War, 1861–1865*, 2 vols. (Trenton: John L. Murphy, 1876), 2:1180-81; Samuel Toombs, *New Jersey Troops in the Gettysburg Campaign* (Orange, N.J.: The Evening Mail Publishing House, 1888), pp. 402-3.
42. Lilian Rea, ed., *War Record and Personal Experiences of Walter Raleigh Robbins, from April 22, 1861, to August 4, 1865* (Chicago: privately printed, 1923), p. 206.
43. Elon J. Farnsworth to John F. Farnsworth, June 23, 1863; Alfred Pleasonton Papers, Library of Congress, Washington, D.C.
44. Pleasonton MSS.

Notes to Chapter Two (*continued*)

45. Warner, *Generals in Blue*, p. 374; Theophilus F. Rodenbough, *From Everglade to Cañon with the Second Dragoons* (New York: D. Van Nostrand, 1875), pp. 444-45.
46. Rodenbough, *From Everglade to Cañon*, pp. 438-39.

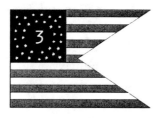

Chapter 3:

Moving through Maryland

HE first intimation that Alfred Pleasonton planned to promote three junior officers from his command over the heads of more seasoned, experienced, and battle-tested veterans came in a letter penned to Congressman John Farnsworth. He stated that:

> . . . Elon Farnsworth has done splendidly and I will make him a B.[rigadier] G.[eneral], What say you? I am sadly in want of officers with the proper dash to command cavalry— having lost so many good ones. . . .[1]

It is unknown whether General Pleasonton actually held his young aide-de-camp in such high esteem or if he was perhaps trying to curry some type of political favor with the congressman for his own career advancement by promoting the youthful Farnsworth. On the basis of the correspondence forwarded to the senior Farnsworth, Elon Farnsworth obviously knew what his commanding general had planned for him along with two of his peers, 1st Lieutenant George A. Custer (U.S.M.A., Class of June 1861) and Captain Wesley Merritt (U.S.M.A., Class of 1860). In the note to his uncle in Washington, written on June 23, the younger Farnsworth reported that:

> . . . The Gen'l. speaks of recommending me for Brig. I do not know that I ought to mention it for fear that you will call me an aspiring youth. I am satisfied to serve through this war in the line in my Reg't as a Capt. or on Gen'l Pleasonton's staff. But if I can do any good anywhere else of course "small favors and etc.". . .[2]

In another of his official reports to Major General Hooker, long-winded and verbose as always, dated June 22, 1863, and sent from the Cavalry Corps headquarters located near Aldie, Virginia, Pleasonton specifically and prominently mentioned another of the three potential promotees—Wesley Merritt. The young Captain Merritt was born on June 16, 1836, and was a recent graduate of West Point. He currently commanded the 2nd U.S. Cavalry Regiment a part of the Regular Brigade of cavalry assigned to General John Buford's 1st Division.

The youthful Wesley Merritt, with only three years of active military experience, was the senior ranking commissioned officer currently present for duty with the regiment. His position in the regiment clearly illustrated the serious vacuum created by the interim exodus of many of the senior field commanders from the Regular Army regiments. During the Civil War, Regular Army officers often took extended leave from their permanent assignments to accept higher ranking and more prestigious commissions in the rapidly expanding volunteer service.

In the middle of 1863 the 2nd U.S. Cavalry Regiment still carried Thomas J. Wood as its colonel on the unit muster rolls, even though he currently served as a brigadier general of volunteers in the Army of the Cumberland. Wood had replaced Philip St. George Cooke as the commanding officer of the old 2nd Dragoons in November 1861 when the latter received a promotion to the rank of brigadier general in the Regular Army.[3]

Within the officer ranks of the Reserve Brigade of General Buford's 1st Division, most notably during the Gettysburg Campaign, only the 6th U.S. Cavalry had a senior field-grade officer, Major Samuel Henry Starr, commanding it. The other three assigned Regular Army regiments in the brigade each had a captain in charge. Unfortunately, after their brief skirmish and shocking defeat at Fairfield, Pennsylvania during the afternoon of July 3, the 6th U.S. Cavalry would have only a lowly lieutenant commanding it. Major Starr received a serious wound, while the rest of the regiment, including both officers and enlisted men, was terribly decimated.[4]

In another of his many letters, this one written to General Hooker, General Pleasonton referred to the young Captain Merritt in most glowing terms by stating that:

> . . . I desire to inform the general commanding that the losses my command has sustained in officers require me to ask for the promotion of good commanders. It is necessary to have a good commander for the regular brigade of cavalry, and I earnestly recommend Captain Wesley Merritt to be made a brigadier general for that purpose. He has all the qualifications for it, and has distinguished himself by his gallantry and daring. Give me good commanders and I will give you good results.[5]

The last individual of the recently recognized trio of junior cavalry officers to be recommended for promotion by Alfred Pleasonton at that time in the war was George Armstrong Custer. Young Lieutenant Custer's most recent assignment was to the newly recruited Troop M of the 5th U.S. Cavalry as the original first lieutenant. Custer was the second-in-command to Captain Edward Henry Leib, a Regular Army officer with a mere two years of actual military experience, scarcely a couple of months more than Custer. Leib, who lacked a West Point education, joined the cavalry branch in April 1861 as a second lieutenant and had only recently received his commission as a captain. Captain Leib's only other military service was as a private in Company H of the 25th Regiment, Pennsylvania Volunteer Infantry.[6] Also serving in the newly formed troop of the 5th Cavalry was 2nd Lieutenant Temple Buford, the thirty-year-old nephew of Brigadier General John Buford.[7]

As luck would have it, Lieutenant Custer quickly found himself detached from his troop and assigned as an aide-de-camp on General Pleasonton's staff. Subsequently Custer never had the opportunity to serve in the field with the members of Troop M, although he did drill them while stationed at Washington. As a

First Lieutenant
George A. Custer,
General Pleasonton's
Aide-de-Camp
(GAR III)

Captain Elon J. Farnsworth,
General Pleasonton's
Aide-de-Camp
(GAR III)

Captain Wesley Merritt,
Commander, 2nd U.S. Cavalry
(GAR III)

first lieutenant, Custer joined the Cavalry Corps commander's staff on May 15, 1863. He was only twenty-three years old in the spring of 1863, having been born on December 5, 1839.[8]

Hundreds and hundreds of volumes have been written about George Custer's life and exploits before, during, and after the Civil War. Many of the books dealt with the fact that Major General Pleasonton considered Custer as his favorite staff officer and that was perhaps one of the main reasons for the young lieutenant's quick rise to the rank of brigadier general and brigade command. While George Custer ultimately became a true favorite of Alfred Pleasonton during the next few months, it seemed unlikely that Pleasonton viewed him as such in the very beginning of their association.

George Custer had served previously on the staffs of generals Philip Kearny, Edwin Vose Sumner, and George B. McClellan. All three general officers, but especially McClellan, undoubtedly held Custer in high esteem while he served on their staffs. Additionally during 1862, George Custer received an appointment as an assistant engineer on the staff of Brigadier General Andrew A. Humphreys, the Army of the Potomac's chief of Topographical Engineers. While serving in the capacity of assistant engineer, Brigadier General William Farrar "Baldy" Smith (U.S.M.A., Class of 1845) had Custer detailed to his staff. At the time, Smith commanded the 2nd Division of the VI Corps.[9]

In April 1863, six months after General McClellan's final departure as the commander of the Army of the Potomac, Custer lost his volunteer commission as a captain. That commission as a captain had been bestowed upon him because of his position on McClellan's staff. McClellan's leaving forced Custer to return to his permanent assignment with the cavalry branch. He reverted to his regular rank of first lieutenant. After serving with the 5th U.S. Cavalry Regiment for a little over a month, mostly around the city of Washington, Custer had the opportunity to transfer to another aide-de-camp position on General

Pleasonton's staff in May 1863. For the young and ambitious Custer, it was almost like beginning his career again. Once he had served on the staff of the Army of the Potomac's commanding officer, but now he found himself a mere lieutenant on the staff of a low-level brigadier general, who happened to command only one small division of cavalry.[10]

Without a doubt, Custer proved his value, mettle, and loyalty to General Pleasonton on any number of occasions during those early days of service together. The boyish Lieutenant Custer was constantly in the thick of the fighting during most contests in which Pleasonton's troopers became involved. Custer's main concern, as with the other staff members, was to transmit his commander's written and verbal instructions and any other orders to the often widely scattered unit commanders. Finding the right brigade or regiment and then locating its commander in the heat of battle was a difficult task, but Custer seems to have excelled at it, as did Farnsworth. Conversely a staff member often relayed information from the regimental level to the corps' commander.

It appears very likely that George Custer, according to many of the contemporary accounts from a number of different sources, was the only one of the three junior cavalry officers who did not truly know that he was in line for a promotion to brigadier general. Lieutenant Custer honestly appears not to have known about the chain of events that would ultimately unfold and give him the opportunity to command a brigade, composed of four volunteer cavalry regiments, by the end of the month of June. In a letter written on July 26, 1863, to his friend, mentor, and political patron Judge Isaac Peckham Christiancy, Custer seemingly confirmed that lack of knowledge concerning his promotion. Judge Christiancy was an associate justice of the Michigan Supreme Court and a future U.S. senator from that state. In the letter, Custer declared that:

> I never supposed that in one sudden leap I
> should change my 1st lieutenant's shoulder

straps (my real rank) for the star of a brigadier.
I was recommended by Gen. Meade and Gen.
Pleasanton and others, and knew nothing whatever of the fact until our arrival at Frederick,
Md. It was on Sunday the 29th [28th] of June,
I believe. General Pleasanton had just returned
from General Meade's Hdqtrs, and called me
to his room. He then informed me that some
time previous I had been recommended to the
President by letter and that day Gen. Meade
himself had telegraphed to the President asking
to have me appointed at once, as the cavalry
was to set out the next day in search of the Rebel army and leaders were needed. I felt highly
complimented, but had not the remote idea that
the President would appoint me, because I considered my youth, my low rank, and what is of
great importance at this time I recollected that
I had not a single 'friend at court.' I was never
more surprised than when I was informed of
my appointment as a Brigadier General. To say
I was elated would faintly express my feeling. I
well knew that I had reason to congratulate
myself. I was but twenty-three years of age, the
youngest general in the U.S. Army. It was a
position I had never in the faintest measure
asked for. Had I obtained appointment through
influential friends and sought for it in person
without having tried to merit it I should have
felt no such pleasant consolation. Gen. Pleasanton's first act was to relieve Gen. Copeland,
his reason for doing so stated to me was that he
"did not know him" and he wanted officers to
command now "whom he knew." He asked me
what he should do with me. I replied that I had
but one request to make which was to assign
me to the command of the Michigan Brigade,
my request was granted.[11]

If any of those three young cavalry officers could claim
General Pleasonton as his own personal benefactor and patron,
it very well could have been Elon J. Farnsworth. Given the tri-
lateral relationship between Major General Alfred Pleasonton,
U.S. Congressman John Farnsworth, and Captain Elon Farnsworth perhaps a case could be made for that point. The younger
Farnsworth, born on July 30, 1837, in Green Oak, Michigan,

probably was Pleasonton's favorite staff officer at that particular period of the war. Farnsworth's premature death on the battlefield at Gettysburg in less than a week prevented anyone from learning what he might have been able to accomplish with a longer career.

Elon Farnsworth had the privilege to serve on General Pleasonton's staff for a much longer period than Custer. He also outranked his West Point-educated associate. His responsibilities were, naturally, greater than those of the newly assigned George Custer. There is no intimation how the two junior officers interacted with each other as they performed their delegated duties before being promoted. Nevertheless, as an indication of the high esteem which Alfred Pleasonton placed in Farnsworth, consider that it was the young Captain Farnsworth to whom Pleasonton loaned a blouse with his recently retired brigadier general shoulder straps attached. The commanding general loaned the coat to Farnsworth on the same day as Elon's promotion at Frederick City—the identical blouse and shoulder straps worn by Farnsworth at the time of his death only five days later.

According to one of George Custer's orderlies, Private Joseph Fought, it was he who scrounged the stars that Custer first used as his insignia of rank after his leap from first lieutenant to brigadier general. Fought remembered his successful search by stating that:

> I went through every place where they kept such things and found scraps for uniform furnishings, but no stars. Finally, late in the night I found an old Jew and in his place he had a box of things belonging to a uniform and some stars. I bought two, and then went back and found the Captain in his room at Headquarters. He was glad to have the stars–but who would sew them on? And where could we get needle and thread? I scratched around and got them, and sewed them on, one on each corner of his collar. The next morning he was a full-fledged Brigadier-General.[12]

Of course not all of General Pleasonton's other brigade and regimental commanders expressed excitement or pleasure about the prospect of the unanticipated elevation of three in-experienced junior officers to brigade commands. Of Pleasonton's six assigned brigades on the 23rd day of June one had a brigadier general in command—Kilpatrick. Four brigades had colonels commanding—Thomas Devin, William Gamble, John Irvin Gregg, and John B. McIntosh. One brigade was under the leadership of a major—Samuel Starr. Additionally, five regimental commanders present for duty with their regiments held the rank of full colonel. They included George Henry Chapman of the 3rd Indiana; Pennock Huey of the 8th Pennsylvania; Josiah H. Kellogg of the 17th Pennsylvania; William Sackett of the 9th New York; and John P. Taylor of the 1st Pennsylvania. One of those colonels, Josiah Kellogg, listed his alma mater as the U.S. Military Academy, where he graduated thirteenth out of a class of forty-one cadets. Newly promoted brigadier general Wesley Merritt, from the same class, graduated twenty-second and was now Kellogg's senior.

Each of the assigned brigade commanders in Pleasonton's command had much more experience in a battlefield environ-ment and in leading large groups of mounted men in combat than the three youthful officers. Most of those officers were even tactically proficient. Even General Pleasonton's most jun-ior ranking brigade commander, though certainly not junior in age, the almost fifty-three-year-old Major Samuel Starr of the Reserve Brigade of General Buford's 1st Division, had more ex-perience than all the young officers combined.

Earlier in the Civil War that veteran of the Mexican and Seminole Wars commanded the 5th Regiment, New Jersey Vol-unteer Infantry as its colonel. Along with that duty, Starr led the infantry brigade in which his unit served until he unexpectedly resigned late in 1862. After his premature resignation from the 5th New Jersey, Starr returned to the 6th U.S. Cavalry Regi-ment. He reverted to the rank of major and assumed command of the Reserve Brigade from Major Charles Jarvis Whiting (U.S.M.A., Class of 1835) of the 2nd U.S. Cavalry Regiment, being the senior ranking officer present in the brigade.[13]

One of General Pleasonton's other brigade commanders, Colonel J. Irvin Gregg, circulated a, not too, confidential memorandum concerning the recent and somewhat surprising and comparatively unpopular appointments.[14] Colonel Gregg served in his first-cousin's division, Brigadier General David McM. Gregg's 2nd Division. J. Irvin Gregg's missive directly questioned the qualifications of Custer, Farnsworth, and Merritt and further stated that:

> . . . I do not think that any reason can be assigned by the most favorably disposed to warrant these appointments. Nor do I think that the subsequent history of these . . . can show anything to justify their promotion over the heads of superior officers commanding Brigades. . . .[15]

In spite of the intrigue, unprofessional jealousy, and petty animosity regarding the unexpected promotions of the three young officers the Army of the Potomac's Cavalry Corps and General Stahel's independent cavalry command still had crucial missions to conduct during the next few days. Those duties were already well under way during the last week of June. The early morning hours of June 25 quietly arrived and showed that Stahel's horsemen were quickly approaching the banks of the Potomac River. The three assigned brigades of General Stahel's command started their journey to the north by crossing the waters of the Potomac River either near the Edwards Ferry ford or at Young's Island ford located two miles to the south.

The Potomac River at Edwards Ferry was less than a quarter of a mile wide and not very deep under normal circumstances. According to the contemporary accounts, the water was perhaps no more than three to four feet deep during average weather conditions. It was just shallow enough for a horse and rider to be able to make their way carefully across the slippery footing without any danger of being swept downstream by the current. The crossing at Young's Island ford was almost a mile wide and normally shallow.

Major General Julius Stahel,
Commander, Cavalry Division
(GAR III)

For the most part, the assigned cavalry regiments of Julius Stahel's division actually waded across that expanse of the river instead of using the recently constructed pontoon bridge. Construction had begun on one bridge, which spanned the waters of the Potomac River at Edwards Ferry, on the evening of June 20. A small contingent of U.S. Army engineers held the ultimate responsibility for getting it in place across the flowing waters. That bridge was the only one in operation for the army's use until a second pontoon bridge was laid across the water on June 25 to accommodate the thousands of men and animals in the Army of the Potomac marching into Maryland.[16]

Some of Stahel's luckier cavalrymen had the opportunity to march their horses across the pontoon bridges and not get their feet wet. Scores of infantry and artillery units, mainly elements from the Army of the Potomac's XI Corps, attempted to cross the bridge during the same period. In addition, the XI Corps' and Stahel's supply and baggage wagons, all attempted to cross at the same time, using the twin pontoon bridges erected by the army's engineers at the Edwards Ferry crossing. The road leading to the ford quickly became impassable because of the thousands of soldiers funneling to the bridge.

Edwards Ferry, situated on the Maryland side of the Potomac River, was a thriving site while the Chesapeake and Ohio (C & O) Canal was in operation during the nineteenth century. Lock number twenty-five of the canal was located at that fording site. Until 1836 a ferryboat operation shuttled paying customers between the Virginia and Maryland shorelines. A small wooden bridge for foot and single-horse traffic eventually was built at that site for the convenience of the many travelers trying to cross the river without the inconvenience of finding another ford. All wagons had to use the larger and sturdier bridge at Conrad's Ferry located almost six miles farther north along the Potomac. Both bridges were destroyed early in the war.[17]

The first regiments of Stahel's command to ford the river and advance onto the free soil of Maryland were those members of Colonel Richard Butler Price's 2nd Brigade. Crossing the Potomac a short distance south of Edwards Ferry, during the early morning hours of June 25 the 1st Michigan, 2nd Pennsylvania, and 18th Pennsylvania were the first regiments of the division to reach the shoreline of Maryland. The cavalrymen did not tarry for long on the slippery banks of the river but immediately crossed over the imperceptibly flowing waters of the C & O Canal. The canal paralleled the Potomac, on the Maryland side of the river, from Washington, D.C. to Cumberland, Maryland.

*Brigadier General
Joseph T. Copeland,
Commander,
1st Brigade, Stahel's Division*
(NA)

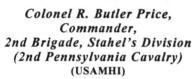

*Colonel R. Butler Price,
Commander,
2nd Brigade, Stahel's Division
(2nd Pennsylvania Cavalry)*
(USAMHI)

*Colonel Othneil De Forest,
Commander,
3rd Brigade, Stahel's Division
(5th New York Cavalry)*
(GAR III)

Taking the Edwards Ferry Road, Colonel Price's brigade traveled a short five miles to the northeast where they reached the small village of Poolesville. At Poolesville, after a brief rest to feed and water their horses, Price's three regiments remounted and continued their journey north toward Frederick City. After traveling an additional dozen miles the Union cavalrymen reached another small village called Urbana. General Stuart and his cavalrymen occupied that place during his raid through Maryland the previous year. The weary horsemen of Colonel Price's 2nd Brigade went into camp in the fields near Urbana for what remained of the day.[18]

The next brigade of General Stahel's command to cross the Potomac River was Colonel Othneil De Forest's 3rd Brigade. Crossing at the Young's Island ford, the three regiments of the 3rd Brigade included De Forest's own 5th New York, the 1st Vermont, and the 1st West Virginia. Passing across the river and canal, they turned their column in the direction of Poolesville, too. After a brief respite at that place, the regiments then continued their march toward the northwest. De Forest's men had to ford the shallow, but rapidly flowing waters of the Monocacy River at Monocacy Junction, which was almost worse than crossing the Potomac. The cavalrymen continued their journey to the tiny community of Licksville where they halted for the night in the shadow of Sugar Loaf Mountain, the highest point, and most easily recognizable landmark, in the immediate area.[19]

Brigadier General Joseph Tarr Copeland's 1st Brigade, composed of the 5th, the 6th, and the 7th Michigan Cavalry regiments, was the last unit of Stahel's command to ford the Potomac River. The Michiganders followed closely on the heels of Colonel De Forest's men. They started across the river at roughly five o'clock in the afternoon on the 25th. General Copeland's regiments, with the 5th Michigan Cavalry in the advance and followed at irregular intervals by the 6th and 7th Michigan, did not get very far before darkness enveloped them on that densely cloudy night. The three regiments crossed the river at an excruciatingly slow pace. Just as the first troopers reached the opposite bank of the river it started to rain lightly, which only added to the discomfort of the tired and already thoroughly wet cavalrymen.[20]

As the 7th Michigan Cavalry crossed the Potomac, one of the troopers upon reaching the banks on the Maryland side of the river decided to desert his troop and comrades. The soldier was Bugler Samuel William Edwards of Troop I. In a curious twist of circumstances Bugler Edwards decided to depart his troop at the place named after the Edwards family. It is unknown if Bugler Edwards was any relation to the family that had given their name to the ferry.[21]

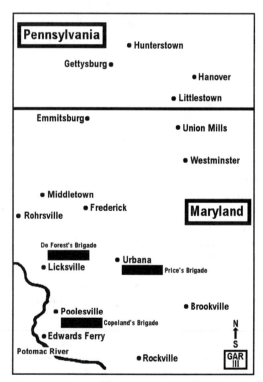

Locations of Stahel's Brigades
Morning of June 26, 1863
(GAR III)

Because of the congestion and mass confusion among men, horses, and wagons at the bridge crossings and because the waters of the Potomac were too high to drive the wagons across to the Maryland side, General Stahel temporarily had to leave his wagon train behind on the Virginia shore. General Copeland's brigade had the tiresome and extremely irksome task of guarding their division's lengthy wagon train. Now, twenty-eight-year-old Major Crawley P. Dake, commanding Troops C and L from the 5th Michigan Cavalry, took his turn to guard it. Major Dake had orders to proceed across the Edwards Ferry bridge as soon as practicable. The members of the two troops guarding the train would continue that same assignment for the next week and miss all the fighting.

As they continued their forward progress in the inky darkness the tired and hungry troopers of Copeland's command, along with their horses, attempted to maintain contact with the rider in their immediate front and any other troopers riding by their sides. It was the only way to travel since nobody could see anything in the blackness of the night. Everybody's movement depended greatly upon those of the surrounding soldiers and their mounts. Another cavalryman, Captain William E. Miller, from the 3rd Pennsylvania Cavalry, assigned to General David Gregg's division, wrote about his experience and the difficulty with a night march:

> To one not familiar with a cavalry night march in the face of the enemy it may be difficult to comprehend why it should differ materially from an advance by daylight, but to those who have had some experience this is easily understood. On a night march, in order to guard against surprise, flankers are thrown out on either side, who are supposed to keep abreast of the advance-guard. These flankers are under the supervision of the officer in charge of the advance, and no matter how dark the night is he must keep them sufficiently deployed to protect the column, and yet always have them well in hand. These flankers encounter all sorts of obstacles, such as ditches,

ravines, fences, underbrush, woods, etc., and
necessarily make slow progress. The time thus
occupied compels the main body in the rear to
make innumerable stops and starts, which are
not only tedious and wearying, but annoying
and irksome, and hard upon the horses, often
causing the men to grow impatient and the officers to become irritable.[22]

It was a very protracted and necessarily slow process for all
of General Stahel's cavalrymen to cross the Potomac and then to
cross the very narrow, but extremely steep-banked, C & O Canal. The roads to all the fords on the Virginia side of the Potomac River were rapidly becoming clogged. Thousands and
thousands of soldiers, along with hundreds of ambulances, wagons, pack mules, cattle, and the other necessary support personnel and equipment, moved into the Loudoun County side of the
river in order to begin their journey across the water.

Upon reaching the Maryland shoreline, the Michiganders of
General Copeland's brigade started along the Edwards Ferry
Road but traveled only as far as Poolesville before calling a
halt. At that place they moved off the road into some muddy
fields and established their bivouac for the remaining hours of
darkness. Throughout the rest of the night the ambulances and
wagons of the division continued to filter into the camp. Chaplain Louis Napoleon Boudrye and Surgeon Lucius P. Woods,
both assigned to the 5th New York Cavalry, traveled with the
wagon train as did most of the other noncombatants in the division.[23] The light rain, that had started to fall earlier in the afternoon, continued until now and made life more miserable for
both men and horses.[24]

On this day General Julius Stahel and the members of his
headquarters staff elected to travel with General Copeland's
cavalrymen, mainly because of the mode of transportation selected by the division's commanding general. Because of the inclement weather, Stahel's chosen method of conveyance was
one that, when seen by any spectator, would not soon be
forgotten.

General Stahel traveled in the grandest of comforts on that miserable day, riding in the rear of a covered spring wagon drawn by four white mules. During the Civil War, it was not unusual for senior commissioned officers to spend time traveling in wagons or ambulances, particularly when encounters with the enemy were not imminent. In that way, they could plot future strategy, reference maps for routes of march, confer with subordinates about changes in orders, or most likely just rest from the rigors of the march.[25]

Riding in the back of the spring wagon, General Stahel crossed the Potomac River at Edwards Ferry using one of the pontoon bridges erected there. Because of the late hour and the increasingly stormy weather, the division commander along with the members of his staff also stopped at the village of Poolesville for the night, just as the Michigan cavalrymen before them had done. As the hectic day came to a close, all the troopers of Major General Stahel's cavalry division found themselves safely on the Maryland side of the Potomac River. However, quite some distance separated the three divisions.[26]

At some time during the early morning hours of June 26, 1863, General Copeland's brigade staff received orders from General Stahel's headquarters temporarily detaching the 7th Michigan Cavalry, commanded by Colonel William D'Alton Mann, from the 1st Brigade. The men from the 7th Michigan received the word to move north. Mann's regiment had only a few scant hours of rest, having gone into camp well after midnight. The regiment received orders to move in advance of the whole division on a scouting mission in the general direction of the passes in the South Mountain.

Colonel Mann's untried and untested regiment, which had only joined their brigade in March, consisted of just ten assigned troops.[27] Upon receipt of their new orders they promptly mounted their tired horses and departed for their newly assigned area of operation. Along their route of march they passed through the village of Urbana and the still encamped regiments of Colonel Price's brigade. Not surprisingly, the men of the 7th Michigan found the traveling quite easy as they made their way toward Frederick. They had overtaken most of the infantry regiments from the Army of the Potomac, except for the advancing units of the XI Corps. Colonel Mann's men were now the leading element of their own division as well. The soldiers of the XI Corps were spread out generally west of Frederick near Boonsboro, Burkittsville, and Middletown. The 7th Michigan Cavalry would eventually pass by many of those infantrymen before halting for the day.[28]

Their ride along the remarkably well-maintained roads leading to the north was now almost enjoyable for the troopers of the 7th Michigan. The rain had ceased and the sun was shining brightly. The roads were somewhat muddy but passable. As they rode along, the men received rousing welcomes and most cordial greetings from many of the small villages and clusters of houses through which they passed. However, not all towns and citizens welcomed the Yankee troopers to their territory. Private Edwin R. Havens, serving with Troop A of the 7th Michigan, recalled with unmistakable disgust one small hamlet through which his regiment had journeyed on that first day in Maryland. He stated that: "After leaving Poolesville we passed through a dirty little village called Bondsville in which nearly everyone was a secesh. . . ."[29]

As the 7th Michigan Cavalry moved toward their objective in the South Mountain, the rest of General Stahel's division received orders to depart their overnight camps shortly after sunrise. The other regiments were to continue their movement to the north and into the interior sections of Maryland. The rainstorm from the previous day had ceased for the present, but the roads were becoming increasingly bad due to the number of marching soldiers, horses, and wagons moving along them.

Unlike the members of the 7th Michigan Cavalry, who were in the lead of the advancing army, the remainder of Stahel's division was much more entangled with the rest of the thousands of soldiers moving to the north. The muddy roads would only continue to worsen as thousands of men and animals tramped along them to Pennsylvania.

General Copeland and the remainder of his horsemen from the 5th and 6th Michigan regiments, along with the division's wagon train, eventually began to move from their overnight camps at Poolesville. They slowly navigated around the base of Sugar Loaf Mountain and continued almost four miles further to the narrow waters of the Monocacy River. There the men from Michigan, as well as the wagon train, forded the rising waters of the river. After crossing that body of water, those troopers had relatively few impediments on their journey and moved rapidly north along the main road and through the small communities of Adamstown and Jefferson with crowds of cheering civilians standing along the route of march. The wagon train started to lag behind.[30]

As General Copeland and his men were moving toward Jefferson, they received orders to leave the division's slowly moving wagon train behind and continue without it toward Frederick. Considering the wagons to be safe with only a few men from the two troops guarding it, General Stahel ordered Copeland to move rapidly to Frederick and then had him continue north to near the Mason-Dixon Line.

As Copeland's men moved out, the teamsters continued their journey, driving the heavily laden wagons very cautiously. Because of the slow-moving vehicles, all traffic eventually backed up behind them along a steep road that entered Jefferson. That road block irritated Brigadier General Buford and his cavalrymen who happened to find themselves caught behind it after they had crossed the Potomac and commenced their journey northward. John Buford's command quickly found another path around General Stahel's stalled wagons.[31]

General Copeland's men had much better luck after divesting themselves of the cumbersome wagon train. They were able to move rapidly toward Frederick City. The two regiments of

Copeland's brigade soon arrived on the outskirts of Frederick, where they stopped for the night.

Colonel De Forest and the members of his brigade traveled along the country roads of Washington and Frederick counties on June 26. As with the other members of the division, reveille sounded all too early for those weary cavalrymen, just after dawn. The 5th New York, the 1st Vermont, and the 1st West Virginia left their bivouac sites at Licksville and marched through the small hamlets of Adamstown, Jefferson, and Burkittsville on their way to the passes of South Mountain. The three regiments crossed that mountain range at Crampton's Gap and did not find any signs of the expected Confederate forces in the immediate vicinity. The tired cavalrymen of De Forest's brigade pushed on for a few more miles to the northwest side of the pass, where they eventually established their camp at Rohrersville for the remainder of the day after sending out numerous scouts and foraging parties.[32]

Colonel Price's men, like their comrades in Stahel's other two brigades, were in the saddle and moving north shortly after sunrise. The colonel's 2nd Brigade moved from near Urbana, north along the Frederick Road, to the city of Frederick, which place they reached about mid-afternoon. Price's troopers did not remain within the city limits too long before continuing their march west for another ten miles to the village of Middletown. At Middletown the brigade encamped for the rest of the day, sending out the necessary scouts and pickets to safeguard their bivouac. Since their wagon train was well behind them, Colonel Price's men unexpectedly found themselves out of rations. They had not brought enough food with them for either themselves or their horses, thinking that their wagon train with its supplies was only a short distance to the rear of their column. With the timely assistance and intervention of General Stahel, Colonel Price was able to obtain enough rations for his men from members of General Howard's XI Corps also currently located at Middletown.[33]

So far during the short history of the campaign, General Julius Stahel, along with the commissioned officers and enlisted men under his direct command, had done everything that they had been ordered to do by their commanders in the Department of Washington. Additionally, they obeyed orders from the various senior field commanders from the Army of the Potomac. Much to their surprise and chagrin the Hungarian-born general and his troops were now being maligned by no less a personality than Major General John Fulton Reynolds (U.S.M.A., Class of 1841), commander of the Army of the Potomac's I Corps. In a status report forwarded on June 26 to General Butterfield, Hooker's chief of staff, Reynolds opined:

> . . . The cavalry sent out by Stahel does nothing. They go into camp behind the infantry, and send out small squads from them. General Stahel was at Frederick to-day, and will be at Middletown to-night. . . .[34]

Specifically, General Reynolds had received a flurry of detrimental reports from some elements of the XI Corps, currently on their way to guard Boonsboro, Burkittsville, and the pass through the South Mountain at Crampton's Gap. Obviously unaware that General Stahel's 3rd Brigade, under Colonel De Forest, had already positioned themselves at Rohrersville, a tiny community northwest of the gap, Reynolds chastised Stahel for his lackadaisical attitude and his seemingly non-aggressive execution of orders in searching for signs of the enemy's movements west of their position.

Except for some infantrymen posted at Boonsboro, the cavalrymen of Stahel's division at Rohrersville were still farther west than the rest of General Howard's XI Corps. In addition, Colonel Mann's 7th Michigan regiment dispatched patrols as far north as within four miles of Hagerstown, which was almost twelve miles north of Boonsboro and well past even the most advanced pickets of the XI Corps.[35]

The cavalrymen identified by General Reynolds as being in "camp behind the infantry" were members of Stahel's 2nd Brigade, commanded by Colonel Price. Major General Reynolds castigated Major General Stahel and his command based upon faulty intelligence from General Howard's infantry most of which had not deployed far enough even to know if the cavalry might be in their front. Those inaccuracies further compounded Stahel's own delay in reporting his actual troop deployment. In an accompanying postscript submitted with his tardy report, Stahel related to Reynolds that: "The foregoing report would have been sent to you last night had I known where your headquarters were."[36]

Julius Stahel did not improve his overall cause by offering a feeble excuse for not getting his report to Reynolds' headquarters in a timely manner. Previously the independent cavalry commander had received directions to send all dispatches to General Reynolds at Poolesville. For whatever reason, Stahel and his staff officers seem to have forgotten the exact locations of the leading infantry elements of the Army of the Potomac, along with their commanders. That was not a very good sign for General Stahel, but it was already too late to save him from his coming fate.[37]

As indicated in General Reynolds' terse report about the cavalry support, Stahel arrived during the late afternoon hours of June 26 with the Michigan members of his cavalry command in Frederick City, where he briefly established his headquarters in the Dill House near the courthouse in the center of town.[38] Upon his arrival at Frederick, Stahel immediately dictated the following report. However he failed to send the information concerning the deployment of his division to Major General Reynolds commanding the Left Wing of the Army of the Potomac, which encompassed the I, III, and XI Corps, until the next day, June 27. General Reynolds' headquarters did not receive Stahel's report until 5:30 P.M.:

I arrived at this place this afternoon [June 26], and have made the following disposition of my troops: I have one brigade [Colonel De Forest's 3rd Brigade] and one section of artillery at Crampton's Pass, patrolling thoroughly on the other side, but without meeting with any enemy whatever; they are supported by one brigade and two sections of artillery of the Eleventh Corps. I have one regiment [Colonel Mann's 7th Michigan] in South Mountain Pass, patrolling in that vicinity, but without meeting any of the enemy. One brigade [Colonel Price's 2nd Brigade] and two sections of artillery are at Middletown, and two regiments [5th & 6th Michigan under General Copeland] about 2 miles from this place, on the road leading toward Lewistown. . . .[39]

Later the same day, General Stahel vacated his comfortable surroundings at the Dill House and proceeded to ride west to Middletown with a small portion of his staff, where he established his field headquarters and decided to spend the night with Colonel Price's brigade. Other members of the division staff remained in Frederick to evaluate and forward any incoming information to their division commander from the other brigades' patrols. Although the night passed peacefully for all the troopers within Stahel's division, the next couple of days showed evidence that they would not be kind for Major General Julius Stahel and many of his senior officers.

Dawn of June 27 found the regiments of Stahel's command still in their assigned patrol areas and their encampments of the preceding night. For most of the day, Othneil De Forest's 3rd Brigade remained in position at Rohrersville, scouting for any signs of the Army of Northern Virginia's movements. Sometime around 4:00 P.M., Colonel De Forest ordered the brigade to mount their horses and proceed back to Burkittsville, a place through which they had passed the previous day. From Burkittsville the three regiments of his brigade moved northeast to Middletown and thence through Frederick, stopping some three miles to the north, where they set up camp along the main pike to Emmitsburg. Colonel Price's brigade remained in the vicinity of Middletown and was allowed some much needed rest.

General Copeland's Michiganders were the most actively engaged on June 27, moving away from their encampment near Frederick in the early morning hours. They rode north along the Emmitsburg Pike to the small town of Emmitsburg nestled near the Mason-Dixon Line. They halted at that town for the night. Emmitsburg, the site of Mount Saint Mary's Catholic College, had sustained severe damage by a fire set by an arsonist less than two weeks previously and the terrible destruction was still obvious to the men from Michigan. The fire destroyed twenty-eight buildings, as well as leaving roughly 190 residents of Emmitsburg without shelter.[40]

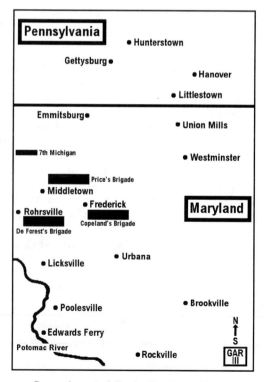

Locations of Stahel's Brigades
Morning of June 27, 1863
(GAR III)

General Stahel's division wagon train, which finally con-
quered the extremely hilly terrain of southwestern Frederick
County, eventually arrived on the outskirts of Frederick City on
June 27. The division's main train would remain parked near
Frederick for the next few days. Only the ambulances, some
supply wagons, and a few other essential vehicles would move
with the cavalry division when it resumed the march and left
Frederick on June 29.

The 7th Michigan Cavalry, still detached from the rest of
their brigade, patrolled the territory near Turner's Gap in the
South Mountain. In a detailed dispatch sent at midnight on June
27 and forwarded to Colonel Price's headquarters, Colonel
Mann reported that:

> . . . a patrol from my command has just re-
> turned from toward Hagerstown, having been
> within 4 miles of that place. They found no
> force. Heard reports that enemy had all left
> Hagerstown this morning, but were said to be
> fortifying at a short distance beyond, toward
> Chambersburg. Four hundred cavalry and three
> pieces of artillery are said to have been sent
> from Hagerstown back to Jones' Cross-Roads,
> on the Boonsborough and Williamsport road,
> this morning, as if to check an expected ad-
> vance. Report says large quantities of stores
> are being sent back to Virginia; stores in
> Hagerstown robbed, &c. With a small re-
> enforcement, or with permission to take my
> entire command from here, I should be pleased
> to make a reconnaissance to Jones' Cross-
> Roads, 8 miles from here, to learn what force
> is there.[41]

Mann's regiment did not receive permission from division or
brigade headquarters to continue toward Jones' Cross Roads in
search of the enemy's forces. The 7th Michigan Cavalry, after
remaining overnight in the area near Turner's Gap, received orders to rejoin their division at Frederick the next day.

Notes to Chapter Three

1. Pleasonton MSS.
2. Elon J. Farnsworth to John F. Farnsworth, June 23, 1863, Pleasonton MSS, LC. The brief military career of Elon J. Farnsworth included assignments as Battalion Quartermaster, 8th Illinois Cavalry – September 1861; Captain, 8th Illinois Cavalry – December 1861; Brigadier General, U.S. Volunteers – June 1863.
3. Rodenbough, *From Everglade to Cañon*, pp. 437-38. The assigned colonels of the other five cavalry regiments in June 1863 were: George A. H. Blake, 1st U.S. Cavalry, serving at Cavalry Corps Headquarters, Army of the Potomac; Marshall Saxe Howe (U.S.M.A., Class of 1827), 3rd U.S. Cavalry, serving at headquarters, XVI Corps in Tennessee; John Sedgwick, 4th U.S. Cavalry, serving as major general of volunteers commanding the VI Corps, Army of the Potomac; George Henry Thomas (U.S.M.A., Class of 1840), 5th U.S. Cavalry, serving as major general of volunteers commanding the XIV Corps, Army of the Cumberland; David Hunter (U.S.M.A., Class of 1822), 6th U.S. Cavalry, serving as major general of volunteers most recently in command of the X Corps in the Department of the South.
4. As the month of June 1863 ended the commander of the 1st U.S. Cavalry was Captain Richard Stanton Chandler Lord from Troop A; the 2nd U.S. Cavalry was commanded by Captain Theophilus Francis Rodenbough from Troop L; the 5th U.S. Cavalry was commanded by Captain Julius Wilmot Mason from Troop K.
5. OR – 3, pp. 912-13. Merritt's forty-five year military career included: Cadet at the U.S. Military Academy – July 1, 1855 to July 1, 1860; Brevet 2nd Lieutenant of Dragoons – July 1, 1860; 2nd Lieutenant, 2nd Dragoons – January 28, 1861; 1st Lieutenant, 2nd Dragoons, May 13, 1861; Captain, 2nd Cavalry – April 5, 1862; Brigadier General, U.S. Volunteers – June 29, 1863; Brevet Major, – July 1, 1863; Brevet Lieutenant Colonel – May 11, 1864; Brevet Colonel – May 28, 1864; Brevet Major General, U.S. Volunteers – October 19, 1864; Brevet Brigadier General, U.S. Army – March 13, 1865; Brevet Major General, U.S. Army – March 13, 1865; Major General, U.S. Volunteers – April 1, 1865; Lieutenant Colonel, 9th Cavalry – July 28, 1866; Colonel, 5th Cavalry – July 1, 1876; Brigadier General, U.S. Army – April 16, 1887; Major General, U.S. Army – April 25, 1895; Retired – June 16, 1900.
6. Samuel P. Bates, *History of Pennsylvania Volunteers, 1861-5*, 5 vols. (Harrisburg: B. Singerly, 1871), 1:10, 228; Constance Wynn Altshuler, *Cavalry Yellow & Infantry Blue:Army Officers in Arizona Between 1851 and 1886* (Arizona: Arizona Historical Society, 1991), p. 201. Originally organized at Pottsville as the Washington Artillery, a three-month unit, it was incorporated into the 25th Regiment as Company H. Edward Leib served for only eight days before accepting a second lieutenant's commission in the Regular Army.

Notes to Chapter Three (*continued*)

7. George F. Price, *Across the Continent with the Fifth Cavalry* (New York: Antiquarian Press Ltd., 1959), pp. 558. Temple Buford's father was Napoleon Bonaparte Buford, John's fifty-six-year-old half-brother. The elder Buford graduated from West Point in the Class of 1827.

8. Custer's military promotions included: Cadet at the U.S. Military Academy – July 1, 1857 to June 24, 1861; 2nd Lieutenant, 2nd Cavalry – June 24, 1861; 1st Lieutenant, 5th Cavalry – July 17, 1862; Captain, Staff – Additional Aide-de-Camp – June 5, 1862; Brigadier General, U.S. Volunteers – June 29, 1863; Brevet Major – July 3, 1863; Captain, 5th Cavalry – May 8, 1864; Brevet Lieutenant Colonel – May 11, 1864; Brevet Colonel – September 19, 1864; Brevet Major General, U.S. Volunteers – October 19, 1864; Brevet Brigadier General, U.S. Army – March 13, 1865; Brevet Major General, U.S. Army – March 13, 1865; Major General, U.S. Volunteers – April 15, 1865; Lieutenant Colonel, 7th Cavalry – July 28, 1866.

9. John M. Carroll, *Custer in the Civil War:His Unfinished Memoirs* (San Rafael, Calif.: Presidio Press, 1977), pp. 74-75.

10. Price, *Across the Continent*, pp. 393-95.

11. Gregory J. W. Urwin, *Custer Victorious:The Civil War Battles of General George Armstrong Custer* (Rutherford, N.J.: Fairleigh Dickinson University Press, 1983), p. 54; Marguerite Merington, ed., *The Custer Story:The Life and Intimate Letters of General George A. Custer and His Wife Elizabeth* (New York: Devin-Adair, 1950), p. 59.

12. Merington, *The Custer Story*, p. 60.

13. Starr's military promotions included: Private, Company G, 4th U.S. Artillery – October 1832; Corporal, Company G, 4th U.S. Artillery – January 1834; Sergeant, discharged – October 1837; Private, Company A, Battalion Engineers – June 1846; Sergeant, Company A, Battalion Engineers – November 1846; Brevet 2nd Lieutenant, 2nd U.S. Dragoons – June 1848; 2nd Lieutenant, 2nd U.S. Dragoons – July 1848; 1st Lieutenant, 2nd U.S. Dragoons – November 1851; Captain, 2nd U.S. Dragoons – June 1858; Colonel, 5th New Jersey Volunteer Infantry – August 1861; Resigned volunteer commission – October 1862; Major, 6th U.S. Cavalry – April 1863; Brevet Major, U.S. Army – May 1862; Brevet Lieutenant-Colonel – June 1863; Brevet Colonel – July 1863; Retired from active service – December 1870.

14. Milton V. Burgess, *David Gregg, Pennsylvania Cavalryman* (State College, Pa.: published by author., 1984), p. 4.

15. John Irvin Gregg, "Private and Confidential Memoranda in reference to appointments of Brig. Gens. in the Cavalry Corps Army of the Potomac," n. d., Gregg MSS, Historical Society of Pennsylvania. This memorandum was penned sometime after the Gettysburg Campaign, probably around September 1863. Gregg had served as a captain in the 3rd U.S. Cavalry; a captain in the 6th U.S. Cavalry; and as colonel of the 16th Regiment, Pennsylvania Volunteer Cavalry before becoming a brigade commander in the Cavalry Corps of the Army of the Potomac.

Notes to Chapter Three (*continued*)

16. Edwin R. Havens, Correspondence File. Michigan State University Library, East Lansing, Michigan. (Hereafter cited as Havens MSS.) Edwin Havens was a sergeant assigned to Troop A, 7th Michigan Cavalry. He received a wound during the cavalry battle on July 3 at Gettysburg.

17. Thomas F. Hahn, *Towpath Guide to the C & O Canal, Section Two, Seneca to Harpers Ferry* (Shepherdstown, W.Va.: American Canal and Transportation Center, 1977), p. 14. Conrad's Ferry is known today as White's Ferry.

18. Publication Committee of the Regimental Association, *History of the Eighteenth Regiment of Cavalry, Pennsylvania Volunteers (163d Regiment of the Line) 1862-1865* (New York: Wynkoop, Hallenbeck, Crawford, 1909), p. 38; *Pennsylvania at Gettysburg: Ceremonies at the Dedication of the Monuments Erected by the Commonwealth of Pennsylvania to Major General George G. Meade, Major General Winfield S. Hancock, Major General John F. Reynolds and to Mark the Positions of the Pennsylvania Commands Engaged in the Battle*, 2 vols. (Harrisburg: Wm. Stanley Ray, State Printers, 1893), 2:887. The date used in both references, but from the same writer, lists June 26, 1863, as the day that the regiment crossed the Potomac River. This date seems unlikely since the other two regiments in the brigade crossed on the 25th and moved to Urbana. Additionally, General Stahel in his report to General Reynolds stated that the whole of Price's 2nd Brigade was at Middletown on the 26th, a physical impossibility if the 18th Pennsylvania did not cross the Potomac until 8:40 that morning.

19. Louis N. Boudrye, *Historic Records of the Fifth New York Cavalry, First Ira Harris Guard* (Albany: S. R. Gray, 1865), p. 63; G. G. Benedict, *Vermont in the Civil War, 1861 - 1865*, 2 vols. (Burlington, Vt.: Free Press Association, 1889), 2:592; 1st Regiment, West Virginia Volunteer Cavalry Regiment; Boxes 4787 – 4791; Muster Rolls, Regimental Papers, Office of the Adjutant General, Volunteer Organizations, Civil War; Record Group 94; National Archives, Washington, D.C. (Hereafter cited as NA RG 94 – 1 WV.)

20. James H. Kidd, *Personal Recollections of a Cavalryman* (Ionia, Mich.: Sentinel Printing, 1908), p. 115.

21. 7th Regiment, Michigan Volunteer Cavalry Regiment; Boxes 1925 – 1929; Muster Rolls, Regimental Papers, Office of the Adjutant General, Volunteer Organizations, Civil War; Record Group 94; National Archives, Washington, D.C. (Hereafter cited as NA RG 94 – 7 MI.)

22. Robert U. Johnson and Clarence C. Buel, eds. *Battles and Leaders of the Civil War, Being for the Most Part Contributions by Union and Confederate Officers, Based Upon "The Century War Series."* 4 vols. (New York: Century Company, 1884-89), 3:398.

23. Louis N. Beaudry, *War Journal of Louis N. Beaudry, Fifth New York Cavalry* (Jefferson, N.C.: McFarland & Co., Inc., 1996), p. 47.

Notes to Chapter Three (*continued*)

24. Samuel Harris, *Personal Reminiscences of Samuel Harris* (Chicago: Rogerson Press, 1897), p. 24; Jno. Robertson (comp.), *Michigan in the War* (Lansing, Mich.: W. S. George & Co., 1880), p. 399; *Michigan at Gettysburg, July 1st, 2nd and 3rd, 1863* (Detroit: Winn & Hammond, 1889), p. 135.
25. Asa B. Isham, *An Historical Sketch of the Seventh Regiment Michigan Volunteer Cavalry from Its Organization, in 1862, to Its Muster Out, in 1865* (New York: Town Topics Publishing, 1893), p. 20. Another senior officer, Colonel John C. Lemmon, 10th Regiment, New York Volunteer Cavalry, used an ambulance as his personal form of transportation. Lemmon was seriously injured when the ambulance in which he was riding overturned while trying to escape from a surprise Confederate attack early in October 1862.
26. Robertson, *Michigan in the War*, p. 399.
27. Troops L and M were just about ready to depart Washington, D.C. Those two troops would join the rest of the regiment at Boonsboro, Maryland on July 8, 1863. Troops L and M had only recently been mustered into service.
28. Robertson, *Michigan in the War*, p. 399.
29. Havens MSS.
30. Ibid.; Kidd, *Personal Recollections of a Cavalryman*, pp. 115-16.
31. OR – 1, p. 926.
32. Boudrye, *Historic Records of the Fifth New York Cavalry*, p. 63; Benedict, *Vermont in the Civil War*, 2:592.
33. Regimental Association, *History of the Eighteenth Regiment of Cavalry, Pennsylvania Volunteers*, p. 38.
34. OR – 3, p. 335.
35. Schildt, *Roads to Gettysburg*, p. 362.
36. OR – 3, p. 335.
37. Ibid.
38. Boudrye, *Historic Records of the Fifth New York Cavalry*, p. 276.
39. OR – 3, pp. 334-35.
40. Schildt, *Roads to Gettysburg*, p. 362.
41. OR – 3, p. 350.

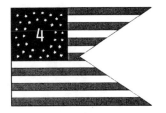

Chapter 4:

Converge on Frederick City

S the sun rose on June 28, 1863, the last Sunday of the month, thousands and thousands of foot-weary infantrymen and saddle-sore cavalrymen, as well as artillerymen and other support personnel, from the North's Army of the Potomac awoke from their all too brief slumbers of the previous night. All the men serving in the vast army, both regulars and volunteers alike, knew that this was the start of what probably would be another grueling day of excruciatingly long marches along worn and rutted roads. At the same time they expected even more long-drawn-out periods of inactivity in the hot and humid summer weather just south of the Mason-Dixon Line. The soldiers' individual units, along with their higher headquarters commands, found themselves still widely scattered throughout a number of small towns and villages in the "Free State" of Maryland. Like many of their senior commanders, the lower-ranking commissioned officers, noncommissioned officers, and enlisted men had little idea where they actually were heading as the sun climbed higher in the eastern sky.

Headquarters for the Army of the Potomac, on the last Sunday in June, was centrally located in Frederick City. Frederick was a bustling community roughly forty-five miles northwest of Washington, D.C. and had a wartime population of roughly 8,500 civilian inhabitants. On this particular morning on the outskirts of the city, a drastic change had already taken effect in the top command tier of the Army of the Potomac. The historic transition in army commanders ultimately hastened its movement to the north and led it into the great three-day battle at the little known Pennsylvania community of Gettysburg.[1]

Major General Joseph Hooker
(NA)

Major General George Meade
(NA)

The newly chosen commander of the Army of the Potomac, Major General George Gordon Meade (U.S.M.A., Class of 1835), who very early in the day had replaced Major General Hooker, was trying desperately to learn the present whereabouts of the scattered units in his new command.[2] Just before dawn, General Meade commanding the army's V Corps was asleep in his tent on the edge of Frederick when he abruptly awoke to the news of his immediate elevation to the command of the entire Army of the Potomac. The messenger arriving from the secretary of war's office by a specially dispatched train from Washington through Baltimore to Frederick was Lieutenant Colonel James Allen Hardie (U.S.M.A., Class of 1843), an assistant adjutant general to General-in-Chief Henry Wager Halleck (U.S.M.A., Class of 1839).[3]

Lieutenant Colonel Hardie traveled incognito, dressed in civilian clothes, and with great secrecy as he personally carried the orders for the change of command. After traveling for hours, Hardie arrived in Frederick around midnight but could not immediately ascertain the exact whereabouts of General Meade's headquarters. He conducted a short and futile search on his own in the darkness, a search that encompassed a number of other camp sites and many false leads as to Meade's location. Hardie then hired a local man who supposedly knew the exact site of Meade and his headquarters. He continued by wagon, ever so slowly through the crowded streets, to General Meade's tent on the outskirts of the town. Even though the hour was very late, hundreds of soldiers and civilians were milling about the streets, preventing quick passage through the town. After he moved only a short distance the wagon could no longer continue along the choked and clogged streets, forcing Hardie to abandon his ride and local guide and finish his journey on foot.[4]

Shortly after two o'clock in the morning of June 28 Lieutenant Colonel Frederick Thomas Locke, George Meade's assistant adjutant general from the V Corps, remembered being brusquely awakened in his tent by someone looking for General Meade. He identified the officer as Lieutenant Colonel Hardie, whom he had met previously. Locke told the lieutenant colonel that the general was asleep in the next tent.[5] Hardie then called at General Meade's quarters with the somewhat foreboding replacement and command orders still in his possession. Those orders, dated from June 17, gave the completely surprised George Meade absolute operational and field control of the Army of the Potomac. That overall responsibility was something that Joseph Hooker had long wanted but had not been granted by President Lincoln and Secretary of War Stanton during his tenure as army commander.

After a tedious process of elimination of many other senior officers in the army Major General Meade received the nomination to command the army. Major generals John Reynolds, John Sedgwick (U.S.M.A., Class of 1837), and Henry Warner Slocum (U.S.M.A., Class of 1852) had summarily declined the tendered appointment when previously offered to each of them. The Army of the Potomac had already seen four top commanding generals since the opening of hostilities in 1861. Major General Irvin McDowell (U.S.M.A., Class of 1838) commanded the army during the opening battles in 1861. Major General George B. McClellan (serving on two different occasions), Major General Ambrose Everett Burnside (U.S.M.A., Class of 1847), and Major General Hooker followed McDowell in rapid succession. After he read the order to himself, George Meade reasoned that he had no option and precious little choice in the actual matter. He reluctantly agreed to accede to the order appointing him as commanding general.

General Meade correctly believed that he had no choice but to accept the tendered nomination. President Lincoln, Secretary Stanton, and General Halleck had grown tired of simply asking someone to accept the command of the army. They, therefore, placed the advancement in the form of an order especially since so many of the other officers had already declined the appointment. Whatever the reasoning behind Meade's affirmation of the order, Lieutenant Colonel Hardie telegraphed his superiors in Washington an hour later with the succinct message: "I have accomplished my mission."[6]

For the rest of that Sunday, generals Hooker and Meade conferred about the exact location and other related matters concerning the disposition of the various units in the Army of the Potomac. Earlier in the beginning of the campaign, as one of his last directives as the army's commander, General Hooker had already ordered a general concentration of his seven assigned infantry corps. In the face of the imminent

Confederate advance into Maryland and Pennsylvania the army's infantry corps had orders to move quickly north from their encampments in Virginia, while Pleasonton's Cavalry Corps received orders to screen their advance.

Some time during the late afternoon hours of June 28, the generals completed the somber business of the command transition. Major General Hooker with several staff members and Lieutenant Colonel Hardie boarded the waiting special train at the passenger station of the Baltimore & Ohio Railroad in downtown Frederick. The officers first traveled south to Monocacy Junction then due east toward Baltimore along the main tracks of the Baltimore & Ohio Railroad. After Hooker and his staff reached the city of Baltimore they continued their journey south to Washington. They arrived in Washington at the Baltimore & Ohio Station, located on New Jersey Avenue, after only a few more hours of travel.[7]

Major General Hooker, the once mighty and powerful commander of the Army of the Potomac, soon found himself dispatched to the western theater of operations. He accepted an offered assignment to the command of the XX Corps in the Army of the Cumberland. Joseph Hooker had one more brief success during the Battle of Lookout Mountain at Chattanooga, Tennessee in November 1863 before being relegated to somewhat tedious and boring desk duty in a variety of military departments around the country before retiring as a major general in the Regular Army in 1868.[8]

On the eve of a possible large-scale engagement with the Army of Northern Virginia, new army commander Meade had no recourse but to concur with his predecessor's general marching plan for the current period. By seven o'clock on that Sunday morning, General Meade had forwarded his response, by telegraph to General Halleck, accepting the command of the proffered army. At the same time, Meade's staff also drafted the following General Order, allowing him to assume the leadership of the Army of the Potomac's top post, while additionally informing the rank and file troops of another all too common change in the command structure:

General Orders,} Headquarters Army of the Potomac,
Number 67,   }   June 28, 1863.

> By direction of the President of the United States, I
> hereby assume command of the Army of the Potomac.
> As a soldier, in obeying this order—an order totally
> unexpected and unsolicited—I have no promises or
> pledges to make. The country looks to this army to re-
> lieve it from the devastation and disgrace of a hostile
> invasion. Whatever fatigues and sacrifices we may be
> called upon to undergo, let us have in view constantly
> the magnitude of the interests involved, and let each
> man determine to do his duty, leaving to an all-
> controlling Providence the decision of the contest. It
> is with just diffidence that I relieve in the command of
> this army an eminent and accomplished soldier, whose
> name must ever appear conspicuous in the history of
> its achievements; but I rely upon the hearty support of
> my companions in arms to assist me in the discharge
> of the duties of the important trust which has been
> confided to me.

[Geo. G. Meade,]

Major-General, Commanding.[9]

In an effort to have the army converge at one particular point, each individual corps commander received detailed directives with their specifically identified routes of march. The Army of the Potomac's I Corps commanded by Major General Reynolds, soon to be a fatality of the campaign, marched from Middletown to Frederick City during that Sunday.

Major General Winfield Scott Hancock's (U.S.M.A., Class of 1844) II Corps received orders to move from their camps near Barnesville to Frederick, but was halted at Monocacy Junction instead. Hancock would become a casualty at Gettysburg in a few more days, being wounded in the thigh during the final assault by the Southern infantry on July 3.

The recently appointed commander of the III Corps was Major General Daniel Edgar Sickles. He led his corps' advance from Middletown through Frederick to Woodsboro. Sickles would also become a casualty of the upcoming fight on July 2 after being wounded in the left leg and later having it amputated. He was the only corps commander presently serving in the command not to have graduated from the U.S. Military Academy at West Point.

Major General George Sykes (U.S.M.A., Class of 1842), Meade's replacement as the V Corps commander, did not move his men from their encampment near Frederick City. Sykes was a veteran of many battles and would survive the war unscathed.

The infantrymen and artillerymen of the VI Corps, commanded by Major General John Sedgwick, traversed the well-worn roads between Poolesville and Hyattstown on that Sunday. Sedgwick's men were the greatest distance from army headquarters.

Leading the XI Corps, Major General Oliver Otis Howard (U.S.M.A., Class of 1854) marched his men from near Middletown, through Frederick, to Worman's Mill. General Howard and his corps would be the second corps, after Reynolds' I Corps, to arrive at Gettysburg to face General Lee's invading army.

The final infantry corps assigned to the Army of the Potomac, the XII, under General Slocum, maneuvered toward Frederick from their encampment near Berlin, located along the Potomac River. They arrived in Frederick City at two o'clock on that Sunday afternoon.[10]

One additional corps assigned to the Army of the Potomac, the Cavalry Corps, found itself congregated reasonably close together in Frederick County, Maryland. On that Sunday morning in June, the recently appointed corps commander, Major General Alfred Pleasonton, found his two assigned mounted divisions, under the experienced and competent leadership of brigadier generals John Buford and David Gregg, positioned on opposite sides of Frederick City.

General Buford's 1st Division, which consisted of three brigades, had encamped at Middletown west of Frederick the previous day. In like manner, the three brigades of General Gregg's 2nd Division were dispersed east of the city of Frederick principally along the Baltimore Pike. Buford's division claimed portions of thirteen regiments within the ranks of its three brigades commanded by Colonel Gamble, Colonel Devin, and Major Starr. Gregg's division also consisted of three brigades and had cavalrymen from fourteen different regiments under the command of

Colonel McIntosh, Colonel Huey, and Colonel J. Irvin Gregg. Colonel Huey replaced Brigadier General Kilpatrick as the 2nd Brigade commander on June 28.[11]

On that propitious last Sunday in June, not only for the Army of the Potomac's newest commander but for General Alfred Pleasonton and his corps too, things were about to change dramatically. Those shifts in official policy would greatly alter the course of the war, especially in favor of the Union horse soldiers. The mounted arm under General Pleasonton was about to confirm its true identity, along with continuing its ongoing and never-ending mission in support of the Army of the Potomac's infantry and artillery units.

During the first two long years of the war, the Union horsemen lacked wide acceptance for their actual capabilities on the battlefield. The Lincoln administration had tried extremely hard in the first year of the Civil War not to accept any cavalry regiments for the volunteer service. Money was a prime factor in denying requests to form mounted units from the various states because of the major expense associated in mounting a fully equipped regiment of cavalry.

Early in 1861, the U.S. government anticipated paying close to $150,000 for only the necessary horses assigned to a ten-company regiment of cavalry. The cost of additional equipment as well as the extra pay for the officers and the enlisted men only compounded the actual cost. However, even with the high cost a few mounted regiments were accepted for Federal service early in the war but, inevitably, were not utilized to the fullest extent of their capabilities. However, all that was now rapidly changing thanks to a change in policy. The old days of dividing a cavalry regiment into detachments, as small as squads for the convenience of general officers and their staffs or for other inconsequential duties, were rapidly coming to an end. The cavalry regiments would hereafter be able to fight as a complete unit instead as much smaller sections. No longer would the men of the cavalry arm have to endure the malicious sarcasm and disdain of their comrades in the infantry and artillery branches of the army. The favorite taunt of "whoever saw a dead cavalryman?" would soon become a thing of the past because many soon would be seen during the current campaign.

The various Union cavalry regiments assigned to the Army of the Potomac had done very well against their Confederate foes in the course of the previous few weeks. General Pleasonton's corps of horsemen held their own in fighting General J. E. B. Stuart's forces at Brandy Station, Aldie, Middleburg, and Upperville during the month of June. Under General Pleasonton's influence, a new breed of young, daring, aggressive, and audacious leader was emerging in the vanguard of the Cavalry Corps. Under those new leaders, along with other tactically proficient and competent officers and noncommissioned officers, the Union cavalry was destined to become a force with which to be reckoned. The enlisted members of the Cavalry Corps given proper leadership proved that they could go saber to saber with their vaunted Southern counterparts. For many of those young cavalrymen the first tests of their ability would be the unexpected engagements with the enemy's cavalry at the two small Pennsylvania towns of Hanover and Hunterstown.

On June 28, Major General Pleasonton, along with many of the senior commissioned members of his staff, was comfortably ensconced in his temporary headquarters at the City Hotel located on West Patrick Street in Frederick. Pleasonton had transferred his headquarters in conjunction with the movement and relocation of Major General Hooker's headquarters command from near Fairfax Court House in Virginia. Crossing the Potomac River at Edwards Ferry with the rest of Hooker's staff on June 26, General Pleasonton had encamped with the commanding general's headquarters near Poolesville later that day.

The next day, June 27, Pleasonton arrived in Frederick and received permission from General Hooker to establish his headquarters in the less than opulent City Hotel. The hotel was not the most impressive in the city but it did supply a comfortable bed and a roof over one's head. The recently promoted major general kept himself, as well as his entire staff, quite busy endeavoring to get everything in order because of the many changes occurring within the mounted branch as the month of June quickly drew to a close. One of the changes included recalling Judson Kilpatrick from his brigade command in General Gregg's division. Kilpatrick was about to receive command of a division, courtesy of General Pleasonton.[12]

During the early afternoon hours the Cavalry Corps commander, as well as the members of his staff, vacated his modestly comfortable lodgings in the hotel because the main body of the army was continuing to rapidly move northward. General Pleasonton relocated the corps headquarters a short distance outside the city limits of Frederick. With deliberate intention, he moved his headquarters to a large farm known locally as Richfield, which coincidentally was the same place where General Stahel and his men had encamped. At the same time that Pleasonton was moving only a few miles from Frederick, the Army of the Potomac's new commander, George Meade, moved his headquarters almost twenty miles to Middleburg, just south of Taneytown and the Pennsylvania border. Before moving north and rejoining army headquarters, Pleasonton requested, and received, some additional time from army headquarters to attend to matters concerning the long-awaited acquisition of a new mounted division.[13]

Situated no more than three miles north of Frederick, along the eastern side of the Emmitsburg Road, the Richfield estate was one of the early Frederick County homes of Thomas Johnson, the first elected governor of Maryland. In June 1863, the main house, along with a considerable amount of the adjoining property, belonged to the Schley family. General Pleasonton's staff officers procured the surrounding, gently rolling, farm land for their immediate headquarters command, their horses, and their baggage wagons.

Fortuitously, a portion of General Julius Stahel's cavalrymen already happened to have their encampment around the same area. Stahel's division wagon train, which had finally completed its slow and tedious journey from the Potomac River crossing, also parked in the fields near the main house. The wagon train remained there for the next couple of days while the rest of the cavalry division moved toward their destiny in Pennsylvania. The area around the Richfield farm would become quite an active place over the next twenty-four-hour period and would earn its own place in the burgeoning history of the Cavalry Corps of the Army of the Potomac.[14]

Shortly before both generals Meade and Pleasonton left the city limits of Frederick on that Sunday morning, they held a brief conference concerning the future of the army's mounted branch. At that meeting, Pleasonton had the opportunity to further malign and slander Julius Stahel's cavalry command, while expounding on his own importance in the forthcoming operations. Having previously merely hinted at wanting Stahel's division incorporated into his own command Pleasonton now directly requested that Stahel's men be reassigned to him. Unbeknownst to him, General Stahel had already been effectively removed as the division's commander and Pleasonton's wishes were about to come true.[15]

In addition Pleasonton wanted the opportunity to place officers of his own choosing in command. During the same meeting he also lobbied for the immediate promotions of Custer, Farnsworth, and Merritt by stating:

> I called his [Meade's] attention to a division of cavalry near Frederick City (3 1/2 miles north) [Stahel's] which he might place under my command, and I would like to have officers I would name specially assigned to it, as I am expected to have some desperate work to do. The General asserted to my request, and upon my naming the officers, he immediately telegraphed to have them appointed brigadier generals. This was his first dispatch to Washington, and on the day afterward, he received the reply making the appointments, and directing the officers to be assigned at once. They were Custer, Merritt, and Farnsworth.[16]

Meanwhile Brigadier General Copeland's 1st Brigade, which now included only the 5th Michigan and 6th Michigan cavalry regiments, was still a considerable distance removed from the main body of General Stahel's still scattered command. The 7th Michigan was still absent. Additionally, the 6th Michigan had just ten troops presently serving with the regiment as they performed their duties at the end of June.

Earlier in February, the 6th Michigan regiment received instructions detaching a hundred men on special duty to search for guerrillas. The commander of the Michigan regiment designated Troops I and M, under the command of twenty-six-year-old Captain Charles W. Deane for that detail. First Lieutenant Robert A. Moon, a thirty-one-year-old businessman from Big Rapids, Michigan led the forty-six enlisted men of the troop while Deane commanded the squadron. First Lieutenant Benjamin Franklin Rockafellow commanded Troop M, being the only commissioned officer present with his troop. Lieutenant Rockafellow's troop carried sixty-three enlisted men on the rolls present for duty. Those two detached troops would eventually find themselves assigned to Major General William Henry French's (U.S.M.A., Class of 1837) command. The Michigan cavalrymen found themselves stationed at Harpers Ferry and the surrounding area during the rest of the Gettysburg Campaign. They would not rejoin their regiment until August.[17]

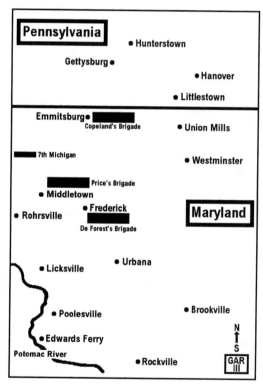

Locations of Stahel's Brigades
Morning of June 28, 1863
(GAR III)

Brigadier General Copeland, who had previously led two-thirds of his brigade out of Frederick City on June 27, was totally unaware of what was about to befall him during the shakeup of Julius Stahel's division. Sunday morning, June 28, found the 5th and 6th Michigan regiments moving slowly from their overnight encampments near Emmitsburg toward the Mason-Dixon Line and Pennsylvania. In obedience to their recent orders, they were constantly searching for information on the whereabouts of the elusive Confederate Army thought to be nearby.

Moving slowly out of Maryland the Michigan cavalrymen crossed into Pennsylvania and arrived in the Adams County community of Gettysburg around one o'clock in the afternoon, immediately after many of the churches in the town were finishing their weekly religious services. Scores and scores of citizens turned out to greet General Copeland and his men and to welcome them to their borough. The town had not seen that many Union cavalrymen since two battalions with over 700 men of the Porter Guard (10th Regiment, New York Volunteer Cavalry) had departed from their community in March 1862, after spending seventy-two days with them.[18]

Captain James Harvey Kidd, the twenty-three-year-old commanding officer of the 6th Michigan's Troop E, recalled the glorious welcome that he and his men received in the streets of Gettysburg on that Sunday afternoon:

> Before we reached the town it was apparent that something unusual was going on. It was a gala day. The people were out in force, and in their Sunday attire to welcome the troopers in blue. The church bells rang out a joyous peal, and dense masses of beaming faces filled the streets, as the narrow column of fours threaded its way through their midst. Lines of men stood on either side, with pails of water or apple-butter, and passed a "sandwich" to each soldier as he passed. At intervals of a few feet, were bevies of women and girls, who handed up bouquets and wreaths of flowers. By the time the center of town was reached, every man had a bunch of flowers in his hand, or a wreath around his neck. Some even had their horses decorated, and the one who did not get a share was a very modest trooper, indeed. The people were overjoyed, and received us with an enthusiasm and a hospitality born of full hearts. They had seen enough of the gray to be anxious to welcome the blue. Their throats grew hoarse with the cheers that they sent up in honor of the coming of the Michigan cavalrymen. The

freedom of the city was extended. Every door stood
open, or the latch-string hung invitingly out.[19]

Copeland's men had arrived in Gettysburg from the south along the
Emmitsburg Road. They marched along Baltimore Street before entering
Gettysburg's center square. At the "Diamond," as the residents called
their center square, the two regiments wheeled to the right onto York
Street and moved to an area east of the town along the York Pike.

On the night of June 28–29 the command established their encampment near the intersection of the York and Hanover roads, not too far
from where the Porter Guard had established their permanent camp early
in 1862. General Copeland ordered the two regiments of Michigan
horsemen to immediately deploy a number of pickets and scouts around
the entire perimeter of the town. The general had only recently received
reports of enemy activity to the west, north, and east and was taking no
chance with the safety of his command. While the rest of his troopers
settled in for the night under their blankets and the stars, General
Copeland established his personal headquarters in a hotel located on the
Gettysburg square.[20]

Captain James H. Kidd,
Commander, Troop E, 6th Michigan Cavalry
(USAMHI)

The Michigan cavalrymen placed strong picket lines a couple of miles from the town in all directions and on all the roads to protect their bivouac from any threat presented by the enemy. One detachment on duty from the 6th Michigan Cavalry threw out their pickets along the road toward Cashtown and Chambersburg to the west. The road through the village of Cashtown would be one of the roads picketed by General Buford's men two days later on the night of June 30 – July 1 at the very beginning of the Battle of Gettysburg.[21]

The detachment tasked with guarding the Chambersburg Pike, composed of Troops E and H, was under the immediate command of Captain Kidd of Troop E. While James Kidd was in overall command of the two troops, First Lieutenant Edward L. Craw led the seventy-seven noncommissioned officers and enlisted men of Kidd's Troop E. Captain Henry L. Wise likewise commanded the roughly fifty-nine troopers assigned to his Troop H.[22]

Years later Captain Kidd, who rose to eventually command the 6th Michigan as its colonel, recalled his unit's brief tour of duty and responsibilities on that Sunday afternoon and evening in the peaceful town of Gettysburg:

> Turning to the right, the command went into camp a little outside the town, in a field of clover, and it made the poor, famished animals fairly laugh. That night a squadron was sent out about two miles to picket on each diverging road. It was my duty with two troops ("E" and "H") to guard the "Cashtown" pike, and a very vivid remembrance is yet retained of the "vigil long" of that July [June] night, during which I did not once leave the saddle, dividing the time between the reserve post and the line of videttes.[23]

While the pickets marched to their assigned posts around the town, General Copeland also dispatched a noncommissioned officer with a small detail of enlisted men to carry the latest reports to General Hooker's headquarters. He now knew that army headquarters was at Frederick, but he did not know about the changes in the Army of the Potomac's leadership. The relatively timely dispatches from Copeland informed the commanding general of what had transpired with the Michiganders' scouting mission since entering Pennsylvania.

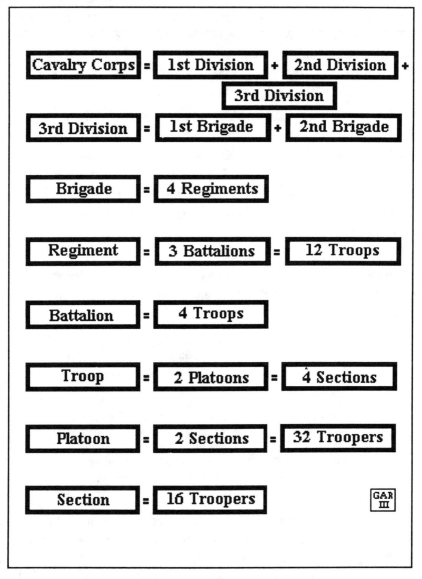

***Structure of the Cavalry Corps,
June 30, 1863***
(GAR III)

During the early morning hours of June 28, the other regiment of Copeland's brigade, the detached 7th Michigan Cavalry, received orders from their division headquarters that recalled them from their outpost duty at Turner's Gap in the South Mountain. The newly received instructions directed those Michigan horsemen to move immediately and as quickly as possible to the division's rendezvous site at the Richfield estate. Traveling along the National Pike, Colonel Mann's regiment passed, again, through Middletown, reached Frederick City shortly after noon and arrived at Richfield a short time after that.

Colonel De Forest's 3rd Brigade had little to do on that auspicious Sunday morning, already being at the rendezvous site north of Frederick. The 5th New York, the 1st Vermont, and the 1st West Virginia, therefore, remained in their overnight camps during the early portion of the day and waited for the expected arrival of the remainder of their division. As the cool of the morning turned into a warm and humid afternoon the men took a brief respite to take care of any personal business along with their number one task of caring for their horses. The Union cavalrymen were finally beginning to realize the importance of their horses.[24]

While the other cavalry units in the division waited for their daily orders to be delivered by the staff members on that Sunday morning, Colonel Price's 2nd Brigade had the distinction of being encamped with the division headquarters. Following the instructions, received personally from General Stahel, the 1st Michigan, the 2nd Pennsylvania, and the 18th Pennsylvania vacated their advanced positions at Middletown in the pre-dawn darkness. They then moved back through the streets of Frederick to the new position at Richfield, where they arrived shortly after sunrise. The troopers dismounted and caught some rest. They then patiently waited for further orders from their officers. This was a well-known scenario for which they had become accustomed in this war.[25]

Shortly after reaching the rendezvous site at Richfield, General Stahel dispatched another short communiqué, his last one as an autonomous cavalry commander, to the Army of the Potomac's chief of staff, General Daniel Butterfield. That final dispatch concerned two vital reports recently received at Stahel's headquarters. One report came from General Copeland's command on patrol near Gettysburg and addressed the enemy's movements. The other intelligence account supplied by the loyal citizens of Gettysburg, through Joseph Copeland, reported the Confederate Army's movements, along with an estimated number of Confederate soldiers who had only recently passed through their town on June 27. The Gettysburg civilians signing the report, forwarded by Copeland, were three of the town's foremost citizens: T. Duncan Carson, bank clerk and teller, Robert G. McCreary, attorney, and David McConaughy, attorney.[26]

With little doubt on that Sunday morning, June 28, Major General Julius Stahel was finally and fully aware of the looming major upheaval about to befall him and his separate cavalry command. On that day, he could not have missed many of the telltale warning signs that his cavalry division assigned to the XXII Corps, Department of Washington, would shortly cease to exist as an independent command. General Pleasonton had wasted precious little time in his bid to absorb the Hungarian's division into his own command. Pleasonton had gotten his plan quickly approved, first by General Hooker, then by General Meade, and finally by President Lincoln and the War Department in Washington. During that fateful Sunday, Stahel's cavalrymen received their official orders permanently transferring them to the Army of the Potomac's Cavalry Corps.[27]

Richfield, Site of Pleasonton's Grand Review, June 28, 1863
(GAR III)

With Major General Pleasonton's persistent pressure and insidious determination in the matter, General Stahel's division of three mounted brigades, all nine regiments, found itself transferred to the Army of the Potomac's Cavalry Corps. The demise of Stahel's division came during the reorganization and expansion that Pleasonton coveted for the revitalization of his own undermanned mounted corps. Under the pretense of needing additional mounted troops to stave off the raids of the Confederacy's J. E. B. Stuart and his cavalry command, Stahel lost his division under the following special order transmitted from General Meade's headquarters:

> Pursuant to instructions which have been received from the General-in-Chief, Major General J. Stahel, U.S. Volunteers, is relieved from further duty with this army and will report to Maj. Gen. D. N. Couch, at Harrisburg, Pa., to organize and command the cavalry in the Department of the Susquehanna. The troops composing General Stahel's command are assigned to the Cavalry Corps, and will be distributed to the division of that corps as the commander thereof may direct. Major-General Stahel will furnish Major-General Pleasonton with a statement of the troops comprising his command and their position.[28]

Upon relinquishing his command, Major General Julius Stahel, along with many members of his staff, lingered at Richfield for only a short time. Major Harvey Baldwin, Jr., Stahel's assistant adjutant general was most adept at making sure that the transition proceeded as smoothly as possible.[29] At Richfield they briefed General Pleasonton and his staff members on the exact locations and strengths of the three old cavalry brigades. Like Pleasonton's two divisions of cavalry during the last several days, Stahel had kept his troopers quite busy scouting and patrolling the Maryland countryside besides sending General Copeland's command across the Mason-Dixon Line into southern Pennsylvania. Unfortunately for the lamentable Stahel and his equally unwanted brigade commanders everything seemed for naught and was quite disheartening to both commissioned officers and enlisted men alike.

Early the next morning, Monday, June 29, upon the completion of his official duties and having transferred his cavalry command to

General Pleasonton, General Stahel rode through all the regimental camps to bid farewell to many of his officers and enlisted men. A small detail of four enlisted men under the command of Corporal Elihu Judy, from Troop A of the 1st Ohio Cavalry, escorted the general, Major Baldwin and a few other chosen members of his staff to the B & O railroad station in Frederick. Stahel and his party departed Frederick on the regularly scheduled afternoon train to Baltimore. Given the suspected close proximity and unknown location of the Confederate cavalry command, Stahel and the others on the train were lucky to avoid contact with Stuart's cavalrymen. General Stahel should have been keenly aware of that fact given the previous day's intelligence reports received from his own troops patrolling near Gettysburg.[30]

Notwithstanding the imminent threat of enemy activity across the Maryland countryside, Stahel's small party arrived safely at Baltimore. Later that day they traveled by another train to Washington and then moved quickly to Fairfax Court House, Virginia. On July 1, he received his official orders to report to Harrisburg, Pennsylvania, where he reluctantly assumed command of the meager cavalry forces in Major General Darius Nash Couch's (U.S.M.A., Class of 1846) Department of the Susquehanna on July 3, 1863. With the unwilling acceptance of his new assignment, Major General Stahel essentially became a commanding officer without a matching command for his rank, a situation that would continue unabated for an additional nine months. On July 20, 1863, he took command of all the U.S. government and state militia forces assigned at Camp Curtin, Camp Couch, and Fort Washington, all located near Harrisburg.[31]

Early in the spring of 1864 Major General Julius Stahel took the field again as a cavalry division commander in the Shenandoah Valley, another humbled soldier assigned to the out-of-the-way Department of West Virginia. He served admirably during that period in his career. For his gallant and heroic actions at the Battle of Piedmont, Virginia on June 5, 1864, he received the Medal of Honor but was also wounded in the shoulder. Because of the extreme pain caused by the wound he was relieved of his command and relegated to duty at Harpers Ferry and Martinsburg beginning on June 9, 1864. Eventually the proud Hungarian immigrant had enough of the War Department's bureaucracy and re-signed his volunteer commission in the U.S. Army in February 1865.[32]

Four of the slandered, maligned, and much disdained foreigners were now stripped of their commands in General Pleasonton's new Cavalry Corps. None of them any longer posed any serious threat along his path to the top. Pleasonton had rid himself of the three highest-ranking foreigners in his command and in the process had gained thousands of additional cavalrymen for his corps from another high-ranking interloper. In a highly unusual circumstance, two of the four men most despised by Alfred Pleasonton eventually went on to win the Medal of Honor for bravery in combat—Luigi di Cesnola and Julius Stahel. Regardless of his general lack of competent character assessment, definitely tainted by his prejudice against foreigners, another of General Pleasonton's ultimate objectives and goals now reached completion.

Judson Kilpatrick, the recently promoted brigadier general, turned out to be the principal beneficiary of General Pleasonton's newest divisional acquisition. Recalled from his brigade command and through Pleasonton's magnanimity, Kilpatrick received the operational and tactical control of the Cavalry Corps' newly assigned and designated 3rd Division while at Frederick City, superseding the hapless General Stahel as the division commander but with less rank than his predecessor. Brigadier General Kilpatrick, the newest, youngest, and most inexperienced of Pleasonton's three division commanders, through no coincidence also controlled the corps' smallest division in terms of the number of brigades and regiments assigned.

Initially, instructions for the 3rd Division's formation consolidated the three brigades of Stahel's command into only two slightly larger brigades under Kilpatrick's purview. General Stahel's three old brigades, commanded by General Copeland and colonels Price and De Forest, were turned over to two of General Pleasonton's extremely youthful and freshly commissioned brigadier generals, the twenty-five-year-old Elon Farnsworth and the twenty-three-year-old George Custer. Pleasonton's plan was almost complete.

All the cavalry regiments assigned to Stahel's former division found themselves transferred to Kilpatrick's new division with the lone exception being the 2nd Regiment, Pennsylvania Volunteer Cavalry commanded by Colonel R. Butler Price, the former brigade commander under Stahel. Immediately after General Pleasonton took control of Stahel's former division, the 2nd Pennsylvania Cavalry received orders to report to the provost marshal general, Brigadier General Marsena Rudolph Patrick (U.S.M.A., Class of 1835). General Patrick served at the headquarters of the Army of the Potomac which on the 28th day of June was moving from Frederick toward Middleburg, Maryland. For the next six months of the war, Colonel Price's Pennsylvanians remained on provost marshal duty with the army headquarters. Ultimately, the 2nd Pennsylvania returned to the Cavalry Corps' 2nd Brigade, 2nd Division in December 1863.[33]

Colonel Price, quite deservedly, should have been promoted to the rank of brigadier general by that period of the war. Regrettably, he was in the same category as many of the other colonels in the army who were considered too old for the rigors of a cavalry field command. The native of Philadelphia was fifty-five years old and repeatedly got passed over for promotion to his first star. He was the oldest brigade commander or regimental commander assigned to either Stahel or Pleasonton's cavalry command. Colonel Price's war record was excellent and unblemished. It clearly justified an advance in rank and command responsibilities. As an added benefit, Price, unlike many senior officers, was popular with his peers and well liked by the junior officers and men in his regiment and brigade.

Earlier in the war, in September 1862, Colonel Price personally captured the lieutenant colonel of the 6th Virginia Cavalry, John Shackleford Green, and won the brevet rank of a brigadier general for that action. Unfortunately, and for unknown reasons, his appointment never received confirmation by the U.S. Congress, as required by law. Price, thus, retained the rank of colonel for the remainder of the war, something that did not particularly please him. Eventually Colonel Price, disgusted by the perceived injustice, officially requested reassignment from his regiment in early 1864. Ultimately ordered to Washington, Price served on various military commissions until the end of the war when he returned to civilian life.[34]

At the time of the official transfer of command, General Stahel's division, minus the twelve troops of cavalrymen from the 2nd Pennsylvania Cavalry, reported a total strength of 239 officers and 3,622 enlisted men present for duty. The actual "paper" strength for the division was slightly higher at 254 officers and 4,280 enlisted men. The discrepancy, between the two sets of numbers, was mainly because many of the officers and enlisted men were away from their regiments. Those soldiers were currently on official leave of absence, special duty, extended detached service, sick leave, or other details as required.[35]

The actual regimental reorganization was effected as follows for the units in Stahel and Kilpatrick's command:

Cavalry Reorganization
Stahel's Division to Kilpatrick's Division
June 28, 1863[36]

Independent Division

Maj. Gen. Julius H. Stahel

1st Brigade

Brig. Gen. Joseph T. Copeland

5th Michigan Cavalry
6th Michigan Cavalry
7th Michigan Cavalry

2nd Brigade

Col. R. Butler Price

1st Michigan Cavalry
2nd Pennsylvania Cavalry
18th Pennsylvania Cavalry
1st Ohio Cavalry (Cos. A & C)

3rd Brigade

Col. Othneil De Forest

5th New York Cavalry
1st Vermont Cavalry
1st West Virginia Cavalry

3rd Division*

Brig. Gen. Judson Kilpatrick

1st Brigade

Brig. Gen. Elon J. Farnsworth

5th New York Cavalry
18th Pennsylvania Cavalry
1st Vermont Cavalry
1st West Virginia Cavalry

2nd Brigade

Brig. Gen. George A. Custer

1st Michigan Cavalry
5th Michigan Cavalry
6th Michigan Cavalry
7th Michigan Cavalry

* Troops A & C, 1st Ohio Cavalry were assigned as headquarters guard for the 3rd Division.

Brigadier General Judson Kilpatrick,
Commander, 3rd Cavalry Division
(GAR III)

For the most part while encamped in the muddy fields outside Frederick many of the cavalrymen of Farnsworth's new brigade, as well as Custer's 1st and 7th Michigan, had a day of relative peace and rest as they arrived at the division bivouac at Richfield. As all veteran soldiers knew, there were always scouting and picketing duties for some of the regiments' less fortunate members. Every day it took scores of men to fill all the various corps, division, brigade, regiment, and troop details. There was always an essential need for the gathering of provisions and wood, the collection of fresh water, as well as other necessities for individual camp life and someone had to perform those duties. In addition all cavalrymen had an additional responsibility and that was to care for their assigned mounts.

Other troopers of General Kilpatrick's new division, having gained some useful experience during their previous months of service under General Stahel, took care of their personal business. They realized that a major battle was looming on the horizon. The troopers took advantage of the free time and wrote letters to their families, got some much needed rest, or foraged for fresh food from the many nearby homes and farms. Many of the men groomed their horses along with refurbishing any damaged and worn-out equipment in preparation for the expected rigors of the upcoming weeks of hard campaigning against the Confederate Army.

Sometime during the early afternoon of that last Sunday in June, General Pleasonton informed his three newest brigadiers, Kilpatrick, Farnsworth, and Custer, of his intention to review the regiments of the newly acquired division. Cavalry Corps headquarters issued an order for a "Grand Review" to be held at five o'clock in the afternoon of that day. All available regiments of Stahel's old division, those encamped at Richfield, received orders to participate in the parade.

It seems highly unlikely that someone as publicity hungry as General Pleasonton would not have invited General Meade to his new division's "Grand Review." However, Meade was not in the official reviewing party due to the pressing demands of his new post as the army commander and the fact that he and his staff were no longer in the Frederick area. Even though the Army of the Potomac was rushing to the north, Pleasonton still found the time to pause from the demands of the war for a totally needless exercise with his new troops. Although he always sought positive publicity for himself, Pleasonton could also deflect any negative comments and would go to great lengths to remove any blame from himself.[37]

Major Henry B. Van Voorhis,
18th Pennsylvania Cavalry,
Assistant Provost Marshal, 3rd Division
(GAR III)

Kilpatrick's division, consisting of Farnsworth's 1st Brigade and just half of Custer's 2nd Brigade, held their review on schedule in the adjacent fields at Pleasonton's headquarters on the Richfield farm. Richfield was also where Custer, Farnsworth, and the other young captain, Wesley Merritt, officially received notification of their especially rapid promotions to the ranks of brigadier general. At the time of Pleasonton's

"Grand Review," the 5th and 6th Michigan regiments from George Custer's brigade were still performing their assigned scouting duties near the towns of Emmitsburg and Gettysburg. They were unaware for now of the immediate changes in their brigade and division and were thus unavailable for the review.[38]

Brigadier General Kilpatrick had some advanced knowledge of his elevation to division command when he presented himself at Cavalry Corps' headquarters on June 28. Being a former brigade commander himself, he brought many of his former staff officers and enlisted orderlies with him from the 2nd Division. However, he still relied on many members of General Stahel's old staff during that period of transition, especially with the prospect of the upcoming battles. General Kilpatrick and roughly sixteen of his 3rd Division staff officers and approximately thirty-five orderlies, buglers, clerks, and other support personnel were present at the "Grand Review" at Richfield on that Sunday afternoon.

On the 28th day of June, Brigadier General Farnsworth's 1st Brigade consisted of the 5th New York Cavalry, Major John Hammond commanding; the 18th Pennsylvania Cavalry with Lieutenant Colonel William Penn Brinton in command; the 1st Vermont Cavalry which was led by Lieutenant Colonel Addison Webster Preston; and the 1st West Virginia Cavalry under the direction of Colonel Nathaniel Pendleton Richmond. Neither the 1st Brigade's new commander nor any of the his regimental commanders serving in the current Gettysburg Campaign had any formal military education nor other martial experience before the beginning of the Civil War.

The young Elon Farnsworth was a student and briefly served in a civilian capacity in General Albert Sidney Johnston's (U.S.M.A., Class of 1826) Mormon Expedition before the outbreak of hostilities of Civil War. John Hammond was thirty-five years old and an iron manufacturer before the war. William Brinton was thirty-one years old and a gentleman from a wealthy Pennsylvania family. Addison Preston commanding the 1st Vermont Cavalry was thirty-two years old and an adventurer and a farmer. Before the start of the conflict, Nathaniel Richmond was twenty-nine years old with a dual role as a lawyer and farmer.[39]

First Lieutenant George A. Custer and Brigadier General Alfred Pleasonton
(LC)

The 1st Brigade's assigned regiments and their commanders, as well as all the other commissioned officers and enlisted men in the regimental ranks, had precious little time to actually acquaint themselves with their new corps, division, and brigades before beginning their advance on the roads to Hanover and Hunterstown. In just two more days General Farnsworth and his new brigade would experience their initial baptisms of fire with their current division.[40]

The young and uninitiated brigade commander, Brigadier General Farnsworth, unlike his immediate superior General Kilpatrick, had very little time and even less opportunity to choose his own personal brigade staff members after receiving official word of his promotion. Many of the six staff officers assigned to Farnsworth had served in similar capacities under the previous brigade commanders in General Stahel's division. All four of Farnsworth's regiments, as well as his commissioned staff members and roughly twenty-five orderlies, clerks, and other enlisted personnel, were present for the division's "Grand Review." His commissioned and enlisted staff would faithfully serve with their new commanding general for the few remaining days of his life.

Brigadier General Custer's 2nd Brigade now included all the Michigan cavalry regiments currently serving with the Army of the Potomac in the east. The venerable 1st Michigan Cavalry, Michigan's oldest cavalry regiment, had been organized in September 1861. Now, they were brigaded with the other three Michigan cavalry regiments serving with General Meade's army, an unusual method for assigning troops but one not without precedence. Colonel Charles H. Town commanded the regiment. The rest of the brigade included the 5th Michigan Cavalry, Colonel Russell Alexander Alger commanding; the 6th Michigan Cavalry, commanded by Colonel George Gray; and the 7th Michigan Cavalry, Colonel William Mann commanding.

Like their peers in General Farnsworth's 1st Brigade, the commanding officers of the four Michigan cavalry regiments also had no pre-war military education or experience. Colonel Town was thirty-five years old and toiled as a machinist before the beginning of the war. Alger of the 5th Michigan was twenty-seven years old and in the lumber business. Prior to the opening of hostilities, Colonel Gray practiced as an attorney at law and was thirty-nine years old. At the onset of the Gettysburg Campaign, William Mann was twenty-three years old, the youngest colonel serving in the brigade. Before the war Mann worked as an engineer and a manufacturer.[41]

As General Custer selected his staff, like the other senior officers in the Cavalry Corps but particularly his mentor Alfred Pleasonton, he appointed only those commissioned officers known personally to him or who were serving within the four regiments assigned to his brigade. Many of the eleven commissioned officers present on his new staff at the end of June eventually were replaced as General Custer became better acquainted with the capabilities and qualifications of the numerous other commissioned officers in his brigade. For now, only a portion of the assigned commissioned officers and the roughly twenty-five enlisted orderlies and clerks of General Custer's 2nd Brigade, would be present for duty on the occasion of the "Grand Review" on June 28. Only the 1st and 7th regiments were present at Richfield, while the 5th and 6th Michigan were still serving at Gettysburg.

Major General Pleasonton's Cavalry Corps had kept very busy during the entire month of June. They fought in many difficult battles against their Confederate foe and traveled hundreds of miles in the course of their duties. Upon their arrival at Frederick many of the corps' men, both commissioned officers and enlisted soldiers, rode tired and worn-out horses. The condition of the horses was extremely poor because of the many days and weeks of extended field service with very little rest and proper food. In addition, too many of the volunteer soldiers still did not take proper care of their mounts. Animals in that poor condition proved almost completely useless in the cavalry's established role of scouting the area and locating the enemy's forces. Even though forage was plentiful and bountiful in Maryland and Pennsylvania at that time of the year, many of the horses were carried on the unit rolls as being in unserviceable condition. A horse listed in unserviceable condition could have something as simple as a missing shoe or it could have something much more serious such as a sore mouth, sore back, or some other debilitating disease.

The constant patrolling and fighting during the month of June had taken a heavy toll on the mounts, as well as many of the men. The Cavalry Corps as a whole used many horses during the previous month's fighting and marching. Many more hundreds of horses would be lost in the future rigors of the Gettysburg Campaign, including scores killed and wounded in combat. The various available unit morning reports submitted by the 3rd Division's regiments for the end of June 1863 showed the total number of horses, both serviceable and unserviceable, in each command as follows:

5th New York Cavalry	–	534 Horses[42]
18th Pennsylvania Cavalry	–	694 Horses[43]
1st Vermont Cavalry	–	723 Horses[44]
1st West Virginia Cavalry	–	450 Horses[45]
1st Michigan Cavalry	–	515 Horses[46]
7th Michigan Cavalry	–	498 Horses[47]
Total	–	3,414 Horses[48]

Notes to Chapter Four

1. Schildt, *Roads to Gettysburg*, p. 271.
2. George Gordon Meade, *With Meade at Gettysburg* (Philadelphia: John C. Winston Company, 1930), p. 20.
3. Warner, *Generals in Blue*, pp. 195, 205.
4. Schildt, *Roads to Gettysburg*, p. 288; Warner, *Generals in Blue*, p. 205. Lieutenant Colonel Hardie received an appointment as a brigadier general of volunteers, to rank from November 1862, but his name never got submitted to the U.S. Senate for confirmation. The promotion was eventually revoked in January 1863. In March 1865 Hardie received the brevets of brigadier and major general.
5. William H. Powell, *The Fifth Army Corps (Army of the Potomac), A Record of Operations During the Civil War in the United States of America, 1861-1865* (New York: G. P. Putnam's Sons, 1896), p. 500.
6. OR – 3, p. 373.
7. Ibid., p. 374.
8. Warner, *Generals in Blue*, pp. 234-35.
9. OR – 3, p. 373; Meade, *With Meade at Gettysburg*, p. 24.
10. Meade, *With Meade at Gettysburg*, p. 28; Schildt, *Roads to Gettysburg*, p. 290.
11. Schildt, *Roads to Gettysburg*, p. 333. The assigned regiments in Gamble's brigade included portions of the 8th Illinois, 12th Illinois, 3rd Indiana, and 8th New York. Devin's brigade included the 6th New York, 9th New York, 17th Pennsylvania, and 3rd West Virginia. General Merritt's brigade listed the 1st, 2nd, 5th, and 6th U.S. regiments, as well as the 6th Pennsylvania. McIntosh's brigade had the 1st Maryland, 1st Massachusetts, 1st New Jersey, 1st Pennsylvania, 3rd Pennsylvania, and Purnell Legion assigned. The regiments in Huey's brigade included the 2nd New York, 4th New York, 6th Ohio, and 8th Pennsylvania. Colonel Gregg's brigade had the 1st Maine, 10th New York, 4th Pennsylvania, and 16th Pennsylvania assigned.
12. OR – 3, p. 373. Special Order Number 175, Headquarters Army of the Potomac, Frederick, Md., June 28, 1863.
13. Schildt, *Roads to Gettysburg*, p. 525. Middleburg, not to be confused with Middletown, was located northeast of Frederick about fifteen miles from the Mason-Dixon Line. Middletown, on the other hand, was situated just west of Frederick.
14. Ibid., p. 320. The home still stands today on the east side of the road between Frederick and Thurmont on present day U.S. Route 15.
15. OR – 1, pp. 59-60. The order relieving Stahel from his command was sent to Hooker's headquarters at midnight on June 27. It was probably not forwarded immediately.
16. Alexander K. McClure, comp., *Annals of the War, Written by Leading Participants, North and South* (Philadelphia: 1879), p. 452.
17. 6th Regiment, Michigan Volunteer Cavalry Regiment; Boxes 1920 – 1925; Muster Rolls, Regimental Papers, Office of the Adjutant General, Volunteer Organizations, Civil War; Record Group 94; National Archives, Washington, D.C. (Hereafter cited as NA RG 94 – 6 MI.)

Notes to Chapter Four (*continued*)

18. Noble D. Preston, *History of the Tenth Regiment of Cavalry, New York State Volunteers, August 1861, to August, 1865* (New York: D. Appleton & Company, 1892), p. 23; George A. Rummel III, *72 Days at Gettysburg: Organization of the 10th Regiment, New York Volunteer Cavalry* (Shippensburg, Pa.: White Mane Publishing Company, 1997), pp. 83-86.
19. Kidd, *Personal Recollections of a Cavalryman*, pp. 120-21.
20. Harris, *Personal Reminiscences of Samuel Harris*, p. 25; Kidd, *Personal Recollections of a Cavalryman*, p. 120; *Michigan at Gettysburg*, pp. 136-37; Robertson, *Michigan in the War*, p. 400. General Copeland spent the night in a hotel identified only as the City Hotel, but there was no such hotel in Gettysburg. If he stayed in a hotel on the square, perhaps it was the McClellan House, located on the northeast corner of the "Diamond," as the center square was known.
21. Kidd, *Personal Recollections of a Cavalryman*, p. 121.
22. NA RG 94 – 6 MI.
23. Kidd, *Personal Recollections of a Cavalryman*, pp. 121-22.
24. Boudrye, *Historic Records of the Fifth New York Cavalry*, p. 63; Benedict, *Vermont in the Civil War*, 2:592.
25. Regimental Association, *History of the Eighteenth Regiment of Cavalry, Pennsylvania Volunteers*, p. 15.
26. OR – 3, p. 370.
27. Dyer, *A Compendium of the War*, 1:378.
28. OR – 3, p. 373. Special Order Number 174, Headquarters Army of the Potomac, June 28, 1863.
29. Major Harvey Baldwin, Jr., twenty-five years old, resigned an earlier commission on March 24, 1863, as one of the original majors in the 119th Regiment, New York Volunteer Infantry. He immediately accepted another commission as a major in the U.S. Volunteers as an assistant adjutant general. The 119th New York Infantry had served in the 2nd Brigade, 3rd Division, XI Corps where he had first come to the attention and served on the staff of Julius Stahel. Baldwin resigned his original commission in order to accompany Stahel when the latter received command of a cavalry division in March 1863.
30. Samuel L. Gillespie ("Lovejoy"), *A History of Company A, First Ohio Cavalry, 1861-1865* (Washington Court House, Ohio: Press of Ohio State Register, 1898), p. 147.
31. OR – 3, p. 730; Special Orders, Number 39, Headquarters Department of the Susquehanna, Harrisburg, July 20, 1863.
32. Warner, *Generals in Blue*, p. 469.
33. Dyer, *A Compendium of the War*, 1:214.
34. Samuel P. Bates, *Martial Deeds of Pennsylvania* (Philadelphia: T. H. Davis & Co., 1876), p. 801.
35. Field Report of the Cavalry Corps, Army of the Potomac, 28 June 1863; Record Group 94; National Archives, Washington, D.C. Of the total number of men present for duty, 8 officers and 331 enlisted men were listed as sick.
36. Dyer, *A Compendium of the War*, 1:378.
37. Regimental Association, *History of the Eighteenth Regiment of Cavalry, Pennsylvania Volunteers*, p. 39; Boudrye, *Historic Records of the Fifth New York Cavalry*, p. 63; Charles N. Bliss Diary, University of Vermont.

Notes to Chapter Four (*continued*)

38. Robertson, *Michigan in the War*, p. 400.
39. Edmund J. Raus, Jr., *A Generation on the March:The Union Army at Gettysburg* (Lynchburg, Va.: H. E. Howard, Inc., 1987), pp. 93, 146, 176-78.
40. Longacre, *The Cavalry at Gettysburg*, p. 166; Stephen Z. Starr, *The Union Cavalry in the Civil War*, 3 vols. (Baton Rouge: Louisiana State University Press, 1979), 1:416-17.
41. Raus, *A Generation on the March*, pp. 45-46.
42. 5th Regiment, New York Volunteer Cavalry Regiment; Boxes 2729 – 2737; Muster Rolls, Regimental Papers, Office of the Adjutant General, Volunteer Organizations, Civil War; Record Group 94; National Archives, Washington, D.C. (Hereafter cited as NA RG 94 – 5 NY.) The unit's Morning Report for the month of June, dated July 28, 1863, was signed at Amissville, Va. by Major Hammond.
43. 18th Regiment, Pennsylvania Volunteer Cavalry Regiment; Boxes 4186 – 4190; Muster Rolls, Regimental Papers, Office of the Adjutant General, Volunteer Organizations, Civil War; Record Group 94; National Archives, Washington, D.C. (Hereafter cited as NA RG 94 – 18 PA.) The unit's Morning Report for the month of June, dated June 30, 1863, was signed at Hanover, Pa. by Lieutenant Colonel Brinton.
44. 1st Regiment, Vermont Volunteer Cavalry Regiment; Boxes 4724 – 4730; Muster Rolls, Regimental Papers, Office of the Adjutant General, Volunteer Organizations, Civil War; Record Group 94; National Archives, Washington, D.C. (Hereafter cited as NA RG 94 – 1 VT.) The unit's Morning Report for the month of June, dated June 30, 1863, was signed at Hanover, Pa. by Lieutenant Colonel Preston.
45. RG 94 – 1 WV. The unit's Morning Report for the month of June is not available. The number used is approximate, based on prior and subsequent months of Morning Reports of serviceable and unserviceable horses.
46. 1st Regiment, Michigan Volunteer Cavalry Regiment; Boxes 1891 – 1898; Muster Rolls, Regimental Papers, Office of the Adjutant General, Volunteer Organizations, Civil War; Record Group 94; National Archives, Washington, D.C. (Hereafter cited as NA RG 94 – 1 MI.) The unit's Morning Report for the month of June is not available. The number used is approximate, based on prior and subsequent months of Morning Reports of serviceable and unserviceable horses.
47. NA RG 94 – 7 MI. The unit's Morning Report for the month of June, dated June 30, 1863, was signed at Hanover, Pa. by Colonel Mann.
48. The Morning Reports for the 5th and 6th Michigan are unavailable.

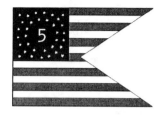

Chapter 5:

Proceed to Littlestown

ONDAY morning, June 29, in Frederick County dawned bright, clear, warm, and slightly humid. A very enjoyable June day in Maryland if one could ignore the thousands of men and animals traveling along the well-worn roads. The weather would remain warm and particularly humid, though not excessively hot, throughout the duration of the forthcoming campaign. It would begin to rain lightly later in the day. Occasionally heavy rainstorms during the previous week had left the roads leading to and from the town of Frederick, as well as those roads of the surrounding towns, a muddy quagmire. The roads were becoming extremely rutted and had numerous depressions from the men, horses, wagons, and artillery of the rapidly marching Army of the Potomac. Thousands and thousands of Union soldiers choked the roads while attempting to make their way as quickly as possible northward in spite of the deplorable condition of many of the main arteries. Many of the infantry corps assigned to the Northern army would eventually pass through or near Frederick on their way to Pennsylvania.

On that exhilarating Monday morning, General Judson Kilpatrick prepared to march his new command out of their encampments around the Richfield estate. Predicated upon the published orders received from General Pleasonton's Cavalry Corps headquarters, Kilpatrick had received exact instructions for the day's route of march for his two cavalry brigades. A portion of the order read:

> II. The Third Cavalry Division, commanded by General Kilpatrick, will move by 8 o'clock this morning as follows: First Brigade and a battery, Brigadier-General Farnsworth, will move, by way of Woodsborough, Bruceville, and Taneytown, to

Littlestown. Second Brigade and a battery, Brigadier-General Custer, will move by Utica, Crea-gerstown, and Graceham, to Emmitsburg; from thence to Littlestown. The trains of this division will move with the First Brigade, and will encamp near headquarters of the corps, at Middleburg. . . .[1]

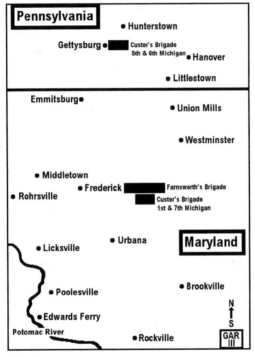

Locations of Kilpatrick's Brigades
Morning of June 29, 1863
(GAR III)

Following a reasonably peaceful night's rest after the excitement of the previous day's "Grand Review," Brigadier General Farnsworth's 1st Brigade began to move north from their camps located along the Em-mitsburg Road. At roughly eight o'clock on the morning of June 29, upon receipt of the detailed instructions for their movement dissemi-nated from Kilpatrick's headquarters, the brigade broke camp.

According to the orders, the brigade was enroute to the small Penn-sylvania hamlet of Littlestown just across the Mason-Dixon Line.

Farnsworth moved to the head of his column, taking his place as the brigade's new commander. At that time in the Gettysburg Campaign, Farnsworth had only a few trusted enlisted men serving him on his headquarters staff. Privates Calvin Tripp and Charles Bond, both from Farnsworth's old Troop K, 8th Illinois Cavalry, and Bugler Gilbert C. Buckman from Troop L, 1st Vermont Cavalry served as the new brigadier's personal orderlies.[2]

Leaving the Richfield farm behind them, Farnsworth and his brigade moved across some cultivated fields for a short distance to the east where they approached the main road to Taneytown. After traveling along that road for a short distance, they crossed over the narrow width of the Monocacy River just before reaching the tiny village of Ceresville. At that point the lengthy cavalry column turned to the north and advanced along the Woodsboro Pike. The brigade moved forward along that road for almost twenty miles in a relatively straight line across the gently sloping hills toward Taneytown in the northeast.

Farnsworth's troopers passed through the several other small communities of Walkersville, Woodsboro, Pipeville, Ladiesburg, Bruceville, and the larger Taneytown enroute to the Keystone State. In each place, no matter the size of the town or the number of residents, the Union troopers received noteworthy welcomes from the mostly pro-Union inhabitants. Extremely impressed with the enthusiastic receptions, the cavalrymen definitely enjoyed the attention at each and every town through which they passed, particularly from the community of young females. The combination of having left the desolation of the Virginia countryside behind them and the passionate greetings of the civilian population tended to lift the spirits of the weary cavalrymen, particularly those members of the 18th Pennsylvania.

For the present day's march, Kilpatrick chose to establish his traveling headquarters with 1st Brigade instead of with Custer's regiments, even though Custer and his troopers would leave Frederick around the same time as Farnsworth's men. Kilpatrick, along with his already numerous staff members, quickly moved from Richfield to near the head of the 1st Brigade's mounted column of troopers. There he joined Farnsworth in the deliberately slow-paced journey toward Littlestown.

Now that he was a full-fledged cavalry division commander, General Kilpatrick opted to travel with his own personal headquarters guard. Although the other two division commanders, generals Buford and Gregg, also had authority to detail a squadron for their own headquarters guard, they chose not to do so. Kilpatrick's newly assigned guard, which had acted in the same capacity for General Stahel, consisted of two troops of Ohio cavalrymen from Colonel R. Butler Price's old 2nd Brigade. During the early morning hours of June 29 at the division's encampment at Richfield, Kilpatrick's new acting assistant adjutant general, Captain Jacob Lyman Greene, formerly of General Stahel's staff, issued the following order to the commander of the 1st Ohio Cavalry: "The First Ohio Squadron will act as General Kilpatrick's escort, and be ready to march in fifteen minutes."[3]

The squadron detailed to General Kilpatrick's command consisted of Troop A and Troop C of the 1st Regiment, Ohio Volunteer Cavalry. The two troops forming the squadron served under the immediate supervision of Troop A's senior officer, twenty-three-year-old Captain Noah Jones. Troop A, commanded by 1st Lieutenant Albert E. Chester while Captain Jones led the squadron, counted seventy-three members within its ranks, having three commissioned officers, five sergeants, seven corporals, and fifty-eight enlisted men serving with Kilpatrick's headquarters guard at the end of the month of June. Troop C was under the direct control of the troop commander Samuel N. Stanford, a twenty-six-year-old captain. Captain Stanford's troop had all three of its assigned commissioned officers, five sergeants, five corporals, and forty-three enlisted men serving as part of the headquarters squadron on June 30. During the same period the rest of the 1st Ohio Cavalry served under Colonel Beroth Bullard Eggleston in the Army of the Cumberland.[4]

As the month of June drew to a rapid close, General Farnsworth's brigade also had one Regular Army artillery battery assigned to it. When the new brigadier's troopers marched away from their bivouacs at Richfield, they traveled with the sixty-five enlisted men of Battery E, 4th U.S. Artillery. As usual, the battery was commanded by First Lieutenant Samuel Sherer Elder, a thirty-two-year-old native Pennsylvanian. Lieutenant Elder's artillery career had begun almost ten years previously in

1853 when he enlisted as a private in the 2nd U.S. Artillery. Shortly after that enlistment he left the military and pursued a new and rather subdued profession as a schoolteacher. Now, on the 29th day of June, as his battery prepared to move into his home state, he was the only commissioned officer currently present for duty and serving with the battery, all other officers being sick or otherwise absent from the unit. Lieutenant Elder's battery included only four 3-inch Ordnance Rifles.[5]

The recently appointed commander of the Cavalry Corps' 2nd Brigade of the 3rd Division, Brigadier General George A. Custer, also arose early on that Monday morning to survey that portion of his command encamped in the trampled and extremely muddy fields surrounding the Richfield estate. Shortly after 8:00 A.M., he gave the roughly 975 cavalrymen of the Michigan Brigade's two available regiments, the 1st and 7th, the order to prepare to mount and move on their assigned route to the north. That route of march happened to be just slightly west of the course used by Farnsworth's troopers.

Additionally on that day, General Custer's brigade moved toward the Pennsylvania border with the four commissioned officers and 125 noncommissioned officers and enlisted men of Battery M, 2nd U.S. Artillery.[6] That battery commanded by 1st Lieutenant Alexander Cummings McWhorter Pennington, Jr. (U.S.M.A., Class of 1860) consisted of six 3-inch Ordnance Rifles. In turn, second lieutenants Robert Clarke, Frank B. Hamilton, and Carle A. Woodruff commanded Pennington's three two-gun sections.[7]

As Custer's men prepared to move from their camps near Frederick, a total of three troops from the 1st and 7th Michigan were absent from their regiments on that morning. At the end of June, Troop D, from Colonel Town's regiment, served on provost guard duty at Alexandria, Virginia. That troop under the command of Captain Thurlow W. Lusk had been detached from the 1st Michigan since November 1862. Lamentably they would remain separated from the regiment throughout the entire Gettysburg Campaign as well as the remainder of the war.[8]

In addition, Troops L and M of the 7th Michigan Cavalry were not with their regiment. They were just preparing to take the field from the comparatively safe environs of Washington where they had reported after their initial organization. Those troops under the commands of two captains, twenty-seven-year-old William H. Clipperton from Troop L and twenty-six-year-old Robert Sproul of Troop M, had been recently recruited and mustered into the service in order to bring the regiment to its full authorized strength of twelve troops. Those additional two troops would not join Colonel Mann's other ten troops in the field until some time during July 8, 1863, when the entire regiment finally united at Boonsboro, Maryland.[9]

After watering, feeding, and grooming their horses, as well as preparing and eating what they could find for their own breakfasts, the Michigan cavalrymen heard the buglers sounding "Assembly." The men packed their pared-down equipment, along with any additional rations for themselves and for their mounts. During the early days of the war, a mounted soldier carried everything imaginable as he rode into combat. Eventually, as the troopers gained more experience, they found much of their baggage was unnecessary, so they discarded most of it, just keeping the absolute essentials. As an added benefit of lightening their loads, they found that their horses would not breakdown as quickly and last longer during marches and charges upon the enemy.

Soon after mounting their horses and forming ranks, the troopers from Michigan moved onto the Emmitsburg Road from their camp sites at the Schley's Richfield farm. They advanced in a mounted column of fours and headed north toward the Pennsylvania border. General Custer mounted his own spirited horse and quickly spurred him to the head of the demi-brigade that was already on the move. Custer and his volunteer cavalrymen moved along the main road, the Emmitsburg Road, toward Emmitsburg, and then toward Taneytown and Littlestown.

Accompanying George Custer on that first morning as a new brigadier, as they would on many other occasions during the remainder of the war, were his two previously assigned personal orderlies. The men delegated to serve him from the ranks of his old Regular Army regiment, the 5th U.S. Cavalry, were buglers Peter Martin Boehm of Troop B and Joseph Fought of Troop D.[10]

Custer carried himself very well on that first full day as a brigadier general, particularly since he had not had the opportunity to practice the evolution of brigade command beforehand, at least not openly and in plain view of his peers. On that morning he led the slow-moving advance elements of his reduced brigade through the Frederick County countryside toward their ultimate destination of Littlestown. The 1st and 7th Michigan regiments, commanded by colonels Town and Mann, moved at a leisurely pace behind the general and his few inherited staff members from General Stahel's division. As always, the regimental commanders sent detachments ahead and on both flanks of the main column to scout the unfamiliar territory for signs of enemy activity and to prevent any surprise encounters or attacks from an enemy that might be nearby.[11]

Unfortunately, the ever boastful and self-admiring Alfred Pleasonton was about to receive some unwanted news. As the three divisions of the Cavalry Corps all moved northward, Pleasonton learned that Major General Meade considered him an essential senior advisor and staff officer, instead of an autonomous corps commander. Unlike the other seven infantry corps commanders, supposedly his equals in both rank and command stature, General Pleasonton received different treatment. Much to his everlasting dismay, he had to maintain his own personal headquarters very close to the headquarters of the commanding general of the Army of the Potomac throughout the Gettysburg Campaign. Except for a few occasions throughout the overall campaign, Pleasonton always established his own command headquarters within a very short distance of the commanding general's headquarters. Whenever Pleasonton strayed too far, General Meade quickly recalled him to his side.

Remaining with the main army's headquarters command was something upon which General Pleasonton had not particularly counted upon or wanted. There was no glory at headquarters. However, he still managed to garner more than enough recognition for others' accomplishments during the campaign. Pleasonton received the additional brevet of colonel in the Regular Army for his subordinate cavalry commanders' efforts mainly on the first and third days of fighting. His promotion citation specifically indicated for "gallant and meritorious services during the Battle of Gettysburg."[12]

The last Monday morning of June was shaping up to be another hot and humid day for the men in the pungent blue wool uniforms, nothing unusual or totally unexpected for the summer months in Maryland. The commissioned officers from major generals to lieutenants wanted to conserve the energy of both men and animals, since the day's march had every indication of being another very long and extremely tiring one.

Upon reaching Utica the first of several small villages on their scheduled route of march, Custer's Michigan men received a very warm welcome from the loyal townsfolk. As with many other locations, the civilians had never previously seen such a large group of men. At that place, as with many others along the way, the cavalrymen heartily received a variety of refreshments from the grateful and appreciative citizens. Not tarrying for very long within the town limits, the Michigan cavalrymen continued north along the straight, but very muddy, road to their next destination.

The youthful William Mann continued to lead the troopers of his 7th Michigan along the well-maintained Frederick Road and through Creagerstown. Although relatively young, Mann hid his youth and some of his inexperience behind a full length and bushy beard. The Michigan men in blue took another short break from the monotonous and exhaustive marching at that small village. Again, as in so many other places during the current march, the residents flooded into the streets offering the soldiers many types of enjoyable refreshments while they rested themselves and their horses. Lingering but a short time, the regiment left the town and continued moving north along the Frederick Road.

Just as the troopers left Creagerstown they came to a small settlement containing but a few houses called Loy's Station. At that place a small body of water known as Owens Creek meandered peacefully through the countryside. The creek was one of many in the area that eventually joined with the Monocacy River, which flowed only a short distance away. A 90-foot long covered bridge spanned Owens Creek at Loy's Station. Custer's cavalrymen, as well as the artillery from Lieutenant Pennington's battery, used the bridge to cross the narrow body of water as they marched north. The covered bridge, built around 1850 with wooden trusses, never ceased vibrating for the next few hours as hundreds of horses with iron shoes on their hooves and the iron-rimmed wheels of the artillery rumbled across it.

Colonel William D. Mann,
Commander,
7th Michigan Cavalry
(GAR III)

Colonel Charles H. Town;
Commander,
1st Michigan Cavalry
(GAR III)

Colonel Charles Town, riding at the head of his 1st Michigan Cavalry, was not feeling very well during the day's incessant marching. He had an affliction that would torment him throughout the remainder of his abbreviated service during the war. His pain was continuous and chronic. Slightly incapacitated with consumption, a contagious disease of the lungs, during the whole Gettysburg Campaign, Colonel Town's time as a soldier was rapidly coming to an extremely premature and painful end. However troubling his health was at the present time he still managed to maintain his position at the head of his regiment, proudly mounted on his horse. Due to his deteriorating condition he eventually received his unwished for discharge from the volunteer military service on August 17, 1864, with the justification of medical disability. Charles Town did not survive too much longer after his discharge from the army, dying on May 7, 1865, from the disease that plagued him for so long throughout his short life.[13]

Continuing on the road to the north, George Custer's regiments passed very close to the tiny village of Graceham on their route of march. Graceham was less than three miles to the west of the Frederick Road. Some of Custer's patrols rode through the town. As always, detachments of troopers kept a constant vigil on both flanks of the cavalry column as they made their way through the various and sundry small towns and villages. General Custer and his brigade moved past the many peaceful farms and homes dotting the sides of the roads enroute to Emmitsburg.

Colonels Town and Mann, as well as General Custer, expected to find the other two regiments of the Michigan Brigade waiting for them near Emmitsburg, but they were disappointed when they were not found there. The 5th and 6th Michigan regiments were still very busy scouting the countryside in the general area south and southeast of Gettysburg. At that very time, the two detached regiments were moving under orders from Cavalry Corps headquarters toward Littlestown, too. General Custer and colonels Town and Mann, along with their regiments, tarried only a short time at Emmitsburg before moving on toward their ultimate destination of Littlestown, where they arrived after dark and encamped for the night shortly after 10:00 P.M.[14]

Colonel George Gray,
Commander,
6th Michigan Cavalry
(USAMHI)

Colonel Russell A. Alger,
Commander,
5th Michigan Cavalry
(GAR III)

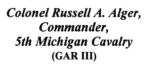

Early Monday morning the unidentified noncommissioned officer and his detail, originally dispatched by Copeland to carry reports to Frederick, arrived back at the Gettysburg encampment of the two Michigan regiments. The cavalrymen returned with dispatches from General Pleasonton's headquarters and with the unanticipated orders that Brigadier General Copeland was summarily relieved of his current brigade command and all associated duties. Copeland's new orders directed him to return immediately in person to the Cavalry Corps headquarters then still located at Frederick for additional orders and reassignment. Taken completely by surprise at the totally unexpected and most unfavorable news, Joseph Copeland, nonetheless took it in stride. Before he left for Frederick he started the process of moving his men out of Gettysburg toward Emmitsburg in the south as previously directed.[15]

The men assigned to the Michigan regiments departed their camps at Gettysburg in the pre-dawn darkness. Around mid-morning of June 29, Brigadier General Copeland bade farewell to most of his brigade staff officers, along with the senior officers of the two regiments that were present with him in Pennsylvania. While the 5th and 6th Michigan Cavalry regiments were somewhere between Gettysburg and Emmitsburg, command of the Michigan demi-brigade passed first to Colonel George Gray and then to Colonel Russell Alger. It is not clear how long Gray held the command position before ultimately relinquishing it to Alger.

Captain Kidd, a member of Gray's 6th Michigan Cavalry, gave his colonel credit for first taking command of the two regiments after Copeland's inopportune departure. His assessment of the situation would seem to have been the proper and appropriate action since George Gray had been the most senior colonel present in Copeland's old brigade with the three Michigan regiments assigned. Now, since the 1st Michigan had joined the brigade, he was junior to only Charles Town in the new brigade structure. As usual during the Civil War, the most senior regimental commander present should have received the command of the brigade unless otherwise incapacitated or unavailable, which is exactly what happened to Colonel Gray.[16]

George Gray's military service records up to the last week in June showed that he had served his entire military career as the colonel of the

6th Michigan Cavalry. Governor Austin Blair of Michigan granted him the position October 1862. Gray was a typical politically appointed commanding officer of the period. He had no military experience, either formal or informal, but did greatly assist in raising his regiment. That undertaking was more than enough to receive a field and staff commission.[17]

A number of critical contemporary reports indicated that the colonel of the 6th Michigan suffered, at various periods during the Gettysburg Campaign, from either a debilitating illness or habitual drunkenness. Colonel Gray was reportedly under arrest at the time of General Copeland's departure for being inebriated some time earlier in the campaign. He was subsequently freed from detention on the eve of the approaching battle, but no date for his release was given. Eventually Gray resigned from the army in May 1864, barely nineteen months after entering on active duty.[18]

As with so many other cases during the Civil War, an arrest simply meant that the charged officer lost his command and side arms while awaiting a possible trial or his return to duty. Usually an arrest took place because of minor infractions in discipline—drunkenness, disrespect to a superior, or breaches of discipline by subordinates. Since officers held commissions from the president or governor of their state, they were considered gentlemen and honorable individuals. An officer's word, theoretically, was his bond, so no armed guards were posted to watch those officers placed under arrest for many of the minor infractions. In many cases, simply having the stigma of an arrest was punishment enough.

Russell Alger was arguably the most experienced officer present for duty among all four Michigan colonels now assigned to Custer's Michigan Brigade. Previously Alger served as a captain in the 2nd Michigan Cavalry, as a lieutenant colonel in the 6th Michigan Cavalry, and finally as colonel of the 5th Michigan. He received his promotion to colonel in mid-June, while serving as Colonel Gray's lieutenant colonel. Alger received a serious wound during 1862 and, in another week, he would receive another wound during a pitched battle in the streets of Funkstown, Maryland.

Alger's military contribution to the war suddenly ended in September 1864 when he abruptly resigned his commission in the volunteer service. Eventually after the end of the war, Alger received the brevets of both brigadier and major general of U.S. Volunteers in June 1865 for his exceptional service in the war. After returning to civilian life, Alger served as governor of Michigan from 1885 to 1887, ministered as U.S. Secretary of War under President William McKinley from 1897 to 1899, and was elected to the U.S. Senate from Michigan in 1902, a position held until his death in 1907.[19]

Turning over the reins of his command to Colonel Gray, Brigadier General Copeland along with a few chosen members of his personal staff then continued back toward Frederick. They moved at a brisk pace along the Emmitsburg Road or through the fields when blocked by advancing infantry units of the Army of the Potomac. One important staff member, who remained with his general and traveled back to Frederick with him, was Captain Freeman Norvell, Copeland's assistant adjutant general.

Norvell, himself a former colonel and commanding officer of the 5th Michigan Cavalry, resigned his colonel's commission in disgrace in February 1863, after being placed under arrest for being intoxicated in the presence of the enemy. Norvell, as well as George Gray, was a prime example of the immoderate use of liquor by some individuals during the war. His arrest was much more serious than the later arrest of Colonel Gray since it occurred in plain view of the enemy. Although not drunk in a battle, which might have gotten him the death penalty, the shame that he felt was overwhelming. He eventually returned to the volunteer service after accepting a much less demanding position as a staff captain and assistant adjutant general.[20]

Only a few brigade staff members joined General Copeland on his sad journey back to Frederick and a perfunctory meeting with General Pleasonton. They included First Lieutenant Phineas G. White of the 6th Michigan Cavalry, who was the brigade's assistant quartermaster; First Lieutenant Frederick A. Copeland (the general's son), of the 5th Michigan Cavalry who was the assistant commissary of sustenance; and an additional-aide-de-camp Second Lieutenant Henry Hamilton Finley also of the 5th Michigan who would tender his resignation in less than a month. During his return trip to Frederick, General Copeland encountered Major General Reynolds along the route to Pennsylvania with the leading elements of the I Corps near Emmitsburg. Before continuing on his journey, Copeland related to Reynolds what he had learned during his scouting mission to Gettysburg.[21]

Upon nearing Frederick some time during the late morning, Copeland ascertained the exact location of Pleasonton's headquarters at Richfield. Luckily for the erstwhile brigade commander, General Pleasonton had not yet started for army headquarters now located at Middleburg, Maryland. Confronting the chief of the Cavalry Corps, Copeland bitterly complained that his relief from command cast a dark shadow over his perceived ability to lead his troops in the forthcoming campaign. General Pleasonton, extremely embarrassed by the controversy created by him, sent Copeland to Brigadier General David Gregg's headquarters then supposedly located near New Market, Maryland. Pleasonton implied that Gregg would grant command of a brigade in his 2nd Division, perhaps Kilpatrick's old brigade, to the exiled Copeland.[22]

General Copeland immediately rode out of Richfield in search of Gregg's headquarters. Meanwhile Gregg had started his command on the road for New Windsor. It is not known at what exact spot Copeland finally located General Gregg's traveling headquarters. The displaced Michigan general awkwardly explained his predicament to a very patient David Gregg, but to no avail. Although both had received their stars on November 29, 1862, technically Copeland outranked Gregg on the promotion list. Copeland's actual date of rank was September, while Gregg's was November. Therefore, the commander of the 2nd Division could do nothing to correct the problem. Gregg sent a thoroughly disheartened Joseph Copeland away with nothing more than that with which he came.

Born in 1813, Joseph T. Copeland was a retired judge when the Civil War broke out. His first war-service was as the lieutenant colonel of the 1st Michigan Cavalry. He then received a commission as the colonel of the 5th Michigan Cavalry, based more upon his political connections than his military capabilities. After accepting a promotion to brigadier general, Copeland received the command of a brigade of three

Michigan cavalry regiments shortly thereafter. His leadership of the brigade was quite acceptable to his superiors, but his one shortcoming was that he lacked the initiative and the innate ability to move his men quickly into and out of action.[23]

One actual reason for Joseph Copeland's removal from the command of his cavalry brigade was the fact that General Pleasonton did not personally know him or anything about his capabilities to lead a brigade of cavalry. Their careers in the U.S. volunteer service had not converged until now. Copeland's perceived advanced age was another obvious excuse for his removal. Additionally, as with David Gregg, Copeland ranked Brigadier General Kilpatrick by almost seven months and Custer and Farnsworth by almost the same time frame. If he remained in General Pleasonton's newest division, General Copeland would have had no valid position within the division or brigade structures with new general officers Kilpatrick and Custer in charge of the Michigan Brigade.[24]

General Copeland did not seem to have any major personality conflicts or other problems with General Pleasonton. He did not appear to have any significant disagreements or disputes with any other high ranking individuals in the command structure of Army of the Potomac or in Washington, D.C. for that matter. He was not a foreign-born officer so that was of no concern in Pleasonton's decision to remove him from his brigade command. Joseph Copeland did everything asked of him by his superiors, but he was in the wrong command position at the wrong time. Soon after the conclusion of the Battle of Gettysburg, Brigadier General Copeland received the command of the U.S. Military Depot at Annapolis Junction, Maryland. He finished the war as the commander of a military post and prison in Illinois.[25]

Meanwhile obeying their recently received but basically unchanged orders from headquarters after General Copeland's departure, the 5th and 6th Michigan regiments continued their march back toward Emmitsburg. Their new orders allowed them to continue their mission of searching for signs of the Rebel army, along with rendezvousing with their new brigade commander at Littlestown. Finding only a few enemy stragglers from the ranks of General Lee's army in the immediate vicinity, the Michiganders proceeded to Littlestown in the east. The Michigan cavalrymen, under the command of colonels Alger and Gray, arrived in the village of Littlestown shortly after midnight on the new day of June 30. They set up their bivouac on the south side of the town for the remaining few hours of darkness.[26]

General Farnsworth's newly assigned brigade traveled over twenty-five miles prior to crossing the Mason-Dixon Line. They arrived at Littlestown shortly before midnight on June 29. The troopers, particularly those from the 18th Pennsylvania Cavalry, cheered excitedly upon crossing into Pennsylvania for now they were truly back on the free soil of their home state, and for some of the men, very close to their own homes, farms, and relatives.[27] The residents of Littlestown provided a much warmer and kinder reception for the Union cavalrymen than anything they had seen previously during their service in the devastated areas of Virginia. A member of General Kilpatrick's escort from the 1st Ohio Cavalry recalled that:

> Here [Littlestown] the people met us with every expression of gratitude and friendship, which was all the more appreciated from our two years' service in Virginia, and especially our recent treatment at Warrenton. A company of young people were on the veranda of the hotel singing patriotic songs, with waving flags and handkerchiefs, while their more thoughtful mothers had provided baskets of provisions, which were appreciated by the tired soldiers.[28]

The march from Frederick had been extremely fatiguing for both the men and horses of General Kilpatrick's division. The roads were muddier than ever, quickly turning into miles and miles of sludge. The thousands of men, horses, and wagons did not help matters any. The poorly constructed and badly maintained roads north of Frederick could not support that volume of traffic in such inclement weather. During their march to the north, Farnsworth's troopers veered off the main road and into even muddier fields a number of times in order to pass the slower moving columns of infantry, artillery, and wagons from the advancing elements of the XI Corps. General Kilpatrick, along with his headquarters staff, also had to travel substantial distances through the fields of ripening corn and wheat to avoid being delayed by the slower marching pace set by General Howard's foot soldiers. In the process of bypassing the slower portions of the Army of the Potomac, the 3rd Division's commanding officer temporarily got separated from the 1st Brigade. Kilpatrick, his staff, and his headquarters guard did not rejoin General Farnsworth's brigade until later in the day near Middleburg, Maryland.[29]

Judson Kilpatrick, along with the members of his new headquarters guard from the 1st Ohio Cavalry, arrived in the village of Littlestown slightly in advance of Elon Farnsworth's saddle-weary troopers. The division's commanding general immediately sought to establish his headquarters in the most comfortable surroundings available in order to change to drier clothing and perhaps get a well-cooked hot meal. A hotel near the intersection of the Gettysburg and Hanover roads, the appropriately named Union House, suited his immediate purpose. Kilpatrick and some members of his staff spent the night in relative comfort, while his subordinate officers and men had to deal with yet another sudden rain shower as they slowly rode through the darkness of the night, across the Mason-Dixon Line, and into town.

Louis N. Boudrye, the chaplain of the 5th New York Cavalry, recalled his regiment's grand reception in the crowded streets of Littlestown:

> . . . where we were received with the greatest demonstrations of joy by the people. A large group of children, on the balcony of a hotel, waving handkerchiefs and flags, greeted us with patriotic songs, while the men made the welkin ring with their cheers. How different was such reception from that we had been accustomed to have given us by the inhabitants of Virginian villages![30]

After their grand entrance into the streets of Littlestown and the spectacular and unforgettable welcome by the people, even though it was late at night and the weather was less than cooperative, the men of General Kilpatrick's 3rd Division slowly continued through the small community. They bivouacked in some vacant fields just northeast of the town. They were obviously oblivious to the possible dangers created from the presence of the nearby Rebel cavalry, whose exact location was still unknown to Kilpatrick and his troopers. The command halted for the remainder of the night and caught some much needed rest as they laid their blankets on the wet ground.[31]

As the month of June ended John Hammond, originally from Crown Point, New York, found himself in command of the 5th New York Cavalry as the senior major present for duty. Colonel Othneil De Forest, recently relieved as a brigade commander serving under General Stahel, had abruptly left the regiment and returned on a leave of absence to his home in New York City for some rest. The colonel, like General Copeland, exhibited signs of irritation at having lost his brigade command. Regardless of the possibility of a forthcoming battle, Colonel De Forest received permission, from whom it is not clear, to leave his regiment before they left Frederick. It was very rare for a senior commander to take an extended leave of voluntary absence when a major battle threatened to erupt. To his credit, Colonel De Forest quickly returned to the regiment on July 9, 1863, after learning of the fight at Gettysburg. It was impossible for him to find any transportation sooner. He reported to his regiment but immediately assumed command of the 1st Brigade as senior colonel present.

Previously, the 5th New York Cavalry's second-in-command, Lieutenant Colonel Robert Johnstone had been relieved of his command and staff duties for improper conduct on June 1, 1863. He was still absent from the regimental roster during the beginning of the Gettysburg Campaign. Johnstone, the originally commissioned lieutenant colonel, eventually was able to return to the regiment again on August 13, 1863, much to the disgust of three of the senior officers then currently serving with the regiment. Majors Hammond, William Bacon, and Amos White, as well as many of the other company-grade officers, considered Johnstone a shirker, a slacker, and a less than honorable individual who seriously lacked all signs of integrity and moral principle. Whenever any members of the regiment needed to accomplish any hard work, whether in camp, on the march, or on the battlefield, Lieutenant Colonel Johnstone was never there. Finally, on September 3, 1863, Robert Johnstone found himself placed under arrest again. The military authorities removed him from the temporary command of the regiment for the final time and cashiered him in disgrace from the service before the end of the year.[32]

On the march through Maryland and into Pennsylvania, Lieutenant Colonel William Brinton was the senior officer present with his regiment and therefore in command of the 18th Pennsylvania Cavalry. He had taken over for the absent colonel of the regiment, Timothy Matlack Bryan, Jr. (U.S.M.A., Class of 1853). Colonel Bryan recently took sick leave from the regiment shortly after reporting as the commanding officer in May 1863. Before receiving the appointment as the original colonel of the 18th Pennsylvania, Bryan served as a second lieutenant in the 10th U.S. Infantry Regiment before resigning in 1857 and as the lieutenant colonel of the 12th Regiment, Massachusetts Volunteer Infantry.

After his transfer from the 2nd Regiment, Pennsylvania Volunteer Cavalry some time in March 1863 and until his muster out in January 1865, Lieutenant Colonel Brinton continued to actively serve with the 18th Pennsylvania Cavalry. He was absent only for brief periods of minor illness and was once taken prisoner but escaped almost immediately. William Brinton had, what could only be termed as a somewhat uneventful and obscure career. He usually served within the ranks of the regiment but he never advanced beyond the rank of lieutenant colonel during the entire war.[33]

Lieutenant Colonel Addison W. Preston briefly commanded the 1st Vermont Cavalry Regiment from June 22, 1863, until Colonel Edward B. Sawyer reclaimed command of the regiment on July 10, 1863, at Boonsboro, Maryland. Sawyer, like Colonel De Forest, had been on an extended leave of absence and, like De Forest, rushed to rejoin his regiment when he learned of the desperate fighting at Gettysburg.

As the regiment's second-in-command Addison Preston was a well-liked and highly respected individual, especially by the enlisted men of his regiment. Other commissioned officers, including many of his superiors, also admired and trusted him to perform all duties assigned to him. During the all-important fighting in the Gettysburg Campaign, Preston discharged his command responsibilities admirably. He commanded the regiment in Sawyer's absence on many other occasions and eventually received his long deserved promotion to full colonel after Sawyer's

Major John Hammond,
Commander,
5th New York Cavalry
(GAR III)

Lieutenant Colonel
Addison W. Preston,
Commander,
1st Vermont Cavalry
(GAR III)

Lieutenant Colonel
William P. Brinton,
Commander,
18th Pennsylvania Cavalry
(GAR III)

Major Charles E. Capehart,
1st West Virginia Cavalry
(GAR III)

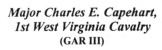

resignation in 1864. Addison Preston served exceptionally well with the 1st Vermont until his unfortunate death at Salem Church, Virginia on June 3, 1864.[34]

Before the beginning of the Civil War, Indiana-born Nathaniel P. Richmond attended Brown University in Rhode Island, as did Addison Preston of the 1st Vermont Cavalry. Richmond briefly served as a lawyer in his native state after his graduation. Eventually he left the legal profession for lack of worthwhile work and turned to farming near Kokomo. At the outbreak of hostilities, he received a commission as a second lieutenant in the 13th Regiment, Indiana Volunteer Infantry. Shortly thereafter Richmond became the original lieutenant colonel of the 1st Regiment, Virginia (Union) Volunteer Cavalry on September 7, 1861. Nathaniel Richmond rose to command the cavalry regiment as its colonel in October 1862. He assumed that position after the originally commissioned colonel, Henry Amisanzel, tendered his resignation from the volunteer service because of ill health some three months earlier. For unknown reasons, Colonel Richmond also resigned his commission on March 18, 1863.[35]

The difficulties or problems that originally caused Colonel Richmond's resignation from the command of the regiment seem to have disappeared within a very short three months. He was re-commissioned as the colonel of the 1st Virginia on June 12, 1863, just in time to lead his regiment in the Gettysburg Campaign. A short time later, the 1st Virginia Cavalry was officially re-designated as the 1st West Virginia Cavalry after West Virginia split from the rest of Virginia and joined the Union on June 20, 1863.

Besides his duties as commanding officer of the 1st West Virginia Cavalry, Colonel Richmond also briefly commanded the 1st Brigade after General Farnsworth's inopportune death during the afternoon of July 3. Upon Colonel Othneil De Forest's return to duty with the 5th New York Cavalry on July 9, Colonel Richmond was relieved from brigade command, De Forest being the senior colonel present, and returned to the command of his West Virginians. Nathaniel Richmond resigned his volunteer commission for the final time in November 1863 because of an injury suffered when his horse fell on him during the previous month.[36]

Four troops from the four assigned regiment's in General Farnsworth's brigade were on detached duty during the brigade's march from Frederick County into Pennsylvania on June 29. Troop I of the 5th New York Cavalry was absent from their regiment and serving in the vicinity of Washington, D.C. under the leadership of twenty-four-year-old Captain George C. Morton.[37] The 1st West Virginia Cavalry had a squadron of roughly eighty men from Troops A and I assigned at Morgantown, West Virginia. The squadron commander was Captain Dennis Delaney of Troop I. Captain Harrison H. Hagans directed Troop A, while First Lieutenant William E. Guseman actually led Troop I while his captain led the squadron. Those two troops of West Virginians served in the Department of West Virginia under Brigadier General Benjamin Franklin Kelley. Furthermore they served in Colonel Rutherford Birchard Hayes' 1st Brigade of Brigadier General Eliakim Parker Scammon's (U.S.M.A., Class of 1837) Division. Captain Delaney died in action at Wytheville, Virginia on July 18, 1863. Lieutenant Guseman received a mortal wound during that battle. Another officer, Charles H. Livingston, the second lieutenant from Troop I received a less severe wound at the same time.[38]

Troop K of the 1st West Virginia, commanded by Captain Weston Rowand, had also been detached from the regiment and was currently serving in the Department of the Susquehanna under the command of General Darius N. Couch.[39] The other two regiments assigned to Farnsworth's brigade, the 1st Vermont and 18th Pennsylvania, had a complete complement of their assigned troops present during the entire campaign.[40]

Notes to Chapter Five

1. OR – 3, p. 400. Special Orders, Number 99, Headquarters Cavalry Corps, June 29, 1863.

2. H. Nelson Jackson, comp., *Dedication of the Statue to Brevet Major-General William Wells and the Officers and Men of the First Regiment Vermont Cavalry* (privately printed, 1914), p. 143; 8th Regiment, Illinois Volunteer Cavalry; Boxes 262 – 267; Muster Rolls, Regimental Papers, Office of the Adjutant General, Volunteer Organizations, Civil War; Record Group 94; National Archives, Washington, D.C.

3. Gillespie ("Lovejoy"), *A History of Company A, First Ohio Cavalry,* p. 147. Jacob L. Greene previously served in the 7th Regiment, Michigan Volunteer Infantry before being detached to serve as a volunteer aide on Julius Stahel's staff. He eventually resigned from the 7th Michigan while continuing to serve on Stahel's staff as a captain. He transferred to Kilpatrick's staff upon the change of command on June 28. The twenty-six-year-old received a commission as a captain in the 6th Michigan Cavalry, effective July 14, 1863, but he declined the appointment. During September 1863, he accepted a captain's commission in the U.S. Volunteers as an assistant adjutant general and continued to serve on Kilpatrick's staff. He was promoted to major and received the brevet of lieutenant colonel after the war for his actions at Trevilian Station in 1864.

4. Ibid., p. 139; W. L. Curry, *Four Years in the Saddle: History of the First Regiment Ohio Volunteer Cavalry* (Jonesboro, Ga.: Freedom Hill Press, Inc., 1984), p. 239; 1st Regiment, Ohio Volunteer Cavalry; Boxes 3496 – 3501; Muster Rolls, Regimental Papers, Office of the Adjutant General, Volunteer Organizations, Civil War; Record Group 94; National Archives, Washington, D.C. (Hereafter cited as NA RG 94 – 1 OH.) Troop A has always been listed as assigned to Gregg's headquarters in all orders of battle for the Gettysburg Campaign. However, much evidence points to the fact that Troop A of the 1st Ohio joined Gregg's division some time after the action at Hanover. They originally served with Troop C, first in Stahel's division and then in Kilpatrick's division. An examination of the unit's muster rolls for the period show casualties from Emmitsburg, Monterey Gap, and Hagerstown. All three of those places saw Kilpatrick's headquarters present and involved in the fighting specifically at Monterey Gap and Hagerstown. Gregg's headquarters was not present at any of those fights, but remained at Gettysburg.

5. John W. Busey and David G. Martin, *Regimental Strengths and Losses at Gettysburg* (Hightstown, N.J.: Longstreet House, 1994), p. 109; Raus, *A Generation on the March: The Union Army at Gettysburg,* p. 164.

6. Busey and Martin, *Regimental Strengths and Losses at Gettysburg,* p. 109; Raus, *A Generation on the March: The Union Army at Gettysburg,* p. 160.

7. Alexander Pennington graduated 18th in the West Point Class of 1860, which was a five-year, instead of a four-year, class. The graduating class, which had forty-one members, was the same class that ranked Wesley Merritt at 22nd and Josiah Kellogg at 13th.

8. NA RG 94 – 1 MI; Robertson, *Michigan in the War,* p. 392.

9. Isham, *An Historical Sketch of the Seventh Regiment Michigan Volunteer Cavalry,* pp. 12, 31.

10. 5th U.S. Cavalry Regiment; Boxes 996 – 1014; Muster Rolls, Regimental Papers, Office of the Adjutant General, Regular Army Organizations, Civil War; Record Group 94; National Archives, Washington, D.C.

Notes to Chapter Five (*continued*)

11. Letter of Amos K. Smith, dated June 30, 1863. Author's collection. (Hereafter cited as Smith Letter) Amos K. Smith was the assistant surgeon of the 1st Michigan Cavalry. He mentioned in his letter that "[Col.] Town was not very well yesterday [Monday, June 29th] when we left Frederick City. . . . our new brig. Coster expressed worry that the col. would not make the trip."

12. Theophilus F. Rodenbough, *From Everglade to Cañon with the Second Dragoons* (New York: D. Van Nostrand, 1875), p. 444.

13. Smith Letter. Colonel Town also suffered from a previous wound received at the 2nd Battle of Bull Run in August 1862.

14. OR – 3, p. 922.

15. Robertson, *Michigan in the War,* p. 400.

16. Ibid., p. 404; Kidd, *Recollections of a Cavalryman,* p. 123. The Michigan Brigade commanding officers and their dates of ranks were: Colonel Charles Town: September 30, 1862; Colonel George Gray: October 13, 1862; Colonel William Mann: December 1, 1862; Colonel Russell Alger: February 28, 1863.

17. Field and staff commissioned officers of a regiment included one colonel, one lieutenant colonel, three majors, one surgeon, one chaplain, one adjutant, one quartermaster, one commissary, and two assistant surgeons. The line, or company-grade commissioned officers for each troop included one captain, one first lieutenant, and one second lieutenant.

18. Military and Pension File of George Gray, 6th Regiment, Michigan Volunteer Cavalry. Records of the Record and Pension Office, Record Group 15, National Archives, Washington, D.C.; George Barbour Diary.

19. Military and Pension File of Russell A. Alger, 5th Regiment, Michigan Volunteer Cavalry. Records of the Record and Pension Office, Record Group 15, National Archives, Washington, D.C.

20. Robertson, *Michigan in the War,* p. 159.

21. Ibid.

22. Letter from Joseph T. Copeland to D. C. Ritter, July 9, 1863, Historical Society of Pennsylvania.

23. Warner, *Generals in Blue,* p. 93.

24. General Pleasonton could easily have avoided any problems if he had truly wanted to keep General Copeland within his new command. Brigadier General Buford outranked Copeland by four months and could easily have had him assigned as one of the brigade commanders. Colonels Devin and Gamble commanded two of Buford's brigades, while the Reserve Brigade listed newly promoted Brigadier General Merritt as its new commander.

25. Joseph T. Copeland to Adjutant General, November 30 – December 1, 1863, Record Group 94, E-159, National Archives, Washington, D.C.

26. OR – 3, p. 992.

27. Regimental Association, *History of the Eighteenth Regiment of Cavalry,* p. 13. Troop E recruited its members in Dauphin County, not too far to the northeast of where they crossed into Pennsylvania.

28. Gillespie ("Lovejoy"), *A History of Company A, First Ohio Cavalry,* p. 148. While encamped around Warrenton, Va. in June 1863, the Union cavalrymen were treated to a series of abuses and profanities from the women of the area.

Notes to Chapter Five (*continued*)

29. Ibid.
30. Boudrye, *Historic Records of the Fifth New York Cavalry*, p. 64.
31. Chamber of Commerce, *Encounter at Hanover*, p. 40; Richard E. Beaudry, *War Journal of Louis N. Beaudry, Fifth New York Cavalry* (Jefferson, N.C.: McFarland & Co., Inc., 1996), p. 48.
32. Phisterer, *New York in the War of the Rebellion*, 1:838.
33. Regimental Association, *History of the Eighteenth Regiment of Cavalry*, pp. 180-81. Brinton transferred from the 2nd Pennsylvania Cavalry, where he was a captain, in order to accept the recently vacated position of lieutenant colonel in the 18th Pennsylvania.
34. Howard Coffin, *Full Duty: Vermonters in the Civil War* (Woodstock, Vt.: The Countryman Press, Inc., 1993), p. 259. The place where Lieutenant Colonel Preston died is also cited as Haw's Shop, Virginia.
35. Theodore F. Lang, *Loyal West Virginia from 1861 to 1865* (Baltimore: The Deutsch Publishing Company, 1895), p. 159.
36. Ibid.
37. NA RG 94 – 5 NY.
38. Dyer, *A Compendium of the War*, 1:383; NA RG 94 – 1 WV.
39. Dyer, *A Compendium of the War*, 1:284.
40. NA RG 94 – 5 NY; NA RG 94 – 18 PA; NA RG 94 – 1 VT; NA RG 94 – 1 WV.

Chapter 6:

Clash at Westminster

EEMINGLY unbeknown to Judson Kilpatrick and his two brigade commanders on June 29 was the fact that Confederate Major General J. E. B. Stuart and a sizable portion, three brigades, of his cavalry division had encamped recently at Union Mills, Maryland. The tiny community of Union Mills was only a short seven miles to the southeast of Littlestown. Kilpatrick's many patrols and scouting parties did not push far enough to the east on their journey northward, believing that the Southern cavalry could not possibly be in that region. Additionally, David Gregg's 2nd Division had the responsibility to patrol the area to the east of Kilpatrick's 3rd Division, while Buford's 1st Division patrolled further to the west. Gregg's cavalrymen, unfortunately, were not advancing to the north as rapidly as the members of Kilpatrick's new command. Gregg's division encountered infantry and artillery from many units in the Army of the Potomac on their way to Pennsylvania, which caused some serious and lengthy delays for the cavalrymen. General Gregg and his three brigades finally reached New Windsor, seven miles southwest of Westminster, on the night of June 29.

Even with General Pleasonton's entire Cavalry Corps screening the advance of the Army of the Potomac his Union troopers failed to locate the Confederate cavalry force operating near Westminster. On the damp and depressing night of June 29, J. E. B. Stuart found himself no more than seven miles from Judson Kilpatrick's cavalry division encamped at Littlestown and an equally short seven miles from David Gregg's division at New Windsor. General Stuart found his command almost caught between Kilpatrick's troopers, Gregg's troopers, and the rest of the advancing elements of the Army of the Potomac. A wrong turn might easily result in a disastrous and unwelcome circumstance for the Southern cavalry.

Major General J. E. B. Stuart,
Commander, Cavalry Division, Army of Northern Virginia
(LC)

Beginning late on the night of June 27, General Stuart's detached cavalry force started across the wide expanse of the Potomac River at Rowser's Ford, roughly eight miles south of where the Union army crossed at Edwards Ferry. The river was high but they crossed with little difficulty during the predawn hours of June 28. As Stuart's troopers prepared to move east and north, they delayed long enough to destroy valuable canal property and confiscate a quantity of U.S. government materials and supplies. In addition, the Confederate cavalrymen had the opportunity to intercept about a dozen small boats being pulled by teams of mules along the placid waters of the canal. The 4th Virginia Cavalry, Stuart's rear guard for the day, captured almost 300 Federal soldiers who were traveling along the canal from West Virginia to Washington, D.C.[1]

During the early morning hours of June 28 a portion of the Confederate cavalry force, led by Brigadier General Wade Hampton, paused briefly as they prepared to enter Rockville, Maryland. Situated some fifteen miles to the north of Washington the thriving town of Rockville sat on the direct road to Frederick located farther to the north. Upon entering the small Montgomery County town, the Rebel cavalrymen quickly cut the telegraph wires along the main pike for a couple of miles in either direction. By destroying the telegraph lines General Hampton's troopers severed any direct communication between Washington and Frederick, where the new commander of the Army of the Potomac, General Meade, was attempting to concentrate his new force.

Wade Hampton's veteran troopers had very little trouble brushing away the limited and totally uncoordinated resistance offered by a small party of two regiments of Union horsemen encountered near Rockville. The two units, the 11th New York Cavalry and the 2nd Regiment, Massachusetts Volunteer Cavalry, had orders to intercept the Southern force when their presence on the Maryland side of the Potomac became known to the U.S. government. The detachment of New Yorkers, also known as "Scott's Nine Hundred," was the regiment in which the recently reassigned Colonel Luigi di Cesnola had served as lieutenant colonel.

The five troops from "Scott's Nine Hundred" for the past few days had been serving near Harpers Ferry on Bolivar Heights. They received instructions to move toward Washington when the magnitude of the Southern threat became apparent to the politicians in Washington.[2] The colonel of the regiment, forty-two-year-old James B. Swain, formerly served as a first lieutenant in the 1st U.S. Cavalry Regiment in 1861. He took extended leave from his regiment in order to recruit the 11th New York Cavalry beginning in April 1862. Colonel Swain was not present when the detachment of his regiment went in pursuit of Stuart's cavalrymen. He remained behind with the rest of his regiment.

Colonel Charles R. Lowell, Jr.,
2nd Massachusetts Cavalry
(GAR III)

Colonel James B. Swain,
11th New York Cavalry
(GAR III)

The seven troops present for duty from the New England regiment were under the personal command of the regiment's newly assigned colonel, Charles Russell Lowell, Jr.[3] Recently commissioned as the commander of the volunteer regiment in May 1863, Lowell served previously as a captain in Troop K of the newly organized 6th U.S. Cavalry Regiment at the beginning of the war. His horsemen from Massachusetts spent a considerable amount of their time trying to capture Major John Singleton Mosby and the elusive members of his partisan band. Only during the previous day had his regiment returned to their former headquarters at Poolesville, Maryland. He had received orders to join Major General Slocum's XII Corps from the Army of the Potomac in pursuit off Lee's army.[4] Colonel Lowell would have an all too brief career in the volunteer cavalry branch; he would receive a mortal wound in action at the Battle of Cedar Creek, Virginia in October 1864.[5]

Colonel Lowell received the overall command of the two individual regiments sent southeast from Poolesville in response to the Confederate incursion. The troops from the lone two Union cavalry regiments initially deceived Wade Hampton into believing that a much larger force was being sent to stop him. Hampton quickly dispatched one of his aides to General Stuart requesting immediate reinforcements based upon his misleading information. Stuart promptly ordered Colonel John Randolph Chambliss, Jr. (U.S.M.A., Class of 1853) to move the men of his cavalry brigade to support Hampton's troopers.

At the same time, the Union forces believed that the Confederates vastly outnumbered them and therefore they did not press the Rebel cavalrymen. Before the Confederate brigades of Hampton and Chambliss could completely deploy, Colonel Lowell and his cavalry detachment quickly retreated back toward the sheltering protection of the Army of the Potomac near Poolesville without attempting a serious demonstration against the Southern raiders.[6]

Meanwhile General Hampton's men busied themselves by cutting telegraph wires and felling the supporting poles all around the town of Rockville and the surrounding area. A small scouting party of Lieutenant Colonel Thomas Jefferson Lipscomb's 2nd South Carolina Cavalry, the leading regiment of Hampton's brigade, reported what appeared to be a heavily laden wagon train approaching the town from the south.[7] Further information gleaned by Lipscomb's men provided General Hampton with the details that the 150 wagons did not have any sizable contingent of armed troops accompanying it as guards. The wagon train, stretching for over eight miles along the pike, had just left the safe environs of Washington a few hours earlier and was heading for the Army of the Potomac's newly established headquarters in Frederick about thirty miles away. The teamsters driving the wagons were shortly to receive a very unpleasant surprise.

In response to the exceedingly interesting information received about the wagons, Stuart hurriedly ordered Colonel Chambliss to send a detachment from one of his assigned regiments, the 2nd North Carolina Cavalry, to intercept the advancing Union wagon train. Colonel Chambliss was the temporary new brigade commander since replacing Brigadier General William Henry Fitzhugh "Rooney" Lee, who had received a serious wound during the engagement at Brandy Station only weeks earlier.[8] Chambliss's Tarheel regiment was one of only two from that state now serving with Stuart's command on the current raid into Maryland.[9]

The North Carolina regiment was under the temporary command of Lieutenant Colonel William Henry Fitzhugh Payne, an 1849 Virginia Military Institute (V.M.I.) graduate. Payne had only recently been detached from his own regiment—the 4th Virginia Cavalry. He took over the command of the 2nd North Carolina after their colonel, Solomon Williams (U.S.M.A., Class of 1858), died while leading the regiment at the Battle of Brandy Station. The regiment's other senior officer, Lieutenant Colonel William George Robinson (U.S.M.A., Class of 1858), received a slight wound and fell into the enemy's hands in April 1862 during an engagement at Gillette's Farm, North Carolina. He never returned to the regiment.[10]

With little difficulty the Confederate cavalrymen swiftly swooped down upon the lightly protected wagons. They easily overwhelmed the few guards and teamsters while capturing the majority of the fully loaded wagons undamaged and with their cargoes intact. A few of the teamsters in the rear of the column attempted to turn their vehicles and get away from their attackers but their efforts only caused a massive tangle of wagons, mules, and men. Chambliss's men captured roughly 125 wagons, each with a fresh team of six mules, and over 400 teamsters, wagoners, and other support personnel. The wagons not captured in the initial assault upon the convoy were otherwise destroyed or badly damaged by the attackers, while their teams of mules also got impressed into Confederate service.[11]

Later in the afternoon of the same day, Brigadier General Montgomery Cunningham Meigs (U.S.M.A., Class of 1836), Quartermaster General of the Union army, acknowledged the loss of such a large number of wagons, mules, and their drivers. In a brusque letter to Brigadier General Rufus Ingalls (U.S.M.A., Class of 1843), Chief Quartermaster of the Army of the Potomac, Meigs bemoaned the loss of the train along with the lack of coordination by stating:

> . . . Last fall I gave orders to prevent the sending of wagon trains from this place to Frederick without escort. The situation repeats itself, and gross carelessness and inattention to military rule has this morning cost us 150 wagons and 900 mules, captured by cavalry between this and Rockville. Yesterday morning a

detachment of over 400 cavalry moved from this place to join the army. This morning 150 wagons were sent without escort. Had the cavalry been delayed or the wagons hastened, they could have been protected and saved. All the cavalry of the Defenses of Washington was swept off by the army, and we are now insulted by burning wagons 3 miles outside of Tennallytown. Your communications are now in hands of General Fitzhugh Lee's brigade.[12]

Brigadier General
Montgomery C. Meigs,
Quartermaster General,
U.S. Army
(LC)

Brigadier General
Rufus Ingalls,
Chief Quartermaster,
Army of the Potomac
(LC)

Major General Stuart now possessed an unanticipated grand and glorious trophy of the war, a prize that delighted him, but also one that ultimately hampered him for the next five days of his mission. Suddenly and totally unexpectedly his cavalrymen had control of a long and cumbersome wagon train filled with commissary and quartermaster stores. Additionally, he added more prisoners to the scores captured since crossing the Potomac.

Acting within the limits of his orders from General Robert E. Lee, Stuart had grabbed the Union wagon train for the supplies that it carried, since everything was of some value to the ill-equipped Southern soldiers. Unfortunately for General Stuart, he had to continue with his raid around the rapidly deploying Union forces. The burdensome extra wagons and hundreds of unwanted prisoners presented many problems not originally anticipated for him and his cavalrymen while they rode so close to the enemy soldiers.

Shortly before the time that Lowell and his detachment started on their mission to harass General Stuart another detail of men from the 2nd Regiment, New York Volunteer Cavalry, Judson Kilpatrick's old regiment, inadvertently wandered into the same general area. That detachment consisted of approximately fifty men from Troops G and K. It was under the capable leadership of twenty-three-year-old New Jersey-native Captain George V. Griggs, commander of Troop K. While Griggs had overall control of the two troops, First Lieutenant William R. Mattison, twenty-three years old, was the senior officer present with Troop K. At the last moment, twenty-six-year-old Second Lieutenant Martin F. Hatch of Troop G had remained with the regiment as acting quartermaster.[13]

Captain Griggs' cavalrymen had been temporarily detached from their regiment and from the Cavalry Corps of the Army of the Potomac during the previous week. They received orders to escort their brigade's unserviceable animals and other captured property to the depots located near Washington. The two troops left their regiment as it began to move toward Maryland from Virginia. At that time the overall command of the detachment evolved upon twenty-three-year-old Captain Henry Grinton of Troop G. Grinton became seriously ill and went on sick leave while in Washington, thus elevating George Griggs to command of the two troops as they attempted to return to the Army of the Potomac.

Upon the completion of their routine assignment the detachment of New Yorkers left Tennallytown, a small settlement located in the northern portion of the District of Columbia. The practice of escorting the broken-down animals had a history of being relatively safe duty and was one constantly performed by all cavalry units assigned to the Cavalry Corps. Hundreds of jaded horses routinely arrived in the Washington area to recuperate or be retired from active service. The officers and men did not mind the duty too much and saw it as an opportunity to get away from the mundane duties of being in the field.

Upon the completion of their mission, the 2nd New York cavalrymen had instructions to return to their regiment, which was a part of

Colonel Pennock Huey's 2nd Brigade of General Gregg's 2nd Division. Captain Griggs and his men hoped to rendezvous with the other troops of Lieutenant Colonel Otto Harhaus' command somewhere in Maryland between Frederick and Westminster. They began their journey during the early morning hours of the 28th. As they moved away from Tennallytown, Captain Griggs and his men traveled with at least two wagons loaded with personal baggage and troop supplies.

Sometime during the afternoon hours of June 28, as Captain Griggs' men moved slowly north through the peaceful Maryland countryside toward Brookeville and Westminster, they began to run into the unmistakable signs of enemy activity in the area, especially just to the west of them. Troops G and K were about seven miles northeast of Rockville when they ran into a small patrol of enemy troopers from Colonel Chambliss' brigade. They assumed that those horsemen were just a small foraging party that had crossed the Potomac River. George Griggs, having received no intelligence about Stuart's cavalry division being in Maryland when he had departed Tennallytown, ordered his men to attack the seemingly small command of enemy cavalrymen. Swinging their horses to the west, the small group of New Yorkers attacked and easily drove the handful of Confederates back toward Rockville.[14]

As the men from the 2nd New York Cavalry shoved the surprised and temporarily outnumbered Confederate scouting party back toward the Potomac River, the number of enemy troopers seemed to grow as the Union cavalrymen neared the outskirts of Rockville. It was now obvious to Captain Griggs that his men had engaged a much larger force than just the members of a simple foraging patrol. Before being completely surrounded and captured, the cavalrymen from the 2nd New York quickly disengaged from their running fight with the Confederate patrol from Chambliss' brigade. They successfully retreated back along the same route over which they had just charged. Most of Griggs' men managed to escape from the closely pursuing Southern cavalrymen and were able to reform near the original starting point of the attack.[15]

The casualties of the 2nd New York Cavalry's two troops included three enlisted men wounded and five other enlisted men presumed captured after the ill-advised attack on the enemy's forces near Rockville.[16]

Stuart's cavalry suffered slightly fewer casualties during his improvident stay near Rockville. Three enlisted men found themselves taken prisoner: two from the 9th Virginia and one from the 13th Virginia.[17] The assumption is that Captain Griggs and his men were responsible for capturing the Southerners since they were the only troops actively engaged during the day.

With contact broken from the enemy's scouts shortly after sunset, the stalwart band of New Yorkers encamped for the night about five miles south of Brookeville. They were perilously close to where the enemy set up their overnight encampment. Captain George Griggs and his detachment, not at all deterred by the outcome of the day's activities, would make another foolhardy attempt to rejoin their regiment during the next day. He and his men still did not sense the magnitude of the danger that may await them.[18]

After the brief clashes with Colonel Lowell's detachment and Captain Griggs' two troops, General Stuart's column continued to push, unmolested for the remainder of the day, through the Maryland countryside. The Confederate cavalry eventually halted for a brief time at a location somewhere between the villages of Brookeville and Cooksville. During Stuart's brief rest stop he paroled the majority of the prisoners captured since crossing the Potomac River. The decision to keep the wagons and to continue to move them with the cavalry column instead of destroying them would plague Stuart, as well as General Lee, throughout the next few days of the campaign.[19]

Stuart recommenced his journey to the north after his successful attack on the wagon train. Colonel Lowell and his detachment of New York and Massachusetts cavalrymen again ventured out from the safety of their fortifications. The colonel and his men continued to shadow Stuart's movements, being careful not to bring on a general engagement. They were unable or unwilling to do anything to stop the much larger Confederate force from resuming their march northward and causing any destruction that the Southern cavalry chief might deem necessary.

Rising early the next morning, June 29, the Confederate cavalrymen continued to push on through the many peaceful Maryland farms and villages toward Sykesville. Their sudden appearance did not cause the same spontaneous outbreaks of celebration from the local inhabitants as the Union forces received but they received cautious welcomes by many nonetheless. The small town of Sykesville was less than twenty-five miles from Baltimore in the east. The Rebel horsemen destroyed all bridges, railroad tracks, railroad rolling stock, and any other assorted station equipment of the Baltimore & Ohio Railroad, including miles of telegraph lines, that they happened to come across during their journey. Cautiously pushing on from Sykesville with the slowly moving wagon train setting the pace, the gray-clad troopers continued heading north some fifteen miles more toward Westminster.[20]

During the early morning hours of that Monday morning Captain Griggs and his men were on the road, once again, attempting to rejoin their regiment somewhere to the north. Their overnight stop had been anything but restful given the proximity of Stuart's men. Meanwhile, the rest of the 2nd New York Cavalry was moving with General Gregg's division between New Market and New Windsor. Unfortunately enemy activity between Brookeville and Cooksville thwarted the forward progress of Griggs' horsemen. Captain Griggs could not have known that this time his detachment would blindly blunder into the main Confederate column encamped near Cooksville. The captain and his men were obviously unaware that during the night Stuart's cavalrymen had, quite by chance, positioned themselves between their two detached troops and the main portion of the Army of the Potomac.

As the small command from the 2nd New York passed to the east of Brookeville and approached Cooksville to the north, they suddenly encountered Stuart's cavalrymen one more time. It remains a tactical mystery how George Griggs could have easily recognized the signs of enemy activity caused by a handful of troops yesterday, but totally missed the warning signals from three full-sized enemy brigades on the same road to his front today. Taken completely by surprise, eleven Union troopers quickly found themselves captured just south of Cooksville by members of Fitz Lee's brigade. The Southerners lost two enlisted men from the 1st Virginia and one from the 2nd Virginia listed as captured.[21]

The remainder of Griggs' horsemen, now only roughly forty-five officers and enlisted men, then finally retreated back toward the safety of

Washington, where they arrived later in the same day. For the next month Captain Griggs and his men remained in the Washington area unable to join their regiment. Troops G and K eventually rejoined their regiment at the end of July having completely missed the whole Gettysburg Campaign. In the meantime, General Stuart's command continued to push his men north toward Westminster and another unplanned and totally unwanted engagement with additional elements of the Union cavalry.[22]

On Saturday evening of June 27, Major Napoleon Bonaparte Knight with Troops C and D of the 1st Battalion, Delaware Volunteer Cavalry held advanced positions at Reisterstown. Equidistant between Baltimore and Westminster, Reisterstown was a moderately sized town. The two troops included approximately six commissioned officers and ninety-five enlisted men. Napoleon Knight, the senior officer currently serving with the 1st Delaware, had little combat experience. However he had served for a brief period in the Confederate Army before seeing the error of his way. Eventually Major Knight received his commission as the lieutenant colonel of the 1st Delaware Cavalry. The unit's colonel, George P. Fisher, had resigned in March 1863 when it became apparent that the 1st Delaware Cavalry would never reach regimental status.[23]

Early the next morning that small detachment from Delaware followed orders from their headquarters in the Middle Department's VIII Corps, commanded by Major General Robert Cumming Schenck, and moved to Westminster. They arrived at that location shortly after 11:00 A.M. just as many of the citizens were attending church services. The two troops of men from Delaware had orders to guard the strategic railroad depot located in Westminster, which was the end point of a branch line running from the Northern Central Railroad. The Westminster depot would become, in a few more days, the main supply point for the Army of the Potomac during and after the Battle at Gettysburg.[24]

Major Knight established his headquarters in the Westminster Hotel on Main Street. Knight's unit spent the rest of that Sunday picketing and guarding the roads around the town, while continuing to search for signs of the Rebel cavalry reported to be in the area. About 9:00 P.M. one of the detachment's pickets came rushing in on his reserve and reported that the enemy's troops were advancing along the Hampstead Road in the darkness from the northeast. Believing that the force could be only General Stuart's Confederate cavalry and that they would be able to strike the rear of his command, Major Knight ordered his horsemen to move out of Westminster to the southeast about three miles. Reaching that point he reformed his command to meet the perceived threat. Upon closer examination of the situation, Knight ascertained that there were no enemy troops to the northeast, the alarm being completely false. The picket mistakenly identified a group of children returning to their homes from singing practice as enemy soldiers. Major Knight and his men then returned to Westminster, where they peacefully camped for the remainder of the night.[25]

The next day, June 29, everything was quiet for most of the day for the troopers from Delaware. They took care of routine business to include shoeing their horses at the local blacksmith shop. Major Knight and his men still did not suspect that a large portion of General Stuart's cavalry division was heading directly toward them. During the late afternoon hours, the two small troops of Union horsemen were about to meet their destiny in the once quiet streets of Westminster. Knight's detachment, composed of Troops C and D, was about to engage in an attack against what they thought to be no more than a foraging party of enemy cavalry. However, the enemy's force was far superior as Captain Griggs had learned the previous day. The cavalrymen of the 1st Delaware Cavalry would soon learn a much more severe lesson than the two troops from the 2nd New York Cavalry.

Around 3:00 P.M. a local citizen observed the leading elements of the Confederate cavalry force advancing along the Washington Pike just south of Westminster. Just minutes before the general alarm sounded the Southern cavalrymen captured the 1st Delaware's pickets assigned to the post on that road. As soon as he learned of the newest alarm, Major Knight gave the order for his command to mount their horses and to prepare to meet the enemy's advance. Of the ninety-five men present for duty with the two troops, including those pickets just captured and other pickets, only seventy of the men had serviceable horses and were capable of obeying the order to mount and move forward. Those troopers had the unfortunate luck to ride out to meet the advancing regiments of Confederate cavalry, while the rest of their comrades and their unserviceable mounts remained behind as the Delaware unit's rear guard.[26]

Shortly before five o'clock on that afternoon, Major Knight committed his meager two troops against the seemingly never ending column of gray troopers stretched before them. Initially, he dispatched Troop C's 2nd Lieutenant D. C. Clark with twelve enlisted men to ascertain the strength and position of the advancing enemy troops. Clark and his men briefly exchanged long-distance shots with the leading Confederate patrol from Company E, 4th Virginia Cavalry before being driven back to Knight's main column drawn up in formation along Main Street. At least one 4th Virginia private from Company E was wounded by the men from Delaware during the abbreviated exchange while they suffered no casualties themselves. Lieutenant Clark reported to Major Knight that a strong force of cavalry was in their front and that the enemy had split their forces and it seemed likely that they were going to attack from both the north and south ends of Westminster.[27]

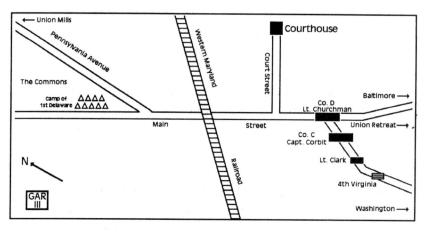

1st Delaware Cavalry Engagement at Westminster, June 29, 1863
(GAR III)

Major Knight then ordered the commanding officer of Troop C, twenty-five-year-old Captain Charles Corbit, to charge the same column of Confederates with his troop's remaining thirty men. Corbit's command had a little more luck than Lieutenant Clark's men a few minutes before, but not much. Clark's men had surprised the Southern cavalry unit that they had hit initially. Unfortunately Captain Corbit's men no longer had the element of surprise on their side. Some fifty additional men from the 4th Virginia Cavalry, led by 1st Lieutenant John William Murray, moved forward to brush the pesky 1st Delaware away.

Momentarily stopped by the sheer audacity of the small band of Delawarens, the Virginians quickly regrouped when the rest of their regiment arrived to support them. The Confederate cavalry severely pressed the Northerners back to Westminster's Main Street. Colonel Williams Carter Wickham, assigned to Brigadier General Fitzhugh Lee's (U.S.M.A., Class of 1856) brigade, commanded the 4th Virginia Cavalry. Lee, a nephew of Robert E. Lee, had only recently resumed command of his brigade after being seriously injured from the kick of a horse a week earlier. He still was not completely well and continued to suffer from the lingering effects of "a painful attack of inflammatory rheumatism" according to General Stuart.[28]

As the fighting quickly escalated, Major Knight then committed 1st Lieutenant Caleb Churchman, commanding Troop D, and his men to the battle. That action proved as futile as Captain Corbit's previous charge. Colonel Wickham's battle-hardened veterans drove the two inexperienced troops completely from the field. Of the six commissioned officers present during the action only Major Knight, Adjutant William W. Lobdell, Lieutenant Clark, and 2nd Lieutenant William J. Reedy, escaped capture. Theirs was a much better percentage than the number of enlisted men who were lucky enough to have escaped. Captain Corbit found himself captured while leading his troop in their mounted charge against the enemy. Corbit's horse was shot between the eyes during the action and went down in a heap in the dusty road with Corbit unhurt but completely surrounded by the Virginians. The few surviving members of the two troops fell back to Reisterstown. Stuart's men captured Lieutenant Churchman as he commanded the rear guard in their retreat to Reisterstown.[29]

Although the action seemed preordained, Major Knight and his valiant band of men succeeded in slowing Stuart's column even more and inflicted a few casualties in the process. In this brief engagement, the 4th

Virginia Cavalry suffered two commissioned officers killed in the initial charge upon the town. The commander of Company E, Lieutenant Murray, and 2nd Lieutenant St. Pierre Gibson of Company D were the only fatalities among General Stuart's force. Two enlisted men from Company E were wounded and captured, while one private from Company G was taken prisoner. A few men from the Virginia regiment had their horses killed or wounded in the skirmish. Lieutenants Murray and Gibson were both buried in the graveyard of the Ascension Episcopal Church on Court Street in Westminster.[30]

The cost sustained by the Delaware troops was extremely high, losing sixty-seven enlisted men either killed, wounded, or missing. Corporal William Vandegrift and Private Daniel Welch were two of Knight's cavalrymen who received fatal wounds during the short, but intense, fighting.[31] Major Knight's men also lost an equal number of horses, along with the command wagon, to the enemy troopers. The wagon carried the regiment's garrison equipment, hospital supplies, and other baggage, as well as the regimental books and papers. Based upon Major Knight's orders, since he did not expect any trouble, the wagon needlessly moved forward from Reisterstown with the two troops. Along with the Union cavalry troopers captured in the attack, a small contingent of Federal infantrymen also found themselves taken prisoner in the streets of Westminster.

That infantry unit, a little twenty-man detachment led by 2nd Lieutenant Pulaski Bowman from Company F of the 150th Regiment, New York Volunteer Infantry, had received instructions to guard the train depot at Westminster.[32] Lieutenant Bowman's men did not offer much, if any, resistance and they all quickly became prisoners of the veteran Confederate cavalry when Stuart's men took absolute control of Westminster. General Stuart was able to parole a few of the new prisoners, but the majority of them accompanied his command on their journey north to Pennsylvania to find General Lee and the rest of the Army of Northern Virginia.[33]

After destroying additional railroad property in Westminster, the Confederate troopers continued their march north and reached Union Mills just after dusk on June 29. The leading elements of General

Stuart's command, the weary troopers of Fitz Lee's brigade, turned off the road and into the fields near the Shriver brothers' homes to get some much needed rest. That site, where the Confederate cavalry forces encamped for the night, was quite unique. Located less than five miles from the Pennsylvania border, Union Mills was the home of the Shriver brothers—William and Andrew. As with many families during the Civil War, the Shriver family had deep divisions in their opinions and beliefs about the war.

William Shriver and his family lived in a large white house, considered by some to be a mansion. The house sat on a hill overlooking the main road running between Littlestown and Westminster. He sympathized with the Southern cause and had at least four sons serving in the ranks of the Confederate Army. Twenty-one-year-old Mark Owings Shriver actually enlisted in Company K of Colonel Drake's 1st Virginia Cavalry as the Southern horsemen passed by his family's home at the end of June 1863.[34]

Another son, seventeen-year-old Thomas Herbert Shriver, also still lived at home with his family. His father allowed him to volunteer his services to General Stuart as a guide, since he was familiar with the local countryside. The young Shriver played a prominent role in attempting to lead the Confederate cavalry around General Kilpatrick's troopers located at Littlestown. General Stuart arrived at Union Mills during the early morning hours of June 30, after having caught a quick nap at Westminster. Upon his arrival he found time to have breakfast with William and his family.[35]

Andrew K. Shriver lived in the family's original homestead across the road from William on the eastern side. He and his immediate family were true to the Union cause even though he owned some slaves and his brother did not. Andrew had one son serving with the Union Army at the end of June 1863. One of his sons, Henry Wirt Shriver, had just been called to duty as a private with Company I of the 26th Regiment, Emergency Militia (Pennsylvania) Infantry during the current Southern invasion.[36]

Notes to Chapter Six

1. *War of the Rebellion: A Compilation of the Official Records of the Union and Confederate Armies* (Washington, D.C., 1880 – 1901), Series 1, Volume 27, Part 2, p. 693. (Hereafter cited as OR – 2.); Henry B. McClellan, *The Life and Campaigns of Major General J. E. B. Stuart* (Boston: Houghton Mifflin & Co., 1885), p. 323.
2. OR – 3, p. 357.
3. The 2nd Massachusetts had Troops E, F, G, H, I, L, and M present for duty in Maryland at that time.
4. OR – 3, p. 354.
5. Warner, *Generals in Blue*, p. 284.
6. OR – 2, p. 694.
7. Longacre, *The Cavalry at Gettysburg*, p. 155.
8. Fairfax Downey, *Clash of Cavalry:The Battle of Brandy Station* (New York: David McKay Company, Inc., 1959), p. 151.
9. Two other North Carolina units the 4th and 5th cavalry regiments of Brigadier General Beverly Robertson's brigade normally served with Stuart. On the occasion of General Stuart's raid through Maryland Robertson's brigade, as well as the two North Carolina regiments, remained with the main body of the Army of Northern Virginia.
10. Krick, *Lee's Colonel*, pp. 324, 400.
11. OR – 2, pp. 322, 694.
12. OR – 3, p. 378.
13. 2nd Regiment, New York Volunteer Cavalry; Boxes 2703 – 2711; Muster Rolls, Regimental Papers, Office of the Adjutant General, Volunteer Organizations, Civil War; Record Group 94; National Archives, Washington, D.C. (Hereafter cited as NA RG 94 – 2 NY.)
14. "A New Jersey Cavalryman," *Northern Monthly* (Volume I, 1867): 554-56.
15. Ibid.
16. Dyer, *A Compendium of the War*, 2:762; NA RG 94 – 2 NY.
17. Compiled Service Records of Confederate Soldiers Who Served in Organizations from the State of Virginia, Microfilm M324; National Archives, Washington, D.C. (Hereafter cited as Records of Confederate Soldiers.)
18. "A New Jersey Cavalryman," pp. 554-56; NA RG 94 – 2 NY.
19. OR – 2, p. 694.
20. OR – 1, p. 66.
21. Dyer, *A Compendium of the War*, 2:762; NA RG 94 – 2 NY; Records of Confederate Soldiers.
22. "A New Jersey Cavalryman," pp. 554-56.
23. Frederic Shriver Klein, "Affair at Westminster," *Civil War Times Illustrated* (August 1968): 32-38.
24. Adjutant General's Office, *Official Army Register of the Volunteer Force of the United States Army for the Years 1861, '62, '63, '64, '65,* 8 Volumes + Index (Gaithersburg, Md.: Ron R. Van Sickle Military Books, 1987), 3:1045. The 1st Delaware Cavalry had mustered only seven troops at that date, not enough for the designation of a regiment. The designation of battalion did not correctly apply either, since a battalion included only four troops.

Notes to Chapter Six (*continued*)

25. "Affair at Westminster," pp. 32-38; OR – 1, p. 202. There seems to be some question who led the Delaware troops during the action at Westminster. Knight's official report is very succinct and informative, but could have been penned by Adjutant Lobdell who was also present at Westminster. Other accounts have the major being either sick or drunk. In James H. Wilson's book, *Captain Charles Corbit's Charge at Westminster,* published in 1913, Major Knight was supposedly drunk at Westminster and departed the town just before the shooting started, leaving Corbit in total command. However, it seems unlikely that Corbit could have been able to coordinate the three distinct attacks upon the 4th Virginia Cavalry if he was leading the second attack himself and was taken prisoner.
26. Ibid.
27. Ibid.
28. David L. and Audrey J. Ladd, eds., *The Bachelder Papers*, 3 Vols. (Dayton, Ohio: Morningside House, Inc., 1994), 2:1201; OR – 2, p. 692.
29. "Affair at Westminster," pp. 32-38; OR – 1, p. 203.
30. OR – 3, p. 695. Lieutenant Gibson's body was eventually removed to Virginia, while Lieutenant Murray's body is still buried in the church's graveyard.
31. Frederic S. Klein, ed., *Just South of Gettysburg, Carroll County, Maryland, in the Civil War* (Lancaster, 1974), pp. 80-81.
32. OR – 1, p. 201; Phisterer, *New York in the War of the Rebellion*, 5:3749.
33. OR – 1, pp. 201-203.
34. Robert J. Driver, Jr., *1st Virginia Cavalry* (Lynchburg, Va.: H. E. Howard, Inc., 1991), p. 227.
35. Ibid.; Chamber of Commerce, *Encounter at Hanover*, p. 21. Thomas Herbert Shriver was born on February 14, 1846, at the family home in Union Mills. He accepted an appointment to V.M.I. in September 1863. Shriver survived the war after briefly serving in the 1st Maryland Cavalry (C.S.A.) and was quite a successful businessman after the war. He died at his ancestral home on December 31, 1916 at the age of seventy.
36. Ibid.; Bates, *History of Pennsylvania Volunteers*, 5:1233-34. The 26th Regiment was organized at Harrisburg on June 19-22, 1863, and mustered out July 30, 1863, after the immediate crisis was over.

Chapter 7:

__Roads to Hanover__

ENERAL Kilpatrick's staff members had already been up for quite some time following another all too brief rest during the previous unsettled night. The 3rd Division's staff officers and orderlies kept very busy dispensing their commander's orders to his two brigade commanders and those leaders' own individual staffs. As dawn broke on the morning of June 30, the regiments in Judson Kilpatrick's division found themselves scattered principally around the outskirts of Littlestown. For the first time since Kilpatrick had taken control of the division, all the Michigan regiments finally were not too far away from each other in one place. Although they had all encamped in the fields around Littlestown, the Michigan cavalrymen would not be traveling together as a brigade just quite yet. The 3rd Division's order of march for that morning saw only two of General Custer's four Michigan regiments, the 1st and 7th, marching with the rest of the division. The other two regiments, the 5th and 6th, received another assignment to complete before ultimately joining their other comrades in the brigade.

After finishing another hastily prepared breakfast, somewhere between four and five o'clock in the morning, the eleven available troops of the 1st Michigan Cavalry led Kilpatrick's division out of their overnight encampments at Littlestown.[1] A still ailing Colonel Town continued to ride at the head of his men, setting an example for others to emulate. Town's regiment carried a total of thirty-eight commissioned officers on the muster rolls present for duty on June 30. The regiment had an additional 596 noncommissioned officers and enlisted men reportedly present within the ranks.[2]

The 1st Regiment, Michigan Volunteer Cavalry was Michigan's longest serving cavalry regiment, originally formed during the months of August and September in 1861. Attached to various commands during the first two years of the war, the Michiganders had the opportunity to participate in many of the larger battles in the eastern theater along with scores of smaller skirmishes. The 1st Michigan Cavalry was the most senior regiment of the eight assigned regiments serving within Kilpatrick's new organization. The regiment's assignment to Custer's brigade provided a stabilizing force of veterans for the other three relatively new Michigan cavalry regiments that were already serving together.[3]

Colonel William Mann and his ten troops from the not wholly battle-tested 7th Michigan Cavalry followed the 1st Michigan in Kilpatrick's line of march as they left their overnight camps. The regiment's muster rolls carried only 27 commissioned officers present for duty along with 447 enlisted men in the ranks of the regiment on the last day of June.[4] Many of the officers and enlisted men listed as absentees from the regiment were either seriously ill or were performing other additional duties.

The formation of the 7th Michigan Cavalry regiment was completed in late 1862. The first ten companies mustered into the Federal volunteer service on January 27, 1863. Those troops then left Michigan during February and moved to the vicinity of Washington, D.C. While stationed at Washington they briefly received an assignment, along with the 5th and 6th Michigan Cavalry regiments, to the Provisional Cavalry Brigade of Major General Silas Casey's (U.S.M.A., Class of 1826) Division in the Military District of Washington. Casey's division eventually got transferred to the XXII Corps.[5] On March 26, 1863, the three Michigan mounted regiments transferred again, this time to Major General Julius Stahel's cavalry division. Colonel Mann's regiment saw only limited action, fighting in no major battles, while assigned to Stahel's division of cavalry for three months.[6]

Before Colonel Mann's regiment left their bivouac at Littlestown on the morning of June 30, the regimental staff discovered that three enlisted men from Troop F and one noncommissioned officer from Troop I had deserted some time during the night. Privates Philander K. Goff, George H. Keeler, Jacob Strouse, and Corporal John C. Lloyd abandoned the 7th Michigan and their comrades after arriving at Littlestown during the hours of darkness. Keeler, Strouse, and Lloyd never returned to the regiment. None of their comrades ever saw them again. Private Goff eventually came back to his troop after a short absence. He honorably mustered out of the regiment in April 1864.[7]

During the Civil War many units, both in the Regular Army and in the volunteer service, suffered greatly from desertion problems. Soldiers in the Regular Army usually received somewhat worse treatment than their volunteer counterparts, but their incidents of desertion were much less than in a volunteer regiment. As the Army of the Potomac moved into friendly territory at the end of June, many volunteer soldiers took advantage of the perceived opportunity to depart their comrades on an unauthorized leave of absence. It was no coincidence that the highest rates of desertion occurred during the winter months of inactivity and just before a big battle.

Shortly after Colonel Town's and Colonel Mann's regiments began to move to the northeast along the Hanover Road, the six guns and caissons of Lieutenant Pennington's battery moved out of their bivouac. Pennington's Battery M, which was marching in a relatively safe position, filled the gap between General Kilpatrick's 1st and 2nd brigades. Battery M of the 2nd U.S. Artillery originally began their initial organization in Texas during January 1861. The battery received orders to report immediately to Washington during the opening stages of hostilities in the Civil War. The artillerymen participated in the Battle of Bull Run, as well as many other significant engagements, before joining the Army of the Potomac in 1862.[8]

On that Tuesday morning Brigadier General Kilpatrick again chose to travel in the vanguard of the division with General Custer and Colonel Town, along with his personal headquarters guard under Captain Jones from the 1st Ohio Cavalry.[9] With Custer at the head of his brigade, the twenty-one troops from the two Michigan regiments quickly spread out along the main road running between Littlestown and Hanover. Marching was not always very well liked by the personnel involved in that activity, particularly in dry and dusty weather conditions or in the mud or in the rain—basically all the time.

The 3rd Division's assigned units were no different from any other cavalry or infantry unit in their general dislike of a brigade or division march. The leading troops of the 1st Michigan Cavalry set the pace for the early morning march from Littlestown. Because they led their brigade and division, the horse soldiers from Colonel Town's regiment had the easiest traveling conditions of all the troops in Kilpatrick's command on that day.

The road upon which the troops traveled was damp but not too muddy from the previous week's occasionally heavy rainstorms, so there was not much dust being raised for the troops in the rear of the column. Eventually the road turned slightly muddy and rutted because of the intermittent rain assisted by the thousands of horses traveling forward on it. As Colonel Town's regiment marched along the Hanover-Littlestown-Frederick road, the units following them had to come to a complete halt at times. At other times the men and their horses in the rear had to move quite rapidly to keep pace with the men in the leading sections who, surprisingly, never changed their pace. The officers and sergeants of each command constantly shouted to their men the order to "close up."

That phenomenon of marching mimicked the actions of an accordion. It had long, drawn-out, slow movements followed by rapid maneuvers to close up the ranks. It proved very frustrating and tiring for all but the men and horses at the very head of the column. It was a chief irritant for all marching soldiers, whether mounted or dismounted. Usually during any long period of marching a different regiment would lead the brigade each day and the brigades would change the leading position within a division on a regular basis, too. The leading units in an advancing column had the easiest time in terms of marching, while the trailing elements had the roughest time. Because of that factor the assigned regiments, brigades, and divisions alternated their positions in the order of march.

It was now between 6:00 and 7:00 A.M. as Brigadier General Farnsworth dispatched the members of his staff with orders for the 1st Brigade to prepare to leave their overnight bivouacs. Those cavalrymen had ample opportunity, unlike their comrades in the Michigan regiments, to heat their coffee and eat their breakfast before packing their equipment, saddling their horses, and moving on to the Hanover Road. The early morning order of march for Farnsworth's troopers had the veteran 1st Vermont Cavalry leading the entire brigade. The new commanding general and his staff chose to travel with Lieutenant Colonel Preston at the head of the 1st Vermont's full complement of twelve troops as they moved away from the friendly citizens of Littlestown.

The 1st Vermont Cavalry, one of the 3rd Division's most veteran and battle-tested regiments, had been in the Federal volunteer service since November 1861 when they mustered at Burlington. The regiment departed the "Green Mountain State" in December of that year and moved by train to Washington, D.C., where they performed insignificant duties for a short period. The Vermonters fought in a wide range of minor skirmishes and major battles throughout Virginia in 1862 and during the early months of 1863 before being assigned to General Kilpatrick's division in the Army of the Potomac.[10] The regiment numbered 38 officers and 703 noncommissioned officers and enlisted men present for duty on June 30.[11]

Colonel Nathaniel Richmond and his troopers of the 1st Virginia Cavalry, the newly re-designated 1st West Virginia Cavalry, took the second place in the brigade's line of march behind the troopers of the 1st Vermont. Colonel Richmond counted only ten troops of his regiment presently serving with the Army of the Potomac. The 1st West Virginia Cavalry was another one of the veteran regiments in Kilpatrick's division, having been recruited between July and November 1861 from the pro-Union populations of Clarksburg, Morgantown, and Wheeling in what eventually became the state of West Virginia in June 1863. In the late months of 1861 the regiment spent most of its time contending with various boring assignments and assorted menial duties within western Virginia and Kentucky. During 1862 the 1st Virginia fought in scores of skirmishes, literally brother against brother, in their native Virginia, usually with just a few troops present.[12] On the last day of June 1863, the regiment counted 30 commissioned officers and 455 enlisted men present on the muster rolls.[13]

The four guns and caissons of Lieutenant Elder's Battery E traveled in the very middle of the 1st Brigade's advancing column. They found themselves safely sandwiched between Colonel Richmond's 1st West Virginia and the next regiment in line, the 5th New York Cavalry. As with the placement of Pennington's battery in General Custer's brigade, Elder's artillery moved in the position considered to be the most secure place during the march, particularly with verified reports of enemy cavalry activity nearby.

Battery E of the 4th U.S. Artillery, another of the Regular Army's light artillery units, had been organized principally in Ohio during 1861. The freshly recruited artillerymen spent almost a year posted to the Department of West Virginia before their reassignment to the Army of the Potomac in 1862. The battery participated in the major battles of Winchester, Antietam, and Fredericksburg, as well as dozens of other minor actions and skirmishes.[14]

On that last morning in June Major Hammond's 5th New York Cavalry had the third place in the brigade line of march with his eleven troops of New Yorkers. The regiment was also known as the 1st Ira Harris Guard in honor of the senator from Albany who had been instrumental in the initial organization of the unit. The regimental organizers started their recruitment between July and September of 1861. The last companies formed finally mustered in on the last day of October at Staten Island. The whole regiment left New York in November 1861 and spent the winter months in camp near Annapolis, Maryland.

After numerous assignments with a variety of commands during the first two years of the war the New Yorkers received orders to report to General Julius Stahel's division early in 1863. The cavalrymen from New York were another combat-tested unit and could be counted upon to stabilize the one raw regiment—the 18th Pennsylvania—assigned to their new brigade. Very shortly they would have the unexpected opportunity to achieve that calling.[15] Major Hammond commanded 28 officers and 449 sergeants, corporals, and privates on June 30, 1863.[16]

While encamped at Littlestown, General Kilpatrick's regiments, as usual in a field environment and in close proximity to the enemy, had the task to maintain security around the town. Troops L and M of the 5th New York Cavalry were two of the many troops placed on the security detail. They, as well as many other troopers, went on picket duty while their brigade was in bivouac in the fields outside Littlestown. Twenty-two-year-old 1st Lieutenant Eugene Dumont Dimmick commanded that portion of the picket detail composed of Troops L and M.

In a few more days, the young lieutenant assigned to Troop M would receive a promotion to fill the troop's vacant position of captain. Unfortunately, Dimmick received a severe wound on July 6, 1863, during the 3rd Division's sharp contest with General Stuart's cavalry at Hagerstown, Maryland. He eventually recovered from his wounds but accepted a discharge for disability nonetheless. In February 1864 he again enlisted, this time in the 18th Regiment, Veteran Reserve Corps, as a second lieutenant. He served until June 1866. In August 1867 having fully recovered from any ill effects of his wounding at Hagerstown he entered the Regular Army. Dimmick began his post-war career, once more, as a second lieutenant initially serving in the 9th U.S. Cavalry, one of the two "Buffalo Soldier" cavalry regiments.[17]

During the early morning of June 30, as the rest of the division was beginning to stir, the lieutenant's outposts received instructions from regimental headquarters recalling them from their picket duty. Shortly thereafter they personally received orders from General Kilpatrick to proceed to Hanover using an alternate route running to the east of the Hanover Road. The primary road between Hanover and Littlestown was the one upon which the main column traveled during the morning. The alternate route closely paralleled the one being used by Kilpatrick's column but pushed Dimmick's troopers far beyond the road used by Stuart's cavalry regiments that would soon be moving from Union Mills.[18]

Lieutenant Dimmick's mission was to protect the right flank of the 3rd Division as it marched toward Hanover. He and his men were only one of many details dispatched by division and brigade headquarters to guard the rear and flanks of Kilpatrick's column. His detachment of New Yorkers, consisting of roughly sixty-six enlisted men, moved away from Littlestown while the main column began moving north. Eugene Dimmick was the lone commissioned officer present for duty on the detail with the two troops. Captain Augustus Barker, the only commissioned officer presently serving in the Gettysburg Campaign from Troop L, remained with the regiment while his men moved on their mission. Shortly he would become intimately involved in the fighting at Hanover. Dimmick and his party moved mainly through cultivated fields and over seldom used farm roads as they rode toward their ultimate destination of Abbottstown.[19]

Close behind the long column of General Farnsworth's three leading cavalry regiments and artillery battery came about twenty-five hospital department ambulances, along with a small number of division, brigade, and regimental wagons carrying ammunition and some food supplies. The main wagon train of the 3rd Division, almost two hundred wagons, remained parked near Frederick while the division moved forward in search of the Confederate Army. Moving with the wagons accompanying the division were a number of herded serviceable and unserviceable horses, and the pack animals, both horses and mules, carrying additional carbine and revolver ammunition. That slow-moving tangle of animals, wagons, and men preceded the last regiment of the whole division. The 18th Pennsylvania Cavalry, also identified as the 163rd Regiment of the Line, with Lieutenant Colonel Brinton at the head of his main column brought up the extreme rear. Portions of the regiment acted as the rear guard of General Kilpatrick's entire division.[20]

The 18th Pennsylvania was another fairly new regiment, having been recruited during the autumn months of 1862. Early in December 1862 the regiment received orders to report to Bladensburg, Maryland located just outside Washington, D.C. After serving in the vicinity of the nation's capitol for the next few months, the regiment eventually joined General Stahel's division in April 1863.

Although they were not the greenest unit in the newly created 3rd Division, they happened to be another of General Kilpatrick's regiments that was, as yet, not fully battle tested. The Pennsylvanians had never seen any hostile action against the enemy as an entire unit. They had only a few minor skirmishes with the enemy to their credit. Their combat skills in a large scale operation were still conspicuously unproven and highly questionable.[21]

It was somewhat unusual for an untried and untested regiment, such as the 18th Pennsylvania, to be given the task of protecting the entire division's rear. The commanding general anticipated no real combat action or danger, after all, they were now in their home state. Additionally, in the marching rotation of the regiments within the division, it was their turn to bring up the rear of the column. Nobody from General Kilpatrick on down through the ranks of the individual cavalrymen expected the scope of the trouble that awaited them just ahead in Hanover. It seemed that all the cavalrymen in the division were unaware of what danger lay ahead of them on that last day of June.[22]

An additional small detail of cavalrymen, like the detachment from the 5th New York, moved away from the main column for another special purpose. That detachment from the 18th Pennsylvania Cavalry, consisting of roughly forty noncommissioned officers and enlisted men from Troops L and M, had the distinction of being the division's actual rear guard. The horsemen in that small detachment were under the immediate command of twenty-five-year-old 2nd Lieutenant Henry Clay Potter the junior ranking commissioned officer of Troop M.[23]

Potter's troopers were the last members of the 3rd Division—at least that part of the division that was in General Kilpatrick's actual line of march on this day—to depart Littlestown sometime around 9:00 A.M. It was Lieutenant Potter's responsibility to ensure that the rear of the long and slow-moving column was protected from any surprise attacks from the enemy's cavalry, now rumored to be nearby. He and his men had the additional duty to drive all stragglers from the division forward to rejoin their troops as quickly as possible, if those men and their mounts were capable of doing so.

Many of Kilpatrick's weary cavalrymen were dropping out of the column by the side of the road because of significant problems with their mounts. The horses became extremely fatigued and sore from the constant marching. After the long, hard marches and lack of rest during the past few weeks many of the men were as equally tired and sore as their horses. Most of the division's stragglers that Potter's men encountered along the route of march pushed on as quickly as they possibly could. Many men, after their horses gave out, continued to trail the Union column on foot in order to rejoin their units rather than remain in the rear. As with any long marches, during the war, scores if not hundreds of men and horses broke ranks for a short respite from the rigors of the march.

The approximately forty men in Lieutenant Potter's detachment comprised a little less than half the assigned cavalrymen of both Troops L and M currently present for duty. Second Lieutenant William L. Laws led the other sixteen troopers from Troop L, while Captain Enos J. Pennypacker commanded the thirty-five cavalrymen remaining in his Troop M. Both depleted troops continued to march with the main body of the regiment toward Hanover as Potter and his men followed behind.[24]

While the Union cavalry regiments of General Kilpatrick's command moved slowly away from Littlestown shortly after the first sign of daylight, the Confederate cavalry under General Stuart was preparing to depart their encampment at Union Mills around the same time. The command structures and formations of the Confederate cavalry regiments that moved out of their camps in Maryland were slightly different from the organization currently used by the U.S. Army.

On July 21, 1861, the Congress of the United States legislated that all volunteer cavalry regiments, as they initially formed in the various states, would consist of twelve companies. Two more companies had been added to all the mounted regiments from the prewar strength of the Regular Army's ten companies. The five oldest regular cavalry regiments, the 1st through the 5th, maintained the old regimental structure of ten companies until July 1862, when they added the extra companies and men. The 6th U.S. Cavalry initially recruited twelve companies when originally formed in 1861.

The organizational structure of the Confederate cavalry, when they formed at the beginning of the war, incorporated the ante-bellum number of companies and the associated level of enlisted strength utilized by the U.S. Army. That system was what most of the former Regular Army officers, now in the Confederate service, were most familiar. Those Southern cavalry regiments maintained the ten-company regimental structure throughout the Civil War. The actual staffing levels authorized a few more men in each company than that of their U.S. Army counterparts. A Confederate regiment consisted of only five squadrons. There were no battalions authorized in the regimental structure. Each squadron consisted of two companies.

Colonel John R. Chambliss, Jr.,
Commander, W. H. F. Lee's Cavalry Brigade
(LC)

Immediately after sunrise on June 30 Colonel John Chambliss, still temporarily at the head of "Rooney" Lee's brigade, took the leading regiments of General Stuart's division on the road north toward Hanover. Brigadier General "Rooney" Lee was absent from his brigade command since his capture by a Union patrol just a few days previously. He was taken prisoner while recuperating from serious wounds received at the Battle of Brandy Station on June 9.[25]

The regiments assigned to Colonel Chambliss's cavalry brigade included all ten companies (A-K) of the 2nd North Carolina Cavalry, also known as the 19th Regiment State Troops. That unit originally recruited its members during May and June of 1861, making it one of the veteran fighting regiments in General Stuart's command. On the last day of June, as the regiment moved toward Hanover, it mustered no more than nineteen officers present for duty, none above the rank of captain.

Additionally a sparse 144 enlisted men, basically enough soldiers for two minimally manned companies, traveled with the regiment. In the preceding weeks the North Carolina cavalrymen had suffered substantial casualties in the several skirmishes fought with the Union cavalry forces. The regimental ranks suffered further losses in the subsequent weeks of additional fighting with General Pleasonton's troopers during the hard fighting in the Gettysburg Campaign. Lieutenant Colonel William Payne, detached from the 4th Virginia Cavalry, temporarily commanded the senior officer-depleted North Carolina unit.[26]

While the 2nd North Carolina moved with their brigade toward the unexpected encounter in the streets of Hanover, Captain William A. Graham, the commanding officer of Company K, was absent from the already diminished ranks of the regiment. The captain led a small detail of enlisted men in search of serviceable horses and essential supplies. Graham commanded only one of the scores of details sent by the Confederate commanders to the nearby homes and farms in the Maryland and Pennsylvania countryside. His detail had relatively minor successes since the civilians, for the most part, prepared themselves for the Confederate advance and had safely removed their valuables to other areas.[27]

The 9th Virginia Cavalry, also assigned to Colonel Chambliss's command, had all ten companies (A-K) present for duty within the brigade on the last day of June. That Virginia regiment, formed in January 1862, counted a scant total of only fourteen commissioned officers present for duty. While short of officers, it listed a rather strong total of 560 noncommissioned officers and enlisted men on their muster rolls for the May 1863 reporting period.

The very recently wounded and imprisoned Brigadier General "Rooney" Lee had previously served as the colonel of the regiment from April to September in 1862. Now the 9th Virginia regiment was under the immediate direction of forty-four-year-old Colonel Richard Lee Turberville Beale. Before the war, Beale received training as a lawyer and served as a member of the U.S. Congress. He began his impressive cavalry career in the Confederate Army as a first lieutenant and finished it as a brigadier general.[28]

Colonel Richard L. T. Beale,
Commander,
9th Virginia Cavalry
(LC)

Colonel J. Lucius Davis,
Commander,
10th Virginia Cavalry
(LC)

Another of John Chambliss's Virginia cavalry units, the 10th regiment, also had all ten of its companies (A-K) serving in the brigade as they marched from their camps at Union Mills on the morning of June 30. Originally organized in 1862, the 10th Virginia Cavalry now reported roughly 26 commissioned officers and a meager 243 noncommissioned officers and enlisted men present for duty within the brigade. Fifty-year-old Colonel James Lucius Davis (U.S.M.A., Class of 1833), the oldest colonel currently present and serving in General Stuart's command, led the Virginians. On July 6, a short week away, he would be seriously wounded and taken prisoner by elements of General Kilpatrick's cavalry at Hagerstown during the Confederate retreat back to Virginia.[29]

The fourth unit serving in Colonel Chambliss's brigade, and one well known to him, was the 13th Virginia Cavalry, his own regiment from which he had been detached in order to assume temporary command of the brigade. The 13th Virginia, formed in July 1862, fielded all ten of its companies (A-K). During the time of the Confederate invasion into Maryland and Pennsylvania, the regiment had a total of only 14 commissioned officers and 341 enlisted men present in the ranks. Thirty-six-year-old Major Joseph Ezra Gillette was the senior officer present and commanded the regiment during Colonel Chambliss's current absence at brigade headquarters. Gillette claimed no prior military experience and was a planter and slave owner immediately before the beginning of hostilities. He became intimately involved in the fierce fighting during the surprise engagement in the streets of Hanover. His career would abruptly end when he received a mortal wound in action at Brandy Station in October 1863.[30]

There is some doubt in the official reports as to who actually commanded the 13th Virginia Cavalry while Colonel Chambliss was serving at brigade headquarters during the Gettysburg Campaign. Ample evidence exists for this study proving that Major Joseph Gillette was in command of the unit. Forty-one-year-old Lieutenant Colonel Jefferson Curle Phillips, identified in many sources as the commander of the 13th Virginia at Gettysburg, was definitely absent from the regiment during that time. According to the service records of the period there are many inconsistencies dealing with Lieutenant Colonel Phillips as the unit commander. The first listed reason for his absence from the regiment was that he was serving on a court-martial board from February 28 – June 30, 1863, in Richmond. Second, he appeared before a court-martial at a place unknown on June 3, 1863, for being absent without leave (AWOL) and being found guilty of the offense. The army temporarily relieved him of his command. Third, General Stuart reported him as being wounded, how seriously is not known, at Brandy Station on June 9, 1863, and absent from the regiment during the first weeks of the Gettysburg Campaign.[31]

Finally, one additional regiment assigned to Colonel Chambliss's command, the 15th Virginia Cavalry, was detached from the rest of the brigade. They remained on patrol and scouting duty in Virginia when Major General Stuart began his raid into Maryland and Pennsylvania in June 1863. That unit's commander was twenty-six-year-old Major Charles Read Collins (U.S.M.A., Class of 1859). Collins, eventually promoted to the colonelcy of the 15th Virginia Cavalry, would be killed in action at Todd's Tavern, Virginia in May 1864.[32]

General Stuart's horse artillery and the burdensome captured Union wagon train followed Colonel Chambliss's brigade in the day's line of march. During the current raid into the Maryland and Pennsylvania countryside, Stuart traveled with just six guns from two assigned artillery batteries.[33] Twenty-six-year-old Major Robert Franklin Beckham (U.S.M.A., Class of 1859), Stuart's chief artillerist, normally commanded the artillery battalion, but he had remained with the main column of the Army of Northern Virginia as Stuart left on his incursion into Maryland.[34]

The artillery units that in actuality moved with Stuart's horse soldiers on his raid included Captain James Breathed's Battery (1st Stuart Horse Artillery) of two 3-inch Ordnance Rifles with approximately two commissioned officers and fifty enlisted men manning the guns. In addition Captain William Morrell McGregor's Battery (2nd Stuart Horse Artillery) of two 3-inch Ordnance Rifles and two 12-pounder Gun-Howitzers (Napoleons) included five officers and one hundred noncommissioned officers and enlisted men.[35]

Brigadier General Wade Hampton,
Commander, Hampton's Cavalry Brigade
(LC)

Brigadier General Wade Hampton's brigade brought up the rear of Stuart's extended column. The Southern cavalrymen continued moving farther to the north as they hoped to join the elusive main body of the Army of Northern Virginia on that last day of June. The brigade's principal assignment was to protect the captured Union wagons from being recaptured by the Yankee cavalry known to be nearby. Hampton's brigade encompassed roughly fifty-four companies from six assigned regiments.

Hampton's brigade included the ten companies, A through K, of the 1st North Carolina Cavalry, also designated as the 9th Regiment State Troops. The regiment was commanded by thirty-three-year-old Colonel Laurence Simmons Baker (U.S.M.A., Class of 1851), who would eventually become a brigadier general in the Confederate service a few weeks after the conclusion of the Battle of Gettysburg. The only other regiment of Tarheels besides the 2nd North Carolina of "Rooney" Lee's brigade currently assigned to this portion of Stuart's command, it was the longest serving mounted regiment from North Carolina, formed in early 1861. The regiment counted roughly 29 commissioned officers along with 437 enlisted men present for duty at the end of June.[36]

The 1st South Carolina Cavalry, with all ten of its companies (A-K), listed thirty-seven-year-old Lieutenant Colonel John David Twiggs as the senior officer present for duty with the command. Twiggs had no prior military experience. His occupation was that of physician before the war. In 1864, Lieutenant Colonel Twiggs died, not on the field of battle, but by the hand of an assailant while on leave at his home in South Carolina. The 1st South Carolina Cavalry listed on its muster rolls 34 commissioned officers present for duty while almost 349 enlisted men also appeared on the rolls of the regiment.[37]

The colonel of the 1st South Carolina, thirty-two-year-old John Logan Black (U.S.M.A., Class of 1850), was absent from the regiment. A fragment of a shell had severely wounded him in the head during the cavalry skirmish at Upperville on June 21. He returned to his home in South Carolina to recuperate before endeavoring to rejoin his regiment. As his regiment began their march from Union Mills toward Hanover, Black was attempting, with great difficulty, to rejoin his command. Unfortunately he did not locate his regiment until after the Confederate Army began their retreat back to Virginia after July 4. However, Colonel Black did perform active service with the Army of Northern Virginia during the Battle of Gettysburg, particularly on the right flank of the Southern army during the third day's intense fighting. At that location he had the unique opportunity to assist in the repulse of the assault by the cavalrymen of Brigadier General Merritt's Reserve Brigade and Elon Farnsworth's 1st Brigade during the late afternoon of July 3.[38]

One more of Hampton's cavalry regiments from South Carolina, the 2nd regiment, listed thirty-year-old Lieutenant Colonel Lipscomb as its current commander. He only recently received a promotion to that position upon the death of Lieutenant Colonel Frank Hampton. Previously serving as second-in-command of the regiment, Wade Hampton's thirty-three-year-old younger brother, died while leading a small contingent of his regiment against a superior force of the 1st Regiment, Massachusetts Volunteer Cavalry at the Battle of Brandy Station on June 9.[39]

Colonel Laurence S. Baker,
Commander,
1st North Carolina Cavalry
(LC)

Colonel Pierce M. B. Young,
Commander,
Cobb's Legion
(LC)

Another senior officer absent from the 2nd South Carolina was its commander, Colonel Matthew Calbraith Butler, who also received a serious wound at Brandy Station. His wound was serious enough to necessitate the amputation of his right foot. He would not return to the command of the regiment until the next year. In his absence, the regiment reported that it had all ten of its assigned companies, A through K, present for duty. The South Carolinians mustered an impressive 34 officers present for duty but listed only a meager 178 sergeants, corporals, and privates under their command.[40]

Cobb's Legion, originally formed in Georgia, had at least nine of its eleven companies, A through L, present for duty in General Hampton's brigade as they prepared on the last day of June 1863 to move out of their camps at Union Mills. One squadron of roughly eighty-five officers and enlisted men from Companies A and H under Captain Crawford was still encamped near Hunterstown. The whole regiment of Georgians reported 30 commissioned officers present for duty and 347 enlisted men in the ranks of their unit. Cobb's Legion was under the capable command of Pierce Manning Butler Young. He was the youngest colonel at twenty-six years of age in J. E. B. Stuart's cavalry division. Colonel Young had entered the U.S. Military Academy in July 1857, but resigned shortly after Georgia's secession from the United States in January 1861. If Young had remained as a member of the five-year class of 1862 he would have graduated early, in June 1861, along with his classmates, including George A. Custer. By mid-September 1863 Colonel Young received his promotion to the rank of brigadier general.[41]

The Jeff Davis Legion reported only six companies, A, B, C, D, E, and F, serving with General Hampton's brigade during the Gettysburg Campaign. Originally formed with men recruited mainly in Mississippi, Alabama, and Georgia, the Jeff Davis Legion listed thirty-one-year-old Lieutenant Colonel Joseph Frederick Waring in the leadership position. The legion's position of colonel had been vacant for the last six months, ever since the promotion of William Thompson Martin to the rank of brigadier general in December 1862. Although it fielded just six companies, the smallest unit in Stuart's immediate command in terms of the number of companies present for duty, the Jeff Davis Legion counted approximately 21 officers and 260 enlisted men present on the rolls as they made their way into Pennsylvania on the last day of June.[42]

The last unit assigned to Wade Hampton's brigade and present with General Stuart's main command in Maryland on the final day of June was the Phillips Legion Cavalry Battalion. Initially formed in Georgia the Phillips Legion was seven companies strong, A through G. The command listed a mere 17 commissioned officers and 252 noncommissioned officers and enlisted men. Forty-year-old Lieutenant Colonel William W. Rich commanded the Phillips Legion.[43]

Brigadier General Fitzhugh Lee,
Commander, Fitzhugh Lee's Cavalry Brigade
(LC)

As J. E. B. Stuart's weary division moved out of their overnight encampments around the Shriver brothers' homesteads, the last brigade of cavalry present for duty moved away from the main column on their newly assigned mission. Brigadier General Fitzhugh Lee's brigade, consisting of five Virginia regiments, had the great responsibility of guarding both the left flank and rear of Stuart's advancing column. Fitz Lee's brigade screened the primary column of Southern horsemen by moving to the west for a mile or two and then heading north on a parallel course with the other two brigades that were already in motion.

Fitz Lee's five assigned regiments included all ten companies (A-K) of his old command, the 1st Virginia Cavalry. The Virginians numbered roughly 25 commissioned officers and 339 noncommissioned officers and enlisted men present for duty at the end of June.[44] Shortly after the regiment's formation at the beginning of the war, the 1st Virginia listed J. E. B. Stuart as its commanding officer and Fitz Lee, a nephew of Robert E. Lee and first-cousin of "Rooney" Lee, as the lieutenant colonel.

As the Confederate horsemen of the 1st Virginia moved to the left flank of the main body, forty-one-year-old Colonel James Henry Drake commanded the regiment. A plasterer and mechanic before the war with only limited experience in the state militia Drake had proved his capabilities on many fields of battle. Unfortunately, he would not survive the war very much longer. Colonel Drake died leading his regiment against General David Gregg's cavalrymen at Shepherdstown, West Virginia on July 16, 1863. The day after his death in a dispatch written to General Samuel Cooper (U.S.M.A., Class of 1815), adjutant and inspector general of the Confederate Army, Robert E. Lee in a rare occurrence specifically referred to Drake's death. He proclaimed that: "I regret to state that Colonel James H. Drake, of the First Virginia Cavalry, was mortally wounded in a charge of his regiment."[45]

The 2nd Virginia Cavalry was formed early in 1861 by consolidating a number of companies recruited around the Commonwealth. The regiment had a full complement of ten companies (A-K). Thirty-two-year-old Colonel Thomas Taylor Munford (V.M.I., Class of 1852) commanded the regiment. He spent the years before the war as a farmer in Lynchburg. Recommended for promotion to brigadier general throughout the war by many of his superiors, including Robert E. Lee, he never got confirmed by the cantankerous members of the Confederate Congress. Munford spent three years as the colonel of the regiment and frequently commanded his brigade. The regiment mustered approximately 28 officers and 420 enlisted men as they moved along the roads of Carroll County, Maryland and York County, Pennsylvania on June 30.[46]

Colonel Thomas T. Munford,
Commander,
2nd Virginia Cavalry
(LC)

Colonel
Williams C. Wickham,
Commander,
4th Virginia Cavalry
(LC)

General Fitz Lee's brigade included all ten companies, A through K, of the 3rd Virginia Cavalry on June 30, 1863. Another of the many regiments formed in early 1861 the regiment now reported 26 commissioned officers and a scant 221 enlisted men in the ranks. Colonel Thomas Howerton Owen (V.M.I., Class of 1856), who had just passed his thirtieth birthday on June 11, commanded the diminished regiment. Colonel Owen, like Colonel Munford of the 2nd Virginia, satisfactorily commanded his regiment for the last three years of the war without receiving a promotion to the rank of brigadier general. He received a slight wound in the hand while leading his command at the Battle of Spotsylvania in 1864 but survived the war.[47]

Another of General Lee's Virginia regiments, the 4th Virginia Cavalry, had just nine companies, A, B, C, D, E, F, G, H, and K, present for duty and currently serving with the regiment. In September 1861 the regiment mustered a number of individually recruited companies from around the state. The 4th Virginia regiment included the famed "Black Horse Cavalry" that originally organized during 1859 in Warrenton and Fauquier County. John Scott became the troop's first captain and then moved on to lead some independent cavalry units during the war. William Payne enlisted in the unit as a private. The "Black Horse Cavalry" eventually was re-designated as Company H of the 4th Virginia.[48] The muster rolls of the regiment showed that a sizable contingent of roughly 34 officers and 594 noncommissioned officers and enlisted men were present for duty during the reporting period. Forty-two-year-old Colonel Williams Wickham directly controlled the regiment. Wickham was a planter, lawyer, and politician before the beginning of hostilities. He eventually rose to the rank of brigadier general but then unexpectedly resigned in 1864 to become a member of the Confederate Congress.[49]

Thomas Lafayette Rosser was only twenty-six years old as he led the ten companies (A-K) of the 5th Virginia Cavalry. The regimental organizers recruited for the ranks in the closing months of 1861. Colonel Rosser attended West Point before the war in one of the five-year classes but resigned just two weeks before graduating with the regularly scheduled Class of 1861. For his distinguished service during the war he ultimately achieved the rank of major general in the Confederate Army.[50]

Colonel Thomas L. Rosser,
Commander, 5th Virginia Cavalry
(LC)

The 5th Virginia Cavalry mustered just an inappreciable seven commissioned officers, the fewest number present by far in any of Stuart's regiments. The number of noncommissioned officers and enlisted men mustered was not much higher at 163. Previous fighting during the month of June had taken a heavy toll on the regiment leaving many vacant saddles within the ranks of the proud regiment.[51]

Acutely aware that General Kilpatrick's cavalry had encamped at Littlestown on the previous day, General Stuart sought a quick and relatively simple route around the cavalry forces of the troublesome 3rd Division. He truly wanted to avoid any manner of contact or actual battle with them. Stuart's column found itself strung out for a considerable distance along the main road between Hanover and Union Mills. Both his men and animals suffered from extreme fatigue after days of continuous marching with little respite. The Southerners were probably much more fatigued than their Union counterparts due to the very taxing nature of their current raid behind enemy lines. Trying to elude the Union forces, while attempting to rejoin the Army of Northern Virginia, the effort easily drained the men both physically and mentally. Additionally, the captured Federal wagon train and prisoners still slowed Stuart's progress considerably. Finally, and probably most importantly, General Stuart was becoming very anxious about the lack of contact or any type of communication for that matter with the rest of the Army of Northern Virginia. His primary concern, at the present time, was to find General Robert E. Lee's main army or at least a portion of it now believed to be near York. For now, J. E. B. Stuart thought that he could reasonably avoid any serious contact with Kilpatrick's Union cavalry by quickly passing through the small community of Hanover.

The Confederate mounted troops advanced cautiously north from Union Mills along the Baltimore Pike toward Hanover. Under the guidance of the young Herbert Shriver, General Stuart's column turned off the main road after only a few miles. They opted to travel along a less used parallel side road with the expectation of escaping detection by Union scouting parties known to be in the immediate area. Unfortunately, and quite unexpectedly, as they traversed that new route they encountered an unexpected obstacle in the form of a fairly steep height known locally as Conewago Hill. It is unknown whether the youthful Mr. Shriver did not know that the hill was there or if he did not know that a heavily loaded wagon would have a slow journey to the top. That steep incline slowed the forward progress of the wagons and artillery pieces even more than they were previously on their journey. The teams of horses and mules became even more exhausted which caused a substantial gap in Stuart's line of march.

While the wagons were slowly falling behind the leading elements of their cavalry escort, Colonel Chambliss and the regiments of his brigade continued to push on toward Hanover at a steady pace. Today's order of march for Chambliss's brigade had the 13th Virginia Cavalry out in front of Stuart's entire force. The 2nd North Carolina followed Major Gillette's regiment and was, in turn, followed by the 9th and 10th Virginia regiments. The companies leading the advance of the Southern cavalry, probably from the 13th Virginia, passed by one of the many local grist mills in the area, this one known as Gitt's Mill. At that place the first somewhat unanticipated, and definitely unwanted, encounter with Judson Kilpatrick's cavalrymen occurred. [52]

Before departing from Littlestown, Lieutenant Potter's forty-man detail from the 18th Pennsylvania received further orders from Lieutenant Colonel Brinton. The additional directive stated that Potter was to allow the division's slow-moving column, which included all the ambulances and other important wagons, to proceed for roughly a mile in front of them before leaving Littlestown. Brinton personally delivered the instructions to his young subordinate before leaving with the rest of the regiment toward Hanover.

Waiting for slightly less than thirty minutes while the last of the division elements left Littlestown, Lieutenant Potter's men moved northeast along the Hanover Road. The lieutenant's detail continued to trail the main column by almost a mile all the way into Hanover. Shortly after leaving Littlestown, Henry Potter was joined on the road by another officer from the 18th Pennsylvania, Captain Thadeus S. Freeland of Troop E, along with his small detachment of ten men. [53]

Captain Freeland, who was only recently released from regimental arrest because of some unknown minor infraction, and his men also had received orders from Lieutenant Colonel Brinton to patrol the flanks of Kilpatrick's advancing column. [54] They were to scout for any signs of the Confederate cavalry now definitely deemed to be in the region. Leaving Littlestown behind, Captain Freeland and his men initially started their mission on a little used road on the left, or western, flank of the column. Eventually Freeland's patrol arrived back on the Hanover Road where he met Lieutenant Potter's rear guard. Freeland and Potter rode together for just a short distance before the captain turned off the main thoroughfare to the east and took another of the area's many side roads. Captain Freeland continued his mission to scout the flank of the slow-moving Union column for signs of enemy activity. Unfortunately, he and his men would soon find ample evidence of J. E. B. Stuart's presence to the east of the Hanover Road. Freeland's orders clearly stated, and common sense dictated, that his patrol was not to engage the enemy. [55]

For good measure as the majority of Kilpatrick's command moved north along the road toward Hanover the 5th and 6th Michigan regiments remained behind at Littlestown as an additional precaution. Colonel Russell Alger's 5th Cavalry received orders to conduct a scouting mission back across the Mason-Dixon Line in the direction of Westminster to the south. During the previous night, disturbing reports had at long last reached General Kilpatrick's headquarters at his Littlestown hotel room dealing with the possibility of enemy cavalry operating nearby. Whether the information was true or false, Kilpatrick had to act upon it because the whole Army of the Potomac was rapidly moving north behind his troopers. If he ignored the information he might possibly find himself cut off from his main supports to the south.

Perhaps the 3rd Division's commanding general had already received the distressing information concerning the rout of the 1st Delaware Cavalry at Westminster on the previous day. A surprise, as a new division commander, was something that he could not afford. To his own credit, General Kilpatrick wanted to make sure that no Confederate troops were trailing him on some of the same roads he had just traversed the previous day. He took all the necessary precautions to make sure that he could remain in contact with the rest of the Army of the Potomac.

Colonel Alger's regiment mustered into the service of the United States in August 1862 at Detroit. However, they did not leave Michigan until December for nominal duty in Washington, D.C. The regiment of Michiganders had seen only limited service during its six months in the field. It was another of Judson Kilpatrick's units that had not seen any battle action as a whole regiment, having been assigned to various scouting missions and patrols around Washington until June 1863. The regiment mustered 30 officers and 633 noncommissioned officers and enlisted men on June 30, 1863.[56]

While the 5th Michigan quickly spurred their horses south toward Westminster, the 6th Michigan Cavalry had orders to remain in Littlestown to guard the route taken by the 3rd Division and to also be alert for any enemy activity nearby. The 6th Michigan Cavalry Regiment mustered into the volunteer service in October 1862 at Grand Rapids. Like the 5th Michigan, the 6th Cavalry did not leave Michigan until

December. Also like the 5th Cavalry, the 6th regiment saw only light service in its six months of service in the field. Mirroring the assignments of the 5th, Colonel Gray's regiment was another of General Kilpatrick's units that had not seen any battle action as a complete regiment. They, too, received a variety of relatively safe assignments and inconsequential patrolling duties around Washington until June 1863. On the last day of June, George Gray's regiment listed 33 officers and a total of 668 enlisted men present for duty in the ten troops currently serving with the regiment.[57]

As an added precaution while still at Littlestown, Colonel Gray ordered Troop A, under the command of twenty-four-year-old Captain Henry Elmer Thompson and twenty-six-year-old 2nd Lieutenant Stephen H. Ballard, to patrol one other road leading toward Union Mills and Westminster. Their mission with only a meager force of seventy-six noncommissioned officers and enlisted men was identical to Colonel Alger's undertaking. Thompson and his men were to locate the Confederate cavalry rumored to be in the vicinity of Union Mills and report that information to General Kilpatrick's headquarters as soon as possible.[58]

Notes to Chapter Seven

1. Isham, *An Historical Sketch of the Seventh Regiment Michigan Volunteer Cavalry*, p. 21.
2. NA RG 94 – 1 MI. The number of enlisted members is based upon an approximate number since some of the muster rolls for June 30, 1863, are not available at the National Archives. The muster rolls immediately preceding June 30 and subsequent to that date gave the approximate totals for Troops A, K, L, and M.
3. Dyer, *A Compendium of the War of the Rebellion*, 3:1269. The 1st Michigan Cavalry had assignments to the Army of the Potomac, Department of the Shenandoah, Army of Virginia, Military District of Washington, and the Department of Washington.
4. NA RG 94 – 7 MI.
5. Dyer, *A Compendium of the War of the Rebellion*, 3:1273.
6. Isham, *An Historical Sketch of the Seventh Regiment Michigan Volunteer Cavalry*, p. 12.
7. NA RG 94 – 7 MI.
8. Dyer, *A Compendium of the War of the Rebellion*, 3:1700.
9. Anthony, *Battle of Hanover*, p. 1.
10. Dyer, *A Compendium of the War of the Rebellion*, 3:1647-48.
11. NA RG 94 – 1 VT.
12. Dyer, *A Compendium of the War of the Rebellion*, 3:1655-56; Busey & Martin, *Regimental Strengths and Losses at Gettysburg*, p. 107. The 1st West Virginia Cavalry originally mustered twelve companies, A to M, (excluding J which was never used in any cavalry organizations). In June 1862 an additional company, identified as N, joined the regiment.
13. NA RG 94 – 1 WV.
14. Dyer, *A Compendium of the War of the Rebellion*, 3:1704.
15. Ibid., 3:1373-74; Boudrye, *Historic Records of the Fifth New York Cavalry*, pp. 17-22.
16. NA RG 94 – 5 NY.
17. William H. Powell, ed., *Officers of the Army and Navy (Volunteer) Who Served in the Civil War* (Philadelphia, 1893), p. 125. Dimmick originally served from April to July 1861 in Company G, 2nd New Jersey State Militia. That three-month regiment saw no combat during its ninety days of service. He re-enlisted as first sergeant in Troop M, 5th New York Cavalry.
18. Anthony, *Battle of Hanover*, p. 101.
19. NA RG 94 – 5 NY.
20. Regimental Association, *History of the Eighteenth Regiment of Cavalry, Pennsylvania Volunteers*, p. 87.
21. Dyer, *A Compendium of the War of the Rebellion*, 3:1567.
22. Regimental Association, *History of the Eighteenth Regiment of Cavalry, Pennsylvania Volunteers*, p. 87.
23. Anthony, *Battle of Hanover*, p. 2.
24. NA RG 94 – 18 PA.
25. Warner, *Generals in Gray*, p. 184.

Notes to Chapter Seven (*continued*)

26. Busey & Martin, *Regimental Strengths and Losses at Gettysburg*, p. 197. After the Hanover skirmish and until the cavalry fight on the third day at Gettysburg the remainder of the depleted 2nd North Carolina regiment was commanded by 1st Lieutenant Randall H. Reese from Company H. He was the senior officer present for duty in the regiment until Captain Graham rejoined the command on July 3.
27. Ladd, *The Bachelder Papers*, 3:1373.
28. Ibid.; Warner, *Generals in Gray*, pp. 20-21.
29. Busey & Martin, *Regimental Strengths and Losses at Gettysburg*, p. 197.
30. Ibid.; Krick, *Lee's Colonels*, pp. 156-57; Daniel T. Balfour, *13th Virginia Cavalry* (Lynchburg, Va.: H. E. Howard, Inc., 1986), p. 77.
31. Confederate Service Records of Virginia Soldiers, Virginia State Library; OR – 2, p. 684.
32. OR – 2, p. 687.
33. Ibid., p. 692. General William F. Smith, in his official report of the action at Carlisle, stated that Fitzhugh Lee shelled Carlisle with seven guns.
34. Chamber of Commerce, *Encounter at Hanover*, p. 23.
35. Busey & Martin, *Regimental Strengths and Losses at Gettysburg*, p. 201. The batteries of Captain Roger Preston Chew, Captain William H. Griffin, Captain James Franklin Hart (South Carolina Military Academy), and Captain Marcellus Newton Moorman (V.M.I., Class of 1856), also part of Stuart's Horse Artillery, were not with Stuart's column as it moved through Maryland and Pennsylvania. Those artillery units moved with the main body of the Army of Northern Virginia and did not rejoin General Stuart until later in the campaign.
36. Ibid., p. 195.
37. Ibid.
38. Ladd, *The Bachelder Papers*, 2:1240-43.
39. Krick, *Lee's Colonels*, p. 177.
40. Ibid.; Warner, *Generals in Gray*, p. 40.
41. Warner, *Generals in Gray*, p. 348; Busey & Martin, *Regimental Strengths and Losses at Gettysburg*, p. 195.
42. Busey & Martin, *Regimental Strengths and Losses at Gettysburg*, p. 195.
43. Ibid.
44. Ibid., p. 196.
45. OR – 2, p. 303.
46. Busey & Martin, *Regimental Strengths and Losses at Gettysburg*, p. 196.
47. Ibid.
48. McClure, *Annals of the War*, pp. 590-93.
49. Ibid.; Warner, *Generals in Gray*, pp. 335-36.
50. Warner, *Generals in Gray*, pp. 264-65.
51. Busey & Martin, *Regimental Strengths and Losses at Gettysburg*, p. 196.
52. Chamber of Commerce, *Encounter at Hanover*, p.16.
53. Regimental Association, *History of the Eighteenth Regiment of Cavalry, Pennsylvania Volunteers*, pp. 87-89; Chamber of Commerce, *Encounter at Hanover*, pp. 253-54.
54. Chamber of Commerce, *Encounter at Hanover*, pp. 253-54. Lieutenant Potter mentioned that Captain Freeland was under arrest for "being the worst forager." He seems to have had a predisposition for stealing personal property from civilians.

Notes to Chapter Seven (*continued*)

55. Regimental Association, *History of the Eighteenth Regiment of Cavalry, Pennsylvania Volunteers,* p. 87.
56. Dyer, *A Compendium of the War of the Rebellion,* 3:1271-72; NA RG 94 – 5 MI.
57. Dyer, *A Compendium of the War of the Rebellion,* 3:1272-73; NA RG 94 – 6 MI.
58. Kidd, *Personal Reminiscences of a Cavalryman,* pp. 125-26.

Chapter 8:

Morning Surprise at Hanover

HE vanguard of General Judson Kilpatrick's division of cavalrymen arrived in the initially quiet borough of Hanover at roughly eight o'clock in the morning on the final day of June. The general, along with his staff members and his headquarters guard, had experienced a relatively effortless ride over the gently rolling hills and through the fertile valleys of south-central Pennsylvania. The weather was quite pleasant, being comparatively warm and sunny during the early morning hours. Marching through the lush countryside the men assigned to the 3rd Division passed a number of small family-owned farms casually dotting the landscape, a common sight in that portion of the United States. At many of those places the pro-Union farmers, along with their delighted families, came out from their homes or stopped their laborious tasks in the fields to watch the soldiers in the dirty blue wool uniforms ride past their houses. A number of them offered food or other refreshments to some of the luckier horsemen.

The Union cavalry column moved unhurriedly along the Hanover Road eventually arriving at a place known locally as Kitzmiller's Mill. The small family-operated gristmill sat alongside the Little Conewago Creek where the shallow flowing waters bisected the hard-packed dirt road running between Hanover and Littlestown. At Kitzmiller's Mill, just a few miles northeast of Littlestown in Adams County, the Northern troopers of General Custer's leading regiment stopped. The members of the 1st Michigan Cavalry received permission to halt momentarily for some cool, fresh water for their thirsty horses and for themselves. John Duttera and his family cheerfully and willingly dispensed buckets and buckets of the refreshing liquid. Duttera was the current owner and operator of the little gristmill. Situated slightly beyond the midway point on the road between Hanover and Littlestown, the mill was in continuous operation since 1738 and was the oldest one operating west of the Susquehanna River.[1]

After their all too brief respite, the two leading regiments of George Custer's brigade continued their seemingly unrelenting journey in pursuit of the ostensibly invisible Confederate Army of Northern Virginia. Less than an hour after halting at Kitzmiller's Mill the leading patrols of Michigan cavalrymen finally entered the well-maintained and quiet streets of Hanover. They tried to pass quickly through the town and continue their journey north along the pike toward Abbottstown and Berlin but to no avail. The begrimed horsemen of the 1st and 7th Michigan regiments had surprised the anxious and extremely nervous residents of Hanover with their completely unexpected and totally unannounced arrival. Since the Michiganders approached the town from the south, the nervous citizens naturally expected to see more Confederate invaders coming from that direction. Perhaps some of the townsfolk thought it might even be Lieutenant Colonel White and his band of Virginia cavalrymen on a return visit through their town. The citizens certainly did not expect to see the regimental standards and troop guidons of the newest division of Union cavalry assigned to the Army of the Potomac. The two Michigan cavalry regiments half-heartedly continued to attempt to make their way along the fairly broad avenues of the town.

Throughout most of the peaceful journey from Littlestown, General Kilpatrick had continued traveling near the leading troops of Custer's brigade. The general arrived in the borough with his headquarters staff and the two troops from the 1st Ohio shortly after the citizens became aware of his division's presence. Kilpatrick and his sizable entourage were able to move only a short distance into the town when they halted in front of a well-maintained private home on Frederick Street near the Center Square. The owner of the house where Judson Kilpatrick stopped was sixty-two-year-old Jacob Wirt. Mr. Wirt was a leading resident of the Hanover community and, even at his present age, still very actively involved in local matters.[2]

Located on the northeastern side of the street and in the first block from the center of town, the Jacob Wirt residence was a large two-story red brick building. On that bright and sunny morning a hastily assembled delegation of Hanover's leading citizens met the general as he dismounted from his horse in front of the house. Among the prominent people greeting the General Kilpatrick were Mr. Wirt, Burgess Joseph Slagle, Constable David S. Tanger, and the Reverend Doctor William K. Zieber. The Reverend Zieber was the pastor of the Emmanuel Reformed Church, located on Abbottstown Street just a short distance from the Wirt residence. Zieber had been in Hanover for only four short years and he was the elected president of the Committee of Safety for the Borough of Hanover.[3]

Following the initial greetings and welcome on the sidewalks of Hanover, General Kilpatrick, along with a number of the town's officials, moved to more comfortable surroundings inside Jacob Wirt's home. The noise and dust raised by the passing Union cavalrymen prevented normal conversation. After just a few minutes had elapsed, George Custer joined his division commander inside the Wirt home. The two general officers, along with a few selected members from their staffs, held a brief conference in Wirt's front parlor with the owner of the house, Mayor Slagle, and the Reverend Zieber. General Kilpatrick voiced an interest in obtaining any information with reference to the recent movements of the Confederate Army. He voiced many questions concerning the exact whereabouts of any of the enemy's forces, whose exact presence was still totally unknown to him.[4]

Generals Kilpatrick and Custer received a briefing from the town's leaders as to what had transpired during the previous few days in the region. The civilians related their tales about Lieutenant Colonel White's earlier visit to their community. They answered the officers' questions to the best of their knowledge. Of course their information had limitations and did not extend much past the borders of their community. Their accounts also were rather old and not exactly current.

To aid the Union cavalrymen in their travels through the unfamiliar though decidedly friendly territory around Hanover, Mr. Wirt granted permission for the Federal cavalry officers to remove a large wall map of

York County from the front room of his home. While the two brigadiers discussed the current circumstances with the civilian committee, General Farnsworth arrived at the Wirt home and joined in the discussion with them. This was one of the rare occasions that all three brigadier generals of the newly created 3rd Division gathered together under one roof.[5]

Besides inquiring about the location and disposition of any Confederate troops known to be around Hanover, Kilpatrick, concerned about the welfare of his men, mentioned the fact that many of his troopers had not yet had a decent breakfast on that day. In a brief statement to the Reverend Zieber, Kilpatrick stated that:

> I pity my men, for they have had no breakfast and they are very hungry. We have been marching hard ever since we crossed the Potomac and have been short of rations for three days. I do not have all my commissary wagons with me.[6]

In a matter of minutes the word about the hungry soldiers filtered through the surrounding homes in the town. The previously cautious citizens anxiously began to flock into the streets, bringing all types of edibles and other refreshments with them. With great joy and happiness after recognizing the begrimed soldiers as friends, the inhabitants of Hanover, those who had not fled to the northern counties or east across the Susquehanna River, began to press into the streets with their offerings. The forward progress of the Union cavalrymen through the streets of Hanover came to a complete halt as the crowd of civilians increased in size and overall exuberance.

Again, as with the many of the other towns and villages along their route of march in both Maryland and Pennsylvania, the Yankee cavalrymen received all types of refreshments and small presents from the loyal citizens of Hanover. Some of the food served to the hungry cavalrymen included recently baked breads, cakes, pies, and gallons of freshly brewed hot coffee. Many of Judson Kilpatrick's soldiers received other small gifts of fresh flowers and some locally produced cigars.

Earlier the troopers from the 3rd Division, before entering Hanover, had ridden past the couple of small structures where they made the cigars. John Butt owned one of the businesses, located just south of

Hanover in the tiny settlement of Buttstown. Along with hand-rolling cigars, Mr. Butt also toiled as a shoemaker during the winter months. Sometime during early May 1863 he raised a U.S. flag close to his place of business. The flag was clearly visible from near the intersection of the Frederick and Westminster roads where the two forces of enemy cavalry first met. Horsemen from both armies rode past it or close to it on their way into Hanover. During the fierce fighting to the south of Hanover, the Southerners were unable to remove it from its pole and it continued to wave defiantly as the fighting roared around it.[7]

Most of the blue-clad troopers enjoyed the food and drink offered by the townsfolk. The cavalrymen assigned to the two regiments from Michigan remained in their saddles. They attempted to continue their slow trek along Frederick Street through the Center Square of the town and out Abbottstown Street to the northeast. Those leading troopers had no orders to halt. The men of Custer's brigade had no opportunity for any leisurely social interchange before continuing on their way toward Abbottstown, but they did manage to garner a respectable share of food and gifts before departing Hanover.

Samuel L. Gillespie was a twenty-four-year-old bugler from Troop A of the 1st Ohio Cavalry. He was also Captain Noah Jones' personal orderly. As a member of General Kilpatrick's headquarters guard he remembered his approach toward Hanover and recalled that:

> We soon came to Hanover, where another royal greeting, with baskets and bouquets of flowers, met us. A large majority of the available population lined the streets with happy faces and cheers of welcome.[8]

Louis Boudrye, the chaplain of the 5th New York Cavalry, recalled receiving the same type of festive welcome from the kind and generous people of Hanover. He observed that:

> The column moved early to Hanover, where we were again enthusiastically received by the citizens, who furnished refreshments liberally to the troopers, as each regiment entered and passed through the town.[9]

Kilpatrick's division presented a somewhat intimidating spectacle for which the citizens of Hanover were not prepared. The streets rippled with the dull thunderous vibrations from the hooves of hundreds and hundreds of horses moving slowly through the town. Buildings clearly trembled on their foundations as the troopers entered the town. Although the clamor created by the heavy horses of the 3rd Division was unique, it palled in comparison to the forthcoming sounds of artillery and carbine fire shortly heard in the streets. In addition, thick clouds of smothering and choking dust rose from the streets as the soldiers and their horses passed through the town. Kilpatrick's six regiments of cavalry and two batteries of artillery were a sight not soon forgotten in Hanover.

Upon the conclusion of their brief meeting with the leading citizens of the town generals Kilpatrick, Custer, and Farnsworth withdrew from Jacob Wirt's front parlor. The information gathered from the citizens had proved to be almost worthless to the Northern commanders. None of the civilian's observations helped to pinpoint the exact location of the enemy's infantry or cavalry regiments. The three Union cavalry brigadier generals remained completely unaware of how close J. E. B. Stuart and his cavalry brigades were to Hanover.

Walking out the front door of the Wirt home and down the half-dozen steps to the sidewalk the three brigadiers remounted their waiting horses. Their enlisted orderlies were waiting with the horses at the curb-side in front of the house. Kilpatrick and Custer rapidly pushed their mounts on through the town square and the growing throngs of people milling about the streets. They quickly rode along the length of Abbott-stown Street. The two general officers overtook the head of the slow-moving column just outside the city limits to the north. In less than an hour Colonel Town's 1st Michigan, still the leading regiment of the 3rd Division and followed closely by the 7th Michigan Cavalry, had already exited the town. Colonel Mann's 7th Michigan followed their specially formed "Guard of Honor" through the streets of the town.

Shortly after its formation and muster the 7th Michigan Cavalry, based upon Colonel Mann's recommendation, formed a special detail of troopers as a reward for excellence and bravery within the ranks of the regiment. Two hand-picked soldiers from each troop acted as a special escort for the U.S. flag and the regimental standard. With only ten troops currently serving with the regiment there were twenty noncommissioned officers and enlisted men presently on the detail. During the Civil War it was a unique honor to guard and care for the flags particularly in any battle action. The flags were the true identity and embodiment of each unit. It was a symbol that every man in the unit swore to protect. Of course the opposition forces equally pledged themselves to try to capture the flags. Scores of Union soldiers received the Medal of Honor for capturing the enemy's flags during Civil War battles.[10]

The fatigued members of the Michigan Brigade continued to push on toward the Pigeon Hills, a prominent elevation located just to the north of Hanover. From the heights of the Pigeon Hills all of Hanover was visible in the valley below. Lieutenant Alexander Pennington's battery of artillery, Custer's last unit in the day's line of march, had just finished rolling their cumbersome cannons and other wheeled vehicles through the town limits as the leading troops of the brigade pushed up the Pigeon Hills.

While generals Kilpatrick and Custer had to travel a few miles to gain the head of the advancing column, General Farnsworth was able to rejoin the leading regiment of his brigade, the 1st Vermont Cavalry, very near the center of the town. Lieutenant Colonel Preston's regiment passed by Jacob Wirt's residence while their commanding general engaged in a brief conversation inside the premises.

It was roughly nine o'clock as the first members of Farnsworth's brigade arrived in the congested and almost impassable streets of Hanover. The brigade's leading cavalry regiment from the Green Mountain State, rode along the road in a column of fours. A column of fours was when four horses and their riders marched side by side followed by another four horsemen and so forth to the end of the column. The Vermonters also entered Hanover from the southwest along Frederick Street. Their orders, like the 2nd Brigade before them, had them continuing through the Center Square and out the Abbottstown Road to the north. Preston's regiment followed the same route that Custer's men had taken previously.

The 1st Vermont troopers, as with the Michigan cavalrymen, received considerable amounts of food and other refreshments by the citizens as they passed through the now crowded and somewhat festive streets of the village. They had barely cleared the center of town when the next regiment rode up Frederick Street and into the square.

Colonel Richmond's West Virginians shared the same experience in Hanover as the previous regiments. People still packed the streets with many people racing back and forth from their homes. They continued to supply treats for the soldiers passing through their town. Frederick Street, the Center Square, and Abbottstown Street were now almost completely impassable with scores of citizens, as well as mounted and dismounted soldiers, blocking the rest of the division's forward progress. It seemed as though almost everybody in the town was standing in the streets to greet the cavalrymen.

Lieutenant Elder's battery of artillerymen followed the ten troops of the 1st West Virginia Cavalry. The lieutenant and his men could scarcely get their four guns through the Center Square because of the throngs of humanity. As the main streets became more and more clogged with people and horses, the advance of the trailing regiments of Farnsworth's brigade came to a complete halt.[11]

Now it was the 1st Ira Harris Guard's turn to share in some of the bounty being freely distributed by the citizens. Because of the oddities associated with the march, many of Major Hammond's New Yorkers had plenty of time to dismount from their horses and visit socially with the citizens. The cavalrymen from New York congregated around Hanover's Center Square and the Public Common. The Public Common sat between Abbottstown and Carlisle streets just north of the Center Square. They received their share of cheers, adulation, and most importantly, food from the local inhabitants. Remembering the depressing circumstances of the previous week and the seemingly never-ending travails of active campaigning the New Yorkers were in no hurry to leave such accommodating and friendly citizens.[12]

Close on the heels of the men from the 5th New York came the recently recruited troopers of Lieutenant Colonel Brinton's 18th Pennsylvania. The Pennsylvanians reached Frederick Street a little after ten o'clock on that fateful morning. They, too, had the opportunity to dismount because of the delay caused by the throng of civilians and other cavalrymen in front of them. The men of the 18th Pennsylvania Cavalry had just started to enjoy the citizen's greetings and the proffered food and gifts when they became the unwitting recipients of another type of reception. That greeting was one that was somewhat surprising and not at all welcomed by the Union troopers.

General Farnsworth's three leading regiments of cavalrymen, as well as a portion of his fourth regiment, the 18th Pennsylvania, experienced a rousing good time in the streets of Hanover. As the main body of Brinton's regiment enjoyed themselves, the rear guard and scouting patrols from his regiment were dealing with a reception committee of a much more serious and dangerous magnitude. Shortly before 10:00 A.M., one of the many patrols dispatched from the 18th Pennsylvania became acutely aware that the enemy was much closer than had been previously anticipated or expected by anyone in the Union ranks. That patrol, under the previously mentioned Captain Thadeus Freeland, shortly would become the first of Kilpatrick's division to engage Stuart's cavalry force on Pennsylvania soil.

Captain Freeland's command was now moving parallel with the main Federal column on the column's right flank. Freeland's small patrol ran into an equally small Confederate scouting party roughly three miles southwest of the Center Square in Hanover. The site of that brief encounter was known as Gitt's Mill. It was where the first battle casualty of the day's fighting around Hanover occurred. A brief exchange of long distance small-arms fire broke out between the two somewhat surprised antagonists. One unidentified cavalryman from Colonel Chambliss's brigade, probably a member of his own 13th Virginia Cavalry, received a fatal wound by a bullet fired by one of Captain Freeland's men. The local citizens buried the Confederate soldier near a barn on the Martin Arnold farm, just north of the steep Conewago Hill and along the Westminster Road. The shot that killed the unlucky Southern cavalryman came from a spot on the William Dresher farm, some two hundred yards distant. Supposedly, according to witnesses, the "Union marksman lay his rifle across the circular well wall of stone bearing windlass and bucket in taking aim."[13]

After only a few minutes of sporadic and mostly ineffectual firing from the opposing parties, Thadeus Freeland's little patrol from the 18th Pennsylvania quickly disengaged from the Confederate forces. They moved rapidly to the north in order to rejoin General Kilpatrick's main column now in the process of moving through the streets of Hanover. The captain wanted to report his unexpected encounter with the enemy to his superiors as soon as possible. Unfortunately, the route along the Westminster Road that Captain Freeland used in order to rejoin his regiment and brigade led directly into the ranks of another, and much larger, patrol from the 13th Virginia Cavalry.

Pushing their already tired horses as fast as they could Freeland and his squad of horsemen overtook another mounted patrol almost within sight of the streets of Hanover. Obviously unaware that any of General Stuart's cavalry could be so close to Hanover so early in the day, Freeland's Union troopers rode right up to the unidentified unit slowly moving in front of them. They mistakenly thought that it was one of their own patrols heading into Hanover. It was virtually impossible for any one individual to be familiar with all the patrols, in addition to all the men assigned to those patrols, dispatched from the 3rd Division in various directions during the morning. After all, it seemed improbable that the enemy could not possibly be already between his patrol and the rest of their division.

Sensing no danger, since both groups were traveling in the same direction toward Hanover, Captain Freeland allowed his small patrol to get too close before they learned of their irreparable mistake. Thadeus Freeland's little detachment found themselves surrounded and captured without a single shot being fired by either side. Since both sides discharged no weapons, the Confederates were able to continue to conceal their exact whereabouts from the rest of General Kilpatrick's troopers. The previously scattered small-arms firing at Gitt's Mill had not been loud enough for the division to hear over the clatter of the moving horses and the racket created by the clanging equipment. Captain Freeland's participation, as well as the participation of the men in his patrol, was abruptly finished in the upcoming battle in the streets of Hanover and the rest of the Gettysburg Campaign.[14]

Meanwhile, shortly after Captain Freeland's scouting patrol found itself quickly and quietly captured by the Confederate cavalrymen, Lieutenant Potter and his forty-man rear guard, were about to come under attack from the same contingent of the enemy's cavalry. As Potter's detachment pushed closer to the southern edge of Hanover, the wagons and ambulances of Kilpatrick's column had just begun to enter the borough along Frederick Street. About that time, Potter called a halt for his command. He allowed his men to take a brief break since they were getting too close to the rear of the main column clearly halted in front of them. Potter's men took the opportunity to water their horses from Plum Creek, a small stream that crossed the Frederick Road very close to Buttstown. Just beyond Buttstown was the southern boundary of Hanover.[15]

Potter recalled many years later what happened next to his command while dismounted near the slowly flowing waters of the creek:

> While watering, a farmer came from a house close by calling to me "The rebs have taken my horses and cows." I went with him to his barn, when he showed me the empty stalls and pointed out in the distance a small body of troops who had with them one of those old-fashioned Conestoga wagons. These troops had on blue coats, and I thought it was Freeland. I told the farmer I would have his stock returned to him and left, not being satisfied in my mind.[16]

Still stopped near the tiny settlement of Buttstown, as the few scattered houses at the intersection of the Westminster and Frederick roads were known, Lieutenant Potter spied the group of mounted men moving in the distance to the northeast of his position. Those unidentified horsemen, traveling north along the Westminster Road, were quickly approaching the same intersection that Potter was about to cross with the rear guard of General Kilpatrick's troops.

Initially, Lieutenant Potter believed those mystery riders appearing in the distance to be Captain Freeland and his small patrol traveling with a commandeered wagon. Potter did not know that Freeland was already a prisoner at that time. Believing them to be Freeland and his men, he was

not too suspicious at the sudden appearance of the unidentified horsemen in his front. Acting cautiously however, he did send a couple of his
men forward to investigate the horsemen. Corporal Isaac I. Dannenhower and Private Frank A. Street, both assigned to Troop M of the 18th
Pennsylvania, rode up the Frederick Road to check the identity of the
soldiers. Incredibly, they advanced only a short distance before returning
with the news that the mysterious cavalrymen were, as previously suspected, members of Freeland's detachment from their own regiment.[17]

Considering the fact that Lieutenant Potter and his men had seen
Captain Freeland's patrol only an hour earlier, Henry Potter should have
known that something was wrong with his men's assessment of the situation. For their part, it is inconceivable how Dannenhower and Street
could have misidentified the sizable force to their right and front as Freeland and his small squad of men. The two enlisted men could not have
possibly identified the dust-covered riders as friends unless, in an unlikely scenario, the Confederate soldiers happened to intersperse some of
Captain Freeland's captured men among them. Perhaps Dannenhower
and Street recognized a familiar face in the crowd.

Second Lieutenant Henry C. Potter,
Troop M, 18th Pennsylvania Cavalry
(GAR III)

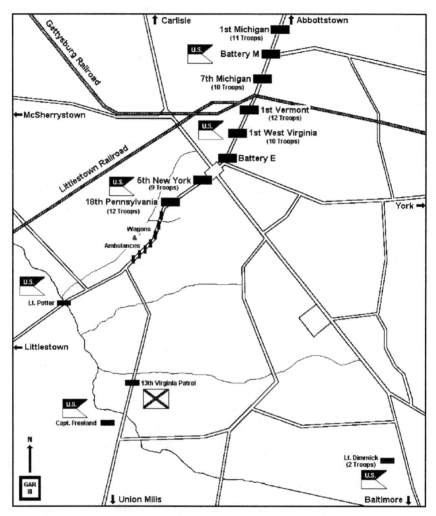

Positions of Union and Confederate Forces June 30, 1863, 9:00 – 10:00 A.M.
(GAR III)

After their capture the Yankee cavalrymen, undoubtedly, found themselves hurried to the rear of the advancing Southern column for immediate interrogation and to join any other prisoners. Captain Freeland's whole detail numbered just ten men, while the suspicious riders in Potter's path totaled at least sixty men and their numbers seemed to be increasing rapidly. Surprisingly, the young second lieutenant took no extraordinary precautions as he prepared to continue his advance into the streets of Hanover, where the rear of his regiment halted.[18]

After their brief respite at the now muddied waters of Plum Creek, Lieutenant Potter gave the command for the men of his detail to remount their horses and to move forward again, at a walk, along the Hanover-Littlestown-Frederick road. As his column of cavalrymen and the questionably identified horsemen in front of him started to converge at the intersection of the Westminster and Frederick roads, Potter was able to get a much better view of the mounted soldiers in his front.

Now the young lieutenant was finally getting increasingly nervous as the two forces slowly moved closer together. As the distance gradually narrowed between the two converging forces of mounted troops, Potter could now positively ascertain that those troops in front of him were from General Stuart's cavalry division and not his own. The lieutenant recalled later that he "was suspicious as their guidon was very red." A very astute observation by the inexperienced lieutenant considering the fact that the distance between the two forces was now less than two hundred yards.[19]

The two columns continued to move closer together. Now fully aware that the suspect horsemen ahead of him were not from his division or even from his army, Lieutenant Potter prepared his men to charge through the enemy's ranks upon his given signal. At what point the troopers of Colonel Chambliss's brigade had identified Potter's command as an enemy force is unknown. Undoubtedly they knew who the Pennsylvanians were shortly after the first sighting, thanks to the capture of Captain Freeland and his men.

Traveling toward Hanover from the slightly elevated ground south of the town, the advanced members of the 13th Virginia Cavalry also had to know that there were a number of Federal wagons and ambulances parked along Frederick Street in their front. Perhaps the men of Major Gillette's regiment thought that they had another wagon train ripe for the picking as in Rockville two days previously. They seem not to have noticed, or decided to totally ignore, any of the additional Union forces moving through and out the other side of the town.

The Southern horsemen, however, chose first to intercept the small Union rear guard where the Westminster Road ended at the Frederick Road near Buttstown. Their quick and decisive action would thus cut off Lieutenant Potter's men from their regiment and sever all hope for any support from the rest of the regiment or brigade. Henry Potter, remembering his first contact with the enemy force, stated that:

> When about a mile from the town the road they were on turned sharply into the one we were on, and about sixty of them came out directly in front of us. They called on us not to shoot, but surrender saying, "We've just captured some of you'ns," and they would not shoot. When we got very close to them we fired and charged (this was the first shot fired); they scattered and we went through them. It did not take them long to recover and they came after us. We ran toward the town and a bend in the road brought into view the rear of our regiment dismounted.[20]

Major Joseph Gillette's leading companies from the 13th Virginia Cavalry were confident that the Yankee lieutenant's small contingent of troops had no alternative but to surrender to them. The Union horsemen completely surprised them when Potter's men suddenly put spurs to their horses and the snorting steeds swiftly bolted forward. The lieutenant and his detachment from the 18th Pennsylvania quickly pushed directly toward the Southerners who were attempting to block their path into town. At that moment Lieutenant Potter knew something that his antagonists apparently did not know. He counted on the fact that his regiment and most of his brigade and division were just a short distance away. Hopefully most of his men would be able to cut their way through the unsuspecting ranks of the enemy and get into the town.

Although slightly outnumbered, Potter gave the prearranged signal to his men as they slowly advanced along the road. Suddenly they emptied their carbines and pistols at the Southerners and rapidly charged through the ranks of the startled Virginians. They then raced for the expected safety of Hanover as the startled enemy troops retreated a short distance back along the Westminster Road. Lieutenant Potter and his detachment continued forward. They soon rounded a slight bend in the road and overtook the rear of their own main column completely stopped along Frederick Street.[21]

After they raced through the enemy's ineffectual roadblock Lieutenant Potter's men quickly came across the parked wagons and ambulances from their division. Many of the wagons had stopped in the very middle of the street with their drivers partaking of the refreshments and gifts made available to them by the people of Hanover. Upon hearing the sudden and intense small-arms firing in their rear, panic quickly set in among the teamsters, especially as Potter and his band passed by them. The lieutenant's detachment then abruptly ran into the rear of their own regiment, which had also dismounted among the shade trees of Frederick Street. The majority of Lieutenant Potter's forty-man detachment escaped unscathed during their swift and surprising charge through the enemy cavalrymen. The relatively minor action, up to that point, was about to escalate rapidly into the pitched battle not wanted by General J. E. B. Stuart.[22]

Somewhere around the same time that Captain Freeland and Lieutenant Potter were encountering various detachments of the enemy, Lieutenant Dimmick and his sixty-six men from the 5th New York also confronted another portion of the enemy. The astute Lieutenant Dimmick was beginning to get very suspicious as he and his men moved northward. There were signs of Confederate activity all along his route of march.

Lieutenant Dimmick and his two troops of horsemen had moved farther to the right of General Kilpatrick's advancing column than any other Union patrol. Ironically, they had moved so far to the right of their column that they had let Colonel Chambliss's brigade move into position between them and the rest of Kilpatrick's division. They seemed to have completely missed that fact until it was too late to correct the error. Unfortunately, the regiments from Chambliss's brigade were not the most pressing problem for the little band of New Yorkers. While it was true that John Chambliss and his troopers were between Dimmick and the main Union column, they happened to be somewhere between one and two miles away. The major concern for the Union troopers was the sudden appearance of the advanced patrols of Wade Hampton's brigade on the rear flank of Lieutenant Dimmick's patrol.[23]

Shortly after leaving Littlestown, Lieutenant Dimmick and his two troops, when about three miles from the town, noticed some men walking in a field on their right flank. Sending forward a couple of men from his patrol they captured two of the men without a struggle. The soldiers were dismounted troopers sent on a scouting mission from Wade Hampton's command. General Stuart's exhausted horses continued to break down all along their route of march, leaving many a Southern trooper to ponder where he would procure his next ride. Given the New Yorker's position at that juncture, the captured Union wagon train, as well as the rest of Hampton's brigade, could not have been very far from Lieutenant Dimmick's patrol.[24]

After the first contact, the two New York troops continued toward Hanover. They then ran into a sizable patrol of the enemy, probably from the 1st South Carolina Cavalry, which was the leading regiment in General Hampton's line of march. After briefly exchanging long-distance carbine fire, the Southern horsemen decided to charge Dimmick's detachment. The young, but veteran, lieutenant commanding the men of the 5th New York immediately recognized that the enemy vastly outnumbered his patrol and quickly decided to disengage.

Unable to move readily forward as planned or back toward Littlestown in the south or even west toward Hanover, Dimmick and his horsemen took to the fields and made a circuitous route to the east and then north. They had decided to give the enemy cavalrymen a wide berth. Eventually Lieutenant Dimmick and his entire command reached Abbottstown later that afternoon, which had been their original destination upon leaving Littlestown earlier in the day. Not knowing that he was going to be detained in Hanover, Kilpatrick's last orders to the young lieutenant had him patrolling the flank of the division as far as Abbottstown.

After their arrival in Abbottstown the lieutenant and his weary men learned of the major fighting at Hanover between Kilpatrick and Stuart. They then immediately started south on the road toward Hanover to rejoin their regiment. Those two detached troops of the 5th New York

Cavalry did not arrive at Hanover until after the fighting had ended for the day.[25]

Shortly before Freeland, Potter, and Dimmick had their unexpected experiences with the Southern troopers of Colonel Chambliss and General Hampton's brigades, General Kilpatrick and his staff had already moved through the center of Hanover. The commanding general of the 3rd Division and his staff followed the leading members of the Michigan Brigade. Custer's brigade continued to advance along the narrow road to Abbottstown. Some six or seven miles from Hanover, Kilpatrick and the members of his staff stopped for a brief rest at another one of the many small communities dotting the roads of Pennsylvania. Situated on a hill, the town of Hendrix offered an excellent panoramic view of the countryside through which the leading regiments of the division had just traveled.[26]

As the Union mounted column continued to move slowly along the Abbottstown Road, the first fatality of the campaign in the new division occurred within the ranks of General Custer's 2nd Brigade. While Lieutenant Alexander Pennington's Battery M was passing near the George Wertz farm at a place known as Hartman's Mill the ammunition chests of one caisson suddenly exploded with a thunderous and deafening roar. The sheer destructive force of the explosion completely shattered a wooden corn barn on Mr. Wertz' property on the side nearest the road. Additionally, a small crater got carved in the middle of the Abbottstown Road.[27]

One unlucky artilleryman Private James Moran an Irish immigrant received a mortal wound while riding on top of the caisson's limber. His comrades from the battery removed his unconscious and horribly mangled body to the Wertz farmhouse, where he was made as comfortable as possible. Unfortunately, Private Moran's wounds proved to be fatal and he died the next day. In addition, two of James Moran's fellow artillerymen received less serious shrapnel wounds and burns. They eventually recovered from their injuries. Of the six horses pulling the accursed caisson, the two closest to the exploding ammunition chests, the wheel pair, also died. Two other horses received less serious injuries in the explosion. Confusion reigned among both men and animals immediately after the detonation of the artillery rounds since it was feared at first that the column was under attack.[28]

Undoubtedly, the cause of the accidental explosion was because of the rough condition of the road, resulting in the ammunition abruptly shifting in its chest, thus causing it to detonate without warning. General Kilpatrick's column came to a complete halt while one of the brigade's surgeons treated the injured men's wounds. Additionally, other artillerymen cut both dead horses loose from their harnesses and then pulled the carcasses to the side of the road. They then removed the ruined caisson, or the remnants of it, from the middle of the road.

Private Moran, a member of the Roman Catholic faith, was initially buried in the Lutheran Church cemetery in Abbottstown. The church's Reverend Doctor Daniel J. Hauer led the burial ceremony. Two months later, after the intervention of the deceased soldier's family members and former comrades in Battery M, Private James Moran was re-interred in the nearby Paradise Catholic Church cemetery.[29]

While the command continued waiting because of the accident, another of General Kilpatrick's patrols reported back from their recently assigned scouting mission. The previous day, June 29, Kilpatrick had dispatched a small detail in advance of the main column toward Abbottstown. That detachment composed of 1st Ohio cavalrymen from Kilpatrick's headquarters guard was under the command of Troop A's junior commissioned officer, twenty-two-year-old Second Lieutenant John N. McElwain.

Lieutenant McElwain's patrol returned from their mission just as the 3rd Division stopped because of the terrible accident in Battery M. The Ohio cavalrymen returned with moderate success, having moved as far north as Berlin, which was just beyond Abbottstown. McElwain and his patrol had captured three Confederate stragglers from General Ewell's corps near Berlin earlier in the day, proving that the Confederate infantry was very close to the 3rd Division.[30]

Shortly before the action was beginning to heat up in the streets of Hanover, Captain Henry Thompson with his Troop A of the 6th Michigan Cavalry advanced his men along the road toward Union Mills and Westminster from Littlestown. They were completely unaware of what was happening just to the north of their current position. Surprisingly, the cavalrymen from Michigan found no enemy forces during their brief reconnaissance, but they did find abundant evidence that General Stuart's cavalry had recently been in the area. Speaking with a number of local residents Captain Thompson learned that all the information and visible signs clearly pointed to a very large body of the enemy's cavalry being in the rear of Kilpatrick's division. Unfortunately, the Southern cavalry seemed to be moving in the same direction toward Hanover as the Yankee cavalry. Wasting precious little time, Captain Thompson immediately began to retrace his steps back to Littlestown with the important information.[31]

Soon after Captain Thompson had begun his scouting mission, an enlisted courier from regimental headquarters overtook his troop and directed that he return immediately to Littlestown. Already in the process of obeying his new directive because of the valuable information that he had learned, the captain continued to withdraw his command back to his original starting point. A short time after he started to move his patrol back toward his regimental headquarters, Thompson and his troop had a brief surprise encounter with a rather large detachment of Southern cavalrymen.

The last Confederate troops to leave the area around Union Mills were members of General Fitzhugh Lee's brigade. Acting as their division's rear guard, elements of Colonel Thomas L. Rosser's 5th Virginia Cavalry were the last of the Confederate cavalry to depart from around the Shriver homestead. Quite by accident as with so many other encounters during the Gettysburg Campaign, both Rosser's horsemen and the mounted members of Thompson's troop crossed paths as they moved in the rear of their respective divisions. The surprised cavalrymen from both sides exchanged a few ineffectual shots from their weapons. Captain Thompson's troopers had the decided advantage with the firepower of their Spencer rifles.[32]

Since both sides had no desire to have a prolonged and protracted fight at that particular time Thompson and his unidentified Confederate counterpart mutually decided to break off contact with each other. As the Southern troops withdrew, they moved farther to the east to avoid any additional contact with the men from Troop A of the 6th Michigan Cavalry. Captain Henry Thompson continued to move back toward Littlestown. Neither side reportedly suffered any casualties in the brief encounter.[33]

After Captain Thompson's arrival at Littlestown, sometime shortly before noon, he received orders to report to Colonel Russell Alger of the 5th Michigan Cavalry. Colonel Gray and the other nine troops of the 6th Michigan had already begun to move toward Hanover, while Alger's regiment was just returning from their scouting foray. Henry Thompson reported his information to Colonel Alger, but it was nothing that Alger did not already know since he, too, had seen many signs of the enemy's activity of the previous day.

Notes to Chapter Eight

1. Chamber of Commerce, *Encounter at Hanover*, p. 41.
2. Ibid., p. 43; Anthony, *History of the Battle of Hanover*, p. 2.
3. Anthony, *History of the Battle of Hanover*, p. 57.
4. Ibid., p. 58.
5. Ibid., p. 143.
6. Chamber of Commerce, *Encounter at Hanover*, p. 108.
7. Ibid., p. 179; Anthony, *History of the Battle of Hanover*, p. 152.
8. Gillespie, *A History of Company A, First Ohio Cavalry*, p. 148.
9. Boudrye, *Historic Records of the Fifth New York Cavalry*, p. 64.
10. Isham, *An Historical Sketch of the Seventh Regiment Michigan Volunteer Cavalry*, p. 14. Shortly after Gettysburg, the "Guard of Honor" disbanded. Too many of the best men from each troop were detached from their units when they could have been solidifying the ranks of their own small commands.
11. Anthony, *History of the Battle of Hanover*, p. 13.
12. Ibid.
13. Chamber of Commerce, *Encounter at Hanover*, pp. 42-43, 163-65. The Southerner, who was killed, was identified as an officer. No commissioned officers from any of Colonel Chambliss's regiments can be identified as having been killed during any of the fighting at Hanover on June 30. Additionally, no officers from either Hampton's Brigade or Lee's Brigade were listed as fatalities during the same period.
14. Regimental Association, *History of the Eighteenth Regiment of Cavalry, Pennsylvania Volunteers*, p. 217. Captain Freeland eventually found himself exchanged but his health was broken and he never returned to the 18th Pennsylvania. He received his discharge from the service on a Surgeon's Certificate of Disability in December 1863.
15. Ibid., p. 87.
16. Ibid., pp. 87-88.
17. Anthony, *History of the Battle of Hanover*, p. 2. Corporal Dannenhower found himself taken prisoner by the Confederates in another six days at Hagerstown, Maryland while participating in a mounted charge. The Confederates then shipped him to Richmond where he died in September 1863. Private Street died in action at the Battle of Fisher's Hill, Virginia on October 8, 1864.
18. Ibid.
19. Regimental Association, *History of the Eighteenth Regiment of Cavalry, Pennsylvania Volunteers*, p. 88.
20. Ibid.
21. Ibid.; Chamber of Commerce, *Encounter at Hanover*, p. 254.
22. Regimental Association, *History of the Eighteenth Regiment of Cavalry, Pennsylvania Volunteers*, pp. 87-89.
23. Anthony, *History of the Battle of Hanover*, p. 101.
24. Ibid.
25. Ibid.
26. Gillespie, *A History of Company A, First Ohio Cavalry*, pp. 148-49.
27. Chamber of Commerce, *Encounter at Hanover*, p. 239.

Notes to Chapter Eight (*continued*)

28. Ibid.; Anthony, *History of the Battle of Hanover*, p. 139. There is a conflicting report that Private Moran's death occurred after Kilpatrick's column had been turned back toward the fighting at Hanover. However, more facts point to the fact that the artillery battery was still heading toward Abbottstown when the explosion occurred.

29. Gillespie, *A History of Company A, First Ohio Cavalry*, p. 149; OR – 1, p. 1000; Chamber of Commerce, *Encounter at Hanover*, p. 239.

30. Gillespie, *A History of Company A, First Ohio Cavalry*, p. 149. Berlin is known as East Berlin today.

31. Robertson, *Michigan in the War*, p. 406.

32. James G. Genco, *Arming Michigan's Regiments, 1862 - 1864*, (n.p., n.d.), p. 96. There is no record of an Ordnance Return for Troop A, 6th Michigan Cavalry for June 30, 1863, in the National Archives. Information from the March 31, 1863, return lists Spencer rifles as the principal arm for the troop.

33. Robertson, *Michigan in the War*, p. 406.

Chapter 9:

Hot Time in Hanover

OUNDS of small-arms fire, along with the unmistakable boom and the reverberation of a cannon, wafted across the borough of Hanover and through the neighboring villages and homes of the surrounding area. It was shortly before 10:30 A.M. when the first assault began against the rear guard of the 3rd Division by members of the 13th Virginia Cavalry. General Judson Kilpatrick saw his division spread out for almost ten miles along the road between the center of Hanover and Abbottstown. The 1st Michigan Cavalry was the regiment located the farthest away from Hanover when the first sounds of the fighting reached them. They still maintained the leading position of the division. Colonel Mann's 7th Michigan was the next regiment in the line of march. They just finished passing through the tiny hamlet of Hendrix when they heard the noise of battle in their rear. General Kilpatrick, his staff members, and his bodyguard from the 1st Ohio Cavalry continued their halt at that place after the caisson accidentally exploded. Private Gillespie of the Buckeye regiment again recalled that:

> While resting here [Hendrix] we heard what seemed to be the report of firearms in the rear of our column. But some one said it was the cracking of the horses' feet on the stones. But as we listened the boom of a cannon was plainly heard, and then the General mounted his horse in haste and rode back to Hanover, it was said, in twenty minutes. Several of our horses were injured in trying to keep up with him as the column opened ranks to let us pass.[1]

General Kilpatrick, upon hearing the apparent roar of battle to the rear of his division, swiftly mounted his already exhausted horse. He immediately turned the animal back toward Hanover and the sounds of the guns. The general quickly retraced his route back along the road he had just traveled. He passed through two of General Farnsworth's regiments, the 1st Vermont and 1st West Virginia, that he met along the way. His staff members and the troopers of the 1st Ohio Cavalry had a difficult time keeping up with the accelerated pace set by an extremely anxious Kilpatrick.[2]

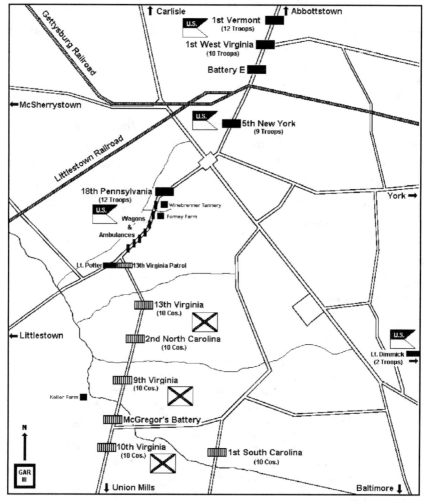

Positions of Union and Confederate Forces June 30, 1863, 10:30 A.M.
(GAR III)

Judson Kilpatrick, and the few members of his entourage able to keep pace with him, stopped for a brief time upon reaching the Pigeon Hills just north of Hanover. The general halted there for just a few minutes at most. He wanted to familiarize himself with the terrain and to observe the quickly escalating encounter between the rear of Farnsworth's brigade and that of Chambliss's troops. The fighting between the two opposing brigades was clearly visible in the distance to the south of the town.

At the Pigeon Hills, General Kilpatrick swung his horse off the Abbottstown Road to the right or toward the west. He pushed his already worn-out horse at breakneck speed through the cultivated fields of ripening corn and golden wheat. The headquarters staff and guard raced behind him for quite a distance, attempting to keep pace.

Bugler Gillespie from the 1st Ohio Cavalry was one of the horsemen who completed the race back to Hanover. He recalled that:

> As we came near the town we met our rear guard cheering lustily over some prisoners and a rebel flag they had captured. They stampeded upon the Fifth New York and First Virginia until these regiments had to go out into the field to let them pass. They then turned back and drove the rebels out of the town, capturing forty-two men and four officers, with their flag, and killing and wounding seventeen. The General quickly formed our men in line and then rode along before them, making a little complimentary speech on their brave charge, and saying: "Boys, look at me. I am General Kilpatrick. I want you to know me, and where I go I want you to follow. Stuart is making a call on us, and we are going to whip him."[3]

After he finally arrived back at the Center Square of Hanover, Kilpatrick found the first phase of the contest between the two rival forces already finished. It was around 11:30 A.M. as General Kilpatrick established his headquarters at the Central Hotel for the remainder of the engagement as well as the remainder of the day. The dependable horse that carried him so rapidly and unhesitatingly over the eight miles or so of roads and fields collapsed and died a few hours after his master's reckless journey back to Hanover. Displaying the brand of "CSA," the unnamed and unheralded horse was a captured Confederate mount. On that occasion Kilpatrick reinforced his nickname of "Kill-cavalry." Some citizens ultimately buried the faithful horse on Bunker Hill after the fighting. Bunker Hill was another elevation of ground to the north of Hanover, just slightly southwest of the Pigeon Hills. Bunker Hill was the same place where the two Union artillery batteries placed their ten guns during the fighting.[4]

Four of the 3rd Division's cavalry regiments, the 1st Michigan, the 7th Michigan, the 1st Vermont, and the 1st West Virginia found themselves strung out along the Abbottstown Road to the north of Hanover. Lieutenants Pennington and Elder's batteries were also moving on the same road with Elder's artillerymen being the closest to the town. An additional two regiments, the 5th and 6th Michigan, were operating to the south of Hanover near Littlestown. That left only two available regiments within the actual limits of the town to meet the immediate threat posed by the sudden appearance of the Confederate cavalry.

Fortunately one of the regiments still in Hanover was the veteran 5th New York Cavalry. Unfortunately Major Hammond's regiment found itself almost completely dismounted and widely scattered around the town square as well as a short distance north along Abbottstown Street. The New Yorkers were still enjoying the refreshments and fellowship being offered by the citizens when the initial sounds of the attack on Lieutenant Potter's detachment reached their ears. The small-arms firing was emanating from somewhere to the south of their position. The first inclination of many of the troopers was that someone was firing a welcome salute in honor of their unexpected arrival. That thought quickly passed after an artillery shell whistled overhead and landed squarely in the town with a resounding boom.[5]

The cavalrymen assigned to the leading troops of the 18th Pennsylvania Cavalry, like the 5th New York regiment before them, found themselves thinly stretched through the town. They had halted and dismounted near the Center Square of Hanover and all along the full length of Frederick Street to the south. The Pennsylvanians were just beginning to relish the food and drink offered by the exuberant citizens of their home state when a great and totally unexpected commotion broke loose behind them on the outskirts of the town.

The rapid popping noise of carbine and pistol firing at the rear of their main column had caused mass confusion among many of the un-tested and untried members of the 18th Pennsylvania. Those troopers closest to the sudden surge of the unexpected attack found themselves particularly vulnerable. The men under Lieutenant Colonel Brinton's command had more than enough sufficient warning to be able to mount their waiting horses. Nevertheless many of them seemed incapable of forming ranks to meet the unexpected attack by the charging and yelling cavalrymen of the 13th Virginia Cavalry. Major Gillette's regiment had mustered roughly 341 enlisted men during the previous month. However, with all the patrols, scouting parties, foraging parties, and other details of men detached from the regiment the main body of the 13th Virginia now charging into the rear of Kilpatrick's division consisted on no more than two hundred soldiers.

There was a primary reason for the 18th Pennsylvania Cavalry's in-ability to offer any kind of unified resistance at the earliest stages of the attack. The rear of the regiment got thrown into confusion because of the unexpected suddenness of having Lieutenant Potter and his forty men and horses, as well as many of the ambulances and wagons, charge through their ranks just before the enemy's appearance. Major William B. Darlington of the 18th Pennsylvania signed his regiment's official re-port about the skirmish at Hanover almost five weeks after the fighting for the absent Lieutenant Colonel Brinton. The major reported what had happened during the first few minutes of the attack. He stated that:

> Several squadrons had formed, when some am-
> bulances, which were in the rear, were driven by the
> frightened drivers through our ranks, creating so
> much confusion that we were compelled to retreat
> through the town, when we reformed.[6]

One small group of Pennsylvanians already mounted and presumably alert while supposedly guarding the right rear flank of Kil-patrick's column was led by 1st Lieutenant Thomas P. Shields. The lieu-tenant was the second-in-command of Troop G. His small detail from the 18th Pennsylvania, a combination of men from different troops in the regiment, had remained mounted along Frederick Street. They, like the rest of the command, were still partaking of the offerings presented by the citizens. The lieutenant's men were pretty well interspersed among the parked wagons and ambulances when the first shots rang out from near the intersection of the Frederick and Westminster roads.

Hearing the sudden commotion behind him as Lieutenant Potter's men drove past the patrol from the 13th Virginia Cavalry, Lieutenant Shields hastily turned his tiny detail, estimated at roughly twenty-five men, off Frederick Street and through an alley to the southeast. Operating with little information as to the identity or number of the attackers, the lieutenant ordered his mixed command to charge down a small side alley off Frederick Street in order to gain the rear of the equally, he believed, small column of attacking Confederates.

The lieutenant and his troopers from the 18th Pennsylvania Cavalry accomplished that maneuver with relative ease, acting much like veterans of many years in calmly moving forward to do battle. Unfortunately as Lieutenant Shields, along with the leading men immediately behind him, exited the alley they entered into a large open field on the southeast side of Hanover between Frederick and Baltimore streets. Much to the lieutenant's surprise and consternation, the advanced mounted elements of Lieutenant Colonel Payne's 2nd North Carolina Cavalry were already deploying through the fields and on both sides of Shields' small party.

In a matter of minutes, Lieutenant Shields and perhaps six or seven members of his command found themselves quickly surrounded and taken prisoner by the North Carolina regiment. The other luckier members of the lieutenant's attacking party, those who had not yet cleared the alley, were quickly able to turn their horses in the narrow alley. They hastened back to their starting point on Frederick Street with more of the enemy's cavalry in close pursuit.

Taken without much of a struggle or prolonged resistance because of the overwhelming numbers of the enemy into which he had run, Lieutenant Shields quickly found himself hustled to the rear of the Confederate line. He joined a growing number of prisoners, many of whom were from his own regiment. Much like Captain Freeland before him, Lieutenant Shields' participation in the war had now ended. Within three months Thomas Shields received his discharge from the U.S. Army in

October 1863. The Confederates exchanged the lieutenant almost immediately after his capture but his health was forever broken.[7]

Meanwhile the main body of the 18th Pennsylvania Cavalry had little option but to flow in the same general direction as their retreating comrades. Interspersed with the confusion of the soldiers were a large number of horses and wagons. The initial impact of the assault was just too much for Lieutenant Colonel Brinton's men to withstand. Two hundred Virginia horsemen and their charging horses quickly slashed and thrust their sabers at the surprised Pennsylvania cavalrymen as well as the almost defenseless teamsters. The free use of the saber caused most of the early casualties during the initial attack, particularly among the teamsters. During the engagement General Farnsworth's men suffered over two dozen casualties directly related to wounds inflicted by the saber, a solemn confirmation of the fierce hand-to-hand fighting.[8]

Just as that bit of chaos from the sudden attack by the 13th Virginia Cavalry ended, the 18th Pennsylvania received another undesired surprise. The 2nd North Carolina Cavalry under the command of the Virginian William Payne quickly charged into the retreating Pennsylvanians in two additional places. A portion, roughly half of the approximately 165 officers and enlisted men assigned, followed-up the success of the 13th Virginia. They moved swiftly along the Frederick Road practically to the town limits behind their Virginia comrades. That section of the North Carolinians pressed the advantage won by the 13th Virginia's sudden attack and plowed into the ranks of the 18th Pennsylvania from just north of the intersection of the Westminster and Frederick roads.

An additional detachment of the 2nd North Carolina swarmed through the side streets and alleys to Frederick Street. Many of those horsemen had crossed through the open fields and followed the retreating troopers of Lieutenant Shields' command. Lieutenant Colonel Payne personally commanded those eighty members of the regiment. The North Carolina troops successfully cut the demoralized and retreating Union regiment into two individual sections with their hurried thrust from the alleys across Frederick Street.

In the meantime, the other section of the 2nd North Carolina continued to pursue the scattered refugees of Lieutenant Shields' thwarted attack. They started to work their way toward the Center Square of Hanover. Both sections of the 2nd North Carolina converged on Frederick Street, trapping some twenty or twenty-five Union vehicles between them. Many of the wagons captured were the division and brigade ambulances, since those were mainly the only wagons traveling with Kilpatrick's command. The North Carolina troopers were soon driving the captured ambulances out the pike toward Buttstown and their own lines farther out the Westminster Road. Those wagons not captured in the initial Confederate attack quickly rumbled north through the center of the town, adding to the confusion.

Luckily for Kilpatrick, most of the 3rd Division's other baggage and supply wagons on the previous day had remained parked at Frederick. On June 30 the division's wagons left Frederick and were approaching Taneytown with the small guard from Troops C and L of the 5th Michigan Cavalry under the command of Major Dake. The wagons would eventually park at Taneytown along with the many other wagons from the rest of the Army of the Potomac. Captain Horace W. Dodge, twenty-eight years old, was the only commissioned officer serving with Troop C. He had roughly sixty-two enlisted men serving in his troop. Thirty-eight-year-old First Lieutenant Benjamin Franklin Axtell was the senior officer presently serving with Troop L. Lieutenant Axtell's command consisted of almost sixty-six enlisted men and one other commissioned officer, Second Lieutenant Robert C. Wallace.[9]

Completely surprised by the unanticipated attack, the 18th Pennsylvania, with over five hundred officers and enlisted men in the saddle, found itself almost instantly routed in the process by a considerably smaller enemy force. The Southern cavalrymen, who attacked by way of the many side streets and alleys, pushed across Frederick Street from southeast to northwest and completely cut Lieutenant Colonel Brinton's regiment into two individual components. They did all that with almost half the men that the Pennsylvania regiment had assigned. The Federal cavalry troopers caught between the two attacking columns south of Hanover made a hasty retreat to the west, away from the closely pursuing Confederate cavalry as well as their own brigade support. Neither the 13th Virginia nor the 2nd North Carolina regiments actively pursued those members of the 18th Pennsylvania, who fled across the open fields to the west of Hanover, very far.

Eventually those panicked Union troopers from Lieutenant Colonel Brinton's broken regiment, those who escaped from possible annihilation, halted their embarrassing retreat and reformed at McSherrystown, almost four miles away. They ultimately returned to Hanover later that afternoon and took up positions with the rest of their regiment.

Colonel Richmond in his official report as the interim brigade commander, submitted over nine weeks after the battle, stated that:

> As the Eighteenth Pennsylvania, which was in rear of the brigade, was entering the town, the enemy's cavalry made a dash upon it, opening at the same time with their artillery, which was posted in a wood about half a mile from the town. Owing to the suddenness of the attack, the regiment was thrown into some confusion and forced back upon the main column, throwing that also into confusion, and for a few moments the enemy evidently had a decided advantage.[10]

In hindsight, if the section of the North Carolina cavalry that had attacked through the side streets had turned their attention to the members of the 18th Pennsylvania caught in the southern part of the street they quite possibly could have captured quite a large group of the isolated Federal horsemen. They additionally could have secured all the vehicles and their teams of horses and mules. As it was, the North Carolinians after starting to move a few captured ambulances back toward their main line along the Westminster Road charged north into the center of town. As they moved into the Center Square they received a rather nasty surprise of their own.

The dismounted Northern cavalrymen from the 18th Pennsylvania and 5th New York regiments enjoying themselves around the town's Center Square quickly retreated when their comrades in the 1st Brigade rode up on them quite unexpectedly. The attacking members of the 13th Virginia and the 2nd North Carolina regiments followed those retreating Federals very closely. Many of the members of the 18th Pennsylvania attempted by any means possible to elude their pursuers. Dozens of them sought to escape by riding down the side streets and alleys of the town, not knowing what may lay beyond their immediate field of sight. Unfortunately, many of those Pennsylvanians found themselves trapped in dead ends with little option but to turn and fight their way out or surrender. To their credit, many of Brinton's men, who retreated to the north, were able to reform just on the other side of the Center Square, near the railroad tracks that crossed Abbottstown Street. At that point they connected with the hastily formed and ready troopers of the 5th New York.[11]

An unusual incident happened to Lyman W. Bliss, the assistant surgeon of the 10th Regiment, New York Volunteer Cavalry, during the charge by the Confederate cavalry along Frederick Street. Assistant Surgeon Bliss had been detached from his regiment, a unit in General David Gregg's 2nd Division, shortly after the June cavalry battles fought in Virginia. Temporarily detailed from his regiment, Bliss went to Hanover in order to establish a temporary hospital for the wounded men of his division. Lyman Bliss was in the Center Square of Hanover conversing with the men of Kilpatrick's division during the initial clash between Farnsworth and Chambliss's forces. One of the men, to whom he was speaking, was the assistant surgeon of the 18th Pennsylvania Cavalry, Samuel C. Williams. The regimental historian recalled the incident in the history of the 10th New York Cavalry. He remembered that:

> Surgeon Lyman W. Bliss, of the Tenth [New York Cavalry], was in charge of the field hospital at Hanover at the time the fight between Kilpatrick and Stuart took place. During the engagement the Doctor noticed a regiment or detachment give way, and then he saw that they appeared to be without an officer to lead them, and, turning to a fellow-surgeon [Assistant Surgeon Williams, 18th Pennsylvania Cavalry], he said: "Those fellows have no officer with them; let's go and lead them," and, discarding all insignia of the medical staff, they each obtained a saber and sailed in, urging the men forward to renew the action, but they appeared somewhat demoralized and refused to stand when another charge was made, but broke, leaving the gallant quinine-dispensers in the hands of the enemy. After making the acquaintance of some of the Confederate leaders, who undertook the useless task of drawing some valuable information from them, they were paroled after being retained two or three days.[12]

Assistant Surgeon Lyman W. Bliss,
10th New York Cavalry
(GAR III)

Assistant Surgeon Samuel C. Williams,
18th Pennsylvania Cavalry
(GAR III)

At the same time that Kilpatrick was rapidly galloping south toward Hanover after hearing the first sounds of the guns, Stuart pushed his own headquarters staff quickly ahead. The Confederates moved north on the Westminster Road. Stuart, who had been traveling with the members of his staff at the rear of Chambliss's brigade, immediately marched to the front and took personal control of the rapidly escalating situation in the streets of Hanover. A portion of Stuart's artillery had quickly maneuvered into position on some high ground south of town when reports arrived concerning the presence of the Union cavalry in Hanover.

Shortly before the initial confrontation, General Stuart had skillfully placed one of his two available artillery batteries in an excellent position on the high ground to the south of Hanover. Captain William McGregor received orders to place his two 3-inch rifled guns on the commanding heights of Rice's Hill to the east of the Westminster Road and directly south of the Center Square of Hanover. The hill was on the farm of John Rice. An extremely youthful but talented nineteen-year-old second lieutenant from Alexandria, William Hoxton, commanded that section of McGregor's battery. Lieutenant Hoxton survived a serious wound at the Battle of Trevilian Station in 1864 and ended his military career as a captain. William Hoxton's older brother Llewellyn was a May 1861 graduate of the U.S. Military Academy. Llewellyn Hoxton resigned his commission three weeks after graduation and entered the Confederate service where he, too, served his entire career in the artillery branch.[13]

Captain McGregor unlimbered the other two guns in his battery, the Napoleons, alongside the red brick farmhouse of Samuel Keller. Second Lieutenant Wilmer Brown commanded the two Napoleons. The artillery pieces sat on the opposite side of the Westminster Road from the Rice home and near a sharp bend in Plum Creek. Samuel Keller's house was almost due west from the position of Lieutenant Hoxton's guns. For now in this early stage of the developing battle, Brown's guns would also face toward Hanover in the north. Colonel Lucius Davis' 10th Virginia Cavalry had the duty of protecting the four guns of the two divided sections of McGregor's Battery.

In the interim, Captain Breathed, commanding the other artillery battery, received orders from a member of General Stuart's staff to press quickly forward and to position his guns on a slight rise along the Baltimore Pike at the Mount Olivet Cemetery. As in scores of other cities and towns across the continent, the elevation was known as Cemetery Hill. His 3-inch rifled pieces faced Hanover directly to the northwest. The section of two guns went into position on the western side of the Baltimore Pike in the actual cemetery grounds. Breathed's artillery sat among the headstones of many of the former inhabitants of Hanover. Temporarily detached from General Hampton's brigade Colonel Pierce Young and his eleven companies of cavalrymen from Cobb's Legion guarded Captain Breathed's two guns from any possible enemy incursion.

Upon the first reports of the seemingly minor contact with the Union cavalry forces, those unlucky troopers of Captain Freeland's small detachment, General Stuart hastily moved forward through the ranks of the men and horses of Colonel Chambliss's brigade. As the Confederate division commander reached the high ground to the southeast of Hanover the only enemy forces that he could see were those of the thinly strung-out 18th Pennsylvania Cavalry as it entered Hanover along the Frederick Road. One thing was certain to Stuart, there were undoubtedly more Union cavalrymen in front of him but he could not be absolutely certain of that unless he probed the enemy's position. Judson Kilpatrick and the horsemen of his 3rd Division, unfortunately for J. E. B. Stuart, were heading for the same pass in the hills to the north. Stuart originally intended to move through the Pigeon Hills along the Abbottstown Road in order to connect with the Army of Northern Virginia.

Perhaps General Stuart thought that Lieutenant Colonel Brinton's Pennsylvanians were just another minor inconvenience across his front. Most likely the Confederate troops could easily brush them aside, much like the luckless members of the 1st Delaware Cavalry in Westminster on the previous day. Perhaps General Stuart thought that the 18th Pennsylvania Cavalry would quickly turn and run instead of fighting with his veteran cavalry division. He was partly right, but he did not count on the appearance of the rest of Kilpatrick's division. Disregarding his original plan to bypass any contact with the Union troops in the region, General Stuart immediately formulated a plan for attacking that Yankee column and breaking through the town on his way to join Lee's army.

Why J. E. B. Stuart planned a vigorous attack on Kilpatrick's troopers instead of avoiding a fight in his haste to join General Lee, as he had originally intended, is unknown. It is true that he wanted to pass through the Pigeon Hills north of Hanover, but that was not the only route open to him. Eventually he moved farther to the east anyway. A detour around the town might have been successfully managed without losing any additional time or resources, considering the wasted time spent fighting the unwarranted battle.

Chaplain Louis N. Boudrye,
5th New York Cavalry
(Boudrye)

General Stuart could have broken off contact with the troopers of the 18th Pennsylvania at any time, even though his men from the 13th Virginia Cavalry had begun an unwanted general engagement with them. Surely the Confederate cavalry commander knew, based upon the latest intelligence reports supplied by his various scouting parties, that there were additional Union cavalry regiments nearby. Additionally a number of infantry regiments from the XII Corps were rapidly concentrating in the area to the south of Hanover. Any attack or delay by Stuart's forces might very well draw those infantrymen into the fight. Worse yet, he might become trapped between all the converging forces. After all, General David Gregg's 2nd Division of horsemen was then near Westminster on their way to Manchester, Maryland just nine miles southeast of Hanover. General Slocum's infantry corps was also just arriving at Littlestown.[14]

Chaplain Boudrye of the 5th New York Cavalry recalled in his regimental history that the reception for the New Yorkers in Hanover was still going strong and that:

This enjoyable state of things continued until about 10 o'clock; and while the Fifth was receiving the attentions of the people, the sudden report of a cannon was heard from one of the neighboring hills. At first this was taken as a friendly salute for our troops, but the deception was soon removed by a fierce charge of Rebel cavalry under immediate command of Gen. Stuart, upon the unsuspecting column in the street, sending terror to the people: especially to the ladies and children, who were paying their compliments to their defenders.[15]

As the battle began, Brigadier General Elon Farnsworth was about a mile north of Hanover at another small cluster of houses along the Abbottstown Road called New Baltimore. He clearly heard the distinctive pops of pistols and carbines firing in the rear of his column as his 1st Brigade continued to move northward. Farnsworth knew that the last two regiments of his brigade were probably still halted in the streets of Hanover and that was where the fighting seemed to be developing. Without waiting for instructions from the division commander, Farnsworth grasped the seriousness of the situation and promptly exhibited the initiative that had helped him to gain his first star. He quickly ordered his two leading regiments to countermarch back to the sound of the guns. Lieutenant Colonel Preston's 1st Vermont and Colonel Richmond's 1st West Virginia reversed their positions in the line of march and rapidly retraced their route to the south. General Farnsworth and the members of his staff, wasting no time themselves, rode down the line of troopers and rushed into the northern fringes of Hanover in the forefront of the returning Union cavalrymen.

Meanwhile the routed elements of Lieutenant Colonel Brinton's 18th Pennsylvania passed rapidly up Frederick Street, through a number of the dismounted members of Major Hammond's 5th New York, and into the Center Square. John Hammond, who upon seeing the panic stricken Pennsylvanians moving away from the sound of the fighting, rode a short distance down Frederick Street to learn the source of the trouble. Along the way he repeatedly admonished the citizens to clear the area and return to their homes and the safety of their cellars since it looked like the beginning of a major conflict.

The major threaded his way along Frederick Street and through the throng of confused Union troopers, as well as their panic stricken horses. Major Hammond's own horse, a nine-year-old Morgan called Pink, calmly carried him along the chaotic street. The horse served throughout the entire term of service of his master. Hammond rode almost half the length of Frederick Street where he came across Lieutenant Colonel Payne's 2nd North Carolina moving quickly toward him.[16]

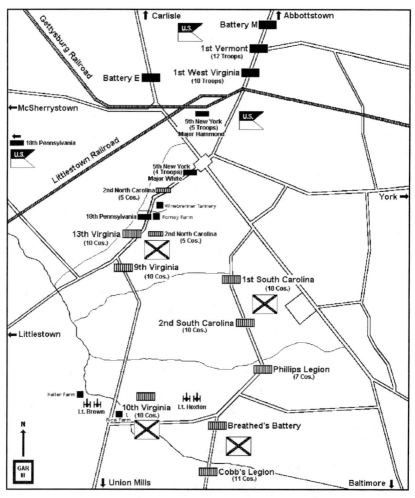

Positions of Union and Confederate Forces June 30, 1863, 11:00 A.M.
(GAR III)

Turning his back on the rapidly advancing horsemen from the 2nd North Carolina Cavalry, Hammond quickly retraced his steps back along Frederick Street and through the Center Square. As he moved away from the advancing Confederates, he gathered the members of his scattered regiment from near the Center Square and along Abbottstown Street. Hammond quickly moved them farther to the north end of town. He ordered the men of the 5th New York to form on the town's Public Common a vacant field recommended by a local resident as a good place to form his regiment. The Public Common sat near the town's railroad station, located one block off Abbottstown Street to the west—between Abbottstown and Carlisle streets. Major Hammond with the capable assistance of Major Bacon and Major White hastily formed the command into a line of battle at the Public Common. Many of the cavalrymen filtering in from the 18th Pennsylvania also joined them.

Major Hammond, in his official report written after the battle, recalled that his command, although initially surprised, was soon ready for the fight:

> While resting, an attack was made upon the ambulances and stragglers in rear of the Eighteenth Pennsylvania, driving them in upon the regiment, and completely breaking up the column, which ran in confusion up the street upon the rear of my regiment, which had faced about, and was trying to clear the streets of the fugitives preparatory to making a charge upon the advancing column of the enemy.[17]

Without waiting for further instructions a battalion composed of four troops from the 5th New York received orders from their officers to draw sabers. Major Amos H. White, along with the adjutant of the regiment 1st Lieutenant Alexander Gall by his side, led the first wave of New Yorkers into the escalating conflict. The hastily organized battalion of Union horsemen moved forward to meet the threat posed by the opening onslaught of the 2nd North Carolina and 13th Virginia cavalrymen. Major White's battalion of New Yorkers moved south along Abbottstown Street first at a walk and then, when the bugler sounded the signal, at a charge through the Center Square.

Lieutenant Potter of the 18th Pennsylvania, who safely led the majority of his men in the rear guard through the ranks of the 13th Virginia Cavalry, stopped when he and his men reached the steady ranks of the veteran 5th New York. He remembered that:

> Hearing the firing in their rear they [5th New York] were mounting their horses and some of them joined us in driving them back. It was here that I was joined by Adjutant Gall of the 5th New York. He rode with me at the head of the first set of fours. He did not get far, when he fell from his horse. We were again driven back and this time the whole regiment joined in and we drove them to a standstill. It was here up a lane, with a high, stiff post and rail fence on each side, the cutting and slashing was done and for a few in the very front it was a hand-to-hand fight.[18]

As they galloped south through the Center Square and out Frederick Street, the 5th New York's first mounted charge temporarily stunned the overconfident and fiercely determined cavalrymen from Colonel Chambliss's Virginia and North Carolina regiments. The quick response from the temporarily surprised Union forces momentarily stalled the Confederate's rapid advance into the center of Hanover. The leading cavalrymen in Major White's gallant charge were mostly members of Troop A. Thirty-three-year-old Captain Luke McGuinn was their commander. His junior officers included First Lieutenant Theodore Boice and Second Lieutenant Frazier A. Boutelle. Troop A sustained the most casualties of any of the 5th New York Cavalry's troops engaged in the brief charge through the streets of Hanover. Lieutenant Boutelle received a serious injury when his horse was killed during the charge and fell on top of him, pinning him until his men could extricate him and remove him from additional danger. Captain McGuinn came through the fight at Hanover without a scratch, but ultimately would be killed in action at Parker's Store during the Battle of the Wilderness on May 5, 1864. Lieutenant Boice survived the battle, campaign, and the war. Eventually he mustered out of the service as lieutenant colonel of the 5th New York.[19]

Captain Augustus Barker, temporarily detached from the command of the 5th New York's absent Troop L, led a segment of the first wave of Union troopers behind Major White. His Troop L, along with Troop M, was now moving under the direction of Lieutenant Dimmick toward Abbottstown to avoid further contact with the men of Hampton's brigade. Captain Barker, only twenty-two years old, received credit later in the battle for the single-handed capture of Captain John A. Billingsley of the 9th Virginia and five Southern privates as the New Yorkers pressed their attack against the outnumbered Confederates. The captain's orderly, Private Phillip M. Place, was not as lucky as his commanding officer. He found himself taken prisoner while riding by Captain Barker's side. Unfortunately, the gallant Captain Barker would only survive the war for another couple of months. He received a mortal wound in another skirmish at Kelly's Ford, Virginia on September 14, 1863, and died four days later.[20]

The initial shock of their mounted counterattack allowed Major White's troopers to easily drive their opponents before them. The two opposing columns met, principally, along the length of Frederick Street and in the many alleys off that main thoroughfare. As in most closely fought actions, it became a life and death struggle between individual soldiers. Numerous hard-fought personal hand-to-hand contests with both sabers and pistols ensued between the determined men from New York, North Carolina, Pennsylvania, and Virginia.

While riding in the first rank of the battalion of charging New Yorkers and while pressing the enemy very hard near the end of Frederick Street, Adjutant Gall suddenly fell from his horse. A bullet had struck him in the head as he quickly evaluated the situation and moved forward with his men. The lethal little projectile killed him instantly by entering through his left eye and passing completely through his head. Slumping from his saddle, he lay sprawled in the middle of the road directly in front of William Wolf's residence. Mr. Wolf's home was on the northeastern side of Frederick Street, roughly five blocks from the Center Square. Blood poured from Lieutenant Gall's fatal wound and slowly seeped into the dirt beneath him as the fighting continued to rage all around his now lifeless form.[21]

His comrades in the regiment hastily recovered Alexander Gall's body before they temporarily withdrew back through the Center Square of the town. Adjutant Gall was originally buried in St. Matthew's

Lutheran Church cemetery on Chestnut Street after the fighting had finally subsided. Eventually his body was removed from that resting place and he was re-interred in the New York section of the National Cemetery at Gettysburg. The thirty-nine-year-old Gall had originally enlisted as a private in the regiment in 1861. He diligently worked his way up through the enlisted ranks to serve as the regimental sergeant major before receiving his commission as a first lieutenant in January 1863.[22]

Also, while still leading his battalion from among the first set of horsemen, Major White suffered a serious gunshot wound to his right foot. As the major and his command approached the intersection of the Westminster and Frederick roads, only a short distance beyond the site where Adjutant Gall received his fatal wound, White felt a dull thud and a searing pain shot up his right leg. A bullet slightly splintered the bone in his foot just below his ankle. Luckily the bullet that hit him was almost spent, otherwise it might have taken his foot off or necessitated its amputation.

Major White's wound proved to be excruciatingly painful and extremely incapacitating as his boot filled with his own blood. However, the major was able to remain on top of his skittish horse, enabling him to retreat back toward the Center Square of Hanover when his battalion's charge ran out of momentum. Because of the debilitating nature of the wound White spent considerable time in one of the locally established hospitals and spent additional time recuperating at home in New York. It would be a long three months before he rejoined his regiment at the end of September.[23]

A thirty-year-old bachelor from Syracuse, New York, White assisted in raising Company D of the regiment in 1861. He mustered into the volunteer service as their original first lieutenant. White served in the regiment for its entire history and finally ended his military career as the colonel of the 5th New York Cavalry. During his time with the regiment Amos White compiled a superb record. He participated in fifty-one engagements, received three painful wounds, and was captured twice. He spent almost three months at Libby Prison in Richmond, Virginia and another four months at the prison in Salisbury, North Carolina. Fortunately, his exchange took place relatively quickly on both occasions.[24]

Major Amos H. White,
5th New York Cavalry
(Boudrye)

Up to the point when their battalion commander received his wound, Major White's men had the enemy's cavalry on the run and immediate victory within their grasp. The surprising audacity and quickness of the Federal cavalrymen had enabled them to charge through the ranks of the thinly spread regiments of the 13th Virginia and 2nd North Carolina. Although the New Yorkers and some members of the 18th Pennsylvania inflicted a substantial number of casualties upon the two Southern regiments, a few killed and wounded of their own would not stop them.

The Yankee troopers easily swept their foes before them. Among the wounded of the 13th Virginia was its commander, Major Joseph Gillette. As he was leading his regiment forward, Gillette suffered a serious gunshot wound to the neck. Taken to the rear area of his brigade by an unknown member of his staff, Major Gillette's participation in the Gettysburg Campaign had come to a premature conclusion. He continued to move with Stuart's column, riding in one of the captured ambulances. Eventually he returned to his home in Virginia to recuperate and rejoined his regiment during August 1863.[25]

In a post-war letter, Captain William A. Graham assigned to Company K of the 2nd North Carolina Cavalry remembered the action that basically devastated his already depleted regiment. Although he did not command his company in the streets of Hanover, Graham recalled that:

> Nearly all of the regt. [2nd North Carolina] present for duty was killed or captured: the other regiment [13th Virginia] of the brigade not supporting it in the charge to "cut through the Federal army at this place." After having gone considerable into the town, finding the enemy closing in on their rear, they attempted to turn and cut their way out by charging down the different streets, but only some forty succeeded in doing so. I learned these facts from Lt. [Randall H.] Reese of "H" Co. who was in the action.[26]

In a very few moments the surprising show of resistance offered by the charging members of the 5th New York and 18th Pennsylvania regiments allowed them to sweep the Confederates back to the very outskirts of the town. Clearing the town limits, the portions of the two regiments quickly passed the Winebrenner Tannery and the Karl Forney farm. They then reached Buttstown along the Frederick Road and continued to drive the enemy's cavalry before them.

Lieutenant Henry Potter and some of his men from the division's rear guard, after reaching Major White's horsemen near the Center Square, turned their horses around and joined in the 5th New York's assault on the 2nd North Carolina and the 13th Virginia. Privates Jacob R. Harvey and John F. Roller, both assigned to Potter's Troop M, were shot and killed as the charging Union horsemen passed near Buttstown. Trooper Harvey received his mortal wound as he rode alongside Lieutenant Potter. Harvey fell off his horse and sprawled onto Potter's horse, where the lieutenant then, unceremoniously, pushed him to the ground. It is uncertain whether Private Harvey was dead before he hit the ground or if he died by being trampled by the scores of horses behind him. In any event, at the end of the charge Jacob Harvey was dead. Two other members of Potter's troop received severe wounds at the same time.[27]

Now as they headed for Buttstown just past the intersection of the Frederick and Westminster roads, the 5th New York and the 18th

Pennsylvania Cavalry's leading troops began to lose their impetus. Thus far the Federals' mounted charge had traveled slightly less than one mile from the Center Square. The Union and Confederate forces fiercely contested every foot along Frederick Street. Both sides were tired and bloodied. Both sides had suffered a number of casualties during only a few minutes of harsh fighting. Initially the Confederate soldiers received a nasty shock when Major White and his battalion of New Yorkers intervened and halted the onslaught of the 13th Virginia and 2nd North Carolina regiments. As the exuberant Union troopers neared the Westminster Road they were about to come face-to-face with yet another unpleasant surprise of their own.

An additional regiment from General Stuart's division, being held in mounted reserve, was waiting near the intersection of the Westminster Road. That unit, the 9th Virginia Cavalry under the command of Colonel Richard Beale, poured a devastating hail of lead into the charging ranks of the unsuspecting members of 5th New York and 18th Pennsylvania regiments. The sudden volley fired by the almost five hundred Virginians emptied many more saddles and included the wounding of Major White. Beale's regiment had more men assigned right now than both the 2nd North Carolina and 13th Virginia combined. The accurate firing from Colonel Beale's men halted the forward thrust of Major White's battalion. Forced to withdraw because of the murderous fire, the New Yorkers and Pennsylvanians moved back along Frederick Street toward the Center Square where they sought additional support from the remainder of their regiment.[28]

Getting pushed back by the sudden appearance of another fresh Confederate regiment from Colonel Chambliss's brigade the men of the 5th New York, with limited support from some members of the 18th Pennsylvania, fell back along the same street through which they had just successfully charged. The street was full of the debris of the recent fighting. Dead and wounded soldiers from both sides, as well as dozens of their dead and wounded horses, littered the length of Frederick Street from the Center Square to the edge of town. The commander of the 18th Pennsylvania's Troop K, Captain David Hamilton, lost his horse in a volley of bullets fired at him from along Frederick Street. Surprisingly, Hamilton suffered no injuries falling from his dead horse.[29] Private Mills E. Powell from Company A of the 13th Virginia Cavalry had his horse shot from under him at the very beginning of the encounter. His horse died near the Forney farm, forcing Powell to beat a hasty retreat on foot back toward the Westminster Road to avoid being captured by any of the advancing Yankees.[30]

Major White's retreating Union cavalrymen did not go too far before they ran into Major William P. Bacon near the Center Square. Major Bacon was in the process of leading the remainder of the 5th New York regiment briskly along Frederick Street toward the sound of the fighting. The retreat of White's battalion away from the enemy's charging troops stopped at that point. Hammond had ordered the last of his men, the final five troops present in his command, into the fray. He hoped that he would be able to successfully defend the town until General Farnsworth's anticipated arrival with the 1st Vermont and 1st West Virginia regiments. Very shortly, Bacon's troops would try to force the Confederates out of Frederick Street for the final time.

In just one hour the fighting between the two antagonists had rapidly escalated and spread throughout the area to the south of Hanover. The heaviest fighting occurred mainly around Frederick Street and included many of the side streets and alleys. Many troopers from both sides fell from their mounts with serious saber wounds, along with critical gunshot wounds, thus underscoring the close contact and furious nature of the engagement.

Major Hammond in his official report of the engagement at Hanover stated that:

> General Farnsworth arriving at this time from the front, the men were reformed, and made another charge, driving the rebels in confusion along the road and through the fields. Private Burke, of Company A, captured a battle-flag from the enemy in this charge, and subsequently turned it over to General Kilpatrick.[31]

The fighting eventually got reduced to smaller groups of men fighting for their lives. Privates Thomas Burke and William Herrick assigned to Troop A of the 5th New York Cavalry spied a solitary figure in gray savagely attacking Sergeant Owen McNulty from Troop C. Both Burke and Herrick knew McNulty, since all had been with the regiment since its formation in 1861. The Confederate attacker, who happened to be the regimental color-bearer of the 13th Virginia Cavalry, used his pistol with lethal accuracy. He had already seriously wounded McNulty in the arm and hand.[32]

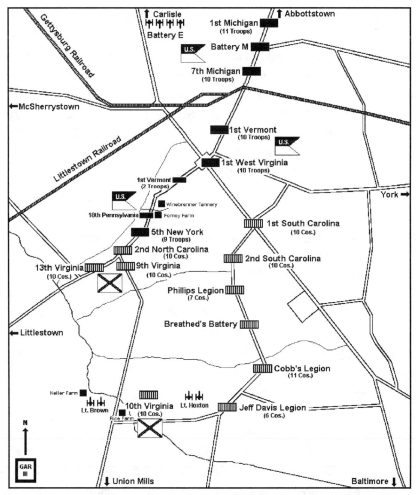

Positions of Union and Confederate Forces June 30, 1863, 11:30 A.M.
(GAR III)

Riding quickly forward to Sergeant McNulty's assistance, Thomas Burke and William Herrick joined the contest. For his efforts Private Herrick was shot and slightly wounded by another assailant before getting too much farther. Private Burke was a bit more fortunate. Using his own revolver, he shot and severely wounded the Southern cavalrymen who had been battling with McNulty. In the process Burke found that he was now the proud possessor of the regimental battle flag belonging to the 13th Virginia Cavalry.

For the action of capturing an enemy's regimental battle-flag an action considered to be quite heroic during the Civil War, Private Thomas Burke received the Medal of Honor. Burke was the only member of General Kilpatrick's division to receive the Medal of Honor for the fighting at Hanover. Private Herrick's wound proved to be very minor and he continued to serve with the regiment. Sergeant McNulty recovered from his two bullet wounds and continued his service with the 5th New York Cavalry. He found himself captured twice during 1864 but survived until mustered out of the regiment at the close of the war.[33]

General Farnsworth, who was a brigade commander for just one full day, arrived back in Hanover shortly after the beginning of Major Hammond's second attack under the command of the twenty-seven-year-old Major Bacon. The young brigadier calmly reformed the rest of his two strung-out regiments, the 5th New York and 18th Pennsylvania, and had them continue the attack through the streets to the south of Hanover. The general also ordered Lieutenant Elder's battery to move north along the Carlisle Road in order to take position on the high ground located there.

Colonel Richmond's 1st West Virginia Cavalry, the next regiment to reach Hanover after Farnsworth's arrival, marched briskly into the Center Square and began to move southeast along Baltimore Street. The mounted troopers of Richmond's command charged only a few blocks along Baltimore Street where they encountered stiff resistance by the Confederate cavalrymen of the 1st South Carolina who were moving toward them from their position near the Mount Olivet Cemetery. The fighting had already spilled over from Frederick Street. Many individual encounters continued between the opposing cavalry forces.

Many of the West Virginians charged along almost the entire length of Baltimore Street. Many found themselves cut off from the main body of their regiment when a small group of Confederate troopers from the South Carolina regiment successfully flanked them and moved in behind them from a side street. The West Virginia regiment lost almost nineteen men captured or missing in action during their initial charge against the advancing units of General Hampton's brigade. After their first attack stalled in the streets, the 1st West Virginia cavalrymen regrouped, fell back a short distance, and were ordered to fight dismounted. The dismounted troopers then advanced forward a few blocks and lapsed into a long range action that would become so prevalent during the fighting of the afternoon. While the dismounted troopers from the 1st West Virginia engaged the enemy along the length of Baltimore Street, every fourth man from the regiment led the horses of three of his comrades back toward the safety of the Public Common.

The majority of the 1st West Virginia's casualties in their initial charge, those killed or wounded, suffered their injuries from the effects of bullet wounds. However, two men from Troop L, Sergeant George Collins and Corporal John Brooks, received serious injuries when an artillery shell from Breathed's Battery posted at the Mount Olivet Cemetery exploded near them. Riding near the middle blocks of Baltimore Street, Sergeant Collins' leg was almost completely torn from his body, mortally wounding him, while his horse was immediately killed. Riding next to Collins, Corporal Brooks received only a slight wound from the shrapnel of the same shell.[34]

Their comrades moved both Collins and Brooks behind the regiment's skirmishers to near the Center Square. Their friends took the two soldiers to the home of George Washington Welsh on the northwest side of the street, only a short distance from the spot where they were wounded. The next day, July 1, Sergeant Collins moved to the hospital established in an empty meeting hall on York Street. He died at that place later that day.[35]

Private Henry Holman, also serving with Troop L, received a gunshot wound in the face during the same assault by the members of the 1st West Virginia. The private laid unconscious on Baltimore Street. His friends in the troop removed him to the home of Mrs. Agnes Spangler, located in the second block of York Street on the northern side. At first, a local doctor from town treated Holman's serious wound. He eventually transferred to one of the hospitals after the battle where he recovered.[36]

The battle action was swirling about Baltimore and Frederick streets and throughout the dozens of side streets and alleys off those two main arteries. As the fighting continued, General Elon Farnsworth made his way, in the company of Major John Hammond, to the roof of William Wirt's house on the northeast side of Baltimore Street and the Center Square. Farnsworth's staff had commandeered the Wirt home and turned the house into the 2nd Brigade's headquarters during the rest of the fighting.[37]

Cautiously standing on the roof of the building, Farnsworth with the aid of his field glasses could clearly discern the positions of the regiments in Stuart's division and particularly Colonel Chambliss's brigade. The general and Major Hammond also noticed that members of Hampton's brigade were beginning to deploy to the left flank of the Union troops, who were still fighting along Frederick and Baltimore streets. By that time, the battle had degenerated into scores of smaller fights all over the southern portion of the borough. Hampton's men were clearly forming in a line of battle to the northeast of the Mount Olivet Cemetery, between the Baltimore and York roads. Additionally, General Hampton had ordered a small portion of Lieutenant Colonel Twiggs' 1st South Carolina regiment forward. They operated against the members of Farnsworth's cavalry as dismounted skirmishers.[38]

The 1st Vermont Cavalry, the regiment that had been leading the brigade earlier in the day as they passed through Hanover, was now the last of General Farnsworth's regiments to return to the streets of the town. From his vantage point on the Wirt roof Farnsworth saw that the Confederate forces were swiftly moving into a position that could easily flank and then completely cut off the gallant men of the 5th New York and 18th Pennsylvania regiments. Colonel Beale had sent a portion of his regiment along the same route that the 2nd North Carolina had taken earlier in the day. The Confederates had started to move through the open fields between Baltimore and Frederick streets.

The newly commissioned brigadier general ordered Lieutenant Colonel Preston, who had just joined him at the Wirt home, to send two troops from his leading battalion from the 1st Vermont to the aid of the New Yorkers and Pennsylvanians along Frederick Street. Twenty-six-year-old Major John W. Bennett commanded the first battalion in the regiment's line of march. Major Bennett was personally riding at the head of his 3rd Battalion, consisting of Troops A, D, K, and M, when half of it was ordered into the fighting on Frederick Street. Bennett selected the first two troops to advance while his other two troops remained in support. Troop D, under the command of Captain William G. Cummings, and Troop M, commanded by twenty-three-year-old Captain John W. Woodward, composed the detail that moved forward. Woodward was the son of the 1st Vermont Cavalry's chaplain, John H. Woodward. The younger Woodward would survive the war for just another short week. He died in the regiment's action at Hagerstown on July 6.[39]

The Vermonters' orders were to support the exhausted members of the 5th New York and 18th Pennsylvania regiments. Major Bennett's detachment consisted of six commissioned officers and roughly 125 non-commissioned officers and enlisted men.[40] Those two troops of the 1st Vermont almost equaled the whole regimental strength of the 2nd North Carolina when they first engaged Kilpatrick's men earlier in the day. The horsemen of Major Bennett's command quickly spurred their horses through the Center Square and out the southern side of the town along Frederick Street. Almost immediately Bennett's troopers captured approximately twenty prisoners from the worn-out 13th Virginia and 2nd North Carolina regiments.

Since that portion of the fight was just about finished, the advancing two troops of the 1st Vermont had very little else to do except to make sure that the Rebel cavalry did not try to flank them. However, the sudden appearance of relatively fresh Federal troops near the Winebrenner Tannery did cause the Confederate command to discontinue any further action on that portion of the battlefield. For the present time Lieutenant Colonel Preston and the rest of the 1st Vermont Cavalry remained near the intersection of Abbottstown and York streets. They were placed as a general support for the 1st West Virginia Cavalry besides acting as a deterrent to the dismounted members of the 1st South Carolina Cavalry, still clearly visible to the southeast.[41]

The 13th Virginia Cavalry secured an initial limited success with their surprise attack on the rear elements of the 18th Pennsylvania Cavalry earlier in the day. That attack was followed by the supporting attack of the 2nd North Carolina. Nonetheless the overall strategy of attacking the Union cavalry force was doomed to failure. The Southern cavalry did capture some additional wagons, a few ambulances, and a number of prisoners but they gained little else for their efforts. General Stuart found his three brigades too widely scattered to be able to coordinate any type of final crushing attack against General Kilpatrick's equally dispersed command. Colonel Chambliss's four regiments, the leading brigade of Stuart's division, found themselves fully committed to the attack, except for the 10th Virginia, which was still guarding McGregor's Battery on Rice's Hill and at the Keller farm.

When General Hampton's men arrived on the battlefield it was already too late to follow up any advantage that the initial attack by Chambliss's brigade had gained. The 5th New York and the 18th Pennsylvania regiments proceeded to force Colonel Chambliss's three forward regiments out of Hanover. General Farnsworth's other two regiments were on the verge of entering Hanover and deploying to cover their comrades' left flank. General Fitzhugh Lee had not yet arrived on the field with his brigade. In addition, General Stuart was about to learn that two more Union cavalry regiments were approaching Hanover from Littlestown, a situation that could possibly put those two units in his rear if he deemed to more fully press the attack into the streets of Hanover. The two regiments, the 5th and 6th Michigan, were moving rapidly toward the sound of the firing and would arrive in the vicinity shortly after the troopers of Farnsworth's brigade secured the town.

Upon the final retreat of Colonel Chambliss's regiments from the streets of Hanover, Lieutenant Colonel William Payne, the temporarily assigned commander of the 2nd North Carolina Cavalry, received a slight wound. Additionally he had his horse shot from under him and embarrassed himself by somehow falling into a vat full of tanning liquid in front of the Winebrenner Tannery on the Frederick Road.

Lieutenant Colonel William H. F. Payne,
Temporary Commander,
2nd North Carolina Cavalry
(LC)

At least two Union cavalrymen, one identified from the 5th New York and one unidentified from the 1st Vermont, claimed credit for capturing Lieutenant Colonel Payne during the fighting near the Winebrenner Tannery. Both stories, undoubtedly, became embellished as the years passed and one of the tales, also, has a number of inconsistencies and untruths within it.[42]

Probably the most widely circulated and, therefore, the most widely accepted story of Payne's capture concerns a member of the 5th New York Cavalry. According to Private Abram Folger of Troop H, he, supposedly, captured the Rebel colonel along with his orderly. Folger's troop advanced in the second wave of the 5th New York's attack concentrated along Frederick Street. As the New Yorkers charged forward, they became involved in their own personal and individual struggles with their counterparts from the 2nd North Carolina regiment. During that time, Private Folger became separated from his comrades and allegedly found himself captured by Lieutenant Colonel Payne and his orderly.[43]

In short order his captors led Private Folger, now dismounted and stripped of his accouterments, to the Confederate rear to the southeast of the town. In one of the story's many inconsistencies, the mounted Payne and his mounted orderly, personally, escorted the dismounted Yankee private back to their lines. It is inconceivable that Lieutenant Colonel Payne, commanding a regiment and in the heat of an undecided battle, would take the extra time involved to bring one lowly Union trooper off the field of combat.

As the story continues, while marching past the Winebrenner Tannery on the Frederick Road, he spotted a carbine lying on the ground. Quickly grabbing that carbine, Folger shot and killed the colonel's horse, causing Payne to tumble into a vat of liquid in the tannery yard. Meanwhile, according to Folger's testimony, the orderly's pistol misfired and, incredibly, Folger was able to make him a prisoner. It is highly unlikely that Folger acquired anything but a single-shot carbine. The dropped carbine could have been from some unfortunate member of the 5th New York, 18th Pennsylvania, or some Confederate trooper. The odds are that it was a single-shot weapon. Unless the carbine that Folger picked up was a repeating rifle, a highly unlikely option on that part of the battlefield at that time, he would have had only one cartridge in the chamber to fire. After shooting the colonel's horse, Folger claims that he took the colonel and orderly prisoner with an empty gun. Would the two prisoners not know the characteristics of a carbine? Would they surrender to a private with an empty gun? What happened to all the other combatants from both armies during this time?[44]

Lieutenant Colonel Payne was definitely a sight to see after his brief swim in the tanning vat. According to Private Folger "his gray uniform with its velvet facing and white gauntlet gloves, his face and hair had all been completely stained, so that he presented a most laughable sight." Private Folger then escorted his two prisoners back toward the Union lines and the Center Square, where he presented them to the proper authorities.[45]

The unidentified trooper from the 1st Vermont Cavalry received far less credit for Lieutenant Colonel Payne's capture and a lot less publicity. Payne's capture still took place at the Winebrenner Tannery. According to this tale, Colonel Payne became unhorsed during the fierce struggle along the Frederick Road. Trying to avoid capture, the colonel ran into the tannery yard and tripped or otherwise fell into one of the large tanning vats. Crawling out of the slimy liquid he took shelter in one of the outbuildings, the loft of a barn, on the tannery property. Lieutenant Colonel Payne then waited for his chance to return safely to his own lines south of his current position.

Shortly the unidentified trooper appeared, having sought shelter in the same building as Payne. Again, as with the scenario involving Private Folger, Lieutenant Colonel Payne personally captured the unknown Union soldier. There, in the loft of the barn, the two men waited for the outcome of the battle raging around them. It would seem highly unlikely that a man of Payne's character would hide in a barn while the outcome of the battle was still unknown. After the passing of some additional time, William Payne considered himself in a perilous position because of the apparent Union victory and surrendered to the unidentified Yankee private. Sergeant Horace Ide from Troop D, 1st Vermont Cavalry reported that:

> Lieutenant Colonel Payne, now seeing that the game was up, told his man that seeing he had been so polite as to surrender to him, he would return the compliment and Payne gave up his arms to him and they both came down and in due course of time Payne was turned over to the Provost Marshal.[46]

The events surrounding the unknown private's capture of Lieutenant Colonel Payne are much more believable than the events related by Private Folger. At the time of the arrival of the 1st Vermont's cavalrymen along Frederick Street, the fiercest hand-to-hand fighting had subsided to a great extent, as is evidenced by the fact that no Vermonters lost their lives or received any serious wounds at that particular place. Troops D and M, the only two Vermont troops involved on that portion of the battlefield, suffered the loss of just six men missing in action and presumed captured.[47]

In any event, there are several facts about Payne's capture by one of Farnsworth's troopers that are indisputable. Lieutenant Colonel William Payne found himself taken captive at the Winebrenner Tannery on Frederick Street. He did fall into a tanning vat that stained his hair, skin, and uniform. Finally, Payne did spend a considerable amount of time as a prisoner of war before being exchanged.[48]

As the contest continued, General Stuart personally directed the movements of additional men onto the field. Stuart and his staff members continued to push their own advance into the southern sections of Hanover. Erroneously thinking that his cavalrymen had cleared the men of General Farnsworth's brigade from that portion of the town, General Stuart found himself riding directly into a sizable group of charging Yankees. Finding himself almost trapped in a field situated between the Westminster and Frederick roads, Stuart turned back toward his own lines. As the troopers of the 1st Brigade pursued him, along with the few accompanying members of his staff, Stuart spurred his horse forward and valiantly attempted to return to the safety of his own lines. General Stuart's thirty-two-year-old chief engineer, Captain William Willis Blackford, recalled that:

> The road was lined on each side by an ill-kept hedge, grown up high, but at some places, fortunately for us, there were gaps of lower growth. Stuart pulled up, and waving his saber with a merry laugh, shouted to me and then lifted his mare, Virginia, over the hedge into the field. . . . I followed him. I had only that morning, fortunately, mounted Magic, having had her led previously, and Stuart had done the same with Virginia, so they were fresh. As we alighted in the field, we found ourselves within ten paces of the front of a flanking party of twenty-five or thirty men which was accompanying the charging regiment, and they called us to halt; but as we let our two thoroughbreds out, they followed in hot pursuit, firing as fast as they could cock their pistols. The field was in tall timothy grass and we did not see, nor did our horses until close to it, a huge gully fifteen feet wide and as many deep stretched across our path. There were only a couple of strides of distance for our horses to regulate their step, and Magic had to rise at least six feet from the brink. Stuart and myself were riding side by side

and as soon as Magic rose I turned my head to see
how Virginia had done it, and I shall never forget the
glimpse I then saw of this beautiful animal away up in
midair over the chasm and Stuart's fine figure sitting
erect and firm in the saddle.[49]

General Kilpatrick arrived in Hanover after the first two assaults by
the combined troops of the 5th New York and 18th Pennsylvania, along
with the additional support from the two troops of the 1st Vermont Cavalry had finished their work. They drove the enemy's cavalry forces
completely out of the town. The Confederates retreated behind their supporting units near the Rice farm along the Westminster Road. Kilpatrick,
after his quick return to Hanover, established his headquarters in the
Central Hotel on the Center Square. He and the members of his staff immediately went up to the hotel's roof to observe the positions of their
own forces as well as those of the enemy to the south of town.[50]

As soon as General Farnsworth's men determined that they had
driven the Southern cavalrymen from the far southern portions of Hanover, soldiers and civilians began to barricade the main streets to the
south—Frederick, Baltimore, and York streets—as well as the numerous
side streets. "Store boxes, wagons, hay ladders, fence rails, barrels, bar
iron and anything that would prevent the enemy from dashing into town
were placed across the streets."[51]

Meanwhile to the north side of town, Lieutenant Samuel Elder's battery, being the closest to the escalating action while originally marching
north along the Abbottstown Road, was the first of General Kilpatrick's
two artillery units to arrive back on the outskirts of Hanover. The battery's guns quickly moved off the main road to Abbottstown, across
some planted fields, and eventually unlimbered on the eastern side of the
Carlisle Pike. That site, known as Bunker Hill, gave the Federal artillerymen a view comparable to that of their Confederate counterparts on the
elevations south of the town. Elder's artillerymen were forced to move
prematurely off the main road between Abbottstown and Hanover because of the threat presented by General Hampton's men to the east of
the community.

Because of their position in the rear of the brigade on June 30, the
5th New York and 18th Pennsylvania received the brunt of the initial

Confederate attack launched against the rear of General Kilpatrick's division. Naturally those two regiments sustained the majority of casualties within the ranks of General Farnsworth's brigade. Dozens of dead and wounded men of both armies, as well as their dead and dying horses, stretched along many of the previous peaceful and serene streets of Hanover. Chaplain Boudrye stated that:

> In less than fifteen minutes from the time the Rebels charged the town, they were all driven from it, and were skulking in the wheat fields and among the hills of the vicinity. The dead and wounded of both parties, with many horses, lay scattered here and there along the streets, so covered with blood and dust as to render identification in many cases very difficult.[52]

As in numerous other battles during the Civil War, many of the surviving members of Kilpatrick's division, those first reported as missing or prisoners, eventually were able to return to their assigned troops after a short time had elapsed. Most of the men became separated from their comrades during the heat of battle. The fighting, originally opened by formations of regiments, battalions, and troops, quickly reverted into struggles of life and death by small squads of men and individual cavalrymen. Some troopers from each army hid themselves to avoid being captured. Some, like a group of the 18th Pennsylvania and Troops L and M of the 5th New York, found themselves miles away from Hanover in an effort to avoid additional contact with the enemy.

Notes to Chapter Nine

1. Gillespie, *A History of Company A, First Ohio Cavalry*, p. 149.
2. Ibid.
3. Ibid.
4. Chamber of Commerce, *Encounter at Hanover*, p. 48.
5. Boudrye, *Historic Records of the Fifth New York Cavalry*, p. 64.
6. OR – 1, p. 1011. Major William Darlington was not present with the 18th Pennsylvania during the fighting at Hanover. He was on sick leave at his home near Harrisburg while the members of his regiment engaged the Confederate cavalry. Upon his return to duty, he received the task of filing the official report of the regiment's actions in Lieutenant Colonel Brinton's absence shortly after the fight. Although he signed the report, his actual contribution to the report written more than likely by regimental Adjutant Guy Bryan, Jr., naturally, would have been limited to only second-hand knowledge.
7. Regimental Association, *History of the Eighteenth Regiment of Cavalry, Pennsylvania Volunteers*, p. 234.
8. NA RG 94 – 5 NY; NA RG 94 – 18 PA; NA RG 94 – 1 VT; NA RG 94 – 1 WV. The majority of the saber wounds inflicted were to the head and shoulders of the victims.
9. NA RG 94 – 5 MI.
10. OR – 1, p. 1005.
11. Chamber of Commerce, *Encounter at Hanover*, p. 45.
12. Preston, *History of the Tenth Regiment of Cavalry*, p. 104. The exact location of Assistant Surgeon Bliss's hospital is unknown, as is the exact number of patients sent from Virginia.
13. Sergent, *They Lie Forgotten*, p. 144.
14. Anthony, *History of the Battle of Hanover*, p. 25.
15. Boudrye, *Historic Records of the Fifth New York Cavalry*, p. 64.
16. *Ticonderoga Sentinel*, June 21, 1972.
17. OR – 1, p. 1008.
18. Regimental Association, *History of the Eighteenth Regiment of Cavalry, Pennsylvania Volunteers*, pp. 87-88.
19. Phisterer, *New York in the War of the Rebellion*, 1:833, 839.
20. Ibid., 1:832.
21. Boudrye, *Historic Records of the Fifth New York Cavalry*, p. 66; Chamber of Commerce, *Encounter at Hanover*, p. 65.
22. Phisterer, *New York in the War of the Rebellion*, 1:836.
23. Powell, *Officers of the Army and Navy (Volunteer) Who Served in the Civil War*, p. 132; Pension File of Amos H. White, 5th Regiment, New York Volunteer Cavalry. Records of the Record and Pension Office, Record Group 15, National Archives, Washington, D.C. (Hereafter cited as White Pension File.)
24. White Pension File.
25. Krick, *Lee's Colonels*, pp. 156-57; Balfour, *13th Virginia Cavalry*, pp. 21, 77.
26. Ladd, *The Bachelder Papers*, 3:1373.
27. Chamber of Commerce, *Encounter at Hanover*, p. 255; NA RG 94 – 18 PA.
28. OR – 1, p. 1008.

Notes to Chapter Nine (*continued*)

29. Regimental Association, *History of the Eighteenth Regiment of Cavalry, Pennsylvania Volunteers,* p. 91.
30. Balfour, *13th Virginia Cavalry,* p. 94. Generally, when a Southern cavalryman lost his horse because of the animal's wounds, illness, or fatigue, the Confederate government would reimburse him for the loss. Unfortunately it was the soldier's responsibility to locate another mount for himself, a feat that was almost impossible to accomplish, especially during the current raid into Pennsylvania. Usually both Union and Confederate troopers found another horse after a battle when some of their less fortunate comrades were killed or seriously wounded and would no longer need their horse.
31. OR – 1, p. 1008.
32. Chamber of Commerce, *Encounter at Hanover,* p. 47.
33. Boudrye, *Historic Records of the Fifth New York Cavalry,* p. 292. Sergeant Owen McNulty survived the war. As luck would have it, or not, he was wounded in action on seven different occasions. It was lucky that he was not killed instead of just wounded.
34. Anthony, *History of the Battle of Hanover,* p. 26.
35. Ibid.
36. Ibid.
37. Chamber of Commerce, *Encounter at Hanover,* p. 49.
38. Ibid.
39. NA RG 94 – 1 VT.
40. Ibid.
41. OR – 1, p. 1012.
42. A third story of Lieutenant Colonel Payne's capture was sumitted by Lieutenant Henry Potter of the 18th Pennsylvania Cavalry. Potter gives the full credit for Payne's capture to the members of his regiment. However, due to many factual inaccuracies in his post-war writings, such as the 18th Pennsylvania being the only regiment involved in the fighting at Hanover and other exaggerated accomplishments made long after the battle, Potter's version is probably the least believable. Additionally, another soldier was given credit by Chaplain Louis Boudrye of the 5th New York Cavalry. The chaplain mentioned in his journal that Second Lieutenant Philip Krohn of Troop G, 5th New York Cavalry, captured Payne.
43. Chamber of Commerce, *Encounter at Hanover,* p. 93.
44. Ibid.
45. Ibid.
46. Horace K. Ide, "The First Vermont Cavalry in the Gettysburg Campaign," *Gettysburg Magazine,* (January 1996): 7-26.
47. NA RG 94 – 1 VT.
48. McClellan, *The Life and Campaigns of Major General J. E. B. Stuart,* p. 327.
49. Chamber of Commerce, *Encounter at Hanover,* p. 73.
50. Ibid., p. 48.
51. Ibid., p. 50.
52. Ibid., p. 65.

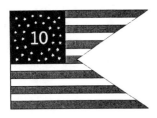

Chapter 10:
Triumph around Hanover

 T was now shortly after the midday hour. Directly overhead in the sky the sun tentatively peeked through a blanket of clouds. However there now was a very thick haze
over most of the borough of Hanover and the surrounding
areas. The discharge from hundreds of weapons during
the morning's fight between Colonel Chambliss's men and those of General Farnsworth's 1st Brigade caused a substantial cloud of thick acrid
smoke to hang just above the rooftops of the homes and businesses.
After almost two hours of stubborn and fierce fighting between two
equally determined foes, peace and relative calm for the present time finally returned to the village of Hanover. Brigadier General Kilpatrick in
his official report concerning the morning's activities, filed five weeks
after the conclusion of the battle, stated that:

> For a moment, and a moment only, victory hung
> uncertain. For the first time our troops had met the
> foe in close contact; but they were on their own free
> soil; fair hands, regardless of the dangerous strife,
> waved them on, and bright, tearful eyes looked pleas-
> ingly out from every window. The brave Farnsworth
> made one great effort, and the day was won. The foe
> turned and field. He had for the first and last time pol-
> luted with his presence the loyal town of Hanover.[1]

All remained reasonably quiet in the town for roughly the next hour
between the two antagonists. Sounds of sporadic firing still emanated
from scattered pockets of continued fighting in the streets of Hanover.
For the most part Stuart's Confederates retreated from within the town
limits and moved back to the safety of their lines to the south and southeast. Many dead and dying cavalrymen from both sides lay in the dusty
and debris-strewn streets and fields around town. There were a

particularly high number of casualties around the Winebrenner Tannery and Karl Forney farm, where the heaviest and most severe fighting took place. Besides the dozens of dead and wounded cavalrymen scattered along Frederick Street, scores of horses were in the same condition as many of their masters.

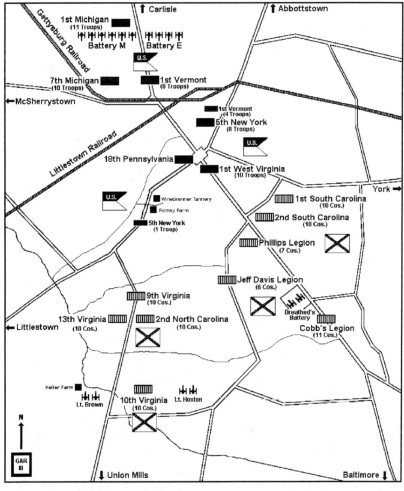

Positions of Union and Confederate Forces June 30, 1863, 12:00 P.M.
(GAR III)

As morning quickly turned into afternoon, many of the citizens of Hanover with additional assistance from the Union cavalrymen, who now held complete and sole possession of the town, immediately began to barricade the southern streets of the town. During the lull they hurriedly placed all types of obstacles across Frederick, York, and Baltimore streets. Soldiers and civilians pulled wagons, carriages, and carts and dragged crates, boxes, fence rails, barrels, bar iron, and anything else into the road and piled it high. The civilians, as well as General Kilpatrick's weary troopers, hoped to prevent General Stuart's horsemen from returning and being able to navigate easily through the town as they had done earlier.[2]

Thus far in the short duration of the battle the untried members of the 18th Pennsylvania Cavalry and their chief opponents from the already depleted ranks of the 2nd North Carolina Cavalry suffered the highest number of casualties. Since the start of the fighting, portions of those two regiments remained in almost constant contact along Frederick Street. Many of the wounded men from both of the opposing forces received medical attention from the helpful and caring citizens of Hanover. Many civilian doctors offered their services to the wounded, as well as helping the surgeons and assistant surgeons from the cavalry regiments. Hanover doctors Alleman, Culbertson, Henry C. Eckert, Hinkle, Smith and William H. Bange (also a dentist) each helped to comfort the number of wounded from both the U.S. and Confederate forces. One unfortunate, but identified, Confederate soldier from the 2nd North Carolina was the recipient of just such humanitarian assistance.[3]

Sergeant Isaac Peale rode with his regiment as they attacked through the side streets and alleys along Frederick Street on the morning of June 30. He was one of the Confederate troopers who chased the members of the 18th Pennsylvania through the Center Square during the initial attack. As he rode into the center of Hanover, a shot rang out from an unidentified Yankee trooper's carbine or pistol. About to charge up Abbottstown Street on the northeast side of the square, a lead projectile struck Peale fully in the chest. The unexpected impact of the bullet knocked him from his horse. As he fell from his saddle he hit his head on the ground, probably on a sidewalk, and severely fractured his skull.

Surgeon Henry Capehart,
Chief Surgeon, 3rd Division
(GAR III)

Surgeon Lucius P. Woods,
Chief Surgeon,
1st Brigade, 3rd Division
(GAR III)

Initially, the Reverend Zieber, in the company of Doctor Hinkle, happened upon the prostrate form of the Southern sergeant as the fighting continued to rage around them. The minister and doctor were the first to offer aid to the hapless noncommissioned officer but the prognosis was not good due to the extent of damage to Peale's head. They eventually moved Sergeant Peale to a hospital set up in either Marion Hall on East Walnut Street or the Flickinger Foundry on York Street where he died in the evening of July 1.[4]

In addition to the many civilian doctors tending to the wounded, some of the surgeons and assistant surgeons from Kilpatrick's division started arriving in town. The 3rd Division's chief surgeon, thirty-eight-year-old Henry Capehart of the 1st West Virginia Cavalry, had not yet arrived in Hanover during the lull in the fighting. He was still trying, as were the majority of General Kilpatrick's staff members, to return from near Abbottstown in the wake of their commander's rapid return. When he finally reached Hanover he kept himself very busy trying to plan properly for the care and shelter of the scores of wounded men. He, along with Surgeon Lucius Woods of the 1st Brigade and Surgeon Samuel Wooster of the 2nd Brigade, was responsible for coordinating the actions of all the surgeons and assistant surgeons assigned within the division and the two brigades.

Within a few months Capehart traded in his surgeon's scalpel for a cavalry saber. Henry Capehart eventually took command of the 1st West Virginia Cavalry as its colonel in December 1863. The surgeon turned soldier received the Medal of Honor for his heroic actions at Greenbriar River in Virginia on May 22, 1864.[5]

The chief surgeon of the 1st Brigade, Lucius P. Woods assigned from the 5th New York Cavalry, was currently present and serving with the brigade in Hanover. The thirty-one-year-old doctor, a graduate from a Massachusetts medical school in 1855, found himself detached from his regiment and detailed as the chief medical officer of the 1st Brigade. He continued to serve in the Union Army until January 1865 when he resigned his commission.[6]

Samuel R. Wooster, temporarily detached from the 1st Michigan regiment, served as the chief surgeon on General Custer's staff. Doctor

Wooster lived in Grand Rapids before the beginning of the war. In 1861 he accepted a volunteer commission as the assistant surgeon of the 8th Regiment, Michigan Volunteer Infantry. In February 1863 he became the surgeon of the 1st Michigan Cavalry. When his term of service expired in October 1864 he mustered out of the regiment.[7]

Surgeon Wooster's time as the brigade's chief medical officer would not last too much longer for he was one of the staff members already in place when Custer took command of the brigade. General Custer eventually replaced the doctor with someone he chose. As the morning slipped into afternoon Doctor Wooster moved back toward Hanover from almost near Abbottstown.[8]

Assistant Surgeon Amos K. Smith,
1st Michigan Cavalry
(GAR III)

All of General Kilpatrick's assigned regiments had at least one medical officer serving with their regiment on June 30. Regulations authorized every cavalry regiment to have one surgeon and two assistant surgeons, each a commissioned officer. The regiment also had two hospital stewards assigned, both from the ranks of enlisted soldiers. Besides the three surgeons detached to brigade and division headquarters, the other surgeons and assistant surgeons included:

Assistant Surgeon Orlando W. Armstrong, 5th New York
Surgeon John J. Marks, 18th Pennsylvania
Assistant Surgeon Samuel C. Williams, 18th Pennsylvania
Assistant Surgeon George W. Withers, 18th Pennsylvania
Assistant Surgeon Ptolemy Edson, 1st Vermont
Assistant Surgeon Perrin Gardner, 1st West Virginia
Assistant Surgeon Arthur K. St. Clair, 1st Michigan
Assistant Surgeon Amos K. Smith, 1st Michigan
Surgeon John P. Wilson, 5th Michigan
Assistant Surgeon Sylvester R. Morris, 5th Michigan
Assistant Surgeon David C. Spaulding, 6th Michigan
Assistant Surgeon George R. Richards, 7th Michigan

Along with the multiple problems created by the many wounded men, the surgeons needed to obtain additional medical materials. The division lost many of its hospital supplies when the Confederates first attacked the rear of the Union column and absconded with some of the ambulances. Assistant Surgeon Perrin Gardner of the 1st West Virginia commanded one of the hospitals after being detached from his regiment. The assistant surgeon remained in Hanover after the rest of his division moved out the next day. He cared for the wounded soldiers from both sides of the fighting. Over the next month his responsibilities expanded and included rendering assistance to a number of casualties sent to Hanover from the three days of fighting at Gettysburg.[9]

A number of temporary hospitals sprung up quickly in many of the more spacious buildings in Hanover as soon as the fierce fighting of the morning subsided. The uppermost thought in many people's minds was the immediate care and comfort of the many wounded from both sides. Albright's Hall on Broadway, Eckert's Concert Hall on the southwestern corner of the Center Square, the J. & P. Flickinger Foundry on York Street, Marion Hall on East Walnut Street, and the Pleasant Hill Hotel on Baltimore Street all became temporary hospitals for the care of the wounded.

The Pleasant Hill Hotel, roughly ten blocks from the Center Square on the southwest side of the street, eventually became the primary hospital for the care of the many wounded in town. Assistant Surgeon Gardner received command of the Pleasant Hill Hotel hospital. Besides the larger hospitals many private homes near the site of the fighting got pressed into service. Some of those homes turned into hospitals for only one or two individuals, thus considerably aiding those wounded men too seriously injured to move.[10]

Cavalry Corps Hospital, Pleasant Hill Hotel, Hanover
(Anthony)

One of the Union cavalrymen taken to a private residence during the break in the fighting was Corporal James A. McGinley from the 5th New York. McGinley, assigned to Troop D, got shot during the initial charge of Major White's battalion. He sustained two gunshot wounds—one to his upper arm and a more serious one to his head. He probably sustained the wounds during his battalion's hasty retreat back through the Center Square. Corporal McGinley fell from his horse somewhere in the second block of Frederick Street.

As the fighting came to a close in the streets of Hanover, somebody took Corporal McGinley to the home of Henry Long. Perhaps some of his comrades, or maybe some civilians, moved him from the street. Mr. Long lived in a house located on the northwest side of Frederick Street in the second block from the Center Square. Long's family nursed the corporal back to health. James McGinley, after almost two weeks at the

Long home, returned to his own home in New York for further recupera-
tion. He eventually returned to his regiment and survived the war after a
brief period as a prisoner of war in 1864.[11]

Lieutenant Colonel Edward Perry Vollum was a military doctor assigned as a medical inspector. The army dispatched him from Washington, D.C. to Gettysburg shortly after the conclusion of the three-day
battle. In his report to Brigadier General William Alexander Hammond,
the Surgeon General of the U.S. Army, he mentioned conditions, and the
extremely helpful civilians, encountered at Hanover as he made his way
to Gettysburg. Lieutenant Colonel Vollum stated that:

> I was detained a few hours, on the 8th [July], at
> Hanover, Pa., where I found about 150 wounded,
> chiefly from Kilpatrick's cavalry, under charge of As-
> sistant Surgeon [Perrin] Gardner, First [West] Vir-
> ginia Cavalry. They were comfortably situated in a
> school-house and in dwellings. The inhabitants had
> furnished them with bunks, bedding, dressings, uten-
> sils, and food in sufficient quantity, the people in each
> street in the town furnishing food, delicacies, nurses,
> &c., two days at a time.[12]

During the short lull in the fighting, General Farnsworth, along with
the members of his staff, kept quite busy attempting to reform and re-
deploy the members of his exhausted regiments. The 18th Pennsylvania
Cavalry was in the worst condition with the largest number of combat
casualties along with the greatest number of missing men. Most of the
missing Pennsylvanians eventually returned to their regiment after taking
a slight detour to a variety of safer spots in both Adams and York counties. The condition of the troopers from the 5th New York was not much
better. They had spent the past hour battling up and down the length of
Frederick Street. Colonel Richmond's regiment also sustained a number
of casualties during the morning. The 1st West Virginia Cavalry lost a
number of good soldiers during their impetuous charge down the length
of Baltimore Street. The 1st Vermont under Lieutenant Colonel Preston
was, by far, the regiment currently in the best condition in Farnsworth's
brigade after the morning's fight. Only two troops actively participated
in the fighting while the rest of the regiment remained in reserve.

Lieutenant Colonel Brinton's 18th Pennsylvania, still reeling from the swift and furious attack mounted against them a couple of hours earlier, slowly regrouped along Frederick Street near the Center Square. The demoralized remnants of the regiment remained near that location for the rest of the afternoon with little additional contact with the enemy. A quick check by the senior noncommissioned officers determined that the regiment was still missing scores and scores of troopers from the mass confusion of the morning. The horsemen, who retreated toward McSherrystown after the initial attack by the 13th Virginia Cavalry, would not return to the regiment until much later in the day. Brinton had no idea if those men simply got separated from the main body or if they were prisoners of war and currently enjoying General Stuart's hospitality. The lieutenant colonel's uncertainty spread up the chain of command to General Kilpatrick, who probably lost some confidence with the performance of the Pennsylvanians in their first major battle.

Around noon the 5th New York Cavalry reformed their injury-depleted troops along the debris-laden streets of Hanover. Major Hammond posted some advanced skirmishers at the edge of town around the Winebrenner Tannery and Karl Forney farm on the Frederick Road. Captain Charles J. Farley, thirty-six years old, received orders from his commander to push forward with a line of dismounted skirmishers detailed from his Troop C. Farley's troop was in relatively unscathed condition having suffered the wounding of only two noncommissioned officers during the morning's action. One of them was the previously mentioned Sergeant McNulty. Sergeant John Kistner sustained a severe slash across the back of his neck from a saber. He was the only other casualty in the troop. Additionally, Private Frederick S. Bogue of the same troop found himself taken captive earlier in the day, but had been quickly released when his comrades in the 5th New York captured his captors.[13]

After posting Captain Farley and his men to the southern edge of the town, Major Hammond returned to where his regiment had reformed near the Public Common. Hammond then received orders from General Farnsworth to withdraw the rest of his men from the town and to move them to the north along the Carlisle Pike. The major's remaining eight troops of New Yorkers were ordered to support Lieutenant Elder's battery of four guns posted on Bunker Hill along the road to Carlisle. The duty was relatively simple and, most of all, safe behind the lines. Elon Farnsworth knew how hard the 5th New York Cavalry had fought during the morning. The duty of guarding the battery was in recognition of that hard fighting and because of the many casualties suffered by them.[14]

Meanwhile, General Kilpatrick had returned to Hanover somewhere around 11:30 A.M. Up to this point in the day, the general was not a real factor in directing his division in the skirmish. After establishing his headquarters at the Central Hotel, Kilpatrick started to move through Hanover to assess the situation. His staff and headquarters guard joined him. Bugler Gillespie from the 1st Ohio Cavalry recalled that:

> He [Kilpatrick] then ordered the fences in our front thrown down and the regiments to be formed in line of battle as they returned, and then moved forward with his escort through the town to where the dismounted men of the Fifth New York were still engaged with the enemy. As we rode through the town, all was silent and deserted, where an hour before the streets were crowded with happy faces. Dead horses were lying along the streets and upon the sidewalks, where the battle had raged, with here and there a gray coat and then a blue, sleeping their last sleep together in the dust.[15]

After returning from near the Confederate lines to his headquarters, Kilpatrick formulated a plan of his own. Before Major Hammond could comply with General Farnsworth's most recent directive, General Kilpatrick superseded those orders. Kilpatrick instructed Major Hammond to move his cavalrymen to the left flank of the division east of Hanover. The division's commanding officer seems to have had no idea how roughly the 5th New York Cavalry was treated during the charges and countercharges of the morning's fight. The New York cavalrymen suffered the second largest total amount of casualties, behind the 18th Pennsylvania, in the division. The troopers showed signs of being completely worn-out and very short on ammunition. Because of Kilpatrick's new orders the eight troops of New Yorkers mounted their horses and marched off to their new position on the eastern edge of the town.

Shortly after returning from his trip to near the intersection of the Frederick and Westminster roads, General Kilpatrick originally wanted Major Hammond's New Yorkers to attempt a flanking movement. He wanted them to capture, if possible, Breathed's Battery currently posted at the Mount Olivet Cemetery. Obeying the orders the 5th New York retraced a portion of their route to a position between Abbottstown and York streets. John Hammond dispatched a line of dismounted skirmishers to probe the enemy's position. He, his men, and the regiment's horses were very near to exhaustion by this time in the day.

Compounding the problem for Major Hammond was the fact that the regiment was woefully undermanned since suffering casualties of over ten percent during the morning's fight. He had only two battalions, or eight reduced troops, of men with him as he placed them in position east of Hanover. Captain Farley's Troop C was currently on the other side of town. Troops L and M, under the command of Lieutenant Dimmick, were on the road somewhere to the north of Hanover. Of course, Captain Morton's Troop I was still at Washington, D.C.[16]

In an extremely peculiar and highly unpopular move, General Kilpatrick directed that the 1st Vermont Cavalry would now guard the battery from the 4th U.S. Artillery. Preston's men replaced the troops of the 5th New York. The Vermonters immediately moved from the Public Common to support Lieutenant Elder's battery on Bunker Hill.

The regiment from Vermont was in remarkably good condition. Ten of the twelve troops from Lieutenant Colonel Preston's 1st Vermont saw no action during the morning's engagement. The movement of a fresh regiment to a position of relative safety and inactivity was very surprising, especially to the commanders of both the 5th New York and 1st Vermont regiments. The 5th New York Cavalry had fought long and hard during the morning. Now they received instructions placing them back on the front line, advancing to the division's unguarded left flank, with highly questionable orders to attack Breathed's Battery.

In another odd decision, Lieutenant Colonel Preston under orders from General Farnsworth placed the 1st and 2nd Battalions in support of Lieutenant Elder while the 5th New York moved to the division's left flank. The 3rd Battalion, now reunited under Major Bennett, was placed to the right of the 5th New York on the front line. The regiment's only two troops, to have taken part in the earlier fighting, now found themselves thrown back into the front line beside the New Yorkers. After their previous advance troops D and M eventually withdrew from their forward position on Frederick Street. They joined the other two troops of the battalion, A and K, near the Public Common at Abbottstown Street.

Major Bennett's battalion, numbering roughly 220 men (minus the few light casualties of the morning), moved forward to set up yet another dismounted skirmish line across York Street. They held a position to the right of Major Hammond's dismounted troopers and to the left of Colonel Richmond's regiment. Giving the order to dismount, Bennett led his men forward from the Center Square on foot. Only 165 cavalrymen moved down York Street to their new positions. Every fourth man, almost fifty-five men, remained behind to hold his horse and the horses of three of his comrades.[17]

Around noon the tired and weary cavalrymen of the 1st West Virginia Cavalry received orders to correct their skirmish line. They did not have very far to move to reform their ranks. Colonel Richmond's regiment maintained their advanced dismounted skirmish positions across Baltimore Street. Although they suffered a number of casualties earlier in the day, they now had firmly entrenched themselves behind barricades along the main road and several side streets and alleys. Their left flank connected with the right flank of the 1st Vermont's battalion. The 1st West Virginia's right flank was in a field to the west of Baltimore Street with additional support from the members of the 18th Pennsylvania, who were now posted along Frederick Street to their immediate rear.

The ten troops of the 7th Michigan Cavalry were the first of General Custer's units to return to Hanover. Colonel Mann had pushed ahead of his command to find his brigade commander. George Custer returned to Hanover very quickly along the Abbottstown Road, as had his division commander. Mann found Custer, who, after conferring with Kilpatrick, had established his headquarters at the Jacob Wirt house on Frederick Street. The Wirt house was the same place where Custer, Kilpatrick, and Farnsworth had stopped earlier in the day as their regiments were passing through Hanover.

Colonel Mann personally received his instructions from General Custer. The general ordered him to move his regiment to a position north along the Carlisle Pike, just to the front of Lieutenant Pennington's deploying battery on Bunker Hill. The 7th Michigan was just arriving near the Public Common when they changed direction and moved north along the Carlisle Pike. After reaching the southern slope of Bunker Hill, a detachment, consisting of troops A, B, F, and G, dismounted and advanced on foot toward the railroad tracks of the Hanover, Hanover Junction and Gettysburg Railroad in their immediate front.

Again, as with the other dismounted members of the command, every fourth man remained behind to hold the horses as the four troops advanced. Roughly 130 cavalrymen from the four troops moved toward the safety of the northwest boundary of Hanover with the horses. Each of those dismounted cavalrymen carried a Burnside (.54 caliber) carbine and a Colt Army (.44 caliber) revolver. The four troops making up the battalion-sized command were under the immediate control of Lieutenant Colonel Allyne Cushing Litchfield. The twenty-seven-year-old second-in-command of the 7th Michigan promptly set up a skirmish line with his troopers and waited for further orders.[18]

Twenty-five-year-old Captain Alexander Walker, of Troop A, led one two-troop detachment from the 7th Michigan. While Walker commanded the detail, thirty-year-old 2nd Lieutenant Franklin P. Nichols led the fifty enlisted men in Troop A. 1st Lieutenant Elliott Gray, thirty years old, commanded the other troop, B, with fifty-two enlisted members present. Troop G's Captain Bradley M. Thompson, twenty-seven years old, commanded the other two troops in the detachment. 1st Lieutenant Joseph J. Newman, thirty-four years of age, commanded the thirty-nine men in Troop G. Troop F had twenty-nine-year-old 1st Lieutenant James L. Carpenter leading the thirty-one noncommissioned officers and enlisted men assigned to the troop.[19]

As Elon Farnsworth was in the process of re-deploying his four regiments, Custer's Michigan regiments were all finally beginning to appear on the scene. Judson Kilpatrick, who had established his headquarters in room number 24 at the Central Hotel upon his celeritous return to Hanover, called for his two brigadiers to join him. The three general officers held a brief discussion about what had transpired thus far and what options were available for continued success against Stuart during the rest of the day.

Lieutenant Colonel Allyne C. Litchfield,
7th Michigan Cavalry
(GAR III)

As the meeting continued the highest ranking Confederate prisoner, Lieutenant Colonel William Payne, arrived at the Central Hotel for an interview with Kilpatrick. In his stained and damp uniform the colonel must have presented quite a sight. The three Union generals probably had to stifle any thought of remarking upon his disheveled appearance. Being the good soldier that he was, Payne informed Kilpatrick that Stuart had his whole division with him consisting of over twelve thousand sabers. Kilpatrick probably knew that Payne was stretching the truth, but his subsequent actions in dealing with Stuart seem to have given credence to the facts as the colonel presented them.[20]

Shortly before the three Union generals met at the Central Hotel, the 1st Michigan Cavalry arrived back in Hanover after their jaunt toward

Abbottstown. Leaving his regiment moving south along the Abbottstown Road, Colonel Town rode into Hanover for further orders. Finding neither Custer nor General Kilpatrick, Town reported the availability of his regiment to General Farnsworth instead. Because of an impending threat to the left flank of the Union line, the commanding officer of the 1st Brigade ordered Town to relieve the 5th New York Cavalry on the eastern side of Hanover. Farnsworth seems to have wanted a fresher regiment to guard the left flank of the division between the Abbottstown and York roads. Riding back to his regiment still a short distance from Hanover on the Abbottstown Road, Colonel Town hastened his troopers forward.

Before Charles Town's regiment had the opportunity to travel too far toward the east of Hanover, General Kilpatrick learned of Farnsworth's directive and sent a staff officer to Colonel Town countermanding his subordinate's order. He then ordered the Michiganders in support of their own artillery from Lieutenant Pennington's Battery M of the 2nd U.S. Artillery on the western side of Carlisle Road. The eleven troops of the regiment remained at that position for the rest of the day and were not actively engaged with the enemy.[21]

As the other regiments of General Custer's brigade arrived on the field, a member of either the brigade or division staff directed them into position. Shortly after the arrival of the batteries of Pennington and Elder on Bunker Hill, the ten guns began to shell Confederate targets across the valley in front of them. The town of Hanover was that valley. The calm, after the morning's fighting, had lasted for slightly less than an hour. Since their arrival earlier in the day the Confederate artillery batteries of McGregor and Breathed had shelled the streets of Hanover with very good results. Their shells had struck quite a few homes in the borough and had killed or wounded a number of Union cavalrymen and their horses. Fortunately no homes sustained any severe damage and, surprisingly, no civilians suffered any wounds from the artillery fire.

Now, as the fighting progressed, the ammunition was running low for the Southern artillery. General Stuart's two batteries could not afford to engage in a long-range duel with the Union artillery located on the heights to the north. They could not waste their valuable artillery projectiles when they were so far away from any supply point. Nonetheless, the

Southern artillerymen from the two sections of Captain McGregor's battery closest to the Keller house aimed and fired their guns very deliberately for close to two hours. The firing had no apparent effect on the guns of lieutenants Pennington and Elder on Bunker Hill.

Central Hotel, Hanover, Site of General Kilpatrick's Headquarters
(Anthony)

Somewhere shortly after 1:00 P.M., within twenty minutes after they had commenced firing at McGregor's battery to the south, the men of Lieutenant Pennington's battery began to cheer wildly. The guns of Lieutenant Brown's section, which were firing from alongside the Keller farm, were withdrawing, or so it seemed. The celebration by Lieutenant Pennington's men was premature and very short-lived. Wilmer Brown's two guns were merely changing front in order to address another perceived threat to their flank and rear.[22]

Following the last orders received from division headquarters Colonel George Gray and his 6th Michigan Cavalry had remained peacefully and undisturbed in Littlestown for most of the morning of June 30. Colonel Gray and his staff dispatched small scouting patrols from the Michigan regiment in all directions. The patrols were seeking any concrete information about General Stuart's cavalry, now definitely known to be in the immediate vicinity. Besides the mounted scouting parties, Gray dispatched several small details of men with some commandeered wagons to forage for supplies in the local area.

A mounted force as large as General Kilpatrick's division always had requirements for any available corn, wheat, and oats that they could obtain for their hungry horses. Additionally the individual cavalryman had certain dietary requirements not usually supplied by the government. They foraged for many treats not normally available through the military supply channels. It was not a hard choice for the soldier to make between crates of hardtack and barrels of salted pork or fresh fruit, vegetables, and milk.

As the morning wore on, probably somewhere around 9:00 A.M., one of Colonel Gray's scouting parties reported that ample evidence existed concerning the position of Stuart's elusive cavalry. The Southern cavalrymen had been just observed moving slightly to the east of Littlestown. All signs seemed to indicate that the Confederate leader and his three brigades were pushing as rapidly as possible toward Hanover, the same place that General Kilpatrick's division was heading.

Although he had numerous other substantiated reports of the enemy's movements to the south and to the east of Littlestown, Colonel Gray did nothing extraordinary. He did apprise his troop commanders to be more vigilant in case the Rebel cavalry chose to visit them. He sent no force to observe the movements of Stuart and his men. It was not until an excited local civilian came running into the village streets of Littlestown with another report concerning a large body of the enemy's troops that Gray became justifiably concerned. Those Southern soldiers observed by the citizen were about five miles to the northeast of Littlestown and were steadily approaching Hanover. That information, if correct, placed the enemy's three brigades of soldiers almost directly between the 6th Michigan Cavalry and the rest of their brigade and division.[23]

The time was now shortly after 10:00 A.M. Colonel Gray's Michigan cavalrymen would shortly hear the outbreak of the fighting at Hanover as they moved toward that place and away from Littlestown. The Confederate troops, seen by the plainly excited civilian, were members of General Fitzhugh Lee's brigade. Fitz Lee's brigade guarded the left flank of J. E. B. Stuart's main column as they continued to move doggedly to the north. That last bit of information was enough to nudge George Gray into uncharacteristic immediate action. Not wishing to get cut off from the main body of his division and therefore his support Colonel Gray gave his regiment the order to prepare to move out toward Hanover along the Hanover-Littlestown-Frederick road.[24]

The nine troops present with the 6th Michigan Cavalry moved rapidly along the Hanover-Littlestown-Frederick road during the anticipated short journey to Hanover. Troop A, still detached from the command, continued with their patrol toward Westminster. When almost within sight of Hanover, Colonel Gray received information from his advanced patrol that the road ahead was covered by a Confederate detachment. The regiment was nearly to Plum Creek where Lieutenant Potter of the 18th Pennsylvania had halted his rear guard force earlier in the day. The leading patrol from Gray's regiment saw considerable evidence of the morning's fight. Additionally, the fighting in front of the 6th Michigan was clearly audible as the regiment moved toward Hanover during the late morning hours. As the sun reached its highest point in the sky, the noise of the battle to their front lessened considerably. At this juncture, Colonel Gray had two directions from which to choose if he expected to find his brigade and avoid any contact with the enemy. He turned his regiment off the Hanover-Littlestown-Frederick road to the east and into a wheatfield. Gray had made his choice, but it would shortly prove to be the wrong option.

As the vanguard of Colonel Gray's regiment crested a small rise in the open field they suddenly came upon the left flank and rear of some of the enemy's cavalry. That force, Colonel Davis' 10th Virginia Cavalry, was still guarding Lieutenant Wilmer Brown's two Napoleons west of the Westminster Road on the Samuel Keller farm. Both the Union and Confederate forces were not expecting any contact. The Confederate cavalrymen undoubtedly did not think that there was another Yankee regiment to their rear. The Michiganders unquestionably thought that they had bypassed any immediate threat or danger from the enemy since they were now so close to Hanover, almost in sight of the rest of Kilpatrick's division.

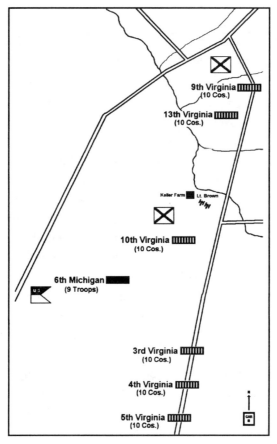

Positions of Union and Confederate Forces,
South of Hanover, June 30, 1863, 1:00 P.M.
(GAR III)

Some of the 10th Virginia's skirmishers were the first of Stuart's command to become aware of the sudden approach of Colonel Gray's cavalrymen as the Union troopers crested a slight rise. The Virginians immediately opened fire on the somewhat surprised members of the 6th Michigan. Momentarily halted back along the road while his men moved forward, Colonel Gray decided to order an attack on the seemingly small group of enemy cavalry to his front. The 10th Virginia regiment stretched thinly for almost a mile from Rice's Hill, across the Westminster Road, past the Samuel Keller farm, to the eastern edge of the Hanover-Littlestown-Frederick road. The ranks of their regiment, nevertheless, did not cross that thoroughfare.

Initially, the horsemen from Michigan, moving in a standard column of fours, met with some limited success. They drove the Confederate skirmishers back almost to the guns of Lieutenant Brown's artillery section. However, they then came across Colonel Davis' main force mounted and prepared for them. Colonel Gray's men were themselves driven back to their original starting point on the Hanover-Littlestown-Frederick road. Also adding to George Gray's problem during that charge was the fact that Lieutenant Brown quickly turned his two guns to the southwest to address the new threat from the rear.

The Confederate guns now faced the Michigan men directly. At the moment Brown's artillerymen had the capability of firing shells toward the Michigan regiment. They did not seem to possess precision accuracy, since no members of the Michigan regiment reportedly received any wounds from artillery projectiles during the brief encounter. That action of changing front by Brown's two guns was what the members of Lieutenant Pennington's Battery M had cheered when observed from their positions on Bunker Hill. Unfortunately for the 6th Michigan Cavalry, Lieutenant Brown's two Napoleons presented an obstacle for which Colonel Gray seems to have been totally unprepared.

Corporal Horace Hart of Troop D, riding with the leading troop of the Michigan cavalrymen, received a mortal wound, from a gunshot wound to the body, in the first charge against the 10th Virginia. After the fighting he was transferred to one of the local field hospitals where he died on July 3. He was first buried in the cemetery of St. Matthew's Lutheran Church but was later re-interred in the Michigan section of the National Cemetery at Gettysburg. Several other men from the 6th Michigan suffered less serious wounds. Many horses also died during the first contact with the enemy troops. Thirty-nine-year-old First Lieutenant Edward Potter, second-in-command of Troop C, had his horse shot from under him. Luckily, he came to no harm and his men picked him up and safely removed him to the rear.[25]

After retreating back to the safety of the Hanover-Littlestown-Frederick road, the 6th Michigan received another unpleasant and unwanted surprise. Hearing the sound of gunfire to their front, the leading elements of General Fitzhugh Lee's brigade urged their tired mounts forward at a faster pace along the Westminster Road. Those soldiers in gray arrived just in time to hit the right flank of the 6th Michigan Cavalry as they moved back across the wheatfield to their starting position on the Hanover-Littlestown-Frederick road. Luckily for the Michigan regiment, Fitz Lee broke off the charge because he had no idea of the exact location of the rest of General Kilpatrick's men. Besides, the rest of his brigade of Virginia regiments still found itself widely scattered along the road toward Westminster. A small number of men from the 6th Michigan Cavalry found themselves captured when the Confederates overran their position on the right flank or southern portion of the field.

Brigadier General Lee showed his reluctance to commit his men in a piecemeal fashion, mainly because of the ever present possibility of a trap. Because of Lee's apprehension, Colonel Gray was able to reform the roughly 31 officers and 590 enlisted men from his nine troops along the Hanover-Littlestown-Frederick road. Determining that the force that was now in his front was definitely from Fitz Lee's brigade and that they "were outnumbered by the enemy six to one," Gray decided that it would be prudent not to attack them with his single regiment. In reality Colonel Gray was facing a force that, if entirely brought forward to face him, was no more than four times greater than his own.[26]

As valuable minutes passed Colonel Gray saw that the Confederate cavalry in his front was gathering its courage and forming ranks for an imminent attack against his position. Within that short time, Gray positively determined that his command was no match for the perceived larger number of enemy cavalrymen. He decided to make what was basically a detour to the left or west of the Hanover-Littlestown-Frederick road to avoid a large-scale and protracted fight. After he circumvented Lee's soldiers he would then be able to head toward the north again. However, if the enemy troops pressed him too severely as he attempted to disengage, he feared that he might lose his whole regiment.

Colonel Gray resolved to take a gamble to save the majority of the 6th Michigan Cavalry. He opted to detach two troops from his regiment and leave them behind to engage the enemy. Troop B, under the command of twenty-one-year-old 1st Lieutenant Daniel H. Powers, and Troop F, led by thirty-seven-year-old Captain William Hyser, acted as the rear guard for the regiment. George Gray entrusted the overall detachment command to twenty-three-year-old acting Major Peter A. Weber, whose orders were to hold the enemy cavalry in check long enough for the main column to break away.[27]

Acting Major Peter A. Weber,
6th Michigan Cavalry
(GAR III)

In two more weeks on July 14, 1863, the young Peter Weber, who was the commanding officer of Troop B, would die at Falling Waters, Maryland. On July 12, Weber received his promotion to the rank of major but never mustered at that grade. Lieutenant Daniel Powers eventually became the captain of Troop B after Weber's death. Captain William Hyser accepted a discharge from the volunteer service in October 1863 because of disability, but returned to the 6th Michigan Cavalry in March 1864 as a captain of Troop D.[28]

Acting Major Weber capably deployed his meager dismounted force on the eastern side of the Hanover-Littlestown-Frederick road. His detail numbered 6 officers (including himself) and less than 125 enlisted men. Again, when the horseholders removed all the horses to the shelter of some trees on the opposite side of the road, his actual number of combatants consisted of less than one hundred troopers. The two troops, B and F, that Colonel Gray left behind to cover the withdrawal of the rest of their regiment, relied on the single-shot breech-loading Burnside carbines and Colt Army revolvers as their primary weapons.[29]

With little time to do anything else, the acting major formed a short skirmish line facing mainly toward the southeast and Fitz Lee's men. The young Weber and his dismounted cavalrymen successfully stopped three separate mounted charges by Brigadier General Lee's attacking regiments by countercharging them on foot. Weber's men had the advantage of being able to hide behind trees, rocks and other obstacles. The casualties suffered by Weber's heroic troopers were relatively light given the fierceness and the number of attacks against them. Two of his men received slight wounds, while roughly eight enlisted men were listed as captured or missing in action. They inflicted a number of casualties on their attackers.[30]

Unfortunately for acting Major Weber and his gallant little band of cavalrymen, General Fitz Lee managed to cut off the Michigan cavalrymen from their projected avenue of retreat toward Hanover. The Confederate cavalrymen moved almost to where Plum Creek and the Hanover Road intersected. The majority of Lee's brigade then faced northeast toward Hanover, while a much smaller group occupied Weber and his men to the south. Because of that complication, Peter Weber and his men were not able to rejoin their regiment until well after the Confederate withdrawal later that evening. Fortunately for acting Major Weber and his valiant band of men, they had some unintentional but timely assistance from the members of the 5th Michigan Cavalry.

While Colonel Gray and his men of the 6th Michigan were experiencing their difficulties with Fitz Lee's brigade, Colonel Russell Alger was preparing to move his regiment toward Hanover. Additionally, Alger had operational control of Captain Henry Thompson's Troop A of the 6th Michigan. He recalled all his patrols from the roads running from Littlestown to Westminster and Union Mills. Colonel Alger reformed his regiment and departed Littlestown shortly after twelve o'clock in the afternoon. Russell Alger attempted to continue his previously assigned mission, received personally from General Kilpatrick earlier in the day. He was to interpose himself between the rest of the 3rd Division and the enemy forces. The 30 officers and 633 enlisted men from the ten troops of the 5th Michigan Cavalry had heard the booms of the cannons firing earlier in the morning. The cavalrymen wondered silently to themselves and aloud to their comrades about what they might encounter as they rode away from Littlestown. Major Dake and his troops, C and L, were still with the division trains at Taneytown.[31]

Moving very cautiously, Colonel Alger, with Captain Thompson's troop bringing up the rear, had barely covered half of the eight miles along the road to Hanover by 2:00 P.M. A little later that afternoon as they finally neared Hanover, the Union troopers received a nasty surprise when they met a large number of Confederate cavalrymen from Fitz Lee's brigade blocking the Hanover-Littlestown-Frederick road. Those were the same enemy troops who had cut off Peter Weber and his men from Hanover. It now seemed as though Colonel Alger's mission was somewhat of a failure. Instead of placing his men between the main column of the 3rd Division and General Stuart's command, it proved to be just the reverse. The enemy now solidly controlled the area between Alger and the rest of Kilpatrick's division.

Shortly after the two opposing forces first noticed each other another sharp engagement ensued. Again, as with other actions throughout the day, the Northern cavalrymen met with initial success, driving the Southern troops for a short distance along the road before them in a brief mounted charge. Colonel Alger then dismounted his entire command to fight on foot along the Hanover-Littlestown-Frederick road. The whole 5th Michigan regiment carried the new Spencer rifle, as did Captain

Thompson's Troop A. The Spencer rifle was capable of firing seven
shots in rapid succession and was relatively simple to reload by just slap-
ping in a preloaded tube of cartridges. Because of its unique capabilities,
Colonel Alger reported that:

> . . . my regiment was armed with the Spencer ri-
> fle, being the only regiment in the brigade, and I think
> in our division, then provided with that weapon. Con-
> sequently I was then and afterwards required to do
> very much fighting on foot.[32]

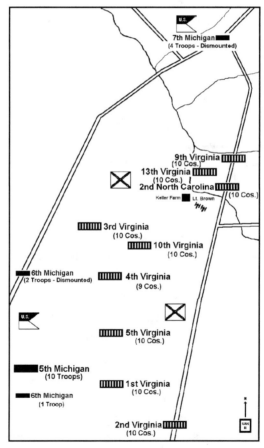

Positions of Union and Confederate Forces,
South of Hanover, June 30, 1863, 2:00 P.M.
(GAR III)

Unknown to them at that time, Colonel Alger and his men stopped along the Hanover-Littlestown-Frederick road before reaching the location where acting Major Weber and his men were fighting their own contest. Both parties could probably hear each other's weapons firing, since they were very close to each other. The 5th Michigan and Troop A of the 6th Michigan, numbering slightly over seven hundred enlisted men, engaged the enemy until near dark, holding off their repeated attacks through the superior firepower of the Spencer rifles. It would be well after dark before the Union troopers arrived in Hanover and rejoined the rest of their brigade.

Casualties were relatively light during the 5th Michigan's engagement with Brigadier General Lee's brigade. One Michigan enlisted man, Private Chauncey Rathburn of Troop D, died in the action, while one officer and four enlisted men suffered minor wounds during the late afternoon's skirmish. Quite by accident Alger and Weber had succeeded in occupying a large portion of Fitz Lee's brigade, thus keeping them from supporting their comrades in Colonel Chambliss's brigade in the main fight at Hanover. Fitz Lee could not easily ignore slightly less than seven hundred enemy cavalrymen on his flank. He might have been willing to totally disregard them, if he knew how uncoordinated their attacks would turn out to be.

Meanwhile, the dismounted skirmishers from Colonel Mann's 7th Michigan regiment, sent south from Bunker Hill and along the western edge of the town, had inched their way across the open fields. They were now very near to the intersection of the Westminster and Littlestown roads, where the battle had opened earlier in the day. Lieutenant Colonel Litchfield and his men came across the carcasses of many dead horses, as well as the bodies of many dead and wounded men from both sides, along the streets. The men advancing from Troops A, B, F, and G kept extremely active firing their carbines at the dismounted enemy troops just to their front, the bloodied remnants of the regiments from Colonel Chambliss's brigade.

Some of Fitz Lee's cavalrymen soon made an appearance to the front of the members of the 7th Michigan and very near to the Hanover-Littlestown-Frederick road. The Confederate soldiers deployed all along

Plum Creek. Although the enemy targets were increasing, the ammunition of Lieutenant Colonel Litchfield's battalion was decreasing. As the men slowly ran out of cartridges for their carbines, they withdrew back to the regimental position across the Carlisle Pike near Bunker Hill. After reuniting with the rest of the regiment, the entire 7th Michigan Cavalry received orders to remain in place near Bunker Hill, while the two artillery batteries operating there prepared to move forward.[33]

Meanwhile, Colonel Gray was moving the 6th Michigan regiment to Hanover by the left of the Hanover-Littlestown-Frederick road to the west. The commander of the regiment detached a number of additional smaller patrols to carefully guard the right and rear flanks of the regiment because of the known presence of the enemy. Upon the regiment's arrival to the northwest of Hanover a short time later, Gray reported to General Custer.

At the time of Gray's arrival both Kilpatrick and Custer were observing the action to the south of Hanover from the steeple of St. Matthew's Church on Chestnut Street. The commander of the 3rd Division, from his observation post at the church, saw that the two guns of Lieutenant Brown's section at the Keller farm apparently had no support. He did not see the 10th Virginia Cavalry or the advancing regiments of Fitz Lee's brigade. The general also could not see acting Major Weber's two troops, or Colonel Alger's 5th Michigan, engaged in their fights against the rest of Lee's brigade. Surely Colonel Gray would have reported his earlier encounter against the enemy's cavalry along the Hanover-Littlestown-Frederick road. With that knowledge, Kilpatrick should not have made an attempt to move some of his men toward the Samuel Keller farm and the two guns of Lieutenant Brown's section.[34]

With orders from his division chief, the young brigade commander at once ordered the seven troops from Gray's regiment to dismount. He wanted them to serve as skirmishers and move to the front. Colonel Gray's dismounted cavalrymen covered much the same ground just left unoccupied by Lieutenant Colonel Litchfield and his four troops from the 7th Michigan Cavalry. At this time in the fighting, the 6th Michigan had less than 350 enlisted men present for the assignment. Thompson and Weber were still sparring with Fitz Lee's men along the Hanover-

Littlestown-Frederick road. The regiment's horseholders moved the mounts near St. Matthew's Church. They aligned the horses along the safety of a side street just northwest of the church and one block west of Carlisle street. There they had shelter from the artillery and were far enough away from any errant bullets. Additionally, they were close enough to the rest of the dismounted members of the regiment in case a retreat became necessary.

The dismounted cavalrymen of the reduced 6th Michigan regiment formed a single, thinly stretched, line of battle that was almost a mile long.[35] They slowly advanced through the relatively flat fields west of Hanover. Crossing over Frederick Street, the Michiganders kept the Winebrenner Tannery on their left. Many of the cavalrymen started to lag behind and had to be urged on by the exhortations of the officers and noncommissioned officers to their rear.

A mounted soldier, by design, had a definite advantage by wearing knee-high boots while mounted on his horse. The leather boots offered some comfort while moving through bushes and shrubs with thorns and sharp needles. Without the protection of the boots the horseman could find his pants, or even his legs, shredded. Unfortunately those boots were not made for walking. The footwear of the period was less than comfortable. Moreover, if the leather got soaked by rain and sweat and then dried and wet again, a cavalryman would find walking to be most troublesome and painful. Add the brass spurs that were most useful in directing the actions of a horse but a total nuisance when tangled in some undergrowth and you have the reason for the large gaps in the advancing line of cavalrymen.[36]

Somewhere around two o'clock in the afternoon the captured Union wagon train, along with a number of prisoners, that had been moving in the rear of General Stuart's advancing column, safely halted some two miles to the south of Hanover. Forced to move very slowly because of human and animal fatigue, the train remained parked for just a few hours before having to continue their sluggish journey northward.

The site where the wagons stopped was along the eastern side of the Westminster Road. They halted in a clearing surrounded by a densely wooded area, very near to the property of Samuel Keller and Henry

Gottwald. While being guarded by members of General Hampton's brigade the teamsters driving the wagons parked them in a circle. As a precaution they piled dried wood, brush, and other combustibles around the wagon wheels. In case the fighting went badly for the Southern troops at Hanover, the men of Hampton's brigade had orders to burn the wagons to prevent them from falling into the hands of Kilpatrick's cavalrymen.[37]

As the 6th Michigan's dismounted cavalrymen started their advance along a mile-wide front, some of the Confederates feared that it was a general advance of Kilpatrick's division. They assumed that the Yankees had spotted the wagon train and that they were now moving to capture it. Captain William Graham from the 2nd North Carolina recalled his reaction to the threat when the Southerners thought that Gray's regiment was moving forward:

> I was in charge of the detail from the regiment, to impress horses from the surrounding country, and did not reach Hanover until the action was over. My "Squad" took part in the movement to repel an attack on the wagon train at this point, but Gen. Fitz Lee's command or a portion of it, coming up, the enemy withdrew. Being "broken down" I continued with my squadron and the captured animals until we reached Gettysburg.[38]

After only an hour of trading shots with the men of Chambliss and Lee's brigades, the cavalrymen of the 6th Michigan Cavalry eventually received orders to pull back. They returned to the vicinity of the tracks of the Littlestown Railroad just west of Hanover. At that juncture their participation in the Battle of Hanover, as well as the participation of most of the other regiments assigned to the division, was pretty well finished.

The artillery duel completely ceased during the mid-afternoon. Each antagonist had been unable to silence their opponent and ammunition, particularly for the Confederates, was running low. The batteries of lieutenants Pennington and Elder moved off Bunker Hill, down the Carlisle Pike, and into Hanover. Because of another perceived threat from General Hampton's brigade to the east, General Kilpatrick directed that the two artillery units take up new positions near the railroad depot and

Public Common between Abbottstown and Carlisle streets. Pennington unlimbered his six guns at the railroad tracks, while Elder wheeled his four guns into the open space of the Public Common.[39]

Also by the middle of the afternoon there was another general lull in the fighting throughout and around Hanover. General Stuart's line of battle still partially encompassed the town from the Hanover-Littlestown-Frederick road in the southwest to the York Pike in the east. They were also solidly posted across the Baltimore Road. All the troops that could possibly be moved forward by Stuart were now in position. Wade Hampton had previously ordered his skirmishers to tear down some wooden fences in front of them along the York Pike. One of his regiments, the 1st South Carolina Cavalry, then pushed their horses forward to the very edge of town before turning off the road and returning to their point of origin. The feint worked because the Union forces immediately began to re-deploy.

Corporal Horace Ide of Troop E, 1st Vermont Cavalry reported his regiment's reaction to Hampton's charging troopers:

> We were deployed as skirmishers and some were engaged pretty lively. The Rebels threw down the fences as though making ready for a charge, and then their skirmishers mounted up. We followed suit and prepared to meet them, but before long they disappeared, and upon our advancing out on our left some distance we found them gone and no trace except tracks in the road.[40]

Major Hammond's exhausted regiment experienced the same defiant challenges from General Hampton's horsemen. The 5th New York regiment also mounted a couple of troops to give chase to the impudent Confederate horsemen, but their results were the same as those of the cavalrymen from the 1st Vermont.

During the afternoon, all along General Kilpatrick's front lines, the regiments from both sides feigned charges, prepared to receive charges, and generally just sniped at each other. Neither side seemed interested in renewing the fierce contest of that morning. Except for an occasional outbreak of carbine and rifle fire, either in the village streets or farther out the many converging roads, everything remained relatively peaceful until dark.

It was now shortly after five o'clock in the afternoon. Only an occasional rifle or carbine shot could still be heard. Farnsworth's brigade did not have the opportunity to participate in any serious action during the afternoon. Lieutenant Colonel Brinton's 18th Pennsylvania was still in formation along Frederick Street and into the Center Square. Colonel Richmond's regiment of West Virginians continued in their positions behind the barricades along Baltimore Street. Major Bennett's battalion of the 1st Vermont still maintained their position across York Street. The rest of the regiment under Lieutenant Colonel Preston was still at Bunker Hill even though Elder's battery had re-deployed. The troopers of Hammond's 5th New York continued their vigilance between York Street and the Abbottstown Road.

At the same time George Custer's brigade did most of the heavy fighting during the afternoon. The 1st Michigan under Colonel Town was, also, still along the heights of Bunker Hill. Colonel Alger's 5th Michigan was still skirmishing with Fitz Lee's cavalrymen along the Hanover-Littlestown-Frederick road. Captain Thompson's Troop A of the 6th Michigan was still operating with Alger's regiment. Colonel Gray's troopers withdrew from near the Westminster Road and relocated near the Littlestown Railroad. The troopers of Colonel Mann's regiment were probably the most active during the late afternoon.

The main body of the 7th Michigan regiment was in formation across the Carlisle Pike just north of Hanover. Late in the afternoon, the colonel ordered three troops under the command of twenty-nine-year-old Major George K. Newcombe into Hanover. In another three days Newcombe would receive a slight wound as his regiment moved into their next major fight at Gettysburg.

The forty-two enlisted men of Troop C, commanded by twenty-seven-year-old Captain Daniel H. Darling, led the dismounted advance into the streets of the town. Captain Wellington Willits, forty-two years old, was the senior officer present with Troop E. The troop counted thirty-four noncommissioned officers and enlisted men in the ranks. Willits became a prisoner of war at Hagerstown, Maryland on July 6, 1863.

He spent the majority of the war in prison and after his release he accepted his discharge from the regiment because of disability. Captain Richard Douglass, the forty-three-year-old commander of the 7th Michigan's Troop H, led the third troop forward. Troop H was the smallest troop currently serving with the regiment and carried only twenty-one enlisted men on the muster rolls. Major Newcombe, along with slightly less than one hundred men, received orders to reenter the town and maintain possession of it until further orders were issued. As in all dismounted operations, one man out of every four remained behind with the rest of the regiment to care for the horses. The troopers were all armed with Burnside carbines and Colt Army revolvers.[41]

Notes to Chapter Ten

1. OR – 1, p. 992.
2. Chamber of Commerce, *Encounter at Hanover*, p. 50.
3. Ibid., pp. 87, 110-11, 113, 161.
4. Ibid., pp. 110-11, 113. Sergeant Peale received the last rites of the Catholic Church and was buried in the Conewago Church Cemetery.
5. Roger D. Hunt and Jack R. Brown, *Brevet Brigadier Generals in Blue* (Gaithersburg, Md.: Olde Soldier Books, 1990), p. 99. Surgeon Henry Capehart received the brevet promotions of brigadier general of volunteers in March 1865 and major general of volunteers in June 1865. Additionally, his brother, Charles E. Capehart, a major also serving with the 1st West Virginia cavalry during the Gettysburg Campaign won the Medal of Honor for his heroic actions during the skirmish at Monterey Gap, Pennsylvania on the night of July 4, 1863. Charles Capehart was commanding the regiment at the time, while Colonel Richmond led the brigade after Farnsworth's death.
6. *New York in the War of the Rebellion*, 1:846; Beaudry, *Historic Records of the 5th New York Cavalry*, p. 237.
7. Robertson, *Michigan in the War*, pt. 3, p. 238.
8. Ibid.
9. Certificate from P. Gardner, dated July 6, 1863, Author's Collection; Anthony, *History of the Battle of Hanover*, p. 46. The temporary hospital operated until August 15, 1863, when the remaining wounded cavalrymen got moved to the larger hospitals in Gettysburg.
10. Anthony, *History of the Battle of Hanover*, p. 29.
11. Chamber of Commerce, *Encounter at Hanover*, p. 63.
12. OR – 1, p. 26.
13. Ibid., p. 84; NA RG 94 – 5 NY. Captain Farley was wounded twice during the war, once in October 1863 and again in August 1864. He remained with the 5th New York Cavalry as a captain until his discharge for disability from the wounds in January 1865. Private Bogue deserted from his regiment as they crossed back into Virginia at the conclusion of the Gettysburg Campaign. He eventually returned to Troop C and completed his term of service.
14. OR – 1, p. 1009.
15. Gillespie, *A History of Company A, First Ohio Cavalry*, pp. 149-50,
16. OR – 1, p. 1009.
17. Ibid., p. 1012; NA RG 94 – 1 VT.
18. Isham, *An Historical Sketch of the Seventh Regiment Michigan Volunteer Cavalry*, pp. 21-22; Robertson, *Michigan in the War*, p. 407; NA RG 94 – 7 MI.
19. NA RG 94 – 7 MI. Captain Walker and 1st Lieutenant Carpenter were both wounded in the afternoon on July 3 at Gettysburg during the confrontation between Gregg and Stuart. First Lieutenant Gray was wounded on July 8 at Boonsboro, Maryland.
20. Anthony, *History of the Battle of Hanover*, p. 5.
21. OR – 1, p. 997.
22. Ibid., p. 1000.
23. Kidd, *Personal Recollections of a Cavalryman*, pp. 125-26.
24. Robertson, *Michigan in the War*, p. 406.

Notes to Chapter Ten (*continued*)

25. Kidd, *Personal Recollections of a Cavalryman*, p. 127; NA RG 94 – 6 MI.
26. Robertson, *Michigan in the War*, p. 406.
27. *Record of Service of Michigan Volunteers in the Civil War 1861 – 1865, Sixth Michigan Cavalry* (Kalamazoo: Ihling Bros. & Everard), pp. 75, 111.
28. Ibid.; Robertson, *Michigan in the War*, pt. 3, pp. 115, 225; Kidd, *Personal Recollections of a Cavalryman*, p. 471; NA RG 94 – 6 MI. Peter Weber died two days after receiving his commission as a major and was never mustered as such. All references indicate that he died as captain of Troop B, while additionally serving in the temporary grade of major.
29. Ordnance Report. Troop F filed an Ordnance Return on June 30, 1863, and listed Burnside carbines as the principal weapon. Troop B filed no Ordnance Report for the period before June 30, 1863, and none immediately after that date. It is possible that they carried Spencer rifles instead of Burnside carbines.
30. Robertson, *Michigan in the War*, p. 406; NA RG 94 – 6 MI.
31. NA RG 94 – 5 MI.
32. Robertson, *Michigan in the War*, p. 404. Colonel Alger was correct when he stated that his regiment was the only one in the division completely armed with the Spencer rifle, at that time during the war. However, Troops A, D, E, and H of the 6th Michigan also used the Spencer rifle. Those were the only Spencer rifles in any regiment in the Army of the Potomac's Cavalry Corps during the Gettysburg Campaign. Contrary to some reports, there were no Spencer carbines used at all during the campaign.
33. Robertson, *Michigan in the War*, p. 407.
34. Gillespie, *A History of Company A, First Ohio Cavalry*, p. 150.
35. Robertson, *Michigan in the War*, p. 406. George Gray's statement that his "line of battle was one mile in length" seems to be a slight exaggeration. Allocating a three-foot-wide front for each of the roughly 350 dismounted troopers would still leave a gap of over twelve feet between each trooper in the mile-long formation. Colonel Gray's single rank dismounted skirmish line would, indeed, be thinly stretched. If the Michigan regiment had one thousand men advancing along the mile-long front the distance would be a much more manageable four feet between the men.
36. Ibid.
37. Anthony, *History of the Battle of Hanover*, pp. 9, 146.
38. Ladd, *The Bachelder Papers*, 3:1373.
39. Kidd, *Personal Recollections of a Cavalryman*, pp. 125-28.
40. Ide, "The First Vermont Cavalry in the Gettysburg Campaign,": 7-26.
41. Robertson, *Michigan in the War*, p. 407; NA RG 94 – 7 MI.

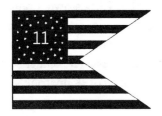

Chapter 11:

On the Road to Hunterstown

FTER the furious skirmishing in the streets and alleys of Hanover and along the roads on the outskirts of town had ended for the day the two antagonists took time to regroup. Brigadier General Judson Kilpatrick spent the night of June 30 – July 1 at the Central Hotel on the Center Square, the site where he established his headquarters earlier in the day. Brigadier General Elon Farnsworth remained in the William Wirt home near the Center Square, while Brigadier General George Custer stayed at his brigade's headquarters at the Jacob Wirt family residence on Frederick Street. Major General J. E. B. Stuart and his three brigade commanders were much less blessed in their choice of overnight accommodations. The four senior officers from the South spent the night in their saddles, as did their subordinates, on the march away from the near disastrous confrontation at Hanover.

As the sudden outbreak of fighting between the Northern and Southern troopers diminished, Judson Kilpatrick found time to dictate a message to his commander. He immediately forwarded it to Cavalry Corps headquarters located at Taneytown. A messenger sent from the 3rd Division headquarters rode back in the direction of Littlestown. At that place he happened upon the skirmish lines of the advanced infantry brigades of General Slocum's XII Corps about a mile north of the town. The infantrymen distinctly heard the sounds of the fighting in the streets of Hanover earlier in the day and were not sure of the outcome, or even who the combatants were.

Allowed to pass through the infantry pickets, Kilpatrick's courier continued into the streets of Littlestown. There he found General Pleasonton's chief of staff and assistant adjutant general, Andrew Alexander.

Lieutenant Colonel Alexander had just arrived in Littlestown along with a small escort of troopers from Cavalry Corps' headquarters. Because of the serious nature of some new intelligence, Pleasonton sent one of his senior staff officers to find Kilpatrick's headquarters. Alexander was to report the news that Stuart was in the vicinity of Kilpatrick's new division.[1]

Lieutenant Colonel Andrew J. Alexander,
Chief of Staff, Cavalry Corps
(USAMHI)

At six o'clock on the evening of June 30 in a message concerning General Kilpatrick's fight at Hanover, Lieutenant Colonel Alexander, forwarded his comments to his commander. Alfred Pleasonton was currently at Taneytown with the general headquarters of the Army of the Potomac. He received the following information from his trusted chief of staff:

> A messenger has just come in from Kilpatrick, asking for re-enforcement. I sent him every cavalryman that I could get hold of. I also informed him of

the infantry at this place. I think there is no doubt but there is a heavy infantry force at Berlin and Gettysburg. Kilpatrick has information that Lee's headquarters are at Berlin. The enemy struck the rear of his column just as it entered Hanover, creating some confusion in one regiment. A charge was, however, immediately made, which resulted in the repulse of the enemy and the capture of about 50 prisoners, one lieutenant-colonel among them. As soon as my horse rests a little, I will come to headquarters.[2]

There is no obvious reason how General Kilpatrick erroneously determined that General Robert E. Lee had advanced his headquarters to Berlin. Due to the fighting in Hanover the 3rd Division did not have any scouting details that traveled that far north on June 30, so no information would have been forthcoming from that source. One patrol, that of Lieutenant Dimmick and his two troops from the 5th New York Cavalry, reached Abbottstown in the afternoon but turned south as soon as possible.

Kilpatrick's cavalrymen could not even discern the numerous and obvious signs, located just north of Hanover, that General Ewell's infantry command had only recently passed through York, Pennsylvania. Undoubtedly, General Kilpatrick based his flawed information upon faulty intelligence from civilians moving around the area. Kilpatrick was quite adept at believing false or exaggerated reports from questionable sources. Most notably, Lieutenant Colonel Payne during his interrogation after his capture boldly deceived Kilpatrick by proclaiming that Stuart had over twelve thousand horsemen with him on his current raid north. That information alone was enough to make Kilpatrick hesitate about attacking the Southern column that ostensibly outnumbered his force by almost four to one.[3]

Nonetheless, General Kilpatrick quite willingly forwarded the erroneous information to his higher headquarters along with the prerequisite request for additional troops to aid in the repulse of the supposedly much larger enemy force. General Pleasonton upon receiving Kilpatrick's message also wished to inflate his own importance and to curry favor with the new commanding general of the army. He indorsed his subordinate's report with the additional remark that "General Lee's headquarters being at Berlin is very important." Luckily for Alfred Pleasonton, the Army of the Potomac, and perhaps the U.S. government, Kilpatrick's message did not arrive at army headquarters until the early morning hours of July 1. To General George Meade's credit, he ignored the exaggerated and insupportable claims presented by both Pleasonton and Kilpatrick. More reliable information had filtered in from the area west of Gettysburg concerning the true location of Robert E. Lee and his army.

In spite of Kilpatrick's grand posturing after the fight at Hanover, he had done quite well as a division commander in his first serious encounter with the combat-tested forces of the enemy. Elon Farnsworth, probably, performed the most capably of the 3rd Division's new commanders. He calmly and coolly directed his regimental commanders into their positions. The young brigadier general took charge of the situation at the opening of the battle, until Kilpatrick's arrival, and did not hesitate in doing his duty as he perceived it. Unfortunately, Farnsworth had many of his orders countermanded by Kilpatrick upon his superior's appearance in Hanover. General Custer, likewise, performed adequately during his first test as a brigade commander, although he had considerably less opportunity to feature his talents in that particular skirmish. He, nevertheless, made a very good impression, particularly among the officers and men of the Michigan Brigade. Captain James Kidd, Troop E, 6th Michigan, related that:

> It was here that the Michigan brigade first saw Custer. As the men of the Sixth, armed with their Spencer rifles, were deploying forward across the railroad into a wheatfield beyond, I heard a voice new to me, directly in rear of the portion of the line where I was, giving directions for the movement, in clear, resonant tones, and in a calm, confident manner, at once resolute and reassuring. Looking back to see whence it came, my eyes were instantly riveted upon a figure only a few feet distant, whose appearance amazed if it did not for the moment amuse me. At first, I thought he might be a staff officer, conveying the commands of his chief. But it was at once apparent that he was giving the orders, not delivering them, and that he was in command of the line.[4]

As the sun began to set over Hanover during that last day of June, the gruesome task of collecting the dead reached its conclusion. The wounded men of both sides were already receiving what aid that they could from the army surgeons, assistant surgeons, and civilian doctors. Unfortunately, more than a few of the seriously wounded died during the next few hours and days. After the wounded received medical care, the U.S. Army and civilians turned their attention to those unfortunate soldiers who had died during the fierce fighting around the town.

The cavalrymen appropriated an empty room in the Flickinger Foundry on York Street where the corpses of the ennobled Union soldiers awaited burial the next day. In an act of compassion by Henry Wirt and many other generous citizens of Hanover, most if not all the dead soldiers from General Kilpatrick's command were furnished with caskets. By nine o'clock that evening the bodies of all the deceased soldiers had been placed in those caskets. The next day, the townsfolk assisted with the burial of the coffins mainly in the cemetery of the Emmanuel Reformed Church on Abbottstown Street. The Reverend William Zieber officiated at the many interment services. Reverend M. J. Alleman conducted additional burials in the graveyard of St. Matthew's Lutheran Church. Many of the dead Confederates were buried in less imposing circumstances in the surrounding countryside.[5]

General Stuart and his brigade commanders had also performed quite capably considering the adverse circumstances with which they had to cope. J. E. B. Stuart, in all probability, should have avoided any contest with Judson Kilpatrick's forces instead of trying to force his way through Hanover toward Abbottstown. Colonel Chambliss, after the initial contact, committed his four small regiments too slowly, but then failed to receive timely support for those troops from the other units in the division. General Hampton's brigade, basically, did not take an active part in the fighting except to show Kilpatrick that he was on the field. Hampton suffered few casualties. The threat of Yankee cavalry on their flank hampered General Fitzhugh Lee's brigade. The presence of the 6th Michigan Cavalry, and then the 5th Michigan, along the Hanover-Littlestown-Frederick road forced Lee to act more cautiously than he otherwise might have. Fitz Lee also had to contend with the threatened advance of the Army of the Potomac's XII Corps moving from Littlestown. Because General Stuart's division was strung-out so far, Lee could not support Chambliss's brigade quickly enough to make a difference in the morning's fight.

As the afternoon's contest ceased and darkness began to blanket the remainder of the day, General Stuart sought the counsel of his three subordinates. They made the decision to withdraw the division from the hills south of Hanover and to move east to Jefferson and then north toward York in search of the main Confederate Army. Stuart's horsemen were now facing another exhaustive all-night march, made that much more grueling because of the day's strenuous activities and lack of a clear victory. In addition, they made another unwanted detour because of the fear of the Union cavalry running into them again, which added precious time and many more miles to their quest to join the Army of Northern Virginia.

Shortly after sundown on June 30, the 125 captured wagons and newly captured ambulances, untouched by any Union incursion during the day, along with the artillery batteries received orders to withdraw from the battlefield. J. E. B. Stuart's prized collection of wagons had now become a seemingly never-ending nightmare for the Southern cavalry commander. The wagons were clearly slowing the progress of his column. As the wagons and McGregor and Breathed's artillery batteries began to move it became very obvious that General Stuart had acquired some additional encumbrances since earlier in the day. His exhausted command now had to contend with added prisoners collected during the battle and, worst of all, dozens of wounded men from their own ranks.

The wagons and artillery batteries began their movement across some cultivated fields and then along some farm lanes south of Hanover. Meanwhile, Fitz Lee's brigade quietly disengaged from contact with the nettlesome men of acting Major Weber and Colonel Alger. His brigade withdrew from its position on the far left flank of Stuart's line near the Hanover-Littlestown-Frederick road. Those troopers then moved to the far right flank and led the wagon train and artillery into the darkness of the east. For now, General Hampton and Colonel Chambliss's brigades maintained their positions to the south of Hanover in case of a belatedly renewed Union attack.[6]

Shortly after ten o'clock on the night of June 30, the weary cavalry-men of Hampton and Chambliss mounted their horses and silently slipped away from their positions at Hanover. The weary Southerners followed the trail left by the horses of Lee's brigade and the wheels of the wagon train through the fields and along the seldom used roads. The tired horses and exhausted men of General Stuart's command slowly inched their way through the unfamiliar nocturnal shadows of York County.

On the first portion of the journey through the night, Stuart's men reached the tracks of the Hanover, Hanover Junction and Gettysburg Railroad. They continued to the east, roughly parallel to those tracks. Never one to pass up the opportunity of destroying a railroad, Stuart had his men tear up a short section of the iron tracks and wooden ties. He also directed that a small railroad bridge over Conewago Creek, midway between Hanover and Hanover Junction, be burned, an order with which his men enthusiastically complied.[7]

Many officers and enlisted men slept in their saddles, while the equally tired horses continued to plod ahead in the blackness. Stuart re-ported the taxing conditions in his official report by stating that:

> The night's march over a very dark road was one
> of peculiar hardship, owing to loss of rest to both man
> and horse. After a series of exciting combats and
> night marches, it was a severe tax to their endurance.
> Whole regiments slept in the saddle, their faithful ani-
> mals keeping the road unguided. In some instances
> they fell from their horses, overcome with physical
> fatigue and sleepiness.[8]

After continuing their ride throughout the night, the sunrise on July 1 found the advanced elements of Fitz Lee's command finally reaching the York Pike at a point roughly seven miles west of York. Major Gen-eral Jubal Anderson Early's (U.S.M.A., Class of 1837) division of Gen-eral Ewell's corps had passed over that road less than twelve hours previously on their way toward Heidlersburg from York. J. E. B. Stuart, not realizing that fact, decided to continue his march farther to the north rather than head west toward Gettysburg along the York Pike. If he chanced to turn west too soon he might inadvertently run into the Federal cavalry again. He did not want another engagement so soon after the trouble at Hanover. Stuart in his report of the campaign commented upon Early's absence:

> Arriving at York, I found that General Early had gone, and it is to be regretted that this officer failed to take any measures by leaving an intelligent scout to watch for my coming or a patrol to meet me, to acquaint me with his destination. He had reason to expect me, and had been directed to look out for me. He heard my guns at Hanover, and correctly conjectured whose they were, but left me no clue to his destination on leaving York, which would have saved me a long and tedious march to Carlisle and thence back to Gettysburg.[9]

Because of the darkness or because of the lack of reliable maps of the area, General Stuart and his men also wasted a seemingly valuable opportunity to visit the vital rail depot at Hanover Junction and destroy it completely. Hanover Junction, only a few miles to the east of Jefferson, was where the Hanover, Hanover Junction and Gettysburg Railroad intersected with the main line of the Northern Central Railroad. The small Confederate force of the 35th Battalion Virginia Cavalry, under Lieutenant Colonel Elijah White, had done some damage to the main depot and some bridges of the Northern Central at Hanover Junction as they passed through York County during the previous week. Although the damage was severe, it was not too bad because the line was reopened within a very short period.[10]

The Confederate cavalry commander's tired men and animals moved for a few more miles to Dover, Pennsylvania, where the column halted and most of the men got some much needed sleep for a few hours. Continuing with his report of the withdrawal from Hanover, General Stuart wrote that upon:

> Reaching Dover, Pa., on the morning of July 1, I was unable to find our forces. The most I could learn was that General Early had marched his division in the direction of Shippensburg, which the best

information I could get seemed to indicate as the point of concentration of our troops. After as little rest as was compatible with the exhausted condition of the command, we pushed on for Carlisle, where we hoped to find a portion of the army.[11]

As usual, some of the more unfortunate Southern soldiers had to accomplish other missions while the majority of their comrades rested. Some had to fill out the paperwork needed to release most of the roughly four hundred prisoners accumulated since the last parole process, one that seemed to have taken place so long ago in Maryland. Additionally, a number of staff officers and orderlies from General Stuart's headquarters moved around the countryside seeking reliable information about the movements of the main Confederate Army. Still other soldiers collected much needed supplies for both men and horses from surrounding homes.

Making sure that everything was in order, J. E. B. Stuart then sat down at the base of a tree and promptly fell asleep. After almost four hours rest, which did almost nothing to refresh man or beast, Stuart determined to move his command toward Carlisle, almost twenty-five miles from Dover.

While his command rested at Dover, Stuart learned that General Early's men moved west earlier in the day. Even though the source of the information was questionable, General Stuart, nonetheless, assumed that Robert E. Lee's army was concentrating somewhere to the northwest of his present location between Carlisle and Shippensburg. Stuart fervently hoped that the main column of the army was not converging at Shippensburg because that meant his tired men and worn-out animals would have to travel close to another forty miles from Dover to join them.

General Stuart dispatched one of his most competent staff officers, thirty-one-year-old Major Andrew Reid Venable, to follow the supposed route of Early's division. Venable's orders were simple. The cavalry commander wanted him to establish contact with General Early's command and find where the Army of Northern Virginia was concentrating. Shortly after sending Major Venable on his journey, J. E. B. Stuart's column resumed its march from Dover. General Fitz Lee also dispatched one of his aides, 1st Lieutenant Henry Custis Lee, to ride generally toward the west to find any signs of the Army of Northern Virginia. Besides being General Lee's aide-de-camp, Henry Lee was also his younger brother. Later in the day, Stuart dispatched another valued member of his staff, Major Henry B. McClellan, with the same directive.

Eventually the persistent searching by Stuart's men reaped some tangible rewards. General Stuart clearly expressed his relief with the good news brought by his returning staff officers. However, for now his three weary brigades continued their slow and tedious movements along the dirt roads of Pennsylvania on July 1 with still no ultimate destination in mind.

From Dover the responsibility for guarding the detestable wagon train passed to the unfortunate men of Colonel Richard Beale's 9th Virginia Cavalry from Chambliss's brigade. As the wagons slowly advanced, the rest of General Stuart's men again mounted their horses and moved through Rossville to the northwest, another tiny Pennsylvania farming community. Constantly having to push his fatigued men forward, the Confederate cavalry commander arrived in the little village of Dillsburg during the early afternoon hours. Lieutenant George William Beale, the twenty-year-old son of the regimental commander of the 9th Virginia Cavalry, in a letter to his mother wrote:

> Weak and helpless as we now were our anxiety and uneasiness grew to be painful indeed. Thoughts of saving wagons were now gone from many of us, and we began to consider only how we ourselves might escape. But this was not so with Stuart. He seemed neither to suppose that his train was in danger nor that his men were not in condition to fight. He could not have appeared more composed or indifferent.[12]

Without halting for a break, General Stuart decided to move immediately toward Carlisle in search of provisions for his men and forage for the animals. The many days spent behind the enemy's lines completely drained his supplies with little opportunity to replenish them. The order of march remained substantially the same as previously in the day. Fitz Lee had the lead of the long and drawn-out column. The 9th Virginia was in the rear of Lee's brigade with the wagons, ambulances, and the six pieces of artillery. Colonel Chambliss's small, battle-scarred, brigade was next in line, while Wade Hampton's brigade brought up the rear of the command. Hampton's officers and men had a rougher trip than most of the rest of the division. They had to push their own tired regimental comrades forward, while collecting the scores of stragglers from all the regiments moving in their front.

As most of his division was passing through Dillsburg, General Stuart's command received the first positive intelligence about the location of the main Confederate Army. He immediately dispatched members of his staff to inform his three brigade commanders about the news. Although the information came too late to halt the entire column's movement toward Carlisle, the men of Hampton's brigade learned that the Army of Northern Virginia was concentrating to the south at a place called Gettysburg. Major Henry McClellan, Stuart's assistant adjutant general and one of the many staff officers sent looking for information, had discovered the army's exact location. Upon reporting to his chief from his successful mission, Stuart sent Major McClellan to find General Hampton's brigade. McClellan reported that:

> . . . Hampton was met at Dillsburg, on the night of July 1, and was turned southward with orders to march ten miles toward Gettysburg before halting. I myself delivered that order to Hampton, and I saw no more of his command until he came on the field of the cavalry battle on the 3d.[13]

General Hampton immediately turned his whole brigade south at Dillsburg, where they were able to march along a well-maintained hard-packed dirt and gravel road, the Harrisburg-Gettysburg Turnpike, for much of the distance to Gettysburg. Hampton and his brigade now became the leading unit in Stuart's line of march. Traveling the ten miles along the road from Dillsburg would have put Hampton's exhausted cavalrymen near Petersburg somewhere around daybreak. After a short rest Wade Hampton and his command continued on the final leg of their journey to Gettysburg.

The brigades of Fitz Lee and John Chambliss, unfortunately for them, continued their march along the road to Carlisle. General Lee was still leading the column with Colonel Chambliss's men spread out some distance behind. The gaps in the line of march were becoming quite pronounced because of the condition of the exhausted horses. Stuart's command had traveled almost forty miles since earlier that morning.

Stuart and his men, after leaving Dillsburg, had to negotiate the northeastern incline of a road over a local height known as Piney Mountain. If the horses did not show signs of fatigue before reaching that point, they surely did after passing over the slope of that mountain. The horses and mules pulling the artillery, wagons, and ambulances had the worst time. They became completely played out and almost worthless after that leg of the journey and many were abandoned before reaching Carlisle.[14]

The town of Carlisle was the site of the U.S. Army's Carlisle Barracks, the former home of the School of Cavalry Practice and Recruiting Depot. British and Colonial troops established the post in May 1757. It continuously served the military, first of Great Britain and then of the United States, in the succeeding years. Founded in 1838, the School of Cavalry Practice once was commanded from 1849 to 1852 by J. E. B. Stuart's father-in-law, Philip St. George Cooke (U.S.M.A., Class of 1827) of the 2nd U.S. Dragoons. The school closed in 1861 when it became the home of the U.S. Mounted Recruiting Service. During its existence, the cavalry school had seen scores of cavalrymen pass through its gates, many of who were now opponents and who were utilizing the knowledge acquired while assigned there.[15]

Major General Stuart never had the opportunity to attend the cavalry school at Carlisle Barracks even though he spent the majority of his ante-bellum career with the 1st U.S. Cavalry. On the other hand his subordinate, Fitz Lee, received an assignment as a brevet second lieutenant to Carlisle Barracks immediately upon his graduation from the U.S. Military Academy in 1856. Lee, who graduated at the top of his class in horsemanship, remained at the School of Cavalry Practice until January 1858 when he finally joined his regiment, the 2nd U.S. Cavalry, in Texas. Fitz Lee shortly proved that the memories from his time spent at Carlisle Barracks were less than favorable remembrances when a portion of the Confederate cavalry column reached that place later in the day.[16]

Brigadier General William "Baldy" Smith,
1st Division, Department of the Susquehanna
(NA)

While Stuart was navigating the unfamiliar roads somewhere between Dover and Rossville, the object of his forced march, Carlisle, welcomed the hastily collected forces in Major General Darius Couch's
Department of the Susquehanna. One of the first units sent from the defenses around Harrisburg in response to an earlier visit from General
Ewell's Confederate infantrymen included the roughly 120 officers and
enlisted men of the 1st Regiment, New York Volunteer Cavalry. Thirty-
eight-year-old Captain William H. Boyd commanded that detachment of
New Yorkers. Originally the commanding officer of Troop C, Boyd's
detachment, also known as the Lincoln Cavalry, arrived in Carlisle early
on the morning of July 1, well before Stuart's exhausted horsemen.[17]

The Department of the Susquehanna's 1st Division was commanded
by the combat-tested veteran, and former commander of the VI Corps,
Brigadier General William Smith, one of George Custer's old commanding officers. Smith had only two small brigades of militia infantry, one
from New York and the other from Pennsylvania, immediately available

to protect Carlisle. However, there were other brigades from the department within supporting distance of Carlisle. All the regiments had only recently mustered into the Federal service for the duration of the current emergency.

Brigadier General John Ewen's command, the 4th Brigade of Smith's 1st Division, consisted of the only two regiments of New York troops actually present for duty at Carlisle. The 22nd Regiment, New York National Guard recruited in New York City had just nine companies present for duty. Thirty-year-old Colonel Lloyd Aspinwall commanded the regiment of New Yorkers. The other regiment assigned to Ewen's brigade was also recruited in New York City. That unit was Colonel Charles Roome's 37th Regiment, New York National Guard. The fifty-year-old Roome counted all ten companies of his regiment present for duty. Ewen's brigade strength was roughly twelve hundred officers and enlisted men.[18]

General Smith's 1st Division also included Colonel William Brisbane's 5th Brigade. One of the regiments included in the brigade was the 28th Regiment, Pennsylvania Militia commanded by Colonel James Chamberlin. Colonel William W. Taylor commanded the other regiment, the 33rd Regiment, Pennsylvania Militia. The two Pennsylvania regiments in Colonel Brisbane's brigade, present for duty at Carlisle, had a total of slightly less than fourteen hundred soldiers in the ranks.[19] Besides the two infantry brigades posted at Carlisle on July 1, Captain Henry D. Landis' 1st Philadelphia Battery was also at Carlisle. The battery consisted of a two-gun section and roughly thirty enlisted men under the command of Lieutenant Rufus King, temporarily detached from the 4th U.S. Artillery.[20]

The forces of General Smith's division arrived in the Cumberland County town of Carlisle around three o'clock in the afternoon of July 1, slightly before General Stuart's cavalrymen. "Baldy" Smith deployed his regiments across the eastern section of the town, running in a north and south direction, in order to halt any incursion into the actual town from that direction. Many of General Smith's men took shelter in several of the town's buildings. Colonel Brisbane and his Pennsylvania regiments guarded the northern most section of the line or the left flank of the command. General Smith personally commanded the center of the line with Colonel Roome's 37th New York and one artillery piece. General Ewen had operational control of the 22nd New York and the other gun on the right flank, or southernmost portion of the line, straddling the Baltimore Pike. The commanding general threw out skirmishers in front of the Federal line. It was well past sunset when the Union troops completed all their preparations.

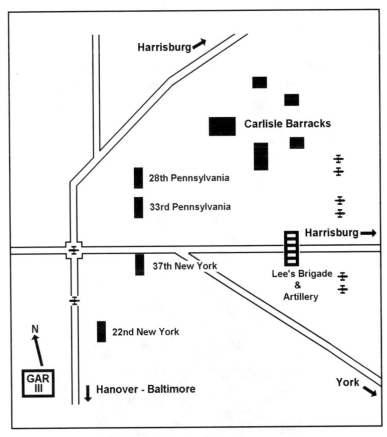

Positions of Opposing Forces at Carlisle,
July 1, 1863, 10:00 P.M.
(GAR III)

General Smith's skillful positioning of his troops protected the town, but left Carlisle Barracks completely and totally exposed on the left flank of the Federal militia troops and to the right of those veteran troops of General Stuart's command approaching from the southeast. Because of the close proximity of the Confederate Army during the last days of June, Captain David H. Hastings from the 1st U.S. Cavalry abandoned Carlisle Barracks six days earlier. Hastings was the current superintendent of the army's Mounted Recruiting Service located there.[21]

The Irish-born forty-nine-year-old David Hastings received a very serious injury in an accident almost six years earlier while assigned to the 1st U.S. Dragoons. His horse had fallen on top of him as he and his command were pursuing a hostile band of Indians along the western frontier. Because of his severity of his injury, he was never able to hold another active field command after being involved in that accident. Serving as Carlisle Barracks' commanding officer was the last assignment in Hastings' mediocre military career. In December 1863, David Hastings retired from the army as a major of cavalry after almost twenty-eight years of active duty service.[22]

Second Lieutenant Thomas McGregor,
Adjutant, Carlisle Barracks
(GAR III)

Before the anticipated arrival of some of the leading elements of
General Ewell's corps almost a week earlier, Captain Hastings had ordered his acting adjutant, Second Lieutenant Thomas McGregor, to pack
up all ". . . the munitions of war and movable public property" and proceed to the safety of Harrisburg.[23] Lieutenant McGregor's Regular Army
regiment, like Hastings, was the 1st U.S. Cavalry. He was on detail from
Troop A as the post adjutant since the end of 1862. Thomas McGregor, a
native of Scotland, had enlisted in the 1st U.S. Dragoons in 1858. He received his commission as a second lieutenant of cavalry in 1862. Now
on June 26 he was spending his twenty-sixth birthday marching the
small contingent of Regular Army soldiers away from the parade and
drill ground of Carlisle Barracks as they abandoned the post. The actual
number of soldiers at Carlisle Barracks included eight officers and 151
enlisted men present for duty.[24] Eventually returning to his regiment,
Lieutenant McGregor received a slight wound at Winchester, Virginia in
1864. His lengthy military career spanned almost forty-six years on active duty from private to brigadier general, when he retired in 1904.[25]

Now, however, the peaceful tree-lined grounds and sturdy structures
of Carlisle Barracks were absolutely deserted and void of any military
activity as the sun set on July 1. Around that same time the advanced
Union pickets of "Baldy" Smith's division spotted the men of General
Fitz Lee's brigade. The Confederates were moving along the York Road
from the southeast. The commanding general of the Union forces did not
wish to expose his recently mustered and extremely green and nervous
troops to a battle with the veterans of General Stuart's command. Smith
reported that he was "determined to content myself till morning with
simply holding the town." Only the previous week had the majority of
General Smith's men mustered into the Federal service.[26]

Short of food for his men and forage for the animals, General Stuart
had no intention of bypassing Carlisle. Hopes were still running high
that they would find some friendly infantry units there. Stuart had set his
sights on the town of Carlisle as a possible place to replenish his supplies, not realizing that the Confederate infantry already had beaten him
there. His prospects for collecting any useful supplies, along with the expectations of his men, promptly got dashed. They learned that Dick

Ewell's troops had vacated the town several hours previously. The Southern infantrymen took wagons loaded with everything that Stuart had hoped to find. Colonel Richard Beale, commanding the 9th Virginia, wrote that:

> . . . nightfall found us in the vicinity of Carlisle,
> where we expected to find our infantry, behind whose
> sheltering muskets we hoped to find one night of
> sweet sleep. Painful was the intelligence that this
> hope must be deffered to some more convenient time
> and place, as our infantry had retired to Gettysburg,
> and the enemy occupied Carlisle.[27]

Instead of finding the hoped for friendly faces along the streets of Carlisle, the Southern cavalrymen instead now found General "Baldy" Smith and his two militia brigades blocking their passage into the town. Stuart ordered Fitz Lee's brigade along with the six artillery pieces of Breathed and McGregor to the very outskirts of Carlisle. The wagon train remained a short distance to the rear with Colonel Beale's troopers still guarding it, while Chambliss and the horsemen of his brigade remained in reserve nearby. General Hampton halted his brigade closer to Dillsburg.

Learning that the force facing him contained only New York and Pennsylvania militia members, Stuart resolved to take the town. He would, therefore, be able to appropriate whatever supplies, so desperately needed, that General Ewell's men missed. However, General Smith had other plans. If J. E. B. Stuart knew the actual size of the other forces heading south from Harrisburg, he might not have paid a call on Carlisle at all. Militia or not, Stuart's ammunition was getting very low for his artillery, as well as for the carbines, rifles, and pistols of the overall command. Stuart had little hope of replenishing the depleted ammunition if he could not find the Army of Northern Virginia and its supply trains. Any prolonged fighting, even with the militia, would not help his current situation.[28]

For the present time the main objective, if General Stuart had one at that time, seemed to be the capture or occupation of Carlisle Barracks. Fitzhugh Lee vividly recalled the area from his earlier tour at the idyllic post shortly after his graduation from West Point. He was able to lead his Virginia cavalrymen right up to the very edge of the federally owned grounds. Both sides exchanged some small-arms fire with each other's advanced skirmishers. As a whole, General Fitz Lee's men were practically unmolested as they maneuvered through the gathering darkness toward the north and the deserted government buildings.

As they moved forward, General Stuart directed that the six guns of Breathed's and McGregor's batteries be carefully deployed. He wanted them to be able to achieve the maximum effect for the limited number of artillery rounds still remaining. Fitz Lee then ordered that a few warning shots be fired into the increasing darkness of the town. In response to that initial attack, Lieutenant King had his sole gun posted in the town square, fire three answering rounds.

Almost immediately after the discharge of those few rounds, General Smith ordered that the Rebel's artillery fire would go unanswered. Smith erroneously thought that his men did not have any solid targets at which to direct their rounds. Additionally, he wanted to save his ammunition in case of an actual attack. He did not want to get involved in a long-range waste of ammunition, particularly in the dark. Even though the Confederate artillery gunners had taken their time in setting up their guns, none of the initial rounds from Breathed or McGregor's artillery pieces struck any of the intended targets. The only casualties seemed to have been some trees on the outskirts of Carlisle.

At approximately ten o'clock, shortly after the Confederate's first attack commenced, it abruptly ceased. A flag of truce from General Stuart's command advanced through the two opposing lines. Fitz Lee, in concurrence with the wishes of J. E. B. Stuart, demanded "the surrender of the town or the removal of the women and children."[29]

General Smith brusquely responded that he would not surrender the town but that his men would notify the women and children to evacuate their homes if they wished to do so. Smith's reply was the only normal response. He did not plan to surrender without a fight. For many months previously, "Baldy" Smith had eagerly sought some combat action as well as some personal glory to stimulate a sagging career. He lost the command of the Army of the Potomac's VI Corps, along with a permanent promotion to major general, because of certain indiscretions

314 ◆ Chapter 11

directed against General Ambrose Burnside, then commanding the Army of the Potomac.[30]

Generals Stuart and Lee took no pleasure from the blunt rebuff from the Union General Smith, particularly since he had the audacity to refuse their demand while commanding only inexperienced emergency troops. Smith's forces should have been extremely frightened at the prospect of a battle with the battle-hardened veterans of J. E. B. Stuart's cavalry and perhaps they were. However, "Baldy" Smith reasoned that the impatient Confederates would need quite some time to carry out their threats. Regrettably, time was something that Stuart and his men did not have. Smith also knew that he had additional support approaching from Harrisburg that could be there the next day. In addition, he already had received reports that the Army of the Potomac was converging in Adams County to the south. Further good news reported that Judson Kilpatrick and David Gregg's cavalry divisions were somewhere behind Stuart's Confederate force to the south or southeast. Considering those facts, General Smith saw no reason why he could not, and should not, wait for Fitz Lee to begin an attack.

Within thirty minutes of the first Confederate solicitation for surrender, the commanding officer of the defending forces received another strongly worded request for capitulation. That demand insisted upon the unconditional capitulation of the entire town. The message stated that they would burn Carlisle to the ground if the appeal did not elicit a positive response. Of course the Union defenders refused that call for surrender too. Because of Stuart's impatience, the women and children in Carlisle hardly had enough time to begin the evacuation process between the surrender demands. Captain James Dougherty, an acting aide-de-camp on the staff of General William Smith, personally delivered the second message from the Confederates to his chief. Dougherty had been captured and his orderly wounded by the Southern forces somewhere along the Harrisburg Road. The two men inadvertently ran into an enemy patrol while trying to deliver an important message to General Couch in Harrisburg concerning the approach of General Stuart's cavalry.[31]

Immediately after the last refusal by "Baldy" Smith to surrender the town peacefully, Fitz Lee ordered his six guns to open fire on the town. During that portion of the bombardment a number of local government buildings as well as some private houses received some slight damage from artillery shells but none seriously. Breathed and McGregor's artillerymen had finally gotten the correct range to targets and were lobbing shell after shell into the center of Carlisle. General Smith reported that 134 shells landed in the town. The Confederate artillerymen preheated many of those shells to cause major damage, specifically by igniting fires in the buildings that they struck. Throughout the short duration of the attack no civilians reportedly suffered any injuries.

Shortly after midnight, General Lee endeavored, one final time, to goad his stubborn opponent into surrendering the town. The Confederates advanced the third demand for submission under another white flag of truce during the early morning hours of July 2. The Union troops in Carlisle returned the same predictable answer. Becoming very annoyed with the redundant response Stuart allowed Fitz Lee to order his troopers to set fire to the Carlisle gas works and an adjacent lumberyard. Both facilities were between the town of Carlisle and the Carlisle Barracks. As an indication of how tired the men were, many of the Confederate horse soldiers, not directly involved in the attack, sought places to get some rest while the cannons roared practically next to them. Again recalling the hardships of the campaign in his letter to his mother, Lieutenant Beale reported the conditions that prevailed around him:

> From our great exertion, constant mental excitement, want of sleep and food, the men were overcome and so tired and stupid as almost to be ignorant of what was taking place around them. Couriers in attempting to deliver orders to officers would be compelled to give them a shake and call before they could make them understand. This was true of Colonels. As for men though in line and in momentary expectation of being made to charge, they would throw themselves over on their horse's necks, and some even down on the ground and fall asleep.[32]

Finally Fitz Lee, with the concurrence of J. E. B. Stuart, ordered that some of the actual barracks buildings, as well as the superintendent's home, be burned. Obviously Lee did not harbor any fond memories of his time spent at Carlisle Barracks. The flames from the burning buildings at Carlisle Barracks, fueled by a quantity of lamp oil, lit up the night sky for miles around Carlisle. All structures torched by General Lee's men became completely engulfed and burned to the ground in a very short period.

After another hour of additional intermittent shelling and other minor depredations upon the town of Carlisle and the surrounding area, the firing suddenly stopped. For the next hour everything was fairly peaceful. Occasional firing continued between the opposing skirmishers. Around 3:00 A.M. an additional three discharges from the Confederate artillery signaled the Southern cavalrymen to begin their withdrawal from Carlisle. Shortly after those final shots, General Smith received multiple reports from his advancing pickets that Fitz Lee's cavalrymen were moving south on the road toward Papertown and Petersburg. General Stuart had finally received orders from General Robert E. Lee to join the Army of Northern Virginia at Gettysburg. He now knew exactly where to proceed to join the rest of the Confederate army.[33]

The citizens of Carlisle ran from their homes and rejoiced in the streets when they learned that General Stuart and his men had departed from the outskirts of the town. At the news of Stuart's withdrawal the members of the New York and Pennsylvania militia regiments also joined in the celebration. General William Smith and his command had been extremely lucky in their brief encounter and ultimate stalemate with Stuart's column of exhausted horsemen. The artillery attack by Fitzhugh Lee had not done very much damage to the town and the Union militia could justifiably claim that they had thwarted the Confederate cavalry's attempt to enter Carlisle.

Brigadier General Smith's reported casualties were relatively minor. None of his immediate command had died during the night time bombardment of the town. Colonel Roome's 37th New York had two officers and two enlisted men wounded and three enlisted men taken prisoner. The 22nd New York, commanded by Colonel Aspinwall, counted one officer and two enlisted men wounded.[34]

Confederate casualties were also very light. Stuart's regiments reported only two soldiers slightly wounded or captured. Fitz Lee's brigade listed one enlisted man from the 2nd Virginia as being captured and one from the 5th Virginia as slightly wounded. Colonel Chambliss and General Hampton's brigades did not participate at Carlisle.[35]

Fitz Lee's horsemen left the Carlisle garrison burning against the northern sky and rode south toward Papertown and Petersburg. The captured Union wagon train was already in motion along the route. Lee's brigade still led the column south, followed by the artillery, wagons, and then by Colonel Chambliss's brigade acting as the rear guard. Wade Hampton had previously received orders from General Stuart to move his command on another road from near Dillsburg through Petersburg toward Heidlersburg. Stuart expected the two columns to reunite at Heidlersburg and then continue the remainder of the journey together to Gettysburg.

Marching along the Hanover Road (also known as the Baltimore Road), Stuart's column from Carlisle re-crossed the steep slopes of Piney Mountain during the early morning hours of July 2. The Southern horsemen now faced another late night march. Colonel Beale of the 9th Virginia Cavalry recalled that:

> A courier delivered General Stuart's request that the command should be kept in the saddle all night, with the further assurance that the promise was fair that Pennsylvania would on the morrow be open to our army. The reply was sent that the request would be cheerfully complied with; but that the utmost verge of endurance by men and horses had been reached, and that whatever the morrow might bring, we feared that neither horses or men could be used either to match or fight.[36]

Finally during the early morning hours of July 2, the Confederate cavalrymen now knew where they had to go to rejoin the Army of Northern Virginia. They were definitely getting closer. General Stuart left Fitz Lee in command of the column while he rushed toward Gettysburg and a meeting with Robert E. Lee. However, the hardships of the exhausted Southern cavalrymen, and their equally tired animals, had not quite finished. As at Hanover, a portion of J. E. B. Stuart's command again met, quite unexpectedly, Judson Kilpatrick's men later in the day.

Meanwhile, during the late afternoon and the remainder of the night of June 30, General Kilpatrick and the men of his 3rd Division had sole possession of Hanover. Obviously aware that his Confederate opponent had withdrawn from his front, but choosing not to do anything about it, Kilpatrick dispatched a report to General Pleasonton at Cavalry Corps headquarters explaining his current disposition by stating that:

> I have gone into camp at Hanover. My command will be in readiness to move again at daylight to-morrow morning. We have plenty of forage, the men are in good spirits, and we don't fear Stuart's whole cavalry.[37]

Elon Farnsworth's four drained regiments established their overnight camps chiefly within the town limits of Hanover. They slept through the night slightly behind the same lines that they had established earlier in the afternoon.[38] Custer's men set up their bivouacs farther north along the Abbottstown Road toward the Pigeon Hills. Colonel Russell Alger's 5th Michigan Cavalry and Captain Henry Thompson's Troop A of the 6th Michigan arrived at the Michigan Brigade encampment some time after midnight. They had finally been able to complete their march from Littlestown, one that started some twelve hours earlier.

The return of many of the men from Lieutenant Colonel Brinton's 18th Pennsylvania Cavalry, those forced to retreat toward McSherry-stown earlier in the morning, greatly bolstered the ranks of Kilpatrick's division. Those men rejoined their comrades during the late afternoon and evening of June 30. Most of the originally reported missing members had finally filtered back to their regiment throughout the hours of darkness. Their return to the regiment significantly decreased the initial casualty reports filed immediately after the cessation of the hostilities. Additionally, Lieutenant Dimmick's two troops, L and M, also found their way to Hanover during the late afternoon.

Seemingly lacking any initiative, Judson Kilpatrick was quite content to break his tenuous connection with the Confederate cavalrymen after their surprise engagement at Hanover. There was also an absence of direct orders from General Pleasonton whether to maintain contact with Stuart's force. The commander of the Cavalry Corps originally tasked General Kilpatrick with the responsibility of screening the movements of the Army of the Potomac as it marched north across the Potomac River from Virginia. Kilpatrick had the center of the Cavalry Corps' advance, while General Buford took the left and General Gregg operated on Kilpatrick's right. Unfortunately Kilpatrick squandered an excellent opportunity to prevent J. E. B. Stuart from maneuvering to the west in an attempt to reunite with the main body of the Army of Northern Virginia. Instead the 3rd Division's commander deliberately wasted precious time lying about Hanover waiting for an attack before finally ordering his two brigades in pursuit of the elusive Stuart.

During the early morning hours of the first day of July, in an effort to reestablish direct contact with the Rebel cavalry, Kilpatrick sent a small detachment of less than one hundred men in pursuit of J. E. B. Stuart's command. Rather than wishing to overtake them, the Union troopers merely trailed the Confederate horsemen as far as Rossville, slightly north of Dover, before turning back to rejoin the rest of the division. Commanded by Lieutenant Colonel Andrew Alexander, General Pleasonton's chief of staff and assistant adjutant general, the detachment captured only a few stragglers and gleaned the important information that the next destination of Stuart's horsemen was Carlisle.[39]

The twenty-nine-year-old Alexander, previously assigned to the 3rd U.S. Cavalry as a captain at the beginning of the war, and his detachment moved slowly along the same route taken by Stuart's three brigades. As that patrol was traveling along the roads to the east of Hanover, Kilpatrick ordered the rest of his division to move north along the Abbottstown Road, the same road many of his men had twice traversed yesterday. In his official report, Judson Kilpatrick wrote that he "marched at daylight to Berlin via Abbottstown to intercept Stuart, but failed." It would seem logical that he would fail since Stuart's force had stolen almost a half day's lead on the Union troopers.[40]

If Kilpatrick and his troops continued pushing through Berlin and marched another dozen miles north toward Dillsburg, they might have struck another blow against Stuart's men. Some time during the late afternoon of July 1, the leading members of Farnsworth's brigade, members of Colonel Richmond's 1st West Virginia, could have intercepted Stuart's column as the Confederates passed through Dillsburg. At that time it would have been the Union cavalry's turn to try to split their opponent's column in two. Unfortunately Kilpatrick did not allow his two brigades to venture beyond Berlin.

Although General Kilpatrick lost all physical contact with the Confederate cavalry after the fight at Hanover, he still was aware of what General Stuart had to accomplish to continue his mission. The 3rd Division's commander attempted to move his horsemen north on July 1, but much too slowly, in an effort to prevent the Confederate cavalry chief from maneuvering west. As a slight excuse for his tardiness, Kilpatrick was not feeling very well. Because of yesterday's bone-jarring ride from near Abbottstown back to Hanover, Judson Kilpatrick was experiencing severe pains in his back. The commanding general of the division moved away from the streets of Hanover while reclining in the rear of an ambulance.[41]

On June 30, after Judson Kilpatrick learned of the preemptory Confederate attack on the rear of his division he immediately rode back to Hanover from near Hendrix. Just hours after his arrival at the Center Square his horse died because of the exertion placed on it by the general. Kilpatrick himself fared only slightly better because of the rough journey. The ride had caused him considerable physical pain in the area of his kidneys, so much pain that he was unable to mount another horse the next day. After spending an understandably restless night at the Central Hotel, he sent a member of his staff to find an ambulance for him to use as the 3rd Division moved from Hanover. Unlike General Stahel, who had used an ambulance previously in the campaign, General Kilpatrick's use of an ambulance seems to have been necessitated by an aggravating medical condition. As his command advanced to the north, Kilpatrick dispensed his orders while laying flat on his back in the slow-moving and bone-jarring ambulance.[42]

The order of march for July 1 found Elon Farnsworth's brigade at the head of the 3rd Division. Colonel Richmond's ten troops of West Virginians was in the leading position. They were followed, in turn, by

the 5th New York, Elder's battery of four guns, and the slightly battered
and bloodied 18th Pennsylvania. Lieutenant Colonel Preston's 1st Vermont was the trailing regiment at the rear of the brigade.

George Custer's Michigan Brigade followed the regiment of Vermonters. For the first time since their assignment to the 2nd Brigade, all
the Michigan regiments were finally together in one place, serving under
one commander, and operating as a brigade. Colonel Alger's 5th Michigan had the leading position of the brigade. The ten troops of the reunited 6th Michigan Cavalry were next in the line of march. Lieutenant
Pennington and his six-gun battery and Colonel Mann's ten troops of the
7th Michigan followed them. As the Union forces moved away from the
borough of Hanover, the 1st Michigan was the last of Kilpatrick's regiments to depart, operating as the division's rear guard. Colonel Town,
like Lieutenant Colonel Brinton on the previous day, dispatched several
patrols from his eleven troops to guard the division's rear and flanks as
they moved toward Abbottstown.

As General Kilpatrick's division moved slowly in pursuit of General
Stuart, scores of his blue-clad troopers remained in Hanover to care for
their many wounded comrades. The ranks of all the regiments probably
had close to three hundred fewer troopers than the previous day. Other
soldiers of the division were detailed from their regiments with wagons
to gather additional supplies from the surrounding countryside. They
would then follow the division at a later time to deliver their cargoes.

Brigadier General Kilpatrick had the opportunity to dispatch another
message to General Pleasonton late on June 30. In a postscript to that report, probably penned on July 1, Kilpatrick stated that:

> The enemy (Stuart's command) is moving toward
> York, cutting his way through the fields. I think there
> is a considerable force at Berlin. I am now midway
> between Abbottstown and Hanover. I cannot well ad-
> vance farther and keep communications open with
> Littlestown. Scouting parties will be sent out in the
> direction of York, Dover, and Carlisle. Stuart is mov-
> ing toward York.[43]

Because Kilpatrick suspected that there was a very large Confederate force encamped at Berlin, the volunteer cavalrymen of his command

moved even more slowly and cautiously than usual. It was, after all, Judson Kilpatrick who had forwarded the supposedly critical information to Pleasonton that Robert E. Lee's headquarters were currently at Berlin. Because of that faulty information, the horsemen of the 3rd Division took most of the day to move a total distance of less than twenty miles.

Eventually upon entering the small village of Berlin, General Farnsworth's troopers found no evidence of a current Confederate occupation. Unfortunately, General Kilpatrick's men completely missed all the unmistakable signs that General Early's infantrymen really had passed through Berlin the previous day on their way to Gettysburg. In the absence of orders from Cavalry Corps' headquarters perhaps Kilpatrick should have detached some of his troopers to harass the men of Ewell's corps as they hurried to join the Army of Northern Virginia. Ironically after the conclusion of the fighting at Gettysburg, Kilpatrick would detach numerous patrols from his command. Their orders were to harass the retreating Confederate Army.

Under orders from Kilpatrick's headquarters Custer and Farnsworth dispatched some additional scouting parties. Those patrols moved farther north toward Rossville and Dillsburg, but the Union troopers did not get close enough to the latter place to detect Wade Hampton's brigade on the northwest side of the town. The 5th New York Cavalry, all eleven troops, under the command of Major Hammond also went on patrol toward York. Hammond's troopers pushed due east in search of Stuart's command. One two-gun section of Lieutenant Elder's battery accompanied the New Yorkers on their mission. Hammond and his men, finding no additional signs of the elusive Confederates, returned to near Berlin around midnight and went into camp with the rest of their brigade.[44]

Most of General Kilpatrick's division, minus some scouting patrols, returned to a point between Abbottstown and Berlin around midnight where they encamped for the remainder of the night. Many a wooden fence rail from neighboring farms found its way onto the hundreds of individual camp fires of the weary Union troopers. The next day, July 2, would find the troopers of Judson Kilpatrick and J. E. B. Stuart crossing sabers, unexpectedly, once again.

Notes to Chapter Eleven

1. OR – 1, pp. 987-88.
2. Ibid.
3. Chamber of Commerce, *Encounter at Hanover*, p. 52.
4. Kidd, *Recollections of a Cavalryman*, pp. 128-29.
5. Chamber of Commerce, *Encounter at Hanover*, p. 163.
6. OR – 2, p. 696.
7. OR – 3, p. 522.
8. OR – 2, p. 696.
9. Ibid., p. 709. There is no other evidence that General Jubal Early received information to watch for General Stuart and his men. Undoubtedly Early and his infantrymen, upon leaving York, heard the sounds of battle from the Stuart and Kilpatrick fight at Hanover on June 30, but it is questionable whether they knew who was fighting.
10. Ibid., p. 467.
11. Ibid., p. 696.
12. George W. Beale, *A Lieutenant of Cavalry in Lee's Army* (Boston: Gorham Press, 1918), p. 114.
13. Ladd, *The Bachelder Papers*, 2:1204.
14. OR – 2, p. 696.
15. Thomas G. Tousey, *Military History of Carlisle and Carlisle Barracks* (Richmond: The Dietz Press, 1939), pp. 236-37.
16. Price, *Across the Continent*, p. 483.
17. OR – 2, p. 221. William Boyd soon resigned his commission from the 1st New York Cavalry in August 1863, and accepted another commission as the colonel in the newly forming 21st Regiment, Pennsylvania Volunteer Cavalry.
18. Ibid., p. 219. One other regiment assigned to General Ewen's brigade was absent from the immediate Carlisle area on July 1, 1863. Colonel Joachim Maidhof commanded the 11th Regiment, New York National Guard but they did not rejoin Ewen's brigade until after the Carlisle incident.
19. Ibid., pp. 215-16. Colonel Brisbane also had another regiment absent from his brigade during the conflict at Carlisle. Colonel Charles S. Smith led the 32nd Regiment, Pennsylvania Militia, which was assigned to other duties during the time of General Stuart's attack.
20. Ibid., p. 224. Landis' battery had four other guns but they were assigned to the other brigades in the division and were not present at Carlisle.
21. OR – 3, p. 344.
22. Altshuler, *Cavalry Yellow & Infantry Blue*, p. 159.
23. OR – 2, p. 344.
24. Ibid., p. 914.
25. Altshuler, *Cavalry Yellow & Infantry Blue*, pp. 215-16.
26. OR – 2, p. 221.
27. Richard L. T. Beale, *History of the Ninth Virginia Cavalry* (Richmond: B. F. Johnson Publishing Co., 1899), p. 84.
28. OR – 2, p. 697.
29. Ibid., p. 221.
30. Warner, *Generals in Blue*, p. 463.

Notes to Chapter Eleven (*continued*)

31. OR – 2, pp. 221, 224-25, 237; OR – 3, p. 492. James Dougherty was a civilian from the Harrisburg area who had volunteered to serve with General Smith's division since he was very familiar with the local network of roads. Upon volunteering, he had received the temporary rank of either first lieutenant or captain, depending upon the source consulted.
32. Beale, *A Lieutenant of Cavalry in Lee's Army*, p. 114.
33. OR – 2, p. 221. Papertown is present day Mt. Holy Springs and Petersburg is present day York Springs.
34. Phisterer, *New York in the War of the Rebellion*, 1: 614, 637.
35. Records of Confederate Soldiers. Some of the injured Confederate soldiers were: Private Andrew Jackson Barnes, Company B, 2nd Virginia – prisoner of war; Private Benjamin Franklin Gosney, Company C, 5th Virginia – wounded in action and prisoner of war.
36. Beale, *History of the Ninth Virginia Cavalry*, pp. 85-86.
37. OR – 1, p. 987.
38. New York Monuments Commission, *New York at Gettysburg*, 3 vols. (Albany: J. B. Lyon Company, 1902), 3:1129.
39. Ibid., p. 992.
40. Ibid.
41. Military and Pension Files of Hugh Judson Kilpatrick, Major General, U.S. Volunteers. Records of the Record and Pension Office, Record Group 15, National Archives, Washington, D.C.
42. Ibid.
43. OR – 1, p. 987.
44. New York Monuments Commission, *New York at Gettysburg*, 3:1129.

Chapter 12:
Advance toward Gettysburg

 HORTLY after sunrise on July 2, General Kilpatrick sent several members of his headquarters staff to awaken the staff officers of his two brigades. The staffs of Custer and Farnsworth, in turn, passed the word to the regimental staff members, who then awakened the peacefully slumbering cavalrymen, both officers and enlisted men, in their respective regiments. The tired Yankee horsemen, while not needing as much sleep as their exhausted counterparts in General Stuart's command, did find that the few extra hours of rest allowed by Kilpatrick benefited both themselves and their equally weary horses.

As the members of the 3rd Division bivouacked in the fields between Abbottstown and Berlin, Kilpatrick received a communiqué from General Pleasonton. The Cavalry Corps commander directed him to prepare his two brigades to move immediately toward the sound of the fighting at Gettysburg, which the members of the division clearly heard at various times during the previous twenty-four hours. Judson Kilpatrick, in his official report, wrote that during the early morning hours of July 2, he:

> . . . received orders to move as quickly as possible toward Gettysburg. I proceeded rapidly across the country in the direction of the firing. Reached the battle-field at 2 p.m. Received orders from headquarters Cavalry Corps, through Brigadier-General Gregg, to move over to the road leading from Gettysburg to Abbottstown, and see that the enemy did not turn our flank.[1]

While the fighting between the two great armies continued for a second day at Gettysburg, mostly in favor of General Lee's army, Major

General Alfred Pleasonton's original intention was for his two available cavalry divisions to guard the Army of the Potomac's vulnerable right flank. In his official report of the Gettysburg Campaign, Pleasonton noted in his orders that:

> Kilpatrick's division on July 2 moved toward Gettysburg from the direction of Heidlersburg [Abbottstown], to prevent the enemy from concentrating his forces by that road, and to protect our right flank from being turned.[2]

Unfortunately General Kilpatrick was nowhere near Heidlersburg on the morning of July 2, but General Stuart's brigades stretched all along the Harrisburg Pike just north of there. If he moved due west from his camps at Berlin on that morning, Kilpatrick might have earned another opportunity to strike a devastating blow to Stuart's force. His 3rd Division could have arrived at Heidlersburg in five or six hours, probably in time to confront at least a portion of Stuart's command as they passed through there. The Union cavalry commander definitely would have had enough time to run into the captured wagon train moving slowly south along the Harrisburg Pike with their guard. Instead, since the two brigades of his division were almost as tired and worn-down as their opponents and because he still had no idea exactly where J. E. B. Stuart had gone, Judson Kilpatrick ordered his men to move back to Abbottstown. There they gained the intersection of the Gettysburg-York road where they were able to move unmolested toward the fighting at Gettysburg in the west.

On that bright and sunny morning, both of General Kilpatrick's brigades eventually mounted, formed into line, and moved out of their camps and back toward the Gettysburg-York pike by 10:00 A.M. Although they complied with the orders from Cavalry Corps headquarters, they certainly had not done so with the great urgency mentioned by Kilpatrick in his report. Various patrols and scouting parties already were moving slightly in advance of the division.

The order of march on that Thursday morning had George Custer leading his whole brigade through Abbottstown and toward the small Adams County village of New Oxford in the west. He rode at the head of his Michigan Brigade in the company of Colonel Gray and the staff of the 6th Michigan Cavalry, the leading regiment in the whole division. William Mann's 7th Michigan Cavalry, Lieutenant Pennington's six guns from Battery M, 2nd U.S. Artillery, and the 1st Michigan under Charles Town all followed George Gray's troopers. Colonel Russell Alger's 5th Michigan Cavalry had the last place in the line of march in the 2nd Brigade during the day.[3]

Elon Farnsworth, riding at the head of his brigade with his few staff members, followed Custer's Michiganders. William Brinton's 18th Pennsylvania Cavalry was in the position of honor as the leading regiment of the 1st Brigade. Addison Preston's twelve troops from the 1st Vermont maintained the next position in the line of march, followed by Lieutenant Elder's Battery E of the 4th U.S. Artillery. The second half of Farnsworth's column had the troopers of Nathaniel Richmond's 1st West Virginia next in line. Today was the 5th New York's turn to act as the division's rear guard. As usual whenever posted as the division's last troops in the line of march the commanding officer split much of his regimental command into smaller patrols and details to guard the rear and flanks of the cavalry column. John Hammond, commanding the rear guard, did not deviate from that practice and soon had his patrols ranging along both rear flanks of the division.

General Kilpatrick's main column quickly reached the Gettysburg-York Pike and immediately turned to the west. The leading regiments traveled about four miles along that road until they reached the small cross-roads community of New Oxford shortly after the midday hour. The division's commanding general allowed his men to take a short rest at that location. Kilpatrick's cavalrymen obtained numerous reports, about the devastating first day's battle, from the many Union soldiers moving away from the sounds of the continuing fighting at Gettysburg. The news extracted from them was less than inspiring for the mounted men in blue. The troopers could not ignore the numerous signs of what looked like another Union defeat at the hands of Robert E. Lee. After the short respite, Kilpatrick's men remounted their horses and continued on their journey toward the right flank of the Army of the Potomac as ordered.

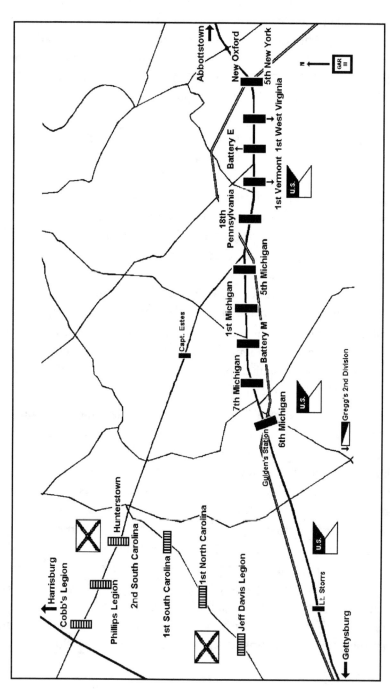

Locations of Union and Confederate Forces, July 2, 1863, 12:00 – 2:00 P.M.
(GAR III)

Captain John Wilson Phillips, the twenty-seven-year-old commanding officer of Troop B, 18th Pennsylvania Cavalry, wrote about the journey as his division neared Gettysburg. He asserted that:

> On the 2d of July, we turned back and moved
> rapidly toward Gettysburg. The sound of the conflict
> was sufficient guide. The peaceful and fertile fields of
> Pennsylvania never looked prettier than they did that
> day, as they waved with their weight of golden grain,
> all unconscious of the carnage that was reddening the
> fields of the beautiful valley of Gettysburg. We all
> felt that the contest was on which would decide the
> Nation's fate. On we rode, no man left his place, no
> man faltered, as with set lips and mayhap blanched
> faces, we moved on to Gettysburg. Passing through
> Abbotstown and New Oxford, we came to Hunter-
> stown late in the evening, and here for the first time
> saw the smoke of the battle and met the enemy.[4]

Captain John W. Phillips,
Commander, Troop B,
18th Pennsylvania Cavalry
(GAR III)

As the 3rd Division's troopers got closer to the sounds of the sporadic early afternoon fighting, the main road between Gettysburg and
York became more and more congested. Hundreds of other soldiers from

the infantry corps in the Army of the Potomac were moving either toward or away from the massive battle. Because of those soldiers and numerous wagons blocking their path, Kilpatrick's mounted column had to move off the Gettysburg-York pike many times. They continued their march by riding through the cultivated fields adjacent to the road when they could and around any obstacles when they could not stay close to the road. The progress of the mounted troopers slowed considerably.

Around 2:00 P.M. General Kilpatrick and his 3rd Division approached Gulden's Station. Located alongside the main pike, Gulden's Station was no more than a whistle-stop along the Hanover, Hanover Junction and Gettysburg Railroad where the tracks bisected the pike. The Yankee cavalrymen, from Colonel Gray's regiment, observed some torn-up tracks along with the charred ruins of the freight depot. General Early's men burned the station to the ground as they passed by it a couple of days earlier.

Just before reaching Gulden's Station, General Kilpatrick and his troopers encountered some of the pickets from General Gregg's 2nd Division. Upon seeing those other cavalrymen, Kilpatrick ordered the head of the Union column, the 6th Michigan, to advance no farther than Gulden's Station. Gregg's pickets patrolled the area near the intersection of the Low Dutch Road and the Gettysburg-York pike, just east of Gulden's Station and roughly four miles east of Gettysburg. An unidentified staff officer from General Pleasonton's headquarters met Judson Kilpatrick near that intersection. The brigadier received directions from Pleasonton's aide to report immediately to David Gregg's headquarters for additional orders. Kilpatrick, along with some of his staff and headquarters guard, moved south on the Low Dutch Road to Gregg's 2nd Division headquarters along the Hanover Road.[5]

Although both Kilpatrick and Gregg held the same rank, the latter was clearly senior by almost seven months. General Pleasonton relied upon the professionalism and competency of David Gregg to impress the seriousness of the situation upon the relatively inexperienced younger brigadier general. Pleasonton, through Gregg, directed that Kilpatrick's division should move into a position to guard the right flank of the Army of the Potomac in conjunction with the two brigades of Gregg's division already posted there.

The 2nd Division previously had received orders to occupy a position primarily along the Hanover Road. Kilpatrick, in the absence of precise orders as to an exact position, chose, with Gregg's concurrence, to move his 3rd Division north of the Gettysburg-York pike. Members of General Ewell's corps controlled that road closer to Gettysburg. Additionally, a move to the north of the road running between Gettysburg and York allowed Kilpatrick the capability to probe the area around Hunterstown, while still maintaining contact with Gregg's division slightly to the south.

It was shortly after 4:00 P.M. when Judson Kilpatrick returned to the leading regiment of his division. Kilpatrick took almost two hours to reach Gregg's headquarters, confer with him, and return to his division. Upon returning to his men, Kilpatrick briefly met with Custer and Farnsworth to inform them of the new orders. The division was moving in another direction. The commanders dispatched their aides to recall the advanced patrols and pickets thrown out to the west along the Gettysburg-York pike. However, one small patrol had already become engaged with some members of General Hampton's brigade. That brief engagement matched the Confederate brigade commander against some very stubborn and nettlesome Michigan cavalrymen.

As Kilpatrick's horsemen marched toward Gettysburg, a small detachment from the 6th Michigan Cavalry received orders to move in advance of the whole division. That patrol formed, principally, from members of Troop G was under the command of Second Lieutenant Charles E. Storrs, the junior ranking officer of the troop. The lieutenant, and roughly twenty men, moved very near to the intersection of the York Pike and Hunterstown Road while the rest of their division halted some miles to the rear of that position. They were about to encounter the leading elements of Wade Hampton's brigade also currently arriving at that intersection after passing through Hunterstown.[6]

Captain George Augustus Drew, the thirty-two-year-old commanding officer of the troop, was absent from his command as they advanced toward Gettysburg. He was, only recently, detached from Troop G to serve as General Custer's acting assistant inspector general. In two more weeks, Drew would receive his commission as major in the 6th Michigan, filling the vacant slot temporarily held by Peter Weber who died at Falling Waters. Captain Drew served as acting assistant inspector general for only a short time before returning to the regiment as a major. However, in December 1863, he was, again, detached from the 6th Michigan and assigned as acting assistant inspector general for the brigade. George Drew finished the war as a major after declining a commission as lieutenant colonel of the 6th Michigan Cavalry. He continued his military career after the war, serving in the 3rd U.S. Cavalry, and retired in 1896 after more than thirty years of continuous service.[7]

Second Lieutenant Charles E. Storrs,
Troop G, 6th Michigan Cavalry
(GAR III)

Because of Captain Drew's latest promotion, a vacancy existed in Troop G. First Lieutenant William Hull, twenty-one years old, should have gotten the promotion, as the next senior officer, to command the troop. For unknown reasons, Charles Storrs jumped over Lieutenant Hull and found himself, in another two weeks, promoted to the rank of captain. The thirty-year-old Storrs sustained a severe wound in a skirmish at Snicker's Gap, Virginia on July 19, 1863. Storrs finished his career as a major in the 6th Michigan Cavalry.[8]

While the 3rd Division halted along the Gettysburg-York pike, General Hampton approached that road from along the Gettysburg-Hunterstown road. Wade Hampton was in the advance of his brigade when he ordered a brief halt. The general moved to the side of the road where he thought he might be able to get a little rest before continuing the march. He knew he was very close to the infantry pickets from General Ewell's corps. What Hampton did not know was that Lieutenant Storrs and his men were also in the area and had spotted him as he placed a little distance between himself and his brigade.

As Wade Hampton sad astride his horse, he heard a bullet buzz close by his head. Alertly scouring the landscape in front of him, he saw nothing except a thicket of bushes almost three hundred yards distant. Pushing his horse forward almost half the distance, Hampton spotted a lone Union trooper, probably from Storrs' detachment, reloading his carbine. The unidentified trooper probably carried a single-shot Burnside carbine instead of the more accurate Spencer rifle supplied to some of the other troops in the regiment. The two men looked at each other over a distance of slightly more than one hundred yards and both fired their weapons almost simultaneously. The enlisted cavalryman's shot missed the brigadier general, while Hampton's pistol shot struck the stump of a tree upon which his adversary was standing.

As Wade Hampton prepared to fire again, his opponent suddenly held up his hand. His weapon had misfired and he signaled Hampton to hold his fire. Clearing his fouled carbine, the unidentified trooper shortly was ready to fire again. This second exchange between the two men saw the bullets get much closer to their intended targets, the Union trooper's bullet grazing the Confederate general. A third, and final, exchange between the two antagonists settled the matter. The Yankee trooper missed his target but Hampton's bullet struck his attacker in the wrist. Wounded, the Michigan cavalryman retreated into the thicket. Hampton had won the long range duel.[9]

No sooner had Wade Hampton sent his first unsuccessful attacker scurrying for safety, then he was beset by another Yankee aggressor. Hampton's opponent this time was the commander of the 6th Michigan's scouting party—Lieutenant Charles E. Storrs.

Lieutenant Storrs had heard, and then seen, one of his men firing at someone in the distance. Furtively approaching Hampton from behind, the lieutenant had almost reached his target when the general fired the shot that forced the irksome Union private from the field. Meanwhile, Storrs reached the Confederate brigadier's position and immediately struck the unsuspecting Hampton with his saber. Had Wade Hampton been mounted on a smaller horse or had he, himself, been shorter in stature, the Southern leader might very well have been killed on the spot. As it was, the blow struck by Lieutenant Storrs opened a serious gash in General Hampton's scalp.[10]

General Hampton was able to stay mounted with blood seeping from the wound and running down his head. The force of Storr's blow had been lessened because of the general's hat and thick hair. He quickly turned his horse to face his assailant and raised his revolver to fire. The gun misfired. Lieutenant Storrs, because the situation had shifted to Hampton's advantage, quickly turned his horse and spurred his mount toward the thicket. A seething Wade Hampton charged after him, still trying to get his revolver to fire. Storrs disappeared into the dense thicket, the same thicket that had swallowed the private only minutes earlier. Wade Hampton abruptly reined in his horse knowing that the Yankee cavalrymen might have additional support on the other side. The slightly wounded, dazed, and infuriated South Carolinian rode the short distance back to his command and found the brigade surgeon, Benjamin Walter Taylor. Doctor Taylor dressed the wound and the general was able to continue on duty for the remainder of the day, but with a slight headache.[11]

After Kilpatrick's return from Gregg's headquarters, he immediately put his division in motion. The 3rd Division's new orders had them turning off the main road at Gulden's Station and moving roughly two miles northwest toward Hunterstown. The members of the 6th Michigan Cavalry, the leading regiment of the division, were the only cavalrymen who had to retrace their steps as the division began their march toward Hunterstown. George Gray's regiment halted along the Gettysburg-York pike between the Low Dutch Road and Gulden's Station. The troopers from the 6th Michigan reversed their order of march and moved the short distance back to Gulden's Station. There they took the narrow and seldom used dirt road alongside the brick farmhouse of Catherine Miller. The rest of Custer's brigade followed them along the dusty road with General Farnsworth's horsemen bringing up the rear of the lengthy column. Unbeknown to the hot and dirty Union troopers was that they were moving to their next unexpected encounter with a portion of J. E. B. Stuart's division.[12]

General Fitz Lee and his brigade left the government buildings of Carlisle Barracks burning in the distance behind them as they marched south in the eerie darkness. General Stuart, after receiving the information pinpointing the exact location of the Confederate Army, left Lee in command of the action as the Southerners continued their unproductive bombardment of Carlisle. Stuart, along with some members of his headquarters staff, moved as quickly as possible toward Gettysburg. Some time around dawn, they caught some much needed rest for an hour or so en route. General Stuart, awakening before the rest of his party, quietly mounted his horse and finished the remainder of the journey to Gettysburg by himself. The errant cavalry commander had his first meeting, since being detached from the army, with Robert E. Lee during the afternoon of July 2.[13]

The troublesome captured Union wagon train continued to slowly roll through the July night. Upon reaching Papertown, Colonel Beale, the commander of the 9th Virginia Cavalry, ordered the first of many halts for the cumbersome wagon train. The fatigue of both animals and teamsters was very evident to even the most casual observer. Because of the general exhaustion among man and beast the convoy had spread out for too great a distance since leaving the vicinity of Carlisle. Richard Beale hoped that frequent short stops would allow the wagons to close some of the increasingly large gaps growing between them. As an added benefit, many of the colonel's equally drained soldiers, those assigned the task of guarding the wagons, were able to catch some beneficial rest while the train stopped.[14]

Meanwhile, Brigadier General Wade Hampton slowly moved his command through the small community of Heidlersburg, which was about four miles south of Petersburg. Continuing to push on, the South Carolinian finally halted his brigade some two miles northwest of Hunterstown. Then, in all likelihood, a small portion of the weary cavalrymen of General Stuart's division finally established contact with the Army of Northern Virginia after days of futile searching. Hampton's men probably found the pickets of General Early's division scattered around the Harrisburg Pike. It was shortly before noon of July 2 as the tired Southern horsemen dismounted after their long and fatiguing march from near Dillsburg. The three-day battle being fought a short four miles to the south was roughly half completed.[15]

As usual, like their Union counterparts, not all members of the brigade were fortunate enough to partake of the unanticipated rest stop. Wade Hampton ordered his regimental commanders to send a number of scouting parties and patrols southeast through Hunterstown toward the York Pike in search of the Union cavalry or the right flank of the Army of the Potomac. The commanders posted additional pickets in front and on the left flank of the brigade while the majority of the men in Hampton's regiments rested for a few hours.

During their brief, and somewhat terse, meeting during the afternoon of July 2, J. E. B. Stuart received succinct instructions from the commanding general of the Army of Northern Virginia. Leaving no room for doubt, Lee directed Stuart to keep the brigades of Chambliss, Fitz Lee, and Hampton on the army's left flank as they arrived along the road from Harrisburg. Robert E. Lee wanted the three brigades to protect the flank anchored by General Ewell's infantry and artillery. General Stuart received instructions to place his men between the York and Harrisburg pikes.

Fortunately for the tired Southern cavalrymen they did not have much farther to advance. Wade Hampton's men stopped just a few miles to the north of Gettysburg along the Harrisburg Pike, while Fitz Lee's leading regiments were just approaching the same area. Colonel John

Chambliss and three of his battered regiments were last in the brigade's line of march. His other regiment, the 9th Virginia Cavalry, still moved ever so slowly with the wagons and artillery.[16]

General Hampton directed his command to advance south along the Harrisburg Pike shortly after receiving Stuart's orders. They were originally going to advance as far as the York Pike. The main objectives for Hampton seemed to be for him to get closer to Gettysburg and then deploy his six regiments on the left flank of Ewell's infantry corps and block the Union cavalry. As the saddle-sore members of his brigade began their march toward Gettysburg in the south, one of his patrols informed him that:

> . . . a heavy force of cavalry was advancing on Hunterstown, with a view to get in the rear of our army. Communicating this information to General Stuart, I was ordered by him to return, and hold the enemy in check. Pursuant to these orders, I moved back, and met the enemy between Hunterstown and Gettysburg.[17]

On the basis of the newly received information and instructions from Stuart, Wade Hampton ordered his six regiments to countermarch. Slowly the Southern horsemen retraced their route of march almost back to their starting point along the Harrisburg Pike. Hampton's troopers in gray then turned their exhausted horses off the main road to the east and took the shortest, and most direct, route toward the village of Hunterstown.

As the begrimed Southerners of Wade Hampton's command neared the center of Hunterstown some of the townsfolk greeted them, although not wholly enthusiastically. The citizens of Hunterstown clearly remembered the first visit by members of Cobb's Legion only three days previously and were more curious than supportive of the Confederate invaders. That previous foraging party had left the residents of Hunterstown in relative peace after their short surprise visit. Captain Crawford and his men remained near Hunterstown and now returned to the center of the town in advance of the main body of troops. Crawford and his party established contact with the Army of Northern Virginia shortly after arriving at Hunterstown. They patrolled near Hunterstown while Stuart and the rest of his division eventually came to them.

General Hampton's men turned southwest as they neared the center of town and continued along the Gettysburg-Hunterstown road. That road ran to the York Pike at which place it ended. The line of march for Hampton's brigade during July 2 had the Jeff Davis Legion under Lieutenant Colonel Waring leading the brigade. Colonel Laurence Baker and the members of his veteran 1st North Carolina Cavalry followed the men from Alabama, Mississippi, and Georgia. The two regiments from South Carolina, the 1st and 2nd, were next in line under lieutenant colonels Twiggs and Lipscomb. Lieutenant Colonel Rich came next with the horsemen of the Phillips Legion. The last regiment in the line of march was Cobb's Georgia Legion led by Colonel Pierce Young. It took well over an hour for the troopers clad in gray to pass through the streets of the village.

Cobb's Legion was the last regiment in Hampton's line of march on July 2. The main body of Colonel Young's regiment moved slowly along the dusty road to Gettysburg. Thirty-six-year-old Lieutenant Colonel William Gaston Delony commanded ten of the eleven companies of the legion, finally reunited, marching away from the streets of Hunterstown. That portion of the regiment was about a mile from Hunterstown when the sudden attack began on their comrades assigned to the rear guard. Without waiting for instructions from brigade headquarters, Lieutenant Colonel Delony countermarched his command and rushed back in the direction of the fighting.

The rear guard of Cobb's Legion consisted of roughly forty enlisted men assigned primarily from Company E. That company remained behind in the streets of Hunterstown while allowing their brigade to move forward a short distance before they themselves continued along the same route. Their objective was identical to Lieutenant Potter's mission on the road tó Hanover only two days earlier—prevent any surprise attacks from the enemy. In an unusual circumstance, Colonel Pierce Young, the commander of Cobb's Legion, remained behind in Hunterstown and personally led the tiny detachment. Regimental commanders rarely led small details of their men.

Because of all the lengthy delays during the 3rd Division's current march toward Gettysburg, it was now getting very late in the afternoon. Somewhere around 4:30 P.M. one of the patrols from General Kilpatrick's division, one that was guarding the flanks, came across the members of the Confederate rear guard less than a mile from the center of Hunterstown. Captain Llewellyn Garrish Estes, Judson Kilpatrick's assistant adjutant general, commanded that particular patrol. That Federal patrol approached the enemy's line of mounted skirmishers almost undetected until the last moment. The quickness with which the Yankee patrol moved, along with the element of surprise, threw the few dozen men from Cobb's Legion into utter confusion. They retreated back to their main reserve posted along the Hunterstown-York road. The cavalrymen from Georgia halted their retreat for a brief period near a schoolhouse at the junction of another road—the same road upon which Colonel Gray's troopers were approaching. At that intersection additional members from the legion's reserve force reinforced them. Upon hearing the beginning of the attack on their comrades, the pickets assigned to other roads fell back toward Hunterstown from their advanced positions.[18]

The nineteen-year-old Llewellyn Estes only recently received a promotion to the rank of captain and assistant adjutant general of U.S. Volunteers on June 18. He previously served as the first lieutenant in Troop A of the 1st Regiment, Maine Volunteer Cavalry. While serving in that capacity he initially joined Judson Kilpatrick's staff as an additional aide-de-camp. Savoring the life of a staff officer, Estes decided to forfeit his burgeoning career in the cavalry branch to stay on Kilpatrick's staff after the latter received the rank of brigadier general. The Maine-native continuously served with the commanding general from February 1863 when Kilpatrick had been a colonel commanding the 1st Brigade of David Gregg's 3rd Division. The 1st Maine Cavalry served in that brigade under him.[19]

Captain Estes remained on General Kilpatrick's staff throughout the rest of the war. The young captain transferred with his general when Judson Kilpatrick got exiled to the western theater of operations in 1864. There they both served under Major General William Tecumseh

Sherman (U.S.M.A., Class of 1840). Later in the war Estes received the Medal of Honor for voluntarily leading a charge over a burning bridge in the fight at Flint River, Georgia in August 1864, while still performing his duties on Kilpatrick's staff. Shortly thereafter he attained the rank of major in the U.S. Volunteers and also received the brevet ranks of lieutenant colonel, colonel, and brigadier general for his overall meritorious service during the war.[20]

Captain Llewellyn G. Estes,
Acting Assistant Adjutant General,
3rd Division
(USAMHI)

Besides their assigned duties, it was not at all unusual for a commissioned officer to lead an assortment of patrols or other details while serving on corps, division, brigade, or regimental staff duty. The expectations were that staff officers would remain away from their regular duties for only short periods. They needed to keep their leadership skills sharp and current for their eventual return to their permanent units. Any experience gained during their period of staff duty greatly helped them to practice the evolution of command instead of only relaying orders to subordinate units. Just yesterday, Lieutenant Colonel Alexander, a senior member of General Pleasonton's staff, led a detachment of troops in pursuit of General Stuart's men as they left Hanover. Additionally, both George Custer and Elon Farnsworth, as junior officers, came to their superiors' attention because of their confident and aggressive skills while leading various elements of the Cavalry Corps on a variety of patrols and into actual battles.

Captain Estes and his detail sprinted on a parallel course to their division as Judson Kilpatrick's two brigades prepared to move from their brief respite near Gulden's Station and the Low Dutch Road. Llewellyn Estes commanded roughly fifty men assigned to Troop A from Lieutenant Colonel Brinton's pummeled regiment, the 18th Pennsylvania Cavalry. The troopers in Estes' patrol were some of the survivors of the chaotic fighting at Hanover. The commanding officer of the troop, 1st Lieutenant Benjamin Franklin Campbell, remained behind with the rest of the regiment while Estes started his patrol on the right flank of the division. Campbell was not feeling too well during the first few days of July. He would be feeling even slightly worse after being wounded by a saber cut during additional fighting by his regiment at Hagerstown, Maryland on July 6.[21]

Edward A. Paul, a *New York Times* correspondent who traveled with General Kilpatrick's headquarters, filed his report of the brief encounter at Hunterstown. In his story, he stated that:

> The column did not reach Hunterstown until 4 o'clock P.M. (on July 2d), when a squadron of the Eighteenth Pennsylvania Cavalry, headed by Capt. Estes, charged through and drove the enemy back upon his reserves to the Gettysburgh road. After surveying the position, Gen. Farnsworth's brigade was ordered on a road to the right leading to Cashtown, and Gen. Custer's brigade was placed on the left.[22]

The Pennsylvania troopers under Captain Estes command pushed the men from Cobb's Legion back into the center of Hunterstown where the Georgians briefly regrouped. The Confederates hoped to make a stand in the center square of the town, but the onslaught of the troopers in blue drove them completely out of Hunterstown. Commissary Sergeant Joseph Cooke from the 18th Pennsylvania went down with a bullet wound that lodged painfully in the side of his head. Luckily the wound was not too serious and he was able to return to duty in a few weeks. The commissary sergeant, of Troop A, survived the war but spent almost six months as a prisoner of war during 1864 after being captured near Cold Harbor, Virginia in June 1864. Sergeant Joseph Cooke was the only reported casualty during Captain Estes quick foray before the arrival of the rest of the division.[23]

Just as the men from Troop A of the 18th Pennsylvania moved to engage the enemy in the center of Hunterstown, the leading regiments of George Custer's brigade arrived on the outskirts of Hunterstown. The 6th and 7th Michigan regiments, moving along the same narrow dirt road since leaving the Gettysburg-York pike a short time earlier, stopped on some slightly elevated ground to the southeast of Hunterstown. General Custer, traveling at the head of his brigade, ordered colonels Gray and Mann to dismount a small portion of their men and establish a skirmish line in the fields and around the farmhouses of Samuel McCreary and Henry Harman. Some of the dismounted soldiers received directions to advance a short distance forward toward the center of Hunterstown as skirmishers.[24]

After the first two of Custer's regiments deployed across the road, Lieutenant Pennington's Battery M of the 2nd U.S. Artillery wheeled into position near the Harman family farm. The artillerymen immediately unlimbered at least one section of two 3-inch Ordnance Rifles on a slight knoll in the clearing in front of the house. Although they quickly deployed the guns, the lieutenant in charge of the section could find no enemy targets in their field of fire and they remained silent for the moment.

Lieutenant Colonel J. Frederick Waring's troopers from the Jeff Davis Legion traveled roughly three miles along the Gettysburg-Hunterstown road after passing through Hunterstown. The legion almost reached the intersection of the Gettysburg-York pike when General Hampton, riding in the vanguard, heard sporadic small-arms fire to the rear of his column. The sounds of the scattered small-arms fire drifted through the warm afternoon air. The volume and intensity of the firing increased rapidly as the commanding brigadier general ordered all his regiments back toward Hunterstown and the sound of the guns. It was readily apparent that at least the rear guard of his brigade, if not other members of his command, had become hotly engaged in a fight with unknown troops.

General Hampton's brigade quickly turned their horses around. The general, after his brief contact with the patrol from the 6th Michigan, raced almost two miles through the ranks of his regiments all the while trying to ascertain the source of the disturbance in his rear. Wade Hampton would not remain in suspense for too long. As he neared the John G. Gilbert farm, located a little less than one mile from the center of Hunterstown, he came across a sight that probably sent a shiver up the length of his spine. A closely pursuing band of Yankee troopers was easily driving the forty or so members of his rear guard from the center of Hunterstown.

The rear guard from Cobb's Legion received directions from Colonel Pierce Young to quickly withdraw from the center of Hunterstown as Captain Estes and his men drove in the scattered Confederate pickets. The veteran members of the legion's Company E moved in the same direction that Wade Hampton's regiments had taken along the Gettysburg-Hunterstown road. While they attempted to withdraw, they were under attack by the troublesome patrol from the 18th Pennsylvania. A running fight continued through the town and to the road stretching toward Gettysburg.

Not wishing to overextend himself, or even worse fall into a trap, Captain Estes broke off all contact with the Confederate rear guard. He, along with the members of the 18th Pennsylvania Cavalry, could not see what was around the first bend in the road. Estes returned to the center of Hunterstown with his determined detachment and their winded horses. Casualties were negligible for the Union troops involved in the initial contact. Southern casualties, if any, were not reported in the opening phase of the fight. Colonel Young, along with the assistance of the capable Captain Barrington Simeral King, quickly reformed his confused detachment of men just north of the John G. Gilbert farm along the Gettysburg-Hunterstown road. Captain King was the twenty-nine-year-old commanding officer of Company E.[25]

Reports from some of his advanced skirmishers filtered back to General Custer with the news that the Rebel cavalry had completely pulled out of the center of Hunterstown. He learned that the Confederate troops were quickly heading south along the Gettysburg-Hunterstown road. Knowing that he should take some action to impede their progress, Custer immediately ordered his men to again advance. The horsemen from the 6th and 7th Michigan, those previously dismounted near the Harman farm, remounted their horses. The two regiments formed in a column of four abreast. Lieutenant Pennington ordered his two guns hitched back up and moved them forward with the rest of the battery. The two cavalry regiments, Colonel Gray's men still in the lead, hurriedly marched past the dozen or so brick and frame houses located along the main street of Hunterstown that ran east and west through the town.

Captain Kidd, assigned to the 6th Michigan Cavalry, mentioned the actions taken by his regiment as they passed through the town and approached the enemy forces:

> When nearing the village of Hunterstown, on a road flanked by fences, the advance encountered a heavy force of confederate cavalry. A mounted line was formed across the road, while there were dismounted skirmishers behind the fences on either side.[26]

The leading troops of the 6th Michigan Cavalry rattled past the few stores in the square, as well as the J. L. Grass Hotel. The two-story brick hotel sat on the southwest side of the square and would serve a dual purpose in the coming fight. First it served as Judson Kilpatrick's headquarters during the early part of the skirmish. Second, after the fighting ended, the hotel served as the largest hospital.

Thirteen-year-old Jacob Taughenbaugh, along with his family, lived on a small farm on the outskirts of Hunterstown, just south of the road that ran toward York. He had been working on the family farm and was talking to his uncle when the Confederate pickets started to hurriedly pass by them in retreat. Some Union cavalrymen closely followed them as the Southerners withdrew. As the young lad watched the troopers go past, General Kilpatrick and his staff approached and stopped near him. The Union officers briefly questioned him concerning the "lay of the land and the size of the enemy force in the village." He responded by telling them that there were less than a hundred enemy soldiers in Hunterstown.[27]

As General Kilpatrick's cavalry took sole possession of Hunterstown the commanding officers of each regiment quickly posted a strong line of skirmishers along all the roads leading into the center of the town from the west, north, and south. General Custer's Michigan Brigade continued to slowly march out the Gettysburg-Hunterstown road to the southwest. Custer's command briefly halted at the top of a piece of high ground. There the leading troops of the 6th Michigan Cavalry cleared the wood line a couple of hundred yards north from the farm of John Felty. A local magistrate, Mr. Felty owned a large two-story brick house and equally large barn, both of which sat on the western side of the narrow road.[28]

The Michiganders surveyed the field in their front and noticed that all the trees had been cut down in at least a half mile square area between the Felty farm and that of his neighbor to the south, John G. Gilbert. The Gilbert farmhouse was much less imposing than that of his wealthier neighbor, but it was another sturdy brick structure so common in that area of south-central Pennsylvania. The lack of trees presented a perfect field of fire for both the Union and Confederate soldiers and any of their artillery. As the Michigan troopers halted their column, they beheld a beautiful sight before them. The wheat and corn, growing in the fields in front of them, slowly swayed in the breeze of a summer day's late afternoon. Under different circumstances the scene would be most enjoyable. However, given the present situation, there was another much less gratifying sight to behold.

Colonel Young halted his rear guard just in front of the Gilbert farm, on the northern side of the house. There they made preparations to receive an imminent attack by the blue-clad cavalrymen. Additionally, George Custer accurately noticed that the enemy soldiers seemed to be forming just south of town. He transmitted that fact by personally reporting to General Kilpatrick, who was just setting up his headquarters at the

346 ◆ Chapter 12

Grass Hotel. After a brief meeting with Kilpatrick, Custer returned to Colonel Gray and the 6th Michigan Cavalry with orders to immediately attack the Confederate troops seen along the road near the Gilbert farm. At the same time, General Farnsworth received orders for his brigade to quickly move forward and occupy the high ground along a ridge to the west of the Gettysburg-Hunterstown road.

George Custer rode to the head of the 6th Michigan regiment and had a brief exchange with the commanding officer of the regiment's leading troop. The general then:

> . . . ordered out Co. A, Sixth Michigan for a mounted charge, and deployed two more companies of the same regiment on foot in a wheat field at the side of the road, so as to rake it with their fire. At the end of the road could be seen a party of the enemy, apparently a squadron. Capt. Thompson commanded Co. A. All was ready, and Thompson was preparing to charge, when to everyone's surprise, the boy general flashed out his long Toledo blade, motioned to his staff to keep back, and dashed out in front of Co. A with the careless laughing remark, "I'll lead you this time, boys. Come on!" Then away he went down the road at a gallop, his broad white hat on the back of his head, while the men raised a short yell of delight and followed him. Down the road in a perfect cloud of blinding dust went the boy general in front of that single company and the next moment they were into the midst of the enemy, only to find they had struck a very superior force.[29]

Brigadier General Custer's stated purpose for the ill-advised attack against an undetermined number of the enemy was to gain enough time "so as to enable our battery [Pennington's] to be placed in position."[30] The officer with whom Custer conversed was Captain Thompson of Troop A. Captain Henry E. Thompson was the very same officer earlier detached from the regiment to fight alongside Colonel Alger's 5th Michigan at Hanover two days previously.

The captain, from Troop A, expressed serious doubts to his brigade commander about one single troop of cavalry being able to overcome the enemy force in their front. Thompson knew that the force in his front almost equaled the strength of his lone troop. The new brigadier general did not want to hear his order to engage the enemy challenged by a subordinate. Additionally, the young captain, though slightly older than his commanding general, saw that the Confederate cavalrymen were no longer retreating. Indeed they had clearly halted their withdrawal and were preparing for the Union horsemen to attack. Captain Thompson had only wondered aloud if his opponents in gray did not have considerable support from other units hidden by the trees.[31]

Nevertheless, the commanding officer of Troop A formed his horsemen in the road along the higher ground just north of the Felty farm. Thompson commanded one of the largest troops in the regiment with two commissioned officers and seventy-six enlisted men currently assigned for duty.[32] Due to the wooden fencing that lined both sides of the road, it is highly unlikely that Thompson's assault column could accommodate more than four troopers riding abreast of each other along the road. A member of Cobb's Legion buttresses that assumption by stating that the "two columns met at a charge in column of four's in the lane, or fenced road."[33] In his haste to advance against the enemy, Custer failed to send out the brigade's pioneers. A pioneer's duty was to move ahead of an attacking force for a safe distance and remove obstacles, such as fences, which might impede or otherwise break up the continuity of the attacking force.

As Captain Thompson, his lieutenant, and noncommissioned officers prepared their nervous men and their excited horses for the mounted attack, the next three troops in the regimental line of march dismounted. Troop E, under the command of Captain Kidd, hurriedly moved forward on foot as far as the red brick buildings of the Felty farm. Many of James Kidd's fifty-eight troopers carried Spencer repeating rifles. Some of his men positioned themselves in the upper floor of the barn. The additional height of the structure enabled them to have a magnificent view of the road, which they could cover with their rifles. Other dismounted cavalrymen from the troop occupied the lower level of the barn as well as positions around the outside of both the barn and the house. As with all dismounted operations, one quarter of the troop members or roughly nineteen enlisted men remained in a protected location in the rear of the skirmish line with their comrades' horses.[34]

Troops C and D, commanded respectively by captains Wesley Armstrong and David G. Royce, also dismounted. Instead of moving directly ahead to the Felty buildings, those two troops deployed obliquely in formation farther to the right, or west, of the Felty buildings. The majority of the sixty-seven men in Troop D carried Spencer rifles, while a few used the single-shot Burnside carbines. Captain Armstrong's sixty-four men took positions farthest from the road and the farm buildings but still maintained contact with the other troop on their immediate left. The twenty-eight-year-old Captain Royce, who would die in less than two weeks at Falling Waters on July 14, had his men take a defensive position closest to the road and the brick farm buildings.[35] They were able to conceal themselves in a field of maturing wheat along the crest of the ridge that had grown almost two feet high.[36]

Colonel Gray's other six troops from the 6th Michigan Cavalry remained mounted and in formation just north of the Felty farm buildings. They directly supported the regiment's dismounted men to their front. The mounted troopers occupied a relatively sheltered position on the western side of the Gettysburg-Hunterstown road at the extreme edge of the wood line. They faced south toward the Felty farm. The horseholders from the three dismounted troops moved to the rear of Colonel Gray's mounted formation and into the safety of the woods.

As the commissioned officers of the 6th Michigan Cavalry finished deploying all their troops, Alexander Pennington's battery arrived just north of the Felty farm buildings. Lieutenant Pennington ordered second lieutenants Clarke, Hamilton, and Woodruff to position their two-gun sections facing south, directly in front of Colonel Gray's mounted force. The six guns of Battery M quickly unlimbered and prepared for action. Pennington strategically and skillfully placed his 3-inch Ordnance Rifles. In case of a full frontal assault by the Rebel cavalry, the dismounted skirmishers of the 6th Michigan found themselves completely covered by the cannons to their rear. Additionally, if the enemy somehow bypassed the Yankee skirmishers and tried to reenter Hunterstown they would get a severe pounding by the battery's ordnance as they passed by on the narrow Gettysburg-Hunterstown road.

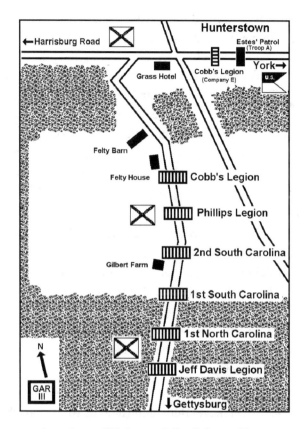

Locations of Union and Confederate Forces,
July 2, 1863, 4:00 – 5:00 P.M.
(GAR III)

Behind the rapidly deploying artillerymen of Battery M came the mounted troopers of Colonel William Mann's regiment. The 7th Michigan Cavalry moved forward along the Gettysburg-Hunterstown road with only eight of its ten troops. Mann's eight troops dismounted and formed a lengthy skirmish line at the edge of the trees and along the ridge line on the eastern side of the road. The regiment had slightly less than three hundred men armed primarily with Burnside carbines on the extended skirmish line. The horseholders moved all the horses to the safety of the trees to the rear.[37]

While the regiment deployed near the Felty farm, two troops of the 7th Michigan Cavalry remained behind to guard and picket the road

leading to the west toward the Harrisburg Pike. Those two troops prevented any additional Confederate cavalry from suddenly appearing and
surprising General Kilpatrick's men and striking them in the rear. Tactically it was a prudent measure on the commanding general's part since
the brigades of Colonel Chambliss and General Fitz Lee were thus far
absent from the conflict at Hunterstown. During the late afternoon
Chambliss and Lee were approaching the intersection of the Harrisburg
Pike and the road toward Hunterstown. That road was the same one that
Hampton's brigade had taken to arrive at Hunterstown earlier in the day.
The intersection was only a short distance from Hunterstown and the recently posted Michigan pickets.

Colonel Town's eleven troops of the 1st Michigan Cavalry were the
next Union soldiers to arrive at Hunterstown. Nine of the troops immediately deployed behind the dismounted skirmishers of the 7th Michigan
on the eastern side of the road. Town's regiment remained as a mounted
reserve behind the tree line and close to the town. If the Confederate
cavalry broke through the 6th and 7th regiments, as well as Pennington's
battery, the 1st Michigan would be the last posted force to block their
entrance into Hunterstown.

Two troops from the 1st Michigan Cavalry were detached from the
regiment and placed on picket duty alongside the two troops from the 7th
Michigan. Colonel Town's men got assigned to the left of the road while
the two troops from the 7th Michigan held the right side of the same
road. The second detachment from the 1st Michigan consisted of troops
B and H under the command of thirty-one-year-old Captain Andrew W.
Duggan from Troop H. Duggan would receive a severe wound during the
fighting at Boonsboro, Maryland on July 8, 1863. 1st Lieutenant Amasa
E. Matthews, twenty-six years old, led the fifty-two enlisted men assigned to Troop H, while his captain directed the overall command. Captain William M. Hazlitt commanded Troop B and had fifty-one
noncommissioned officers and enlisted men assigned to it. Captain
Hazlitt was twenty-three years old and received a slight wound during
the regiment's fight on the next day, July 3.[38]

Notes to Chapter Twelve

1. OR – 1, p. 992.
2. Ibid., p. 914. On July 2 General Pleasonton had allowed John Buford's division, consisting of Gamble's and Devin's brigades, to move from the left flank of the Army of the Potomac. They marched to Westminster. David Gregg's division, consisting of McIntosh's and J. Gregg's brigades, was just arriving on the right flank of General Meade's position. Judson Kilpatrick's division was moving to roughly the same position as Gregg's horsemen before being diverted late in the day to the left flank of the army.
3. Kidd, *Recollections of a Cavalryman*, p. 134.
4. Regimental Association, *History of the Eighteenth Regiment of Cavalry, Pennsylvania Volunteers*, p. 78.
5. OR – 1, p. 992.
6. Letter of Charles E. Storrs, July 5, 1863. Author's collection.
7. NA RG 94 – 6 MI; Robertson, *Michigan in the War*, pt. 3, p. 70; *Record of Service of Michigan Volunteers, Sixth Michigan Cavalry*, p. 48. For unexplained reasons, General Custer's 2nd Brigade had three officers assigned as acting assistant inspector general at the beginning of July 1863. There should have been only one officer assigned. One A.A.I.G., Captain Frederick W. Armstrong from Troop M, 2nd New York Cavalry was a holdover from the previous staff and would soon leave the brigade.
8. NA RG 94 – 6 MI; *Record of Service of Michigan Volunteers, Sixth Michigan Cavalry*, pp. 74, 134. The twenty-one-year-old William Hull saw previous service as a sergeant in the 1st Regiment, Michigan Volunteer Infantry before joining the 6th Michigan Cavalry as a second lieutenant.
9. Manly Wade Wellman, *Giant in Gray: A Biography of Wade Hampton of South Carolina* (Dayton, Ohio: Press of Morningside Bookshop, 1988), p. 115; Edward G. Longacre, *Custer and His Wolverines:The Michigan Cavalry Brigade 1861 – 1865* (Conshohocken, Pa.: Combined Publishing, 1997), p. 140. The exact time and location, where the two foes met, are unknown, as is the true identity of Wade Hampton's attacker. Wellman, in his biography of Hampton, identifies the attacker as Private Frank Pearson, nineteen years old. Unfortunately, there is no Frank Pearson listed on any of the muster rolls of the 6th Michigan Cavalry. That name does not appear on any of the other regimental muster rolls for the other three Michigan units. Another source states that Hampton's foe was twenty-five-year-old Private James C. Parsons of Company I, 6th Michigan Cavalry. At the time of the attack, Private Parsons was still detached from his regiment and serving as an orderly for Brigadier General Copeland in Washington, D.C. He was one of Joseph Copeland's staff members allowed to accompany the general to Washington D.C. and then to the general's next assignment. Additionally, Private Parsons' military record shows no wound received during the Gettysburg Campaign. James Parsons was one of six privates assigned to General Copeland during his reassignment from General Stahel's division. The other orderlies included: Emory Abby, Troop K, 6th Michigan; Christian Briesh, Troop K, 5th Michigan; Ulrich L. Crocker, Troop M, 6th Michigan; David Cummins, Troop I, 5th Michigan; Cornelius Gavin, Troop I, 5th Michigan.
10. Wellman, *Giant in Gray*, p. 116; Longacre, *Custer and His Wolverines*, p. 140.
11. Ibid.

Notes to Chapter Twelve (*continued*)

12. Paul M. Shevchuk, "The Battle of Hunterstown, Pennsylvania, July 2, 1863." *Gettysburg: Historical Articles of Lasting Interest* (Dayton Ohio: Morningside, Inc., July 1989): 93-104.
13. McClellan, *The Life and Campaigns of Major General J. E. B. Stuart*, p. 332.
14. Beale, *History of the Ninth Virginia Cavalry*, p. 84.
15. Beale, *A Lieutenant of Cavalry in Lee's Army*, p. 115.
16. Beale, *History of the Ninth Virginia Cavalry*, p. 85.
17. OR – 2, p. 724.
18. Wilbur S. Nye, "The Affair at Hunterstown," *Civil War Times Illustrated* 9 (February 1971): 22-34.
19. Dyer, *Compendium of the War*, 1:326; Edward P. Tobie, *History of the 1st Maine Cavalry, 1861 – 1865* (Boston: Press of Emery & Hughes, 1887), p. 465; 1st Regiment, Maine Volunteer Cavalry Regiment; Boxes 1495 – 1500; Muster Rolls, Regimental Papers, Office of the Adjutant General, Volunteer Organizations, Civil War; Record Group 94; National Archives, Washington, D.C.
20. Hunt, *Brevet Brigadier Generals in Blue*, p. 197; Tobie, *History of the 1st Maine Cavalry*, p. 465.
21. Regimental Association, *History of the Eighteenth Regiment of Cavalry, Pennsylvania Volunteers*, p. 183; Robertson, *Michigan in the War*, pp. 412-13; NA RG 94 – 18 PA. The regular commander of Troop A was Captain William C. Lindsey, who had been just recently assigned to the regiment's Field and Staff as an acting major. He actually led the members of his troop into the streets of Hunterstown on July 2. Lieutenant Colonel Brinton was the only field grade officer serving with the regiment at the end of June 1863. The colonel and all three majors were absent from the regiment—sick, detailed, or under arrest and about to be dismissed. Acting Major Lindsey died at the Battle of Hagerstown on July 6, 1863.
22. Robertson, *Michigan in the War*, pp. 412-13.
23. Letter of Joseph Cooke, July 14, 1863. Author's collection; Regimental Association, *History of the Eighteenth Regiment of Cavalry, Pennsylvania Volunteers*, p. 184.
24. Shevchuk, "The Battle of Hunterstown, Pennsylvania, July 2, 1863," pp. 93-104; Nye, "The Affair at Hunterstown," pp. 22-34.
25. Letter of William G. Delony, MSS Collection. University of Georgia. (Hereafter cited as Delony Letter.)
26. Kidd, *Recollections of a Cavalryman*, p. 134.
27. T. W. Herbert, "In Occupied Pennsylvania," *The Georgia Review*, vol. 4 (The University of Georgia, Athens, 1950): 103-13.
28. Shevchuk, "The Battle of Hunterstown, Pennsylvania, July 2, 1863," pp. 93-104.
29. Frederick Whittaker, *A Complete Life of Gen. George A. Custer* (New York: Sheldon & Co., 1876), p. 173.
30. OR – 1, p. 999.
31. D. A. Kinsley, *Favor the Bold*, 2 vols. (New York: Holt, Rinehart and Winston, 1967), 1:142.
32. NA RG 94 – 6 MI.
33. *Gettysburg Compiler*, December 10, 1901.
34. NA RG 94 – 6 MI; Kidd, *Recollections of a Cavalryman*, p. 134.

Notes to Chapter Twelve (*continued*)

35. NA RG 94 – 6 MI. Troops C and D each had lost one enlisted man during the fighting at Hanover on June 30. The type of weapon used by the members of Troop C is unknown.
36. Kidd, *Recollections of a Cavalryman*, p. 134.
37. NA RG 94 – 7 MI.
38. NA RG 94 – 1 MI; OR – 1, p. 998.

Chapter 13:
Encounter at Hunterstown

T was now somewhere around five o'clock in the afternoon. General Custer and Captain Thompson started to
move the anxious members of Troop A forward toward
the position of Colonel Young and the rear guard of his
legion. With sabers drawn, Custer and Thompson moved
to near the head of the short column of horsemen. The Union troopers
started their horses first at a walk. After only a short distance, they
passed the Felty house and moved into a trot. Finally, as they quickly
covered almost half the distance to the Gilbert farm, the troopers from
Michigan forcefully spurred their frenzied horses forward at an all out
gallop. They rapidly closed the short distance between themselves and
the Southern soldiers.[1]

As Captain Thompson's troop neared the Gilbert home at a full gallop they struck the stationary ranks of Pierce Young's men. Thompson's
troopers slammed into the ranks of Captain King's Company E with a
sickening thud. Just before the two forces became intermingled, the
mounted members of the legion's rear guard fired a volley that was
mostly ineffective upon the rapidly charging Yankee horsemen. The initial impact of a swiftly advancing body of men and horses, into another
group that was not moving, was far too great for the Southerners to overcome. Their skirmish line stretched thinly along the road. They gallantly
tried to resist, but to no avail. In a matter of seconds Colonel Young's
rear guard retreated in mass confusion past the Gilbert farmhouse and
into the rear of their regiment.

At the start of the charge everything looked good for the attacking
members from Thompson's Troop A. They fired their weapons and
wildly slashed at the enemy troopers with their sabers. All the while they

continued hastily to advance in the wake of the legion's inauspicious retreat. The seemingly one-side fighting flowed quickly south past the Gilbert farmhouse. Thompson's men expressed their extreme elation at the ease with which they pushed the Rebel cavalry back. Suddenly, Custer and his Michigan troopers received a very unpleasant surprise and a nasty reminder of the ebb and flow of battle. Colonel Young had dismounted some of his men before Custer ordered his charge. The unseen Confederate skirmishers, hidden in the wheatfield around the Gilbert house, opened a severe fire on Captain Thompson's column moving along the road.

A slightly incapacitated Brigadier General Hampton quickly reversed his order of march when he learned of the trouble in his rear. The main body of Cobb's Legion arrived on the edge of the contested field shortly before Custer's assault. They halted, and remained mounted, along the road just south of the Gilbert farm and along the tree line to the south. To their immediate left, facing north, were the seven companies of horsemen from the Phillips Legion. Lieutenant Colonel Rich deployed his men in the field behind the Gilbert house. He also advanced at least one company, dismounted, a short distance into the wheatfield as skirmishers. To the right of Cobb's Legion were the companies of the 2nd South Carolina. Lieutenant Colonel Lipscomb, likewise, advanced at least one of his ten companies as skirmishers and sharpshooters. Wade Hampton's other three regiments, the 1st North Carolina, the 1st South Carolina, and the Jeff Davis Legion, had not yet arrived as George Custer clearly threatened to overrun Colonel Young's rear guard from Cobb's Legion.

Colonel Pierce Young found himself caught in the melee between his men from Company E and the men from the 6th Michigan's Troop A. The commanding officer of Cobb's Legion hastily turned his horse's head southward and withdrew from the front line just as his men received the first attack from Captain Thompson's charging horsemen. Fortunately for Pierce Young, Barrington King, and their men, they did not have to retreat very far to gain some semblance of safety. After moving south for only a few hundred yards, they ran into the leading company of Cobb's Legion returning to assist them. Company C, commanded by 1st Lieutenant Thomas Houze, had been the last company in the line of march, but now they were in the very forefront of the action. Bugler Henry C. Jackson, serving with Company C, remembered the sudden chaotic arrival of Colonel Young and the disorganized men from Company E in a letter to some of his former enemies:

> I was in front and came near being killed. General P. M. B. Young came flying down the pike, hat in hand, with your men in close pursuit, firing at him constantly. He ordered a charge, and the two lines rushed at each other and had a hand to hand conflict.[2]

Just as Colonel Young reached the expected safety offered by the rear ranks of his steadfast legion his horse was shot and killed. As his horse's legs buckled under him, Young found himself unceremoniously dumped to the ground. Luckily, he was unhurt in the tumble. Jumping to his feet immediately, Colonel Young ordered his legion's Company C and the next company in the regiment's line of march, Company H, to attack the now disorganized and somewhat surprised Michiganders. First Lieutenant Cicero C. Brooks commanded Company H as they, and Lieutenant Houze's mounted men, immediately complied with their commander's order.[3]

Until now, the action was all in favor of Custer and his men. His valiant cavalrymen from Thompson's troop had driven the Southerners easily before them. Then the unthinkable happened to the rapidly charging Union troopers from the 6th Michigan Cavalry. The enlisted men suddenly found themselves without a leader. Custer, Thompson, and the only other commissioned officer participating in the initial assault, 2nd Lieutenant Stephen Ballard, all went down as the frenzied contest continued along the road.

Before all else, the fair-haired Custer found himself sprawled on the ground when his horse dropped dead in its tracks after being hit by a bullet. Fortunately, as with Colonel Young before him, Custer received no major injuries or wounds as he fell to the ground. Unfortunately, many of the nearby Rebel cavalrymen saw him go down and set their sights on the now dismounted brigadier. The stars, that Joseph Fought had sewn to Custer's collar only days beforehand, served as tempting targets for the

Confederate soldiers. Again, as with many other situations throughout the war, "Custer's Luck" prevailed on this occasion. George Custer escaped from serious injury or probable capture because of the heroic and courageous efforts of one of his accompanying staff members from the Michigan Brigade.[4]

Private Norvill F. Churchill, only recently assigned as an orderly to Custer's brigade staff from Troop L of the 1st Michigan Cavalry, happened to be the closest Union trooper to his commanding officer's perilous position. One Southern soldier, in particular, approached General Custer with the idea of making him a prisoner. Churchill, pushing his horse quickly forward, shot the impudent attacker before he could harm the newly commissioned brigadier general. The twenty-three-year-old Private Churchill then grabbed his commanding general and pulled him onto the back of his horse. Churchill's horse beat a hasty retreat and brought both riders back to the safety offered by the rest of the Michigan Brigade near the Felty farm.[5]

Captain Henry E. Thompson,
Commander,
Troop A, 6th Michigan Cavalry
(USAMHI)

At almost the same time that General Custer was unhorsed, Captain Thompson also went down in the jumble of men and horses. He sustained a serious gunshot wound to the body that knocked him from the saddle. The seemingly indefatigable captain escaped certain capture only because of the timely intervention by one of his men. Thompson's savior plucked the profusely bleeding officer from the very midst of the enemy soldiers. The gallant, but unidentified, Michigan trooper pulled the semi-dazed officer up behind him on his horse. Together the two members of Troop A quickly retreated along the road toward the regimental skirmish line at the Felty farm, which they safely reached. Captain Henry Thompson eventually recovered from his wound but never again returned to field duty with the 6th Michigan. In June 1864 he received his discharge because of wounds sustained in action at Hunterstown.[6]

Lieutenant Stephen Ballard was not as lucky as either his brigade commander or troop commander. Ballard suffered a slight wound during his troop's furious charge against the members of Cobb's Legion. After being wounded he was thrown from his horse and crashed to the ground. Although his wound was relatively minor, he was unable to remount his skittish horse. The young lieutenant stood all alone, a solitary figure in blue, in the swirling maelstrom around him. None of his troopers could reach his position to rescue him as they had done with Captain Thompson.

Quickly surrounded by Colonel Young's troopers, they relieved the disgusted lieutenant of all his weapons and hustled him to the rear of the Confederate lines beyond the Gilbert farm. Lieutenant Ballard's captors eventually turned him over to one of the numerous details from the Army of Northern Virginia's provost marshal. Since his wound was not serious, the Confederates marched him to Richmond along with hundreds other prisoners captured during the Gettysburg Campaign. The once youthful lieutenant spent the next twenty months of the war incarcerated at the infamous Libby Prison. Stephen Ballard belatedly returned to the 6th Michigan Cavalry after his release from confinement, just before the end of the war, in March 1865.[7]

In a matter of minutes, the cavalrymen from the 6th Michigan Cavalry found the tide completely turned against them. Their charge had pretty well stalled in the road. Seeing that his companies were gaining the upper hand over the Michigan cavalrymen, Lieutenant Colonel Delony ordered additional companies from Cobb's Legion to move forward. Delony tasked two companies to support the men of lieutenants Brooks and Houze. Companies A and I quickly advanced, charging the intermingled mass of blue and gray troopers as they moved in mass confusion toward the Felty farm buildings. First Lieutenant J. W. Cheeseboro commanded the enlisted men of Company A, while Captain William B. Young led the Georgia troopers assigned to Company I.

Lieutenant Colonel Delony personally led the two additional companies of the legion forward along the Gettysburg-Hunterstown road. As they passed the Gilbert farm, the members of the legion pitched headlong into the raging conflict. The popular thirty-six-year-old Delony pushed his horse "Marion" onward to the head of his attacking column and straight toward the Yankee line. The lieutenant colonel was now fighting in the fray among the leading members of the legion's Company C and Captain Thompson's Troop A. Private Wiley C. Howard of Company C, Cobb's Legion, remembered that:

> Col. Deloney leading the charge on his prancing bay Marion was unhorsed, his charger being shot, fell upon him so that with great difficulty he extricated himself from his prostrate position. Our men had passed him meantime, driving and routing the force in front, when three Yankees seeing his almost helpless position and that he was an officer of note, dashed upon him to subdue, capture him or kill him, shooting and cutting him from their horses. But this superb fighter, with his Hugunot blood boiling, raised himself on one knee and with his dexterous and wiry arm fenced and parried their blows, Charley Harris who was helping him, being wounded, until Bugler H. E. Jackson of Company C, Cobb Legion, who was coming up from the rear, spurred his horse to the fray and to Deloney's aid, fencing with these daring assailants, at last by a dexterous movement successfully thrust one man through the side, the others escaping with saber wounds from Deloney's shimmering blade as he rose to his feet. Jackson's bugle, coat and shirt were cut through with saber blows and his sword.[8]

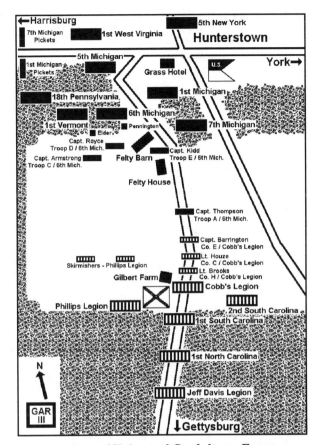

Locations of Union and Confederate Forces,
July 2, 1863, 5:00 – 6:00 P.M.
(GAR III)

Bugler Henry Jackson also recalled what happened to his lieutenant colonel during the same encounter. His recollections, written to a former opponent, were that:

> Your three front men made at Deloney and my-self, and soon the left and rear man of these struck my colonel over the right eye near the temple, and he fell paralyzed on his horse's neck. Seeing this, the middle man gave him a thrust and would have killed him, but I knocked his saber up. Meanwhile the third man was fighting me. After my colonel was helpless I had to combat all three of you, and narrowly escaped death.[9]

Fortunately, Lieutenant Colonel William Delony survived the fierce, savage, and hand-to-hand fighting at Hunterstown, but he sported a rather nasty scar across his face from the saber slash by one of his attackers. Unfortunately for Lieutenant Colonel Delony, he would not survive the war much longer. He received a mortal wound in September 1863, during another cavalry engagement at Jack's Shop, Virginia. After his wounding, the Federals took him prisoner and removed him to a military hospital in Washington, D.C. Although in great pain, the lieutenant colonel of Cobb's Legion refused the amputation of his leg, which might have saved his life. William Delony died from an infection in his leg on October 2, 1863, just before receiving command of the legion after Colonel Young's promotion to brigadier general.[10]

Immediately after running into the fresh reinforcements from Cobb's Legion, the troopers of the 6th Michigan Cavalry became totally disorganized, and, worst of all, demoralized by the sudden turn of events. Without any firm leadership or orders to the contrary, the Michigan troopers started to fall back along the same route that they had just traversed. Captain Thompson's men, once again, had to pass the Gilbert home. There some members from Company E of Cobb's Legion, from their dismounted positions around the house, again took the opportunity to pepper the chaotic Union cavalrymen as they rode past.

All during this time, the men assigned to companies C and H from Cobb's Legion closely pursued the panicked horsemen from Troop A. It is highly unlikely that if the three commissioned officers, Custer, Thompson, and Ballard, had remained mounted and in control of the troop that they would have been able to stop their men from retreating. Perhaps the outcome might have been different if at least one of those three officers remained in command. More than likely the outcome would have remained the same.

As the troopers in the dirty and sweat-soaked blue uniforms moved back toward the north they encountered the ghastly sights resulting from their initial attack. One of Henry Thompson's men, thirty-year-old Saddler Charles C. Krauss, lay dead and sprawled awkwardly in the road.[11] Krauss had sustained a ghastly gunshot wound through his head during the initial charge with his comrades. After the impact of the gunshot knocked him from his horse, the other horses behind him trampled his prostrate body as they continued to race along the narrow road. Such unavoidable injuries, usually resulting in a fatality, were extremely common during the war. The wounds sustained from the iron-shod hooves of scores of charging horses, who found themselves driven to near madness from fear and noise, almost always resulted in a critical injury to anyone caught in their path. Along with Saddler Krauss, a number of other troopers from both sides remained behind with a variety of gunshot and saber wounds as Troop A retraced their steps back to the Felty farm. All tolled Troop A of the 6th Michigan lost two officers wounded and at least seven enlisted killed, wounded, or reported missing. Those were the only confirmed losses reported.[12]

While the battle action was hotly swirling between the Gilbert and Felty farms, the rest of Judson Kilpatrick's division under General Farnsworth arrived in Hunterstown and finished deploying to their assigned positions. Farnsworth's 1st Brigade quickly moved through the center of the small town. They followed the same route through Hunterstown taken by Custer's brigade earlier. Completing their march, General Farnsworth's four regiments then took their positions in support of General Custer's brigade.

Lieutenant Samuel Elder's Battery E, 4th U.S. Artillery turned off the Gettysburg-Hunterstown road just to the north of the John Felty farm. Moving to the west the battery passed in front of the already positioned guns of Lieutenant Pennington's battery. Elder then unlimbered his four guns facing to the south. Elder's battery was now to the immediate right of Battery M. The 18th Pennsylvania and 1st Vermont regiments moved into supporting positions to the right of Lieutenant Elder's battery. Lieutenant Colonel Brinton's regiment was the first of Farnsworth's regiments to turn off the Gettysburg-Hunterstown road and move into position. They followed Elder's battery to the west, passed by the artillerymen and continued to move into the woods. The regiment remained mounted and in reserve as the late afternoon turned into evening.[13]

Lieutenant Colonel Preston's men were next in the day's line of march. They followed the 18th Pennsylvania Cavalry until they reached the tree line in front of the Pennsylvanians' position. The Vermonters' position was slightly in advance, and to the right, of Lieutenant Elder's battery. Preston received orders to dismount a portion of his regiment. He had them advance as skirmishers into the wheatfield directly to their front.[14]

The last two regiments assigned to General Farnsworth's brigade, the 1st West Virginia and the 5th New York, proceeded to deploy to the right and rear of the entire division. At that time the sounds of the running fight between Captain Thompson's troop and the five companies of Colonel Young's legion got louder as the combatants moved closer to Hunterstown. Colonel Richmond's West Virginians and Major Hammond's New Yorkers found themselves pretty much out of the fighting at Hunterstown and relegated to guarding the division's rear.[15]

The exhausted remnants of Captain Thompson's troop raced back down the same road over which they had proudly moved only a short time beforehand. When they began their attack the ranks of the troop were neat and orderly. Now as they neared the Felty farm buildings the troop was totally disorganized and in utter chaos. Both men and horses showed signs of confusion and exhaustion. The majority of Henry Thompson's horsemen reached their regimental skirmish line unscathed. However, some of the members in the rear of the retreating column became intermingled with the enthusiastic and determined men from companies C, E, and H of the closely pursuing legion.

Believing that they had effectively routed the members of Troop A, the leading companies of Confederate horsemen raced to overtake the Union troopers before they totally escaped from them. Unfortunately, the Southern officers commanding those companies failed to control their exuberant men. More than likely, they, themselves, became careless because of their apparent success. Because of that, their elation quickly turned into terror as they reached the red brick buildings of the Felty farm.

The troopers in both blue and gray, some of who remained closely intermixed, reached the Felty buildings while they continued to fire their weapons and slash at each other with their tightly gripped sabers. Frightened horses, most soaked with their own sweat and some with blood, carried their riders past the house and around a slight curve in the road. Most of the Union troopers had, by this time, managed to put a little distance between themselves and their pursuers.

Rounding the slight bend in the road, the Southern horsemen from Cobb's Legion suddenly received a vicious volley from the previously concealed members of the 6th Michigan's Troop E. Captain Kidd's dismounted troopers opened a withering fire with their repeating Spencer rifles on the attacking Confederates. The dismounted Union cavalrymen's aim was quite accurate since most of casualties suffered by Colonel Young's men occurred at this point in the fight.

Many of the men from the legion's Company E, the rear guard that had initially opened the fighting, now became heavily engaged in the contest again. Both Captain Barrington King and 1st Lieutenant Ebenezer F. Smith, the second-in-command of Company E, had their horses shot from under them during the searing attack from the dismounted Michigan troopers on the western side of the road. Captain King received no serious injuries in his fall from his horse and escaped back to his own lines on foot. A much more unlucky Lieutenant Smith was slightly wounded in the charge and taken captive.[16]

Bugler Henry Jackson, Company C, Cobb's Legion, remembered what occurred to his comrades in Company H as the encounter between the two antagonists came to a deadly climax:

> Finally we ran into your dismounted men, who were on both sides of the road, and into a large barn on the left. Every door and window was a blaze of fire, and every man who was with me fell.[17]

At this point in the fighting, the Confederate's assault started to lose all its momentum. Their attack, much like Captain Thompson's charge at the other end of the road, came to an abrupt halt. Lieutenant Houze, commanding Company C, and Lieutenant Brooks from Company H continued to futilely push their few remaining men forward. After passing by the 6th Michigan's searing rifle fire at the Felty barn, the Southern horsemen were only able to continue their attack for another few hundred feet up the sloping terrain to the north before coming to a complete halt.

Surprisingly, especially to them, the members of the attacking companies of Cobb's Legion received little support from the other regiments
in their brigade during their valiant charge against Thompson's troopers.
In their zealousness to drive Captain Thompson's lone troop from the
contested field, lieutenants Brooks and Houze advanced their commands
too far. Their commanders, particularly Lieutenant Colonel Delony, tried
to stop them from moving too far in advance of their own lines. Delony
wrote to his wife on July 7 that:

> Had I not been wounded so early in the action I
> feel confident I could have saved him [Houze] and
> Pugh and Brooks. They charged too far after the field
> was cleared and were killed by Yankee sharpshooters.[18]

The small Confederate force that remained near the Felty farm was
now facing the combined might of the 6th and 7th Michigan regiments,
along with a well-directed cannonade from Lieutenant Pennington's battery. Private Wiley C. Howard, also assigned to the ranks of Lieutenant
Houze's Company C of Cobb's Legion, recalled his participation in the
unsuccessful attack, and the ultimate consequences of that charge, by
stating that:

> . . . our command had a thrilling experience and
> while charging a body of cavalry down a lane leading
> by a barn, ran into an ambuscade of men posted in the
> barn who dealt death and destruction upon us. Within
> five minutes some four or five officers were killed or
> wounded and about fifteen men were slain or
> wounded.[19]

A series of unwarranted events transpired to force the Confederate
cavalrymen to suddenly retreat. First, the two advanced companies of
Cobb's Legion, C and H, ran into the extended skirmish line of Colonel
Mann's 7th Michigan Cavalry. Opening fire with their Burnside carbines, the dismounted Yankee cavalrymen totally destroyed the last ves-
tiges of organization that the Southern attackers could summon.
Additionally, Lieutenant Pennington's battery opened fire on the assail-
ing column, who, given the odds against them, came surprisingly close
to the cannons before being repelled. Finally, the dismounted skirmishers of the 6th Michigan Cavalry, those troopers assigned to support

Pennington's battery, simultaneously opened fire on the confused horse-men in gray. The courageous assault by the undaunted band of Georgi-ans was completely doomed.

Twenty-three-year-old William Baird, a farrier assigned to Troop C of the 6th Michigan Cavalry, related his activities in assisting to repulse the Confederate cavalry assault. His troop had dismounted and went into position in support of Lieutenant Pennington's six guns. He remembered that:

> We were hastily dismounted and sent out in sup-port of our Battery and we scarcely got into position when the Rebels made a desperate attempt to drive us back and capture our Battery a few Rebels rode right over us on and up to our guns of the Battery and it was then that hand to hand encounter with the saber until every one that reached the guns was hewn down with the saber or shot to death with Revolvers.[20]

Now the fighting turned desperate for all the Southern cavalrymen involved on the northern end of the contested field. The casualties were quite appalling for the members of Colonel Young's command. Cobb's Legion counted four commissioned officers present for duty from both companies C and H. The legion lost all four of those officers in the charge. The four officers were either immediately killed or mortally wounded as they collapsed from the hail of lead fired by the dismounted troopers of the 6th and 7th Michigan regiments.

Lieutenant Thomas Houze, commanding officer of Company C, top-pled from his horse while he was very close to the dismounted Union line by the Felty buildings. A bullet pierced his skull causing the lieuten-ant's instantaneous death, most likely before he hit the ground. Lieuten-ant Cicero Brooks, commanding Company H, likewise died not far from where Houze fell. Second Lieutenant Nathan S. Pugh, assigned to Com-pany H, also received a fatal wound during the ineffectual charge to the very muzzles of Pennington's guns.

After the fighting along the road southwest of Hunterstown sub-sided, Union medical personnel removed Lieutenant Pugh's unconscious body to the temporary hospital established at the Grass Hotel where he died later that night. Second Lieutenant J. W. Cheeseboro, the second-in-command of Company C, suffered a mortal wound somewhere between the main Union battle lines and the John Felty farm buildings. He, too, was taken to the Grass Hotel for treatment. As with Nathan Pugh, Lieutenant Cheeseboro succumbed to his wounds later that night, too. Besides the four dead officers, roughly fifteen enlisted men from the two farthest advancing companies of Cobb's Legion were killed or wounded during the assault.

The Union cavalrymen fared somewhat better than their Confederate opponents. They did not sustain many additional casualties beyond those suffered by the members of Troop A. Unfortunately a few soldiers proved to be extremely unlucky during the fighting. Some of the dismounted Michigan cavalrymen received wounds from the indiscriminate firing of their own comrades posted behind them. First Lieutenant Seymour Shipman, the thirty-five-year-old second-in-command from Captain Royce's Troop D of the 6th Michigan, received a serious wound from a gunshot during the fight. Instead of being shot by the enemy one of his own men wounded the lieutenant from behind. The wound proved serious and troublesome enough for the lieutenant to force him to accept a discharge in 1864.[21]

Another commissioned officer from Troop D also received a very serious injury during this same phase of the battle. It is unknown whether the wound was from friend or foe. Second Lieutenant Horace B. Rogers received a life-threatening gunshot wound to his lower chest. The twenty-five-year-old lieutenant's wound looked so serious that nobody thought him capable of surviving through the night. After the cessation of fighting, his comrades removed the young lieutenant to another temporary hospital established in the store and home of Abraham King in the center of town. Jacob Taughenbaugh recounted Lieutenant Rogers' initial time spent at the hotel turned hospital. The teenaged resident of Hunterstown recalled that:

> The Union doctor had a lieutenant who had been shot through the chest. The bullet had gone in just below the ribs and come out the back. The doctor had bound up the wound, but the lieutenant was still in a bad way. One of the people of the town asked if the Union doctor would mind having the Confederate doctor come over and look at the man. He said it

would be alright, and the Confederate was fetched. As
soon as the Confederate doctor saw the man he said
another method would have to be used. He asked the
woman who lived in the house if she had any warm
water. She said she hadn't, but soon would have.
Pretty soon she brought some in a coffee pot. The
Confederate took off the bandage and opened the
wound in the lieutenant's chest and began pouring in
the water, a little at a time, from that coffee pot. He
said he wanted to pour it in until the water came
through and dripped out the back. It did, too, for I
saw the bloody water first start a trickle and then pour
through to the floor.[22]

Surprisingly, Lieutenant Rogers eventually recovered from the life-
threatening wound received in the action at Hunterstown. He even corre-
sponded with some of the local citizens who aided him in his recovery.
However, his military career abruptly ended because of the serious nature of the wound. In September 1863, Horace Rogers received his discharge from the 6th Michigan Cavalry because of physical disability
from wounds received in action.[23]

Two noncommissioned officers were also gravely injured during the
attack on the dismounted skirmish line of the 6th Michigan Cavalry.
Corporal John W. Soule, assigned to Troop D, sustained a severe injury
from a gunshot wound to the leg. The fatal wound, thought not serious at
first by those attending him, necessitated the amputation of his right leg
at the thigh. Corporal Soule died on July 29 after being removed from
Hunterstown to the larger U.S. hospital at Frederick, Maryland.[24]

Charles W. Cox, the twenty-one-year-old first sergeant of Troop C,
was another noncommissioned officer listed as a casualty from the 6th
Michigan Cavalry. Sergeant Cox received a very painful and mortal
wound from a gunshot to the bowels. Farrier Baird recounted his sergeant's wounding by stating that:

> It was while we were supporting the Battery
> [Pennington's] that Comrade Charles Cox our
> Sargeant was shot through the Bowels and after the
> Rebels had left I carried him to a Barn where the Sur-
> geons were caring for the wounded. . .[25]

Whether a cavalryman wore blue or gray, it was not a very good day to be a commissioned officer in the vicinity of Hunterstown on July 2. Brigadier General George Custer and Colonel Pierce Young both had been severely shaken during their participation in the opening stages of the Hunterstown fight. Neither officer played a deciding factor in the battle after their individual and dramatic escapes from any personal injury. Both returned, safely, to their own lines and did not venture forward again. Additionally, the respective seconds-in-command along the Gettysburg-Hunterstown road, Lieutenant Colonel William Delony and Captain Henry Thompson, both received rather nasty wounds from their initial participation in that portion of the action. Lieutenant Stephen Ballard of the 6th Michigan was wounded and also captured. Eight other company-grade officers from both antagonists were either killed or wounded.

The sun finally started to set on that Thursday as the shattered remnants of the attacking companies of Cobb's Legion fled back down the Gettysburg-Hunterstown road to the south. They finally reached the safety of their now fully deployed, though tardy, brigade. The first line of battle consisted of three regiments from General Hampton's brigade. Phillips Legion, the other unengaged companies of Cobb's Legion, and the 2nd South Carolina had been in position for over an hour just north of the John Gilbert farm.

As darkness started to envelop the area, the other three regiments of the brigade were only now finally marching into position a short distance behind the first three regiments. The 1st North Carolina Cavalry stretched across the Gettysburg-Hunterstown road with their left flank slightly touching a heavy wood line immediately behind the mounted members of Cobb's Legion. Hampton posted the 1st South Carolina Cavalry on the North Carolinians' right flank and partially behind a portion of the mounted troopers of the 2nd South Carolina. Lieutenant Colonel Waring's six companies of the Jeff Davis Legion held the right rear flank of the brigade.

Considering that they were much closer to Gettysburg when they received word to march to that place, General Hampton's brigade arrived in the vicinity well before the brigades of John Chambliss and Fitz Lee.

J. E. B. Stuart's three brigades had not reunited at Heidlersburg as previously planned. Since the lengthy wagon train and artillery, both Breathed and McGregor's batteries, still traveled with Colonel Chambliss's brigade, Wade Hampton had no artillery support at Hunterstown as the fighting between him and Kilpatrick escalated. The two Union batteries, already in position, opened an accurate and devastating fire upon the retreating companies of Cobb's Legion and then opened upon the rest of Hampton's brigade. Wade Hampton clearly felt the necessity for some artillery and sent an urgent message to General Stuart's headquarters requesting some artillery assistance.

First Lieutenant Alexander C. M. Pennington, Jr.,
Commander, Battery M, 2nd U.S. Artillery
(NA)

.Due to the absence of his own artillery batteries, J. E. B. Stuart forwarded Hampton's request to Lieutenant Colonel Hilary Pollard Jones, the twenty-nine-year-old acting chief of General Ewell's artillery. Ewell's Second Corps was the closest command to Wade Hampton's brigade on the left flank of the Army of Northern Virginia. Lieutenant Colonel Jones immediately ordered a section of two ten-pound Parrott guns from Captain Charles A. Green's Louisiana Guard Artillery to General Hampton's position near Hunterstown. Captain Green received the orders to move his guns shortly before sunset. The two guns and their crews, consisting of one other officer and roughly thirty enlisted men, left their positions along the Carlisle-Gettysburg road and moved the roughly three miles toward Hunterstown.[26]

The veteran artillerymen of Captain Green's abbreviated command reached the scene of the hard-fought cavalry action south of Hunterstown somewhere around dusk. They immediately deployed their two cannons on the western side of the Gettysburg-Hunterstown road in front of the tree line and just slightly to the rear, or southwestern side, of the John Gilbert house. From their new position in the trees, where they withdrew to avoid the deadly accurate artillery fire of lieutenants Pennington and Elder, Lieutenant Colonel Rich's Phillips Legion supported the artillery section. Green immediately sighted his two guns. They boldly kept up a steady fire against the overwhelming superiority of the Union artillery for the next hour or so.[27]

Captain Green's men put up a gallant struggle against the larger artillery force but suffered severely in doing so. The two Union batteries had ten guns compared to Green's single two-gun section. By the end of the brief artillery duel, Green lost one enlisted man killed along with one sergeant and fourteen enlisted men wounded. The Union and Confederate cannons continued to pound each other's emplacements in the darkness. Streaks of light from the muzzles of the guns illuminated the night skies and enabled each side to more accurately pinpoint their opponent's position. Although Captain Green's Louisiana Guard Artillery lost roughly half the men in their section as casualties, he managed to inflict some damage against his foe, too. His section of guns killed four horses, wounded three enlisted men, and disabled one wheel, all in Lieutenant Pennington's battery.[28]

As the darkness completely enveloped the participants, all action finally ceased. General Hampton still maintained control of the southern portion of the Gettysburg-Hunterstown road. Some time shortly after eleven o'clock the brigade commander ordered his six cavalry regiments and Captain Green's artillery section to withdraw from their forward positions near the Gilbert farm. Leaving a number of pickets behind, Wade Hampton moved most of his command about a mile farther down the road to the south and went into camp for the remainder of the night. The two other brigades that participated in General Stuart's journey through Maryland and Pennsylvania finally arrived and encamped in the rear of Hampton's line. General Hampton's regiments moved as far south as the William Stallworth farm, located on the western side of the Gettysburg-Hunterstown road.[29]

Also somewhere around eleven o'clock on that warm July night, Judson Kilpatrick, who still controlled Hunterstown, received an unexpected visit from a staff officer from Cavalry Corps headquarters. He was to immediately move his division to Two Taverns, a small settlement along the Baltimore Pike, almost due south of Hunterstown. The 3rd Division had orders to reinforce the left flank of the Army of the Potomac, which had been without cavalry support since early in the afternoon of July 2.[30]

After completing their heroic delaying action during the morning of July 1, John Buford's two brigades under colonels Devin and Gamble moved to a position to cover the left flank of the army. Somewhere around noon Alfred Pleasonton pulled General Buford and his horsemen from their newly assigned position and sent them toward Westminster. The cavalry troopers were relieved, primarily, so that they could provide security for army supplies at Westminster and refit after their fight of the previous day. General Daniel Sickles' III Corps, on the left side of the Army of the Potomac, now had virtually no cavalry support. Partially because of General Buford's departure from the left of the army, General Longstreet was able to move his infantry to that area for an attack during the afternoon of July 2.[31]

Now as the second day of July was about to turn into the third day with a strong prospect of additional heavy fighting, General Pleasonton proposed to partially uncover the right flank of the army by moving Judson Kilpatrick's division again. General Kilpatrick on the evening of July 2 had his 3rd Division fairly well entrenched around Hunterstown. They held the high ground just south of the town. Union casualties were relatively light in the division. The two batteries of lieutenants Pennington and Elder covered one of the basic avenues of approach. A number of small stands of trees dotted the area around Hunterstown, making maneuverability for large-scale, sweeping, mounted cavalry operations most difficult. Additionally, David Gregg's 2nd Division was not too far away and could offer invaluable support for Kilpatrick if the circumstances deemed it necessary.

Instead of being able to get some much needed rest, the troopers of General Kilpatrick's cavalry division started on another long and thoroughly hated night march. Moving very quietly through the darkness, so as not to alert the enemy's pickets, General Custer's brigade took the lead and moved back along the same dirt road traversed earlier in the afternoon. Shortly they arrived back on the Gettysburg-York pike, which they crossed and continued toward the south where they headed for Two Taverns along the Baltimore Pike.

During the early morning hours of July 3, General Hampton learned from his pickets that Judson Kilpatrick's command had surprisingly disappeared from the streets of Hunterstown some time during the night. The Confederate brigadier ordered his men to cautiously move forward and occupy the deserted streets of Hunterstown. As the Southern cavalry rode north along the Gettysburg-Hunterstown road they passed some of the carnage from the previous day. Scattered along the length of the road were the bodies of many devoted horses, faithful to the last. At least a dozen horses were killed or seriously injured around the John Felty and John Gilbert farms. By the time Wade Hampton's men advanced into town, most of the wounded men from both sides at least those capable of being moved a short distance, had been taken to the shelter of a nearby building.

Some of the more seriously wounded cavalrymen, particularly those from the 6th Michigan regiment, moved only a short distance into the Felty barn. Friends, of Corporal John Soule of Troop D and 1st Sergeant Charles Cox of Troop C, carried them both inside the barn. Undoubtedly, Assistant Surgeon David C. Spaulding of the 6th Michigan Cavalry held the responsibility for caring for the wounded of his regiment at the barn turned hospital.[32]

After the Confederate cavalrymen took possession of Hunterstown they threw out their pickets to the north and east. They then turned their attention to searching the houses in the town and the surrounding area. Hampton's men found more wounded soldiers who were unable to travel. Both Union and Confederate wounded found themselves quartered and well cared for at the Gilbert and Felty farms, the Grass Hotel, the Great Conewago Presbyterian Church, the King's grocery and general store, as well as Abraham King's home.[33]

A few of General Kilpatrick's wounded troopers were taken to the almost empty store of eighty-year-old Abraham King. The Kings removed most of the major and valuable items in the store for safe-keeping. What had remained in the shop had been "appropriated" during the occupation of the town by the soldiers of both North and South. The King's store was along the northern side of the Harrisburg-York road near the center of town. Abraham's son, Hugh, probably managed the store for his elderly father. Some of the less fortunate soldiers who died from their wounds, mostly members of Cobb's Legion, were laid in a somber row in front of King's store. The lone local undertaker, Benjamin Detrich, accepted the responsibility for preparing the bodies of the fallen soldiers for burial.[34]

The compassionate citizens of Hunterstown, like their distant neighbors in Hanover only two days previously, opened their homes and hearts to the dozens of wounded and dying cavalrymen. They wholeheartedly tried to make the many wounded men as comfortable as possible, regardless in which army they happened to serve. Everybody in Hunterstown, as a rule, did everything within their power to alleviate their suffering.

An extremely common occurrence during the Civil War was that members of the same family would often serve together in a company, troop, or battery. Too often the results would be devastating for that family when one or more relatives died or received serious injuries in battle. July 2 had proved this once again. Bugler Henry Jackson suffered a personal misfortune as he entered Hunterstown and saw something that he had hoped he would never observe during the course of the war. However, he surely suspected the worst possible outcome when Lieutenant Thomas Houze had not returned from the severe fighting of yesterday. With true regret, he recalled that:

> My brother-in-law [Thomas Houze] had been killed and his pockets had been turned inside out. His watch, knife, spurs, and all he had were gone. His hat lay by his side with two holes in it, made by the ball which passed through his head. Two or three of us were detailed to bury these men, and we placed them in a corner of a field near where they fell, under a big cherry tree.[35]

Notes to Chapter Thirteen

1. A walk was at a speed of four miles an hour. A slow trot covered six miles an hour. A maneuvering trot covered eight miles an hour. A maneuvering gallop had a speed of twelve miles an hour. An extended gallop could cover sixteen miles an hour, though not for a very long period.
2. H. E. Jackson, *Confederate Veteran Magazine* (September, 1889) VII, p. 415.
3. Delony Letter.
4. Whittaker, *A Complete Life of Gen. George A. Custer*, p. 173. Custer made a grand gesture by telling his brigade staff to remain behind as he prepared to lead the charge. However, at least one orderly and quite possibly two or three others accompanied their general on the assault.
5. Ibid., p. 174. Private Churchill was only recently detailed from the 1st Michigan Cavalry as an orderly for the new brigadier general. Hunterstown was the first of many battles in which the young Churchill would participate while on the brigade staff.
6. NA RG 94 – 6 MI. Captain Henry Elmer Thompson received an appointment to the regiment's vacant lieutenant colonel's position with the effective date of June 10, 1863. However, he did not muster in that grade until September 1863. Up to the date of his wounding he was still acting as the commander of Troop A. Thompson filled the position vacated by Russell Alger when the latter accepted the colonelcy of the 5th Michigan Cavalry. Thompson also received the brevet rank of colonel for "gallant and meritorious service during the war."
7. Ibid. Second Lieutenant Ballard received the rank of first lieutenant when Captain Thompson and the original first lieutenant of the troop, Manning D. Birge, had gotten promoted on June 10, 1863 (mustered in September). Unfortunately, because of his capture at Hunterstown, Ballard never mustered at the new grade.
8. Wiley C. Howard, *Sketch* of *Cobb Legion Cavalry and* Some *Incidents and Scenes Remembered,* United Confederate Veterans, August 19, 1901, p. 9.
9. Jackson, *Confederate Veteran Magazine,* p. 415.
10. Krick, *Lee's Colonels,* p. 117.
11. Ibid. A saddler was assigned to each troop and was responsible for making repairs to the horse equipment and other leather accouterments of the assigned cavalrymen. Each regimental headquarters also had a saddler sergeant assigned in a supervisory role.
12. Ibid. The official reports, filed shortly after the fight, listed a total of thirty-two casualties in the brigade, not just in the charge of Troop A. Other reports that were filed listed two officers and twenty-five enlisted men as casualties in Troop A. Only seven enlisted men could be found as casualties on the unit's muster roll, casualty sheets, and after-action reports. The same reports listed Captain Thompson as being mortally wounded, even though he survived the war.
13. OR – 1, p. 1011.
14. Ibid., pp. 1012-13.
15. Ibid., p. 1018.
16. Delony Letter.
17. Jackson, *Confederate Veteran Magazine,* p. 415.
18. Delony Letter.
19. Howard, *Sketch* of *Cobb Legion Cavalry,* p. 9.

Notes to Chapter Thirteen (*continued*)

20. Letter of William Baird, Michigan Historical Collections, Bentley Historical Library, University of Michigan. William Baird originally enlisted as a farrier in Troop C, 6th Michigan Cavalry. A farrier was responsible, primarily, for shoeing horses. Surviving the skirmish at Hunterstown, Baird got wounded in action the very next day, July 3, during the fighting between Gregg and Stuart. Early in 1864 he received a discharge to accept a commission as a first lieutenant in the 23rd U.S. Colored Infantry. (Hereafter cited as Baird Letter.)
21. NA RG 94 – 6 MI.
22. Herbert, "In Occupied Pennsylvania," pp. 103-13.
23. Ibid.; Robertson, *Michigan in the War*, pt. 3, p. 182.
24. NA RG 94 – 6 MI; John W. Busey, *These Honored Dead: The Union Casualties at Gettysburg* (Hightstown, N.J.: Longstreet House, 1996), p. 360.
25. Baird Letter; Entry of July 2, 1863, George W. Barbour Diary, Robert Brake Collection, United States Military History Institute. First Sergeant Charles Cox died early the next day, July 3, at Hunterstown.
26. OR – 2, p. 497.
27. Ibid.
28. OR – 1, p. 1000. The disabled wheel was, presumably, on one of Pennington's guns. However, the wheel could have been on a caisson or a limber since the loss of it received scant mention.
29. OR – 2, p. 497.
30. OR – 1, p. 992.
31. Ibid., p. 914.
32. NA RG 94 – 6 MI; Baird Letter.
33. Gregory A. Coco, *A Vast Sea of Misery: A History and Guide to the Union and Confederate Field Hospitals at Gettysburg, July 1 – November 20, 1863* (Gettysburg: Thomas Publications, 1988), p. 109.
34. Ibid.; *Philadelphia Record*, September 15th, 1901.
35. Jackson, *Confederate Veteran Magazine*, p. 415.

Chapter 14:

Roads to the Potomac

ERY little had been accomplished by the two unexpected clashes between J. E. B. Stuart's Confederate brigades and the Union troopers assigned to Judson Kilpatrick's 3rd Division of the Cavalry Corps. The commander of the Army of the Potomac's newest division clearly failed in his first attempt, since taking command, to defeat decisively the tired and exhausted Southern soldiers at Hanover. After fighting to a virtual draw at Hanover, Kilpatrick then compounded his woes by neglecting to maintain physical contact with Stuart's cavalry. For most of the next two days Stuart continued his search for the Army of Northern Virginia, while Kilpatrick continued his mission to find Stuart. Imagine not being able to find the trail left by over ten thousand horses in the heat of July. Evenly poorly fed and fatigued animals would leave a number of signs in the middle of any roads traveled or any fields traversed.

At the end of those first two days in July the 3rd Division's two brigades under George Custer and Elon Farnsworth confronted the single brigade of Wade Hampton at Hunterstown. General Kilpatrick failed to grasp another great advantage afforded him. He squandered another valuable opportunity to conquer conclusively a portion of General Stuart's command.

On the other hand, General Stuart had his own shortcomings. He failed to keep General Robert E. Lee apprised of the sudden turn of events that ultimately would culminate in the Battle of Gettysburg. Because of the uncharacteristic speed with which the Army of the Potomac marched northward in pursuit, the Confederate major general had to move too far away from the rest of the Confederate Army. Additionally, the extra miles added to the route of his evasive march did more harm to his horses and men than could be calculated at the time. The almost constant skirmishes since crossing the Potomac River with a variety of Union cavalry also took its toll on the morale of his troopers. During their separation from the rest of the Army of Northern Virginia, both Stuart's men and horses endured harsh physical deprivations that were truly amazing.

The losses for both sides at both Hanover and Hunterstown were quite minuscule given the number of horsemen involved and when compared to other similar actions during the Gettysburg Campaign. Kilpatrick's official losses for his division at Hanover totaled 183 combined casualties in killed, wounded, or missing for both officers and enlisted men. The Union losses for the brief action at Hunterstown, which included only the 2nd Brigade, listed thirty-two killed, wounded, or missing for both officers and enlisted members.[1]

The exact losses of generals Stuart and Hampton during the fighting at both Hanover and Hunterstown received no official acknowledgment by either officer. The best estimate counts slightly more than one hundred officers and enlisted men as being injured or captured at Hanover. Colonel Chambliss's brigade experienced the greatest loss of men at Hanover since they launched the initial attack on the 18th Pennsylvania. The 2nd North Carolina Cavalry suffered more than fifty casualties during the fighting, while the 13th Virginia Cavalry sustained almost twenty-five killed, wounded, or missing cavalrymen.[2]

Wade Hampton's losses at Hunterstown were less than twenty-five officers and enlisted men. Naturally, since Cobb's Legion played the major role in the attack on General Custer's brigade, they suffered nearly all the casualties. Among the two hundred officers and enlisted men engaged in the skirmish, Colonel Young's regiment lost, roughly, three killed, five wounded, and seven missing.[3] The other big loser during the fighting at Hunterstown was Captain Green's section of artillery from the Louisiana Guard. They lost fifteen enlisted men during the early evening hours of the fight.

The next day, July 3, would be a day that the members of the brigades of Custer and Farnsworth would long remember. Both the Union and the Confederate cavalrymen sustained a high number of casualties near the John Rummel farm, located between the roads running to Hanover and York. The numbers of dead, wounded, and missing men counted during the July 3 fight made the cavalry casualties sustained during the previous few days pale in comparison.

General Gregg's two brigades, commanded by colonels McIntosh and J. I. Gregg, with the division's artillery support and George Custer's 2nd Brigade with Pennington's battery faced Stuart on the afternoon of July 3 on the left flank of the Confederate line, not very far from the previous day's fight at Hunterstown. Both sides essentially fought to another stalemate, but the casualties suffered, particularly by the Michigan Brigade, were particularly appalling.

On the morning of July 3, Judson Kilpatrick moved his two brigades from near Two Taverns to the left flank of the Army of the Potomac. Kilpatrick had orders to guard that flank, which had been without cavalry support since the previous day when Pleasonton pulled Buford's horsemen out of line. The whole 3rd Division originally started toward the left flank with Elon Farnsworth's brigade in the lead. As Custer's 2nd Brigade moved along in the rear of Kilpatrick's column, General Gregg diverted them in order to reinforce his own brigades. Generals Kilpatrick and Farnsworth continued to move to their originally ordered location. Instead of just maintaining his newly assigned position as originally intended, the 3rd Division commander ordered a late afternoon attack by the men of the 1st Brigade.

Judson Kilpatrick ordered his subordinate, in conjunction with Brigadier General Wesley Merritt's Reserve Brigade of Buford's division, to attack the entrenched enemy lines with a mounted force. Merritt had just arrived with his new brigade at a position along the Emmitsburg Road from near Mechanicstown, Maryland. Shortly after 5:00 P.M., General Farnsworth moved forward with troopers primarily from the 1st Vermont and 1st West Virginia regiments with support from Brinton's 18th Pennsylvania and Hammond's 5th New York.

The results of the charge were tragic for the Union troopers involved. A number of promising officers needlessly lost their lives during the futile charge, including the youthful Farnsworth. A number of enlisted men also died during the attack. Elon Farnsworth's brief career as a brigadier general came to an unexpected conclusion. The attack, in retrospect, seems to have been extremely ill-advised since the selected portion of the battlefield was not at all conducive to mounted cavalry operations.[4]

On July 4 the two brigades of Kilpatrick's 3rd Division reunited and started to move toward Maryland in pursuit of Robert E. Lee's defeated and retreating army. Colonel Nathaniel Richmond of the 1st West Virginia Cavalry now temporarily commanded the lamented Elon Farnsworth's brigade. Colonel Othneil De Forest would eventually supersede Richmond when the former returned to duty with his 5th New York Cavalry on July 9.

The next ten days of July were full of activity for the two brigades in Judson Kilpatrick's division. There would be very little time for rest for neither man nor beast as the division, in conjunction with the rest of the Cavalry Corps, moved in pursuit of the defeated Confederate Army. The horsemen from Michigan, New York, Pennsylvania, Vermont, and West Virginia gained additional glory for themselves and their regiments during a series of small skirmishes and battles. The surviving cavalrymen serving within the ranks of the 3rd Division would long remember the places with the names of Monterey Gap, Smithsburg, Hagerstown, Williamsport, and Boonsboro. Scores of their less fortunate comrades gave their lives and much more at those little-known places in Maryland as the Army of Northern Virginia tried to maneuver back across the Potomac River.

Many have considered the cavalry actions at Hanover and Hunterstown but small segments in the overall history of the Gettysburg Campaign. Neither fight, according to many, had a major impact on the outcome of the main battle action at Gettysburg. One could argue that the chance attack at Hanover served to deny Robert E. Lee of the services of J. E. B. Stuart for another two days. Perhaps if General Stuart had been able to take the more direct route to Gettysburg, along the York Pike, maybe some portion of the three-day affair at Gettysburg might have been altered.

To those cavalrymen who gave their lives or suffered severe wounds, the fights at Hanover and Hunterstown were just as important to them as any other battlefields in the Civil War. To the families of those cavalrymen, the names of Hanover and Hunterstown would always be a painful reminder of the sacrifice made by their loved ones. To those cavalrymen who surrendered a portion of their body, the towns of Hanover and Hunterstown would always harbor memories of the furious struggles at the end of June and beginning of July. Finally to the cavalrymen who served their countries, both North and South, and survived the fighting, the names of Hanover and Hunterstown would remind them of the hard fought actions where each side, begrudgingly, acknowledged the martial skills and abilities of their opponents.

Notes to Chapter Fourteen

1. OR – 1, p. 992. See Appendix A for verified casualties from the action at Hanover, which reflect a higher number than officially reported. Conversely, although Kilpatrick stated his loss in the 2nd Brigade at Hunterstown as thirty-two officers and men, only those soldiers listed in Appendix B can be verified as being casualties during the fighting, a figure that is considerably less.
2. See Appendix C for a partial, though incomplete, listing of identified Confederate casualties.
3. Robert K. Krick, *The Gettysburg Death Roster: The Confederate Dead at Gettysburg* (Dayton: Morningside Press, 1985), p. 16. Jacob Taughenbaugh, the teenager from Hunterstown, remembered seeing thirteen graves "on the ridge where the Federal artillery had been in position." Lieutenants Cicero Brooks and Thomas Houze were, supposedly, two of those buried on the ridge just north of the Felty farm.
4. OR – 1, p. 993.

Appendix A

3rd Division Casualties
at
Hanover - June 30, 1863

		Officers	Enlisted
KIA	Killed in action	2	9
MWIA	Mortally wounded in action	0	4
WIA	Wounded in action	5	65
POW	Prisoner of war	3	60
MIA	Missing in action	0	47
	Total	10	185

5th Regiment, New York Volunteer Cavalry

Field and Staff
Major Amos H. White – WIA – Gunshot to right foot
Adjutant Alexander Gall – KIA – Gunshot to head

Troop A
2nd Lieutenant Frazier A. Boutelle – WIA – Injured by falling horse
1st Sergeant Selden D. Wales – KIA – Gunshot
Quartermaster Sergeant Dennis O' Flaherty – POW
Sergeant Michael James Hayes – WIA – Saber cut in shoulder
Sergeant John Malley – POW
Private William Clark – MIA
Private John Glowdell – MIA
Private William Herrick – WIA – Gunshot
Private Patrick O'Donnell – MIA
Private Thomas Ritchie – WIA – Gunshot bruise in leg
Private Brad Wessart – WIA – Saber cut in head

Troop B
Sergeant George Gardells – WIA – Gunshot
Private George Brown – MIA
Private James Kelly – POW
Private John R. Updyke – WIA – Saber cut in head
Private George T. Whaley – MIA
Private Elias Wheeler – MIA

Troop C
Sergeant Owen McNulty – WIA – Gunshot in arm and finger
Sergeant John Kistner – WIA – Saber cut in neck

Troop D
Sergeant Jeremiah J. Callahan – WIA – Saber cut in hand
Corporal James A. McGinley – WIA – Gunshot in arm and head
Private John Langier – KIA – Gunshot
Private Peter McGovern – POW
Private Peter Schemerhorn – WIA – Gunshot bruise

Troop E
Acting 2nd Lieutenant Elam S. Dye – KIA – Gunshot
Sergeant John S. Trowbridge – MWIA – Gunshot in thigh
Corporal Sylvester F. Updegrove – WIA – Gunshot in hip
Private Bradley Alexander – WIA – Saber cut in head (Ambulance Corps)
Private Henry W. Monroe – WIA – Gunshot in side
Private Franklin Olmstead – POW
Private Newton C. Rew – WIA – Saber cut in face (Ambulance Corps)

Troop F

Corporal Donald J. McMillan – WIA – Saber cut in head and shoulder
Private John W. Barnard – MIA (Ambulance Corps)
Private Wynant H. Bennett – POW
Private Clark C. Knowlton – MIA (Ambulance Corps)
Private Emile Portier – WIA – Gunshot in left shoulder and arm
Private James Henry Tuthill – WIA – Injured by falling horse

Troop G

1st Sergeant John H. Wright – POW
Corporal Newel Barnum – WIA – Gunshot in arm and neck
Private Samuel Gordon – MIA
Private George Payne – POW

Troop H

Private Walker E. Johnson – POW
Private Carlos A. Jordan – POW (Ambulance Corps)
Private William Lamson – WIA – Saber cut
Private William Lively – WIA – Saber cut in arm and neck
Private Erastus McGowan – POW
Private William Sampson – WIA – Saber cut in arm and foot

Troop K

Private Edwin A. Campbell – WIA – Gunshot
Private Michael O'Neil – POW

Troop L

Private Phillip M. Place – POW (Captain Barker's Orderly)

18th Regiment, Pennsylvania Volunteer Cavalry

Field and Staff
Assistant Surgeon Samuel C. Williams – POW

Troop A
Corporal John Evans – POW
Private William Cole – WIA – Saber cut
Private Moses Harrison – WIA – Saber cut in head
Private Elisha Jefferies – WIA – Gunshot in arm
Private Henry C. Mankey – POW
Private Michael Radlonghafer – POW

Troop B
Sergeant Osborne Buck, Jr. – MWIA – Gunshot
Private Eber F. Cady – MWIA –Gunshot
Private Samuel P. Grey – POW
Private John Herrick – WIA – Gunshot in back
Private Leon Kissel – POW
Private Jesse H. Little – WIA – Saber cut in head and shoulder
Private John Moorehouse – WIA – Saber cut
Private Alfred W. Stone – WIA – Gunshot in head
Private Winfield S. Stricer – POW

Troop C
Corporal Reuben Saunders – WIA – Saber cut
Private William Crawford – KIA – Gunshot
Private John Durbin – WIA – Saber cut in face
Private John Jones – MIA
Private James Kimball – MIA
Private John P. Staggers – MIA

Troop D
Corporal Matthew D. Kerr – POW
Corporal Francis M. Magee – POW
Bugler John Doyle – WIA
Private Ralph Conover – WIA – Saber cut in head and neck
Private Joseph Groner – WIA – Saber cut in head
Private Matthew B. Micksell – WIA – Saber cut in back
Private David W. Winans – KIA – Gunshot

Troop E
Captain Thadeus S. Freeland – Commanding Troop – POW
Quartermaster Sergeant George F. Wingard – POW
Sergeant John H. Boalt – POW
Corporal John Hoffacker – KIA – Gunshot

Troop E (*continued*)

Corporal Jerome B. Long – POW
Private Frederick Boyer – WIA – Saber cut in back
Private James Lyons – WIA – Saber cut in head
Private Henry C. Martin – POW
Private William McCool – POW

Troop F

Captain John Britton – Commanding Troop – WIA – Saber cut
Corporal John Montgomery – WIA – Saber cut in head
Private Clark L. Baker – POW
Private James S. Jones – POW
Private Samuel Jones – WIA – Gunshot in back
Private Allison Louderbach – WIA – Injured in fall from horse
Private Peter Mcready – POW

Troop G

1st Lieutenant Thomas P. Shields – POW
Sergeant Shadrack M. Sellers – WIA – Broken leg in fall from horse

Troop H

Corporal John P. Ross – WIA
Private Peter Albert – POW
Private James Newberry – WIA-MIA

Troop I

Private Israel Blessing – MIA
Private Edward A. Hildreth – MIA
Private William Jacob – WIA
Private Lymon B. Simon – WIA – Saber cut
Private William Smith – WIA – Hit in hip by shell

Troop L

Bugler Henry Juhrs – WIA – Gunshot in leg

Troop M

Corporal William Willard – WIA
Private Jacob R. Harvey – KIA – Gunshot
Private William Nott – POW
Private Andrew Pipher – WIA – Gunshot
Private George Roberts – MIA
Private John F. Roller – KIA – Gunshot

1st Regiment, Vermont Volunteer Cavalry

Troop A
Private Horace Blinn – MIA

Troop D
Private Ira S. Bryant – MIA
Private Joseph S. Clark – MIA
Private Levi P. Howland – MIA

Troop G
Private Parker L. Hall – POW
Private James McMahon – POW

Troop K

Private Frederick H. Holdridge – MIA (Ambulance Attendent)

Troop M
Sergeant Joseph L. Southerland – MIA
Bugler Albert F. Hackett – MIA
Private Thomas McGuire – WIA

1st Regiment, West Virginia Volunteer Cavalry

Troop B
Quartermaster Sergeant Hamilton H. Bell – POW

Troop C
Corporal Thomas H. Marshall – MIA
Private Henry Braden – MIA
Private Colby W. Brown – MIA
Private John Dinnethorn – MIA
Private Michael O'Hara – MIA
Private Frederick Wolf – MIA

Troop D
Sergeant Harrison Allum – POW
Sergeant William Heskett – MIA
Bugler Charles Geissler – MIA
Private Uriah W. Halsted – POW
Private Thomas Todd – MIA

Troop E
1st Lieutenant Newberry W. Wheeler – POW
Corporal Frederick M. Satow – MIA
Private Washington M. Flinn – POW

Troop F
1st Lt. Maxwell Carroll – Commanding Troop – WIA – Gunshot in leg
Quartermaster Sergeant Garrett C. Selby – KIA – Gunshot in head
Corporal Joseph Gabbert – MIA
Private Hamilton Butcher – WIA– Gunshot in thigh

Troop G
Corporal John M. Underwood – WIA

Troop H
Private John H. Brown – POW

Troop L
Sergeant George Collins – KIA – Hit in leg by shell
Corporal John W. Brooks – WIA – Bruise from shell
Private John Durbin – MIA
Private Henry Holman – WIA – Gunshot in face

Troop M
Private Augustin Graber – POW
Private Thomas McGuire – WIA – Gunshot in thigh

1st Regiment, Michigan Volunteer Cavalry

Troop B
Sergeant William H. Ingersoll – WIA-POW

Troop E
Private George W. Weller – MIA

Troop H
Private Milan Canfield – MIA

Troop L
Private Colby Short – POW

5th Regiment, Michigan Volunteer Cavalry

Troop D
Private Jasper Brown – WIA – Gunshot in chest
Private Chauncey Rathburn – KIA – Gunshot

Troop I
Captain George N. Dutcher – Commanding Troop – WIA
Private Gabriel Cole – WIA
Private Charles Taylor – WIA

Troop L
Private Milton S. Burson – WIA (Ambulance Teamster)

6th Regiment, Michigan Volunteer Cavalry

Troop B

Farrier James D. Gay – MIA
Bugler John Newton – MIA
Private Thomas McGowan – POW
Private Oscar Stout – POW
Private William J. Tuffs – MIA (Troop Teamster)
Private Walter W. Wait – POW
Private Charles W. Watkins – POW

Troop C

Private Thomas A. Edmonson – POW

Troop D

Corporal Horace Hart – MWIA – Gunshot in body

Troop F

Commissary Sergeant Frank Konkle – MIA
Sergeant Latham H. Averill – WIA
Private Thomas C. Borden – WIA
Private George W. Sanders – MIA

Troop G

Farrier Andrew B. Culp – MIA
Private Charles Glosser – POW
Private Henry Hopkinson – MIA
Private Nelson A. Madden – POW

Troop H

Private Charles Hayes – MIA

Troop K

Private Lewis Blackman – POW
Private Manson Buck – MIA
Private Justin A. Smith – MIA

Troop L

Private Adumea A. Russell – POW
Private Francis O. Vandersluice – WIA

7th Regiment, Michigan Volunteer Cavalry

Troop A
Private Henry Allen – POW

Troop B
Private William Carouth – POW
Private William Gleason – POW
Private William Hawthorn – POW
Private George H. Heddon – POW

Troop F
Corporal William H. Armstrong – POW (Provost Marshal)
Corporal James Livingston – WIA – Gunshot

Troop H
Private Arthur Kemp – WIA

Appendix B

3rd Division Casualties
at
Hunterstown - July 2, 1863

		Officers	Enlisted
KIA	Killed in action	0	1
MWIA	Mortally wounded in action	0	3
WIA	Wounded in action	4	3
POW	Prisoner of war	0	2
MIA	Missing in action	0	9
	Total	4	18

5th Regiment, New York Volunteer Cavalry

Troop C
Sergeant Patrick Q. Lincoln – MIA

18th Regiment, Pennsylvania Volunteer Cavalry

Troop A
Commissary Sergeant Joseph Cooke – WIA – Gunshot in head

1st Regiment, Vermont Volunteer Cavalry

Troop B
Private Eli Hibbard – WIA

1st Regiment, Michigan Volunteer Cavalry

Troop H
Private Alfred G. Ryder – MWIA

6th Regiment, Michigan Volunteer Cavalry

Troop A
Captain Henry E. Thompson – Commanding Troop – WIA– Gunshot
2nd Lieutenant Stephen H. Ballard – WIA-POW
Sergeant Darwin P. Swain – MIA
Saddler Charles C. Krauss – KIA – Gunshot in head
Private Alexander Bevard – POW
Private William Dalziel – MIA
Private James M. Davis – WIA – Gunshot
Private Reuben B. Douglass – MIA
Private John Holcomb – POW

Troop C
1st Sergeant Charles W. Cox – MWIA – Gunshot in bowels

Troop D
1st Lieutenant Seymour Shipman – WIA – Gunshot
2nd Lieutenant Horace B. Rogers – WIA – Gunshot in chest
Corporal John W. Soule – MWIA – Gunshot in leg

7th Regiment, Michigan Volunteer Cavalry

Field & Staff
Private Carlton Llewellyn Cornell – MIA (Orderly)

Troop E
Private Joseph Stanford – MIA

Troop G
Corporal Francis H. Cunningham – MIA
Private Phelix Henon – MIA
Private Benjamin Wilds – MIA

Appendix C

Confederate Casualties
June 28 - July 2, 1863

June 28, 1863 - Rockville and Cooksville, Maryland

1st Virginia Cavalry
Private James F. Arnett, Jr. – Company D – POW
Private Joel William Mottley – Company G – POW

2nd Virginia Cavalry
Private Charles Alexander Andrews – Company G – POW

9th Virginia Cavalry
Private James W. Rowe – Company B – POW
Private G. Smith – Company E – POW

13th Virginia Cavalry
Private Simon E. V. Seward – Company E – POW

June 29, 1863 - Westminster, Maryland

1st Virginia Cavalry
Private George B. Edwards – Company E – POW
Private Henry Dewitt Clinton – Company K – WIA / POW
Private John Hammond Owings – Company K – POW
Private John William Pitts – Company K – POW

2nd Virginia Cavalry
Private Burwell D. Mitchell – Company A – POW
1st Lieutenant Hiram Claiborne Burks – Company G – POW

4th Virginia Cavalry
2nd Lieutenant St. Pierre Gibson – Company D – KIA
1st Lieutenant John William Murray – Company E – KIA
Private John Townes Leigh – Company E – WIA
Private James Oscar Martin – Company E – WIA / POW
Private John Allan Randolph – Company E – WIA / POW
Private John W. Pate – Company G – POW
Corporal John Scott Nicholas – Company K – WIA

10th Virginia Cavalry
Private E. Bruno Brunschwitz – Company E – POW
Private Andrew Jackson Fought – Company G – POW

June 30, 1863 - Hanover, Pennsylvania

2nd North Carolina Cavalry
Sergeant Isaac Peale – MWIA
Corporal John Eaton – Company D – KIA

1st Virginia Cavalry
Corporal Isaac Bare – Company C – POW
Private Adam Bare – Company C – WIA / POW
Private James M. Brownlee – Company E – MWIA
Private Christian H. Koiner – Company E – WIA / POW
Private William Henry Rader – Company E – WIA / POW

4th Virginia Cavalry
Lieutenant Colonel William H. F. Payne – F & S – Detached 2nd N.C. – POW

9th Virginia Cavalry
Private Charles James French – Company A – POW
Private John William Irvine – Company A – POW
Private Walter F. Chapman – Company B – POW
Private William H. Franklin – Company C – POW
Private Edwin D. Brown – Company C – WIA
Private Philip T. Gatewood – Company F – WIA
Private Andrew Jackson Eubank – Company G – WIA
Private William Henry Tisdale – Company G – WIA / POW
Private Harmon H. Littlepage – Company H – KIA
Captain John A. Billingsley – Company I – POW
Sergeant Alexander Frank – Company I – POW
Private Lorenzo Green – Company I – POW
Private John Lawson Lunsford – Company I – POW
Private William Page – Company I – POW
Private Meredith M. Mozingo – Company K – POW
Private Richard H. Quesenberry – Company K – POW

10th Virginia Cavalry
Captain William Hartman Kable – F & S – Quartermaster – WIA
Private Joseph Watson – Company A – POW
Captain James L. Dickinson – Company K – KIA
Private Zenus P. Bennett – Company K – POW

13th Virginia Cavalry

Major Joseph Ezra Gillette – Field & Staff – WIA
Private Thomas N. Briggs – Company A – POW
Private Thomas H. Crumpler – Company A – POW
Private Mills E. Powell – Company A – WIA
Private Samuel Abram Riddock – Company A – WIA / POW
Private Jefferson J. Woodard – Company A – WIA
Corporal William Neal – Company C – WIA
Private John T. Councill – Company C – MIA
Corporal Phocean Rolfe – Company E – POW
Private Rupert Church – Company F – POW
Private James E. Gorman – Company F – POW
Private Andrew J. Miller – Company F – POW
Private Robert J. Gwaltney – Company H – POW
Private St. George Tucker Mason – Company H – WIA
Private George Washington Milby – Company K – POW
Private George H. Morrow – Company K – POW
Private R. S. Scarborough – Company K – POW

July 1, 1863 - Carlisle, Pennsylvania

2nd Virginia Cavalry

Private Andrew Jackson Barnes – Company B – POW

5th Virginia Cavalry

Private Benjamin Franklin Gosney – Company C – WIA / POW

July 2, 1863 - Hunterstown, Pennsylvania

Cobb's Legion

1st Lieutenant Thomas Houze – Company C – KIA
2nd Lieutenant J. W. Cheeseboro – Company C – MWIA
1st Lieutenant Ebenezer F. Smith – Company E – WIA / POW
1st Lieutenant Cicero C. Brooks – Company H – KIA
2nd Lieutenant Nathan S. Pugh – Company H – MWIA

Appendix D

3rd Division Staff Roster
June 30, 1863

Headquarters Staff

Brig. Gen. Hugh Judson Kilpatrick	Commanding Division	
Maj. Charles F. Taggert	Assistant Inspector General	F&S-2 Penna.
Surg. Henry Capehart	Chief Surgeon	F&S-1 W. Virginia
Capt. Llewellyn Garrish Estes	Assistant Adjutant General	U. S. Volunteers
Capt. Jacob Lyman Greene	Act. Asst. Adjutant General	U. S. Volunteers
Capt. Zachariah J. McMasters	Additional Aide-de-Camp	K-5 New York
1st Lt. Jacob Bristol	Asst. Commissary Musters	C-5 Michigan
1st Lt. Eli Holden	Additional Aide-de-Camp	C-1 Vermont
1st Lt. Edward W. Whittaker	Additional Aide-de-Camp	C-2 New York
2nd Lt. Edmond Blunt, Jr.	Additional Aide-de-Camp	M-5 New York
2nd Lt. George W. Chandler	Additional Aide-de-Camp	C-1 West Virginia
Sergeant William A. Appleton	Clerk	A-2 Pennsylvania
Sergeant Hiram R. Ellis	Clerk	I-5 Michigan
Sergeant Abel Jones	Farrier	A-1 Massachusetts
Sergeant Miram Judy	Color Sergeant	A-1 Ohio
Sergeant Ansel Smith	Orderly	E-1 Maine
Corporal James Donnely	Orderly	D-2 New York
Corporal Henry E. Johns	Orderly	C-2 New York
Corporal Charles Smith	Orderly	F-2 Pennsylvania
Private Edwin F. Beckett	Orderly	A-2 Pennsylvania
Private William N. Borts	Orderly	G-6 Ohio
Private Alfred H. Cator	Orderly	C-1 Michigan
Private Michael J. Coleman	Clerk	B-5 New York
Private Joseph R. Curtis	Orderly	I-1 Maine
Private Peter Denny	Orderly	F-2 Pennsylvania
Private Frederick Fabrey	Orderly	A-10 New York
Private William H. Farnano	Bugler / Orderly	G-1 Maine
Private Charles D. Furbush	Orderly	A-1 Maine
Private Edward Gilley	Orderly	C-1 Maine
Private Charles Gilpatrick	Orderly	D-1 Maine
Private Willard Jackson	Orderly	F-1 Vermont
Private James Moore, Jr.	Orderly	C-1 Ohio
Private Michael O'Neil	Orderly	M-1 Vermont
Private James B. Peakes	Orderly	A-1 Maine
Private Josiah Sager	Orderly	H-7 Michigan
Private James Sloan	Cook	C-18 Pennsylvania

Headquarters Staff *(continued)*

Private Everhart Snyder	Orderly	F-2 Pennsylvania
Private Rawson Stoddard	Orderly	I-10 New York
Private George H. Warner	Orderly	F-2 New York
Private Charles Werkhaiser	Bugler / Orderly	B-2 New York
Private Jacob H. White	Orderly	H-2 New York
Private James White	Orderly	D-5 New York
Private Rudolph Winkelried	Orderly	M-18 Pennsylvania
Private Charles Wright	Orderly	D-5 New York

Division Band Members

Private James Perry	A-6 Michigan
Private Henry G. Servis	D-6 Michigan
Private Gardner W. Simonds	I-6 Michigan
Private Henry J. Simonds	I-6 Michigan
Private Albert Stuck	I-5 Michigan
Private George W. Warner	M-6 Michigan

Ambulance Corps Staff

1st Lt. Clark P. Stone	Ambulance Officer	F-1 Vermont
2nd Lt. George Washington Hill	Asst. Ambulance Officer	G-7 Michigan
Sergeant Bradley Croninger		M-6 Michigan
Corporal John C. Lusk		L-5 Michigan
Private H. Dwight Smith	Clerk	K-1 Vermont

Commissary Staff

Capt. William P. Dye	Acting Commissary of Subsistence	E-5 New York
Private Andrew J. Bennington	Butcher	B-1 Michigan
Private Permenio Casey	Teamster	M-5 Michigan
Private Robert G. Dilly	Teamster	B-5 Michigan
Private William Gripman	Teamster	B-5 Michigan
Private Harvey Hyde	Teamster	E-7 Michigan
Private Charles Little	Teamster	M-5 Michigan
Private James Mills	Teamster	M-5 Michigan
Private Charles B. Thomas	Teamster	F-5 New York

Provost Marshal Staff

Maj. Henry B. Van Voorhis	Assistant Provost Marshal	FS-18 Pennsylvania
Sergeant Isaac Lake		B-5 Michigan
Sergeant Samuel Smith		D-6 Michigan
Corporal Orrin D. Hough		D-5 Michigan
Corporal John M. Sheardon		B-5 New York
Private William Criddle		B-5 New York
Private George R. Decker		K-5 Michigan
Private George S. Decker		K-5 Michigan
Private John M. Gardner		D-5 Michigan
Private Cornelius Gorten		B-5 New York
Private George Lord		B-5 Michigan
Private David Martin		C-1 Michigan
Private Amos Miller		B-5 New York
Private John M. Overton		A-5 Michigan
Private Daniel Parker		D-6 Michigan
Private Alonzo Rockwell		L-2 Pennsylvania
Private Perry Soules		L-2 Pennsylvania
Private John C. Thompson	Clerk	K-1 Vermont
Private Stephen W. Thompson		B-5 Michigan
Private John A. Tubbs		D-5 Michigan
Private Charles B. Van Dyne		D-5 Michigan
Private George L. Van Dyne		D-5 Michigan
Private James Welsh		D-5 New York

Quartermaster Staff

Private Oliver D. Bacon	Train Guard	C-2 New York
Private Nehemiah Barnes	Teamster	K-10 New York
Private Samuel H. Clark	Teamster	A-1 Vermont
Private John Cummings	Teamster	A-1 Vermont
Private Charles E. Hyde	Train Guard	E-7 Michigan
Private Christopher Stone	Train Guard	C-1 Michigan

Division Teamsters

Private Charles S. Lewis	H-1 Vermont
Private James W. Welch	C-1 West Virginia
Private George W. Williams	L-1 West Virginia

Company Teamsters & Wagoners

Private Abraham Aldrich	Wagoner	A-1 Ohio
Private Robert Bryan	Teamster	C-1 Ohio

Headquarters Guard
1st Regiment, Ohio Volunteer Cavalry

2 Troops (A-C)
6 Officers & 123 Enlisted Men
June 30, 1863

Troop	Officer	NCO	B'smith	Bugler	Farrier	Saddler	Private
A	3	12	0	2	1	1	54
C	3	10	2	1	1	1	38
Totals	6	22	2	3	2	2	92

Troop A

Captain Noah Jones - Commanding Squadron
1st Lieutenant Albert E. Chester - Commanding Troop
2nd Lieutenant John N. McElwain

Sergeants

1st Sergeant Marcus T. C. Williams
Quartermaster Sergeant John Backenstoe

Justus V. Elster James A. Gunning Abraham Thomas

Corporals

George W. Hughes Elihu Judy Henry Keifer
William McMaster William Milliken Henry C. Painter
James P. Squier

Farrier Simon Doron Bugler Samuel L. Gillespie
Bugler Thomas D. McElwain Saddler Amos Thornton

Privates

Frederick W. Backenstoe	John Hidy	Samuel Rodgers
John C. Ball	Thomas J. Howe	John A. Sanders
William H. Baxley	Nelson B. Jenkins	Lycurgus Saxton
Wyatt D. Blakemore	Henry Judy	Richard Saxton
Samuel Brindley	Henry E. Kingman	Reuben B. Short
Daniel B. Clark	Andrew J. Lewis	Anthony Shreckengast
Edward N. Coleman	Henry S. Limes	Jacob Smith
John Collins	John C. Lively	Madison Squier
Henry C. Denions	William McClellan	John H. Straley
William Devorz	Jonathan McLaughlin	Anthony T. B. Terry
John Dickey	Jacob D. Miller	Lewis Campbell Thomas
George W. Duffee	Thomas J. Mooney	George W. Thurston
John Dumon	George W. Phares	Robert Tweedale
Archelaus Dyer	Spencer C. Phares	George McJ. Ustick
Richard D. Evans	Granville Plumley	Robert W. Vincent
Peter Getz	William H. Price	William Vincent
Michael Givens	James Priddy	William Welch
Jacob A. Harper	Abner R. Riggin	Wenton Wells

Troop C

Captain Samuel N. Stanford - Commanding Troop
1st Lieutenant Jacob K. Kuhn
2nd Lieutenant Charles W. Florence

Sergeants

1st Sergeant Daniel S. Tenycke

Gustavus A. Springer	Daniel Donovan
Henry Krumdick	Presley Neville

Corporals

William A. Auth	D. Mixer	John H. Shields
Daniel Valadine	James Wyland	

Bugler David H. Cummings	Farrier Henry Hertz
Blacksmith James Kirk	Saddler Alexander J. Proctor
Blacksmith Ernest Benner	

Privates

Benjamin F. Bird	George W. Holloway
George Bowers	Joel D. Hull
Stephen Briechl	Marcus Hummel
Edward Burns	John W. Johnston
John Camm	Philip Kleiber
John Ciford	John Lewis Koehler
Alfred Collins	William W. Lawson
William Davies	William S. Malden
John Diehm	Henry Neargarter
James Douseau	William Ormston
Paul During	Augustus Pete
John Fell	James L. Price
Christian Flattich	George Roemer
David Fouts	Henry Schnitker
Jonathan J. Gaddis	Henry Stephens
John Garleson	Albert Webb
Francis H. Gilker	James M. White
Henry Grottendick	Anthony Willhauck
William Hampton	Frederick Yockey

Appendix E

3rd Division, 1st Brigade Staff Roster
June 30, 1863

Headquarters Staff

Brig. Gen. Elon John Farnsworth	Commanding Brigade	
Maj. Benjamin Franklin Chamberlain	Act. Asst. Inspector General	F&S 1 W. Virginia
Surg. Lucius P. Woods	Chief Surgeon	F&S 5 New York
Capt. Andrew Cunningham	Additional Aide-de-Camp	D-18 Pennsylvania
1st Lt. Herman Harnburger	Act. Asst. Adjutant General	L-18 Pennsylvania
Corporal John Braden	Orderly	B-5 New York
Corporal Sidney E. Wolcott	Orderly	A-1 Vermont
Private Arthur Alexander	Orderly	B-1 Vermont
Private Albert C. S. Ball	Orderly	C-1 West Virginia
Private Charles Bond	Orderly	K-8 Illinois
Private Gilbert C. Buckman	Bugler / Orderly	L-1 Vermont
Private William Coblins	Orderly	B-18 Pennsylvania
Private George M. Conner	Orderly	M-1 Vermont
Private Malcolm S. Corse	Orderly	B-1 Vermont
Private James Covil	Orderly	M-1 Vermont
Private Joseph Demarro	Orderly	M-1 Vermont
Private Robert H. Edwards	Clerk	E-1 West Virginia
Private John W. Hayes	Orderly	F-5 New York
Private Charles H. Holcomb	Postmaster	H-5 New York
Private Joseph Hutchinson	Wagoner	D-1 Vermont
Private John J. Jeffries	Orderly	F-5 New York
Private Thomas A. Johnson	Orderly	D-1 West Virginia
Private John Kelly	Orderly	M-18 Pennsylvania
Private Jacob Leaphart	Cook	B-18 Pennsylvania
Private Emanuel Moses	Orderly	K-18 Pennsylvania
Private John C. Murray	Orderly	M-1 Vermont
Private Eugene Pratt	Wagoner	F-5 New York
Private David H. Robbins	Orderly	H-5 New York
Private Valentine Savage	Orderly	M-1 West Virginia
Private James Sinclair	Orderly	L-1 West Virginia
Private Alder Smith	Orderly	I-18 Pennsylvania
Private Frank A. Street	Orderly	M-18 Pennsylvania
Private Calvin Tripp	Orderly	K-8 Illinois

Ambulance Corps Staff

Sergeant Almon B. Gibbs		F-1 Vermont
Corporal Elisha Whitney		F-5 New York
Private Bradley Alexander		E-5 New York
Private John Allen		B-1 West Virginia
Private Julius R. Austin	Attendent	B-1 Vermont
Private John W. Barnard		F-5 New York
Private William Blackmore		D-18 Pennsylvania
Private Christian Boehrs		M-1 West Virginia
Private Edgar C. Boyleton		E-5 New York
Private Jude Brown		B-1 Vermont
Private James T. Burty		D-5 New York
Private James Butts		D-1 West Virginia
Private Michael Carr	Attendent	C-1 Vermont
Private Theodore Clark		F-5 New York
Private John M. Coleman	Teamster	E-1 West Virginia
Private John Dingman		G-5 New York
Private Hubbard J. Eastman		F-1 Vermont
Private Christian Ehman		E-5 New York
Private Theodore Hilldore		E-1 West Virginia
Private Frederick H. Holdridge	Teamster	K-1 Vermont
Private Carlos A. Jordan	Teamster	H-5 New York
Private Lorenzo D. Keyes	Teamster	F-1 Vermont
Private Clark C. Knowlton		F-5 New York
Private George Mallonee		D-1 West Virginia
Private William J. Mattick		N-1 West Virginia
Private Martin Van Buren McCollough		F-1 West Virginia
Private John McConaughy		N-1 West Virginia
Private Augustus McKinn		E-1 West Virginia
Private Jonathan Milburn		D-1 West Virginia
Private William C. Morey		F-5 New York
Private Philo Neef		M-5 New York
Private Merritt H. Parker	Teamster	D-18 Pennsylvania
Private William Phillips		N-1 West Virginia
Private Newton C. Rew		E-5 New York
Private Cyriel E. Scripter	Teamster	D-5 New York
Private Andrew Seary	Teamster	L-1 West Virginia
Private William Seely		N-1 West Virginia
Private Edward F. Smith		N-1 West Virginia
Private Daniel W. Sollars		N-1 West Virginia
Private John A. Templeton	Teamster	L-1 West Virginia
Private William M. Veazey		G-1 West Virginia
Private Thomas Wallace		B-1 West Virginia
Private Robert L. Warren	Teamster	E-1 West Virginia
Private Austin B. Wellman		H-1 Vermont
Private James H. Wilson		C-1 West Virginia

Commissary Staff

1st Lt. John S. Beazell	Acting Assistant Commissary of Subsistence	F&S 18 Penna.
Private John P. Ferris	Teamster	F-5 New York
Private Henry Hurd	Teamster	D-5 New York
Private Michael McHale	Guard	B-5 New York
Private Nelson M. Newell	Teamster	D-5 New York
Private Lorenzo L. Razey	Teamster	E-5 New York
Private Milton D. Rew	Teamster	E-5 New York
Private Thomas Shelly	Butcher	C-5 New York
Private George Weber	Clerk	A-1 Vermont

Provost Marshal Staff

1st Lt. Hiram H. Hall	Acting Assistant Provost Marshal	E-1 Vermont
Sergeant Farwell H. Hathorn		K-1 Vermont
Sergeant Samuel T. B. Pitcher		M-5 New York
Corporal Charles Beers		B-5 New York
Corporal Henry J. Hicks		M-1 Vermont
Private Royal G. Austin		E-5 New York
Private Charles H. Blinn		A-1 Vermont
Private James Burns		M-5 New York
Private James H. Chase		E-5 New York
Private Eugene Chilson		K-1 Vermont
Private Frank Guyett		K-1 Vermont
Private George J. Hull		B-1 Vermont
Private Erskine W. Lyford		H-5 New York
Private George Macha		K-1 Vermont
Private Peter McAllister		M-5 New York
Private Patrick O'Rourke		M-5 New York
Private Camiel Pesea		K-1 Vermont
Private Chester C. Reynolds		B-1 Vermont
Private Charles R. Shambo		K-1 Vermont
Private Charles Smith		M-5 New York
Private Samuel F. Whitlock		K-1 Vermont
Private Francis Young		K-1 Vermont

Quartermaster Staff

1st Lieutenant John Greeley Viall	Act. Asst. Quartermaster	H-5 New York
Sergeant Charles F. M. Mansfield	Quartermaster Sergeant	G-1 West Virginia
Sergeant Liberty C. Abbott		E-5 New York
Sergeant Charles N. Chilson		H-5 New York
Sergeant Adelbert E. Gould	Clerk	E-5 New York
Sergeant Samuel W. Sortore	Teamster	E-5 New York
Corporal Foster S. Dickinson		E-5 New York
Corporal William L. Murray	Teamster	N-1 West Virginia
Corporal Henry C. Streeter		F-1 Vermont
Private Henry Aldrich		F-1 Vermont
Private John Benjamin	Teamster	C-1 Vermont
Private George Blake		F-1 Vermont
Private Henry R. Brannock	Teamster	E-1 Vermont
Private Ichabod D. Cheney	Teamster	C-1 Vermont
Private James W. Ellis		F-1 Vermont
Private Patrick Gleason	Teamster	K-5 New York
Private Lewis J. Gorman		H-5 New York
Private William B. Hart	Teamster	M-18 Pennsylvania
Private Martin L. Henry	Teamster	C-1 Vermont
Private George Hill	Teamster	C-1 Vermont
Private Henry Jackson		H-1 Vermont
Private William C. Joyce		F-1 Vermont
Private Sumner E. Kilmer		E-5 New York
Private Michael Kinney	Wagoner	K-5 New York
Private Andrew J. McElhenny	Blacksmith	E-5 New York
Private Chauncy Merrill	Teamster	A-5 New York
Private Frank A. Remington		F-1 Vermont
Private William F. Ring	Teamster	C-1 Vermont
Private Frank C. Robinson	Teamster	D-1 West Virginia
Private Albert M. Shaw		K-1 Vermont
Private Marshall W. Sias		I-1 Vermont
Private Hanford H. Sortore	Teamster	E-5 New York
Private William O. Stickney	Teamster	C-1 Vermont
Private Joseph Suddarth	Teamster	E-1 West Virginia
Private Edwin D. Thrall	Teamster	E-5 New York
Private Simon Town		H-5 New York
Private Henry Trombley	Teamster	C-1 Vermont
Private John Upham, Jr.	Teamster	A-1 Vermont
Private George E. Vance	Teamster	L-1 West Virginia
Private Van Buren Warner	Teamster	A-1 Vermont
Private William W. Watkins	Teamster	D-5 New York
Private Joseph Westcott	Saddler	H-5 New York
Private John B. Woodruff	Wagonmaster	E-5 New York
Private Leonard M. Worthington	Teamster	E-5 New York

Brigade Teamsters

Private Frank Bronson	E-5 New York
Private Thomas B. Bryant	E-1 Vermont
Private Asa Burke	G-1 Vermont
Private George Burke	G-1 Vermont
Private Lorrin A. Butler	B-1 Vermont
Private Warren W. Conger	B-1 Vermont
Private Joseph G. Crawford	I-1 West Virginia
Private John T. Day	D-18 Pennsylvania
Private William H. Edwards	B-1 West Virginia
Private Linsey Fonner	B-1 West Virginia
Private George H. Gilpin	L-1 West Virginia
Private John L. Jones	B-1 West Virginia
Private Preston L. Manross	D-18 Pennsylvania
Private Edward Martin	C-5 New York
Private James Martin	D-1 West Virginia
Private John Newman	B-1 West Virginia
Private Arthur Perry	D- 5 New York
Private Reuben Saunders	D-5 New York
Private Charles Schmidt	M-1 West Virginia
Private William S. Williams	B-18 Pennsylvania
Private William Wilson	B-1 West Virginia

Regimental Teamsters & Wagoners

Private George P. Thompson	Wagonmaster	F-18 Pennsylvania
Private William A. Adams	Teamster	G-5 New York
Private Jedediah Anson	Teamster	M-5 New York
Private Alfred L. Blanchard	Teamster	F-1 West Virginia
Private David Brown	Teamster	H-1 West Virginia
Private Edmond S. Brown	Teamster	C-1 West Virginia
Private George L. Brown	Teamster	H-1 Vermont
Private George W. Burnes	Teamster	L-1 West Virginia
Private Thomas Finney	Teamster	H-5 New York
Private William T. Gaines	Wagoner	N-1 West Virginia
Private John Gordon	Teamster	L-5 New York
Private Leonidas R. Hollenback	Wagoner	G-1 West Virginia
Private Thomas Letson	Teamster	H-5 New York
Private George W. Middaugh	Teamster	G-5 New York
Private Harmon Miller	Teamster	H-5 New York
Private James S. Pennell	Wagoner	E-1 West Virginia
Private Jonas Stinehiser	Wagoner	F-1 West Virginia
Private Joseph Thornburg	Wagoner	D-1 West Virginia
Private William H. Titus	Teamster	C-5 New York

Troop Teamsters & Wagoners

Corporal Ebenezer Parlow	Teamster	B-5 New York
Private George A. Baker	Teamster	H-5 New York
Private Michael Barkheimer	Wagoner	K-18 Pennsylvania
Private Reuben Brooks	Teamster	I-1 Vermont
Private William Brown	Teamster	L-5 New York
Private Loren Chase, Jr.	Wagoner	D-1 Vermont
Private Henry Chiott	Wagoner	B-1 Vermont
Private James A. Davis	Teamster	B-1 Vermont
Private Eubert Davison	Teamster	G-5 New York
Private Solomon Eagon	Wagoner	A-18 Pennsylvania
Private Hiram S. Hall	Teamster	G-1 Vermont
Private Edward Hinkley	Teamster	H-1 Vermont
Private Henry Howard	Teamster	K-18 Pennsylvania
Private Joshua Lash	Teamster	F-18 Pennsylvania
Private Charles McMullen	Wagoner	E-5 New York
Private Levi Montgomery	Wagoner	C-18 Pennsylvania
Private Erastus Northaway	Teamster	B-5 New York
Private David H. Oakes	Wagoner	B-18 Pennsylvania
Private John M. Polm	Teamster	E-18 Pennsylvania
Private William P. Russell	Wagoner	L-5 New York
Private Edward S. Sheets	Teamster	F-18 Pennsylvania
Private George De Thompson	Teamster	G-5 New York
Private Samuel Thompson	Teamster	E-18 Pennsylvania
Private George Wilber	Wagoner	A-5 New York

Hospital & Medical Department Staff

Corporal Truman C. Narramore	Nurse	A-1 Vermont
Private Chauncey M. Allen	Attendent	C-1 Vermont
Private Louis Bonnah	Attendent	B-1 Vermont
Private Howard H. Burge	Attendent	K-1 Vermont
Private Martin Carroll	Orderly	B-1 West Virginia
Private John W. Davis	Cook	E-1 West Virginia
Private Nathan C. Dimmick	Attendent	A-1 Vermont
Private Harry Duncan	Nurse	I-1 West Virginia
Private Loren Durken	Nurse	B-1 Vermont
Private John P. Durno	Nurse	H-5 New York
Private Frederick Elberfield	Nurse	M-1 West Virginia
Private Augustus Forsyth	Nurse	G-5 New York
Private Joseph O. Gallup	Nurse	E-5 New York
Private Thomas Hand	Nurse	I-1 West Virginia
Private Frederick H. Holdridge	Attendent	K-1 Vermont
Private Nathan B. Howe	Attendent	F-1 Vermont
Private John Ingram	Attendent	C-1 Vermont
Private William T. Morrow	Nurse	F-1 West Virginia
Private William C. Page	Clerk	B-5 New York
Private Charles R. Petze	Nurse	L-5 New York
Private J. Hale Powers	Clerk	D-1 Vermont
Private Patrick Quinlan	Nurse	C-5 New York
Private George Savery	Teamster	C-1 Vermont
Private Warren Smith	Nurse	B-18 Pennsylvania
Private Henry Spaulding	Cook	H-5 New York
Private Joseph Tierney	Cook	G-5 New York
Private Alfred K. Wanzer	Cook	B-1 Vermont

5th Regiment, New York Volunteer Cavalry

11 Troops (A-B-C-D-E-F-G-H-K-L-M)
28 Officers & 449 Enlisted Men
June 30, 1863

Troop	Officer	NCO	B'smith	Bugler	Farrier	Saddler	Private
F & S	8	7	1	1	0	0	2
A	3	14	1	1	1	1	21
B	1	10	1	0	1	0	21
C	2	14	0	0	1	1	18
D	3	12	1	1	1	1	32
E	2	10	0	1	1	1	15
F	3	14	1	1	1	0	42
G	2	14	1	1	0	1	17
H	1	11	0	0	2	0	49
K	1	11	1	1	1	0	21
L	1	9	0	0	1	1	19
M	1	14	1	1	0	0	20
Totals	28	140	8	8	10	6	277

Field & Staff

Major John Hammond
Major William P. Bacon
Major Amos H. White
Adjutant Alexander Gall
Commissary Joseph A. Phillips
Quartermaster Linson S. De Forest
Chaplain Louis Napoleon Boudrye
Assistant Surgeon Orlando W. Armstrong

Sergeant Major Frederick M. Sawyer
Chief Trumpeter Robert Heisser
Commissary Sergeant Merritt N. Chaffee
Quartermaster Sergeant Dewitt H. Dickinson
Acting Saddler Sergeant David F. Wolcott
Veterinary Surgeon John Young
Hospital Steward Richard Marvin
Hospital Steward Isaac N. Mead
Blacksmith John C. French
Private John Brown (Major White's Orderly)
Private James Campney (Major Hammond's Orderly)

Troop A

Captain Luke McGuinn
1st Lieutenant Theodore A. Boice
2nd Lieutenant Frazier Augustus Boutelle

Sergeants

1st Sergeant Selden D. Wales
Commissary Sergeant James B. Bolt
Quartermaster Sergeant Dennis O'Flaherty

James H. Gallagher	James H. Hayes
John Mally	William Murray

Corporals

Justin Babby	William Freeman	John Lambert
Jeremiah McDonald	James Rickey	Patrick Shaughnessey
George Walker		

Blacksmith Barclay McGeary
Bugler John Catlin
Saddler Arthur Neil
Farrier John Peterson

Privates

Frederick Berhardie	Thomas McGovern
Thomas Burke	Charles McGuire
William Clark	Patrick McNieve
Henry Colvin	Thomas O'Connor
James Donohue	Patrick O'Donnell
John Glowdell	Christopher Philips
Rollin C. Goodwin	Thomas Ritchie
Patrick Healy	William Taylor
William Herrick	Brad Wessart
Daniel Martin	Alexander Whitmore
Robert McCauley	

Troop B

Captain Abraham H. Hasbrouck

Sergeants

1st Sergeant Jabez Chambers
Commissary Sergeant Silas Miles
Quartermaster Sergeant Patrick Tierney

George Gardells   Edward Price
Herman Richards   Charles Stadley

Corporals

Thomas Butterworth   John S. Smith   Edward Snyder

Blacksmith Charles Stewart
Farrier William Young

Privates

Edward S. Borst   William P. Reeves
George Brown   Silas A. Rix
Tracy Burnap   W. H. Sampson
William Cooney   John Smith
Keyes Davenport   John R. Updyke
Charles Ellis   John Waghorn
James Hogan   James Walsh
John Horr   William Walsh
James Kelly   George T. Whaley
Edward McNally   Elias Wheeler
John L. Morse

Troop C

Captain Charles J. Farley
1st Lieutenant Benjamin M. Whittemore

Sergeants

1st Sergeant Robert Harper
Commissary Sergeant John Evans
Quartermaster Sergeant Sylvester Meade

Patrick Q. Lincoln — Owen McNulty
Timothy O'Connor — Michael Wheaton

Corporals

Albert D. Burgess — James Highland — Michael Howland
John Kistner — John C. Lucas — Patrick Tiffany
Arthur F. Tileson

Saddler Mark D. Moonement
Farrier William Jones

Privates

James Adams — Henry Hill
Robert S. Anderson — Daniel Hurley
Frederick S. Bogue — James Michaels
William Brennan — William H. Norcott
John Buckley — Henry Pynes
Michael Coffee — John Smith
Martin Finley — Matthew Southard
Edward H. Fitch — John Stein
Lawrence Hand — John Withers

Troop D

Captain Seth B. Ryder
1st Lieutenant William Watson
2nd Lieutenant Henry I. Appleby

Sergeants

1st Sergeant Charles H. Greenleaf
Commissary Sergeant Ransom A. Perkins

Jeremiah J. Callahan Michael Donigan
William H. Marshall Henry Stone

Corporals

Stephen H. Greeley Peter Matthews James A. McGinley
Hiram Smith John Tierney John Tucker

Blacksmith John P. Cole
Farrier James W. Reed
Bugler Thomas Reynolds
Saddler John Watson

Privates

Edmund Barber Harmon Rogers
Edwin Bennett Edgar Schemerhorn
Patrick Bowler Peter Schemerhorn
Farquier Chapman Sanford Shearer
Patrick Gallagher William Shehee
John Guyatt James Smith
Norman Hazleton Frederick B. Stone
Peter Higgins John Sullivan
Richard Kenwill Michael Sullivan
John Langier Robert Taylor
Thomas Lynch Hyland Thomas
Dennis Mahoney Michael Tobin
Charles Matthews John Vaughn
Peter McGovern James Welch
James Moffitt Joel J. White
George Parris John P. Williams

Troop E

1st Lieutenant Daniel B. Merriman
Acting 2nd Lieutenant Elam S. Dye

Sergeants

Quartermaster Sergeant William H. Waterhouse

Henry C. Miner	Franklin S. Smart	John S. Trowbridge

Corporals

Roswell N. Boyington	Michael Maloney	Charles M. Newton
William G. Peckham	Matthew Strait	Sylvester F. Updegrove

Saddler Henry C. Brown
Bugler Frederick J. Clark
Farrier Aaron Eaton

Privates

John Burke	Cornelius W. Miner
L. Umberto Davis	Henry W. Monroe
Frederick J. Ehman, Jr.	James K. Morgan
Isaiah V. Filkins	Edward L. Morris
Sherman K. Ford	Franklin Olmstead
Andrew Jackson	Russell A. Paddock
Oscar S. Keyes	Truman Pascella
George W. Lamb	

Troop F

Captain William D. Lucas
1st Lieutenant Edward D. Tolles
2nd Lieutenant William B. Pickett

Sergeants

1st Sergeant George D. Lawrence
Commissary Sergeant William H. Nieman
Quartermaster Sergeant Marvin Wight

George W. Dodge	Alfred W. Nourse	Asa Suther
Miles Wells	Charles Whitney	

Corporals

John Hooper	John W. Jackson	John B. Jones
Donald J. McMillan	William W. Sowersby	Thadeus K. Whitlock

Blacksmith Nelson E. Cummings
Farrier William Coulston
Bugler Luke S. Williams

Privates

Merritt Austin	William B. Hutton
Anthony Baker	Edward Kinney
Wynant H. Bennett	Henry Leilores
William Blake	Charles H. Lewis
Henry J. Brooks	John B. McMillan
Ira Brown	Franklin B. Moore
William J. Brown	James Moore
Samuel Bullock	Wallace Moore
Philip Carney	A. Judson Oliver
Nelson Clark	Charles Porter
John Coulon	Emile Portier
Ysidro De La Rosa	Charles H. Richardson
John Devanney	Victor D. Smith
Thomas Donlon	Walter Church Smith
Hiram H. Earl	Hosea B. Stewart
Colonel Fuller	James H. Tuthill
Waterman Galuaka	Nelson Updyke
John Gregg	George Wells
Everett Hawley	William H. Wells
William Hawley	Daniel Wight
Philip Hazleswast	Nicholas Zahler

Troop G

1st Lieutenant James Bryant
2nd Lieutenant Philip Krohn

Sergeants

1st Sergeant John H. Wright
Quartermaster Sergeant Charles R. Wilcox
Commissary Sergeant Byron G. Wilmot

Peter Conlan	William H. Knight	Philip Ryan

Corporals

Eugene B. Barns	Newel Barnum	James Mallory
James M. Pollard	Abijah Spafford	John Tribe
William Turner	Peter White	

Blacksmith Allan Barney
Bugler Stephen D. Green
Saddler John Williams

Privates

Rodney Bovee	Samuel Gordon
William Butman	Wheeler C. Green
John Daniels	David Lane
Henry F. Davis	Cyrus B. Norton
Chauncey Deyo	George Payne
Timothy Dolan	John Thorn
Theodore Doremus	Clarence O. Van Winkle
John Doyle	Joseph Weiss
Johnson Foster	

Troop H

Captain James A. Penfield

Sergeants

1st Sergeant Eugene B. Hayward
Commissary Sergeant James A. Murdock
Quartermaster Sergeant Lucius F. Renne

James Bryan
Silas J. Mason

Robert A. Dunlap
Clark M. Pease

Corporals

Fayette H. Baker
Alphasis H. Moore

Alvin Bassett
Henry Wyman

Farrier Hiram Underhill
Farrier Charles Wells

Privates

Russell W. Baker
George D. Barber
William Barrows
Charles A. Boudrye
Wesley Brown
Duransie S. Carr
Oliver Cornell
Charles W. Curtis
D. Dean
George Delehan
George C. Durns
Abram Folger
Warren R. Fuller
Henry Giles
Stephen T. Glidden
Horace Graves
Walker E. Johnson
Ervin W. Jones
Jaleez Knights
Lewis Labounty
Joseph J. Lam
William Lamson
James Lively
William Lively
Warren McGinniss

Erastis McGowan
Patrick McLaughlin
Edward McManus
Abner B. Mead
David B. Miller
John Minor, Jr.
Albert Moncrief
J. Moore
Orville J. Moore
James Nelson
Henry Odle
Horace Orr
Amos Pierce
Robert W. Porter
William Sampson
William Sartwell
Albert W. Shattuck
George W. Smith
John Smith
John E. Starks
George L. Town
Benjamin F. Washburn
John Wilson
Edward A. Winters

Troop K

2nd Lieutenant Henry A. D. Merritt

Sergeants

1st Sergeant Robert Black
Commissary Sergeant James Nulan
Quartermaster Sergeant Jeremiah Noonan

George W. Dinsmore   Thomas O'Keefe
Lewis B. Parker   Nathaniel Talmadge

Corporals

John Dooling   John Mack
George W. Toms   Horace M. Wright

Blacksmith John Fox
Bugler James Madden
Farrier James Welsh

Privates

Aaron Aldrich   Edward McDonald
Dominick Bridon   George A. Munroe
Edwin A. Campbell   Michael O'Neil
John Donnell   Anthony Perry
James D. Dowd   Warren Russell
Charles Erriger   David Scofield
John Holden   Thomas Stafford
Abraham Howard   James Telfer
Robert Jasper   Amos Wilkins
Michael Keely   James Wilkins
William McCullough

Troop L

Captain Augustus Barker

Sergeants

1st Sergeant Benjamin Turner
Commissary Sergeant Sidney B. Lockwood
Quartermaster Sergeant Charles H. White

Anthony Cross   Henry S. Davenport   Peter McMullen

Corporals

Esek Bowen   James G. Smith   Samuel Townsend

Saddler Michael Henretty
Farrier Dennis O'Brien

Privates

William Caine
Edward Companion
Lewis Cooper
Frederick Harvey
Martin Hohn
Joseph Hurd
James Kilby
George Lamb
George Lang
John McEvan

Joseph Metzler
Phillip M. Place
Jesse Purdy
James Riley
William Runney
Pierre Sehe
John Smith
Joseph Tagle
Edward Unwin

Troop M

1st Lieutenant Eugene Dumont Dimmick

Sergeants

1st Sergeant Wilbur F. Oakley
Commissary Sergeant Peter Rafferty
Quartermaster Sergeant Orlean De Witt

William H. Bogardus	Philip H. Moore
Olney Paine	William H. Whitcomb

Corporals

Andrew Bridgeman	John Feen	James Fryhorn
Samuel Phister	George W. Ruff	John Spahn
	Justus Travis	

Bugler Louis Erdman
Blacksmith Erastus D. Marston

Privates

Joseph Bebon	Henry Kiveland
Walter Bishop	John Lock
George Bogardus	John F. McCann
Michael Davis	John Moam
John Dougherty	Edward Morton
Godfried Frank	Thomas Murray
John Freeling	John Myles
Charles Frike	William Rowell
James Garvey	Elisha B. Scott
William Haddle	Edward Sharkie

18th Regiment, Pennsylvania Volunteer Cavalry

12 Troops (A-B-C-D-E-F-G-H-I-K-L-M)
30 Officers & 546 Enlisted Men
June 30, 1863

Troop	Officer	NCO	B'smith	Bugler	Farrier	Saddler	Private
F & S	7	3	0	0	0	0	3
A	1	8	1	0	1	0	47
B	3	9	0	0	1	0	34
C	2	13	0	0	0	0	37
D	1	11	1	0	2	0	30
E	3	14	1	0	2	1	37
F	2	11	0	0	1	1	32
G	3	11	0	0	1	0	28
H	2	11	0	0	0	0	24
I	1	8	0	2	1	0	37
K	2	6	2	1	0	0	31
L	1	10	0	2	0	1	21
M	2	8	0	1	0	0	39
Totals	30	123	5	6	9	3	400

Field & Staff

Lieutenant Colonel William Penn Brinton
Acting Major William C. Lindsey
Adjutant Guy Bryan, Jr.
Quartermaster James C. Golden
Surgeon John J. Marks
Assistant Surgeon Samuel C. Williams
Assistant Surgeon George W. Withers

Quartermaster Sergeant John R. Winters
Saddler Sergeant Thomas Vanata
Veterinary Surgeon Samuel Dodd
Private William Franklin (Butcher)
Private William Harrison (Lt. Col. Brinton's Orderly)
Private John Marshall (Forage Master)

Troop A

1st Lieutenant Benjamin Franklin Campbell

Sergeants

1st Sergeant Roseberry Sellers
Commissary Sergeant Joseph Cooke
John B. Gordon

Corporals

John Evans	Henry Lashire	Job T. Morris
Samuel S. Rhinehart		Robert J. Tewkesberry

Blacksmith Everly L. Dow
Farrier Frederick Ramer

Privates

John Ammonds	Henry C. Mankey
George W. Boyers	Philip C. Martin
George W. Bryner	William H. Martin
William A. Bryner	Lemuel H. Millaneer
George Chapman	Joseph C. Morris
William Cole	Salathiel Murphy
Henry Cooke	Cavalier Poland
Thomas Eagon - Color Bearer	John W. Poland
Azariah Evans	Michael Radlonghafer
Caleb Evans	David Reese
John Finnegan	Levi Rush
John Fry	Frederick Shape
Joseph R. Gallatine	Isaac W. Sherrick
Freeman Gardner	John R. Smith
Moses Harrison	Henry Straight
Henry Hinerman	William Tewkesberry
James Huffman	John Thomas
Elisha Jefferies	Henry Ulum
Ellis J. Johns	Jonas Whisskey
George W. Kent	James D. White
Nicholas J. Kent	Andrew Wilson, Jr.
Warren Kneel	Alexander Yates
William Knox	Hazlett Yates
John Lapping	

Troop B

Captain John Wilson Phillips
1st Lieutenant David T. McKay
2nd Lieutenant James W. Smith

Sergeants

1st Sergeant Thomas J. Grier

Joseph Brown   Osborne Buck, Jr.

Corporals

| Edward Baldwin | Alvin J. Frey | William A. Moorehouse |
| Daniel Rice | David Smith | Samuel R. Smith |

Farrier Aaron Mosier

Privates

Thomas Adams	Andrew S. Pettigrew
Simeon Z. Bailey	Herman B. Rice
Robert Bender	Nelson Rice
Eber F. Cady	Hugh G. Rick
Edwin Carr	Osmond W. Rockwell
William J. Carrier	Isaac Sayers
DeWitt C. Childs	William Sheppa
Samuel Davis	James H. Shoemaker
John W. Davison	Franklin Skiff
Samuel P. Grey	George C. Slaven
John Herrick	Francis M. Southwick
James C. Higley	Orville Stager
Leon Kissel	Alfred W. Stone
Jesse H. Little	Winfield Scott Stricer
James McKay	Thomas G. Sweeney
John Moorehouse	Caleb W. Todd
James F. Morgan	Elijah N. Tubbs

Troop C

1st Lieutenant Samuel Montgomery
2nd Lieutenant James R. Weaver

Sergeants

Quartermaster Sergeant William McGlumphey

James Burns	Albert L. Montgomery	Alexander Montgomery
Martin Supler	Eli J. White	

Corporals

John M. Ashbrook	Francis Clutter	James H. Courtwright
Jonathan Gregory	Wilson Manford	Jonathan B Morse
Reuben Saunders		

Privates

James Allen	John Jones
Porter Allums	James Kimball
Andrew J. Barger	John R. Kimball
Wilson Barnhart	Richard J. Leonard
Maxwell Bayles	Joseph Masters
Daniel Carter	James McDonald
Addison Clutter	Alexander McKean
Seeley B. Clutter	Joel McNutt
William Crawford	Dennis Murphy
Elisha Daily	Thomas Philby
William B. Day	William Philby
Abraham V. Dille	Thomas Poland
John Durbin	Samuel H. Roach
George W. Gump	William Rum
Philip Gump	Jacob Shultz
James Haggerty	John P. Staggers
Morgan Hickman	Daniel W. Vanata
James L. Hughes	John M. Wright
John D. Johnson	

Troop D

1st Lieutenant Bethuel R. Mackey

Sergeants

Acting 1st Sergeant Noah Jones
Quartermaster Sergeant Elias Allen

Robert Henderson
Hugh St. Clair

Oliver H. P. Rouse
Obed W. Stackpole

Corporals

Henry B. Aldrich
Nathan Morey

Matthew D. Kerr
Samuel J. Ward

Francis M. Magee

Bugler John Doyle
Farrier Joseph A. McCutcheon
Farrier John Shoemaker

Privates

Charles A. Akin
Jonathan W. Alcorn
Alexander L. Anderson
Charles F. Arnold
William H. Bear
Lafayette Burton
Ralph Conover
Joseph Groner
John Hasbrouck
Harmon Holdridge
Garrett C. Hummer
John F. Hummer
David G. Kerr
John W. Kerr
Hugh Lafferty

James E. Lash
John Mack
Paul Martin
Mathew B. Micksell
John Peterson
Daniel A. Pomeroy
Daniel Richard
Samuel St. Clair
Garrison Shelmadine
Martin S. Sherwood
James C. Snedaker
Archibald Steward
Thomas R. Thompson
David W. Winans
Jackson W. Winans

Troop E

Captain Thadeus S. Freeland
1st Lieutenant George W. Nieman
2nd Lieutenant Samuel H. Treasonthick

Sergeants

1st Sergeant Hiram C. Fraley
Commissary Sergeant James H. Daddow
Quartermaster Sergeant George F. Wingard

John H. Boalt	Peter F. Dunkle
Aaron C. Etzweiler	Charles P. Sheaff

Corporals

Gilbert Depew	William L. Fulkenson	Jacob Greenewalt
George W. Hoch	John Hoffacker	Jerome B. Long
William Stephens		

Saddler William J. L. Ettinger
Farrier William F. Polm
Bugler Wilbur J. Shepherd
Farrier James H. Treasonthick

Privates

George Anderson	Henry C. Martin
William A. Baylor	William McCool
Jacob Beller	Franklin Meads
John A. Berry	Charles D. Mocherman
Frederick Boyer	William Mocherman
Edward Brown	Joseph S. Morrison
Daniel Carbaugh	Henry Neff
Benjamin Garman	Amos Noble
George Garrison	Henry Painter
Barnhard Gruber	William M. Poffenberger
William B. Hess	Samuel Ritston
John D. Hoover	Sawara S. Snyder
John H. Hoover	Philip Strominger
Adam Hurling	Solomon S. Updegrove
Joseph H. Kawel	John Warner
Adam Kurtz	Isaac N. Williamson
Josiah Lehn	Absalom A. Wilt
Robert Lowe	William J. Woodside
James Lyons	

Troop F

Captain John Britton
1st Lieutenant James Moffitt

Sergeants

1st Sergeant Samuel H. Fox
Quartermaster Sergeant Simeon T. Jackman

Leander N. Beazell	John W. Ward	William A. Young

Corporals

John Chew	David V. Donley	James Irwin
John Montgomery	John J. Moore	Aaron Pritchart

Saddler Benjamin R. Follansbee
Farrier Joseph R. Phillips

Privates

Samuel Anthony	James S. Jones
Clark L. Baker	Samuel Jones
William Ball	Allison Louderbach
John W. Bates	Morgan S. Louderbach
Henry M. Blakely	Archibald Marshall
Jacob Britton	Johnson Mayhorn
John A. Chester	Henry McNelly
William E. Childs	Peter Mcready
John B. Dodd	Finley Patterson
Lobingnier L. Dougherty	William Peebles
William Farrow	Harmon Perrin
Jackson Fry	William Pitman
Samuel Fry	William M. Rimmel
John Hazelbaker	William J. Weaver
Martin Howley	Joseph H. Wilson
Isaac K. Jackman	Joshua Worrell

Troop G

Captain Marshall S. Kingsland
1st Lieutenant Thomas P. Shields
2nd Lieutenant Benjamin Franklin Herrington

Sergeants

1st Sergeant John Rogers
Quartermaster Sergeant William Scott

Charles H. Hook	Zenas Jewel
Shadrack M. Sellers	Thomas Thompson

Corporals

John Coe	John C. Shields	William H. Six
David Thorpe	William H. Webster	

Farrier Rhinehart B. Church

Privates

Isaac Anderson	James Mahan
Theophilus L. Bunson	Samuel Martin
John C. Church	John McKeever
John B. Cooper	John Phillips, Jr.
Henry Cumley	Stephen Rush
Reuben Edgar	Amos P. Ryan
Benjamin Gray	Joseph M. Schofield
George W. Hart	James Staggers
Jonathan D. Headlee	Isaac Stiles
Roseberry Hughes	Jordan Strosnider
Nicholas Ihart	Charles T. Webster
Peter W. Kerns	George Whitlach
Leroy W. Kintyhitt	Isaac Wise
Henry Lyons	Jesse Yeager

Troop H

Captain Frederick W. Utter
2nd Lieutenant Benjamin A. Austin

Sergeants

1st Sergeant Irwin W. Fritchman
Commissary Sergeant William Fox

John Hulings	Frederick A. Lang
John Raymond	Harry Wilson

Corporals

Walter A. Clowes	Hamilton Gillespie	Isaiah Klinglesmith
Ralph Patrick	John P. Ross	

Privates

Peter Albert	Peter A. Jack
Charles Borton	Solomon King
Remar Bush	Jacob Kunkle
Charles Butler	Jacob Letler
Thomas Caldwell	James Newberry
James Forsythe	Charles Norris
Hiram Gillespie	George W. Nunn
Michael Glenn	Frank A. Powell
James Goldsmith	Samuel B. Reed
John Hand	Jacob Sindorf
William Hand	Edward Smith
Samuel P. Huff	Alexander Zimmerman

Troop I

2nd Lieutenant Samuel H. McCormick

Sergeants

Acting 1st Sergeant David R. Foresman
Commissary Sergeant Peter R. McCoy
Quartermaster Sergeant Benjamin G. Alliger

Jesse Crawford   Frederick Gohres   James D. Welshaus

Corporals

Daniel Stackhouse   Elias O. Wise

Farrier David Bishline
Bugler Charles Bohne
Bugler Ulrich Deiber

Privates

Samuel Atkins
Henry Baker
James Barr
Charles S. Beck
Israel Blessing
William Bordenhart
William M. Bradbury
Thomas B. Brady
Eli Cleveland
John Degraw
Jacob Fogel
George Folmsbee
William H. Harriet
Edward Hildreth
George W. Holdbrook
George W. Hottenstine
William Jacob
Charles M. Keller
Edward Litzenberg

William J. Lohr
Patrick McLaughlin
John Moon
Edward Musselman
John O'Dell
John C. Pierce
John F. Renn
James Rinebold
John Simmons
Lymon B. Simon
William Smith
John Still
John Strelz
Dareus Townsend
James C. Tripp
John K. Welliever
Michael Welsh
Smithson Williams

Troop K

Captain David Hamilton
Acting 2nd Lieutenant Henry J. Blough

Sergeants

1st Sergeant Augustus Dorsey
Commissary Sergeant Horace G. Hill
James L. Coleman   Robert H. Owens

Corporals

Levi S. Hoover   William Lowery

Blacksmith John Gull
Blacksmith Stephen S. Kelley
Bugler Henry Lohr

Privates

George Beaner   James McCurdy
James F. Bissel   William Morgan
Silas T. Bitner   William N. Nelson
Thomas Cooper   Benjamin T. F. Oliver
John Eisley   Adam Poorbaugh
Conrad B. Feigh   William Raily
Daniel E. Fritz   George W. Ringler
Elias Gibbs   Barney Shriver
Samuel M. Gibbs   Peter Smith
John Graham   Wolfgang Smith
Solomon W. Hensel   John A. Snowberger
Christian Holsoppel   George Strimel
George Karmichael   Noah Weaver
George Kelley   Calvin Weed
Peter Knepp   Moses Wisel
Isaac H. Koon

Troop L

2nd Lieutenant William L. Laws

Sergeants

1st Sergeant William H. Ferrell
Commissary Sergeant John W. Hudson

George Cornish   James H. Gordon
Lewis Oldfield   Peter L. Peterson

Corporals

Lawrence Fiegenshuh   Jeremiah Geaney
Charles C. Jones   John H. King

Bugler John Huber
Bugler Henry Juhrs
Saddler George W. Schultz

Privates

John W. Aler   Jacob Heller
Louis Bingham   Thomas Hill
Frederick Booth   Richard H. Hulse
Gustave Brauen   Michael Mullett
John M. Brown   John Nichols
John R. Brown   Louis A. Quinlin
Edward Buckhart   Byron Robinson
William Dottery   Joseph Schmidt
John Ehni   William T. Smith
Charles Fisher   Leonhardt Wetzel
Charles S. Griffith

Troop M

Captain Enos J. Pennypacker
2nd Lieutenant Henry Clay Potter

Sergeants

Acting 1st Sergeant Samuel Rodebaugh II
Commissary Sergeant Emanuel Coykendall

Jonas Beckwith	John L. Dougherty
John L. Keys	John Smith

Corporals

Isaac I. Dannenhower	William Willard

Bugler Henry Flentgo

Privates

John L. Adams	Christian Nollinger
Charles Bechtel	William Nott
John Bush	Andrew Pipher
Emil Fisher	John Puter
Nelson E. Fountain	Daniel B. Reed
Patrick Foy	George Roberts
Samuel Gilbert	Adam Rodebaugh
William G. Guest	Samuel Rodebaugh
Simeon Hamill	John F. Roller
Jacob R. Harvey	Daniel D. Rosecrans
Anthony Heither	Josiah Ruth
Daniel C. Horton	Albert Schultz
Thomas Jackson	Jeffry W. Smith
Alexander Kulp	William Speilhoffer
John W. Litts	Luther Stephens
James McBeth	Phillip Stewart
John McCarthy	Frank A. Street
Daniel McClurey	John Sullivan
John McKowsen	Joseph Wanner
Adam Morris	

1st Regiment, Vermont Volunteer Cavalry

12 Troops (A-B-C-D-E-F-G-H-I-K-L-M)
38 Officers & 703 Enlisted Men
June 30, 1863

Troop	Officer	NCO	B'smith	Bugler	Farrier	Saddler	Private
F & S	9	7	1	0	0	0	2
A	2	14	1	1	0	1	43
B	3	13	1	2	0	1	48
C	2	12	1	2	0	1	30
D	3	15	0	1	0	1	44
E	2	13	2	1	0	1	39
F	2	12	2	1	0	0	36
G	2	11	1	2	1	1	38
H	3	14	2	1	0	1	37
I	2	11	1	2	0	1	50
K	2	14	0	2	0	0	24
L	3	16	2	1	0	1	57
M	3	14	1	2	0	1	45
Totals	38	166	15	18	1	10	493

Field & Staff

Lieutenant Colonel Addison Webster Preston
Major John W. Bennett
Major Josiah Hall
Major William Wells
Adjutant Clarence D. Gates
Commissary Mark H. Wooster
Quartermaster Charles V. H. Sabine
Chaplain John H. Woodward
Assistant Surgeon Ptolemy O'Meara Edson

Sergeant Major Brainard M. Parker
Commissary Sergeant Lorentio H. King
Quartermaster Sergeant John H. Parson
Saddler Sergeant William Sparrow
Veterinary Surgeon Hosea Stone
Hospital Steward George W. Brush
Hospital Steward Joel H. Fisk
Blacksmith Joseph Gauthier
Private William H. Hayward (Armorer)
Private William Russell (Clerk)

Troop A

1st Lieutenant Ellis B. Edwards
2nd Lieutenant Cornelius W. Morse

Sergeants

1st Sergeant Warren Gibbs
Commissary Sergeant Rufus G. Barber
Quartermaster Sergeant Edward P. Whitney

Atchinson Blinn	Malcolm G. Frost	Reuben Hayes
Patrick Hogan	Henry O. Wheeler	

Corporals

Josiah H. Adams	James Kelley	William J. Langshore
Ichabod W. Mattocks	Michael Quinlan	Henry C. Smith

Saddler Christopher C. Gordon
Acting Blacksmith Samuel B. Roberts
Bugler James C. Squires

Privates

Jarious Alger	Francis B. Macomber
George Anson	Alonzo D. Marshall
Homer Bliss	Daniel W. Morehouse
Julius Bushaway	James A. Palmer
Charles Daniels	Thomas Ralph
Daniel Dixon	William B. Renouf
Ezra S. Doty	Orville Rounds
Albert George Edwards	Albert Shatzel
Josiah Emery	George D. Sherman
Frederick Falkner	Henry J. Smith
Henry F. Farnsworth	Sylvester Sprague
Irving E. Fay	Henry H. Stone
Oscar B. Ferguson	Willard S. Stowe
Lester Green	Henry E. Sweet
Lewis Green	Levi A. Taft
Jerome H. Grow	Milo S. Taft
Alexander Hall	Charles M. Wait
Jeremiah Haskins	Ephraim W. Wheeler
Guy Haynes	George Wheeler
John Hughes	Edward J. Whipple
George Keese	Edgar E. Wright
Frederick A. Lyon	

Troop B

Captain William M. Beeman
1st Lieutenant John Sawyer, Jr.
2nd Lieutenant Horace A. Hyde

Sergeants

1st Sergeant Samuel Ufford
Commissary Sergeant Orris P. Beeman
Quartermaster Sergeant John W. Erwin

Charles M. Cook	Frank B. Eustace
Harmon D. Hull	Mark N. Rogers

Corporals

Rufus M. Bliss	Benjamin G. Chapman	Samuel F. French
Hannibal S. Jenny	Myron J. Patten	Daniel F. Wilder

Blacksmith John B. Caraway
Saddler Deforest Shattuck
Bugler Nathan E. Skinner
Bugler Lucius G. Stiles

Privates

George W. Austin	Oren C. Farnsworth	Andrew E. Miller
George H. Baker	Joseph B. Farrand	William H. Perley
Alphonzo Barrows	Reuben R. Field	Harrison H. Perry
William H. Barrows	Antoine Fortuna	Nelson M. Perry
Orson T. Bigelow	Rodney R. Foster	Daniel H. Rogers
Philo Booskey	John Henry	William W. Rogers
Joseph E. Bowes	Eli Hibbard	Marshall St. Germain
Edwin B. Brewer	William C. Humphrey	Mitchell Sharrow
Antepas Brigham	John Hutchinson	John Smith
Azel N. Brush	Peter P. Hutchinson	William O. Sporr
Ossian Burleson	Edward N. Jacquier	Lafayette Stanhope
James Cavanaugh	Frank B. Jocelyn	Horace B. Stetson
George Currier	Peter King	Francis Touchett
Noble A. Daniels	Francis B. Kinney	Lucian G. Town
Luther H. Davis	James M. Lake	Lyman C. Wright
Simon Dufar	Benson J. Merrill	Edmond Yates

Troop C

Captain Henry M. Paige
2nd Lieutenant Perley C. J. Cheney

Sergeants

1st Sergeant Edmond Pope, Jr.
Commissary Sergeant Henry C. Phillips
Quartermaster Sergeant Jerome B. Hatch

Harlan P. Aldrich
Daniel J. Hill

Martin Heath
Lester K. Stiles

Corporals

Orange A. Baldwin
Pliny M. Morffitt

David P. Freeman
Marcus M. Rice

Edward McEvoy

Blacksmith George Brown
Bugler Charles Nownes
Bugler George W. Nownes
Saddler Merritt H. Stone

Privates

John Bancroft
Edward S. Bryant
Eliphalet E. Bryant
Chester L. Dwyer
Henry L. Edson
William Farnham
Gilbert E. Fisk
James W. Gordon
William R. Grove
Randall L. Hall
Samuel B. Hidgdon
Alonzo A. Hoyt
Dennis G. Leahy
Deforest L. Lewis
Arthur P. Lovejoy

Munroe Lyford
Lorenzo D. Mallory
William P. Mason, Jr.
Thomas S. May
Malon Norris
William Nownes
Philander A. Preston
James T. Reed
Gilbert O. Smith
Joel J. Smith
George W. Sterling
Noah W. Vincent
Tertullus C. Ward
Henry S. Waterman
John A. Wheeler

Troop D

Captain William G. Cummings
1st Lieutenant Jacob Trussell
2nd Lieutenant Harris B. Mitchell

Sergeants

1st Sergeant Josiah H. Moore
Commissary Sergeant Darwin J. Wright
Quartermaster Sergeant George P. Blair

Anson L. Chandler	Barney Decker
Horace K. Ide	John W. Woodbury

Corporals

Joseph O. Clark	John S. Coombs	John C. Gracey
Warren G. Norris	Edwin W. Southworth	Martin Van Buren Vance
James Wright	Frederick C. Wiggins	

Saddler George W. Cook
Bugler Milo J. Corliss

Privates

James B. Abbott	Rodney Eames	Lucius F. Reed
Daniel Adams	Patrick C. Gilligan	Martin V. Reinell
Harvey J. Allen	Orin S. Hendrick	William R. Roundy
George A. Austin	Samuel L. Higgins	Francis N. Rowell
Bartlett S. Bard	Levi P. Howland	Curtis L. Stacy
Harrison K. Bard	John Hutton	John S. Tilton
Joseph T. Bemis	Azro H. Kemson	Lineas V. Vance
George F. Bennett	Silas B. Kingsley	Daniel C. Walker
Charles W. Bickford	Sylvanus Lund	Samuel Washburn
Luman Blaisdell	Henry A. Moore	William M. Wheaton
Ira S. Bryant	Byron Morrill	Mark M. Wheeler
Joseph S. Clark	John F. Morse	William W. Whitney
Commodore W. Clifford	Chester Orr	John Woodward
Antipas H. Curtis	Frank H. Powell	Loren W. Young
Hiram P. Danforth	Frederick A. Powers	

Troop E

Captain Oliver T. Cushman
2nd Lieutenant Alexander B. Chandler

Sergeants

1st Sergeant Richard A. Seaver
Commissary Sergeant Joseph W. Bailey
Quartermaster Sergeant Charles N. Jones

Charles W. Bishop	George W. Everest
Jarvis Wentworth	Charles Wheeler

Corporals

Eugene H. Abels	William Hanley	Lamister Milan Parks
Lafayette M. Perham	Barney Rubenstein	Henry C. Williams

Blacksmith David B. Daniels
Saddler Miles H. Dodge
Bugler John E. Locke
Blacksmith William Stafford

Privates

Albert W. Allen	John Jellison
Austin G. Allen	Albert A. Kendall
Carlos Bryant	Orvis F. Kimball
Henry F. Buckman	Amos S. Lamson
Constant Carter	John Morse
Joseph Champlain	Oramel Morse
Albert S. Clapp	Oscar M. Parkhurst
George A. Curtis	William H. Pond
Clarence E. Cushman	Samuel Priest
Mitchell J. Finney	Riley G. Rogers
Franklin P. Flynn	Daniel H. Ryan
William A. Ford	Charles B. Sisson
Franklin Gould	Charles T. Sleeper
Hiram Gould	Henry A. Smith
Major Gould	Sylvester M. Snow
Horace Hall	Edmund Stone
Reuben W. Hayward	Vallorous Thurston
Michael Hogan	Wesley Watts
Henry O. Hutchinson	John H. Willard
Theodore H. Hutchinson	

Troop F

Captain Robert Scofield, Jr.
2nd Lieutenant Stephen A. Clark

Sergeants

1st Sergeant Thomas E. Bartleff
Commissary Sergeant Charles R. Farr
Quartermaster Sergeant John E. Whipple

Charles W. Forbush	Joseph A. Hyatt
Henry E. Smith	Jason A. Stone

Corporals

Henry M. Cook	Douglas Edmonds	Eli Metcalf
John M. Nash	Edwin A. Puffer	

Blacksmith John W. Curtice
Bugler George M. Taylor
Blacksmith James H. Woodburn

Privates

John Bathrick	Samuel C. Hinkley
Franklin M. Beterly	Rosalvo A. Howard
Charles W. Brigham	Andrew Howe
Lorin M. Brigham	John S. Jillson
Thomas Brigham	George B. Mattoon
William C. Butler	Eugene McCarthy
John C. Carol	Norman A. Morrice
Edwin Clemons	Loren Packard
Charles A. Corea	Herbert S. Pierce
George R. Crosby	John T. Pierce
Nathaniel P. Dickinson	George B. Roundy
Charles A. Dinsmore	Ovid Seymour
George H. Forbush	Mason A. Stone
Henry Gardner II	John A. Thwing
Henry Gervais	Laomia Ware
Rinaldo G. Gillmore	Myron C. Warner
George W. Haskell	Theodore Witt
Jesse S. Heath	Charles L. Wooley

Troop G

Captain Frank Ray
1st Lieutenant Gilbert Steward

Sergeants

1st Sergeant James E. Hadaway
Quartermaster Sergeant John M. Vanderlip
Stephen B. Chellis   Alvah R. Haswell   Irvin W. Hurd

Corporals

Joseph Courtright   Fayette Dyer   William J. Fuller
Charles Sherwood   Philip Vaughn   Hiram W. Waters

Blacksmith Lorenzo D. Atherton
Bugler James Barrett
Bugler Horatio N. Leach
Saddler Samuel D. Preston
Farrier Daniel E. Waters

Privates

William H. Belding
Eugene F. Bellows
Homer Benson
Oscar Bracy
George H. Calkins
Edward Carl
Palmer Clapp
Stephen Clapp
William E. Colby
Winslow Colby
Lewis Conger
Frederick W. Cook
George W. Curtis
David Darling
Joseph C. Farnum
James C. Frazer
Oliver Green
Henry H. Hadaway
Parker L. Hall

Thomas G. Hard
John H. Hill
Silas J. Hurd
Henry Jones
Morte Kerce
Charles Mattison
James McMahon
William T. Moncrief
Clark Nelson
Vitale Reulo
Lyman L. Russell
James Saunders
Matthew Short
Dexter Smith
Samuel Snell
Charles Stewart
William W. Warner
Leander White
Alonzo R. Wilson

Troop H

Captain Charles A. Adams
1st Lieutenant John H. Hazelton
2nd Lieutenant Carlos A. Barrows

Sergeants

1st Sergeant Emmet Mather
Commissary Sergeant Nathaniel B. Lewis
Quartermaster Sergeant Samuel P. Bailey

George D. Bucklin   Samuel Dowling
James Everson, Jr.   Lensey R. Morgan

Corporals

Henry W. Cooke   Stephen Corey   Henry O'Meara Edson
William E. Fitzgerald   George M. Gorton   Henry W. Pratt
Daniel D. Warren

Blacksmith Patrick Callaghen
Blacksmith Theophile Champeau
Saddler William O'Brien
Bugler Alonzo M. Ritterbush

Privates

Frank J. W. Baldwin   Jeffrey Hart
Luther S. Barnes   George W. Knights
Royal C. Bostwick   Ralph Locklin
Stephen L. Braxton   John McIntire
Joseph Buffum   Ira C. Monroe
John Cantrell   Dean W. Reed
Anthony P. Clair   James O. Riley
Charles Cowley   George A. Rogers
Frederick Cowley   James M. Ross
James M. Cowley   Abner E. Sanderson
Willard Crandall   John C. Smith
Donald C. Davis   Frank Snay
Solon D. Davis   Royal J. Stevens
Alonzo E. Doty   James A. Stewart
Martin Dwyer   James Stone
Darwin E. Eames   John Sulham
George J. Everson   Ira C. Warren
William Flynn   Henry M. Worthen
Joseph Guertin

Troop I

1st Lieutenant Eben Grant
2nd Lieutenant Patrick H. Caldwell

Sergeants

1st Sergeant George A. Hyde
Commissary Sergeant Franklin E. Sawyer
Quartermaster Sergeant Aaron M. Crane

William W. Foster   Benjamin F. Perry   Luther B. Persons

Corporals

William H. Hall   Charles C. Hoyt   Harvey Lilley
Martin R. Sargent   Mark Warner

Bugler Joseph W. Allen
Bugler William Chamberlain
Saddler William Dutton
Blacksmith Samuel H. Kaiser

Privates

Benjamin O. Aiken	Silas Hines	Albinus F. Raymere
Elias W. Barry	George W. Jackson	Warren M. Reed
Herbert A. Boomhower	Albert A. Kingsley	Frank A. Russell
Adoniram J. Burr	Henry Laxford	Samuel Sargent, Jr.
Samuel B. Clark	James M. Manchester	George E. Skinner
Oscar E. Collins	Franklin S. Mead	Theodore P. Skinner
Alanson E. Coon	Ephraim Miles	Eliab Smith
Albert E. Cowles	George W. Miso	George S. Spofford
Russell W. Cowles	Charles Nelson	Jonas F. Stevens
William H. Currier	Augustus L. Newland	Samuel Stratton
Warren J. Dane	Levi A. Newland	Jonas G. Sulham
William H. Daniels	George B. Nimblet	Chauncey C. Thurston
Joseph Enos	Aaron S. Ober	Robert S. Tice
George H. Gilman	Harry B. Pettengill	Edward A. Washburn
James F. Goin	Watson S. Pierce	Abijah F. Whitney
James Greaves	Reuben C. Piersons	Thomas Wisewall
George W. Hemingway	Elias M. Quimby	

Troop K

Captain Andrew Jackson Grover
1st Lieutenant John Williamson

Sergeants

1st Sergeant Jonas R. Price
Commissary Sergeant Benjamin Sheldon
Quartermaster Sergeant Charles K. Spencer

Ozro F. Cheney	Charles B. Goodrich
Horace Lapham	Charles A. Sanborn

Corporals

Hazard Bennett	Frank Goodnow	Walter H. Goodnow
Charles W. Lamorder	Charles N. Lapham	John Marshall
John Shelly		

Bugler William F. Lewis
Bugler Allen Walmarth

Privates

Robert B. Barry	Alfred Mossey
Israel Blair	Hiram Noble
Thaddeus A. Canfield	Joseph S. Perkins
David S. Dillon	Alexander W. Ross
John Gavin	Eli C. Ross
O. Judson Green	Edwin Russell
Herman H. Heitman	James H. Sanborn
John W. Jackson	Bradford Sherwood
William F. Johnson	Sanford Sherwood
Edwin E. Jones	Edgar P. Sloan
David H. Lewis	Hiram E. Tupper
John McSorley	Arthur H. Wilcox

Troop L

Captain Henry Chester Parsons
1st Lieutenant John W. Newton
2nd Lieutenant Alexander G. Watson

Sergeants

1st Sergeant F. Stewart Stranahan
Commissary Sergeant William H. Eastman
Quartermaster Sergeant Herbert Brainerd

George W. Duncan	Willard Farrington	William L. Greenleaf
George Miller	Seymour A. Brainerd	

Corporals

Joseph A. Brainerd	William A. Clapp	Henry A. Curtis
Beach T. Knight	George L. McBride	Robert Pollenger
Ira E. Sperry	Hiram L. Waller	

Blacksmith Loren Brow
Blacksmith Francis L. Pedneau
Bugler Sanford H. Potter
Saddler Josiah Sturtevant

Privates

Seymour Avery	Reuben A. Everts	J. Scott Merritt
Joseph Bener	Arabut E. Fobes	Hugh Mooney
Charles C. Bennett	Josiah A. Fobes	William H. H. Muncil
Leonard E. Blatchley	Albert Girardeau	Hosea B. Nash
Horace C. Blinn	Albert R. Greene	Ahira H. Perkins
Albert Blish	Samuel A. Hale	William A. Perry
Charles H. Bradley	Charles D. Harvey	John Pierce
Joseph P. Brainerd	Charles W. Hayward	Isaac Ryan
Otis H. Brainerd	Calvin A. Irish	Albert F. Sawyer
George S. Brownell	Homer C. Irish	Andrew A. Smith
Walter H. Burbank	Horace A. Irish	Edward A. St. Louis
Abram Burlett	Gilbert D. Isham	Rufus D. Thompson
Hezekiah B. Carr	William H. Jure	Samuel S. Watson
Charles B. Chapin	Timothy Keefe	William G. Watson
Thaddeus H. Clark	John Labarei	Truman B. Webster
Charles M. Cornell	Eben T. C. Lord	William H. Welshman
Clarence A. Cornell	Willis Lyman	Thomas Wilson
Albert H. Drury	Sanford H. Marshall	Edgar J. Wolcott
Charles Erwin	Charles H. McCarroll	Curtis S. Woodward

Troop M

Captain John W. Woodward
1st Lieutenant George Washington Chase
2nd Lieutenant Ebenezer K. Sibley

Sergeants

Commissary Sergeant Eugene C. Hinman
Quartermaster Sergeant John H. H. Quimby

Eugene Consigny	James Kinehan	George C. Lewis
Joseph L. Southerland	Samuel F. Stearns	

Corporals

Alexander Blo	Charles Harding	John Kinehan
Harry G. Sheldon	Schuyler Smith	William H. Thompson
James Ward		

Acting Blacksmith Ezra E. Aldrich
Bugler Albert F. Hackett
Bugler Azro F. Hackett
Saddler Jone Stone

Privates

John Aldrich	Franklin Doyle	Robert McLellan
Joseph Armstrong	Cotton Fletcher	James A. McNeily
George Bellores	Patrick Flynn	Hesakiah P. Nichols
Alexander Bessiallon	Benjamin Gordon	David Niles
John Bourke	Peter Hughes	Thomas O'Brien
Patrick Brannon	Francis Jordan	Albert Partlow
Carmichael A. Brown	Henry Labonty	James Quirk
George Brown	Joseph Laplant	Dennis Rafferty
John Brown	Edwin B. Leavitt	Joseph Rober
George Buchanan	William Malcolm	James Ryan
Joseph Buchanan	John Mansfield	Lenord Sartwell
Michael Curren	Joseph Martin	Henry Shattle
Patrick Curren	Thomas McGuire	Charles St. Michael
Alonzo Davis	Daniel McKenty	Peter St. Peter
Hiram A. Dean	Charles McLaughlin	Allen Wright

1st Regiment, West Virginia Volunteer Cavalry

10 Troops (B-C-D-E-F-G-H-L-M-N)
30 Officers & 455 Enlisted Men
June 30, 1863

Troop	Officer	NCO	B'smith	Bugler	Farrier	Saddler	Private
F & S	8	7	1	0	0	0	6
B	2	13	0	0	1	1	25
C	2	15	0	1	1	1	40
D	2	14	1	1	1	1	37
E	3	15	1	1	1	1	29
F	1	9	0	0	1	1	22
G	3	16	1	0	0	1	20
H	3	11	1	0	0	0	22
L	2	16	1	0	0	0	32
M	2	13	1	0	0	1	40
N	2	11	1	0	0	0	19
Totals	30	140	8	3	5	7	292

Field & Staff

Colonel Nathaniel Pendleton Richmond
Major Charles E. Capehart
Acting Major Harvey Farrabee
Adjutant Sidney W. Knowles
Commissary Henry C. Durrett
Quartermaster S. C. W. Dunlevy
Chaplain F. W. Vertican
Assistant Surgeon Perrin Gardner

Sergeant Major Richard B. Sowers
Chief Trumpeter Charles Schorn
Quartermaster Sergeant William C. Steward
Saddler Sergeant David Turner
Veterinary Surgeon William Gill
Hospital Steward James Dean
Hospital Steward Ebenezer M. Woods
Blacksmith George W. Jeffers
Private John N. Elliott (Foragemaster)
Private George W. Bardsley (Orderly)
Private Thomas Cunningham (Orderly)
Private Clinton H. Potter (Orderly)
Private Charles Ruble (Orderly)
Private Philander Smith (Surgeon Gardner's Orderly)

Troop B

1st Lieutenant Hugh P. Boon
2nd Lieutenant William W. Wilson

Sergeants

1st Sergeant Samuel Grim
Commissary Sergeant John W. Day
Quartermaster Sergeant Hamilton H. Bell

James P. Allum	William H. Bell
John R. McCoy	Stephen Stickle

Corporals

Samuel H. Barnett	John M. Conkey	Franklin Jones
Andrew B. Porter	Thomas B. McGlumphy	James H. Walton

Farrier William Fox
Saddler David Howell

Privates

Robert Allison	Watson Karrh
Nelson Booth	George H. Klinefelter
William J. Brown	George W. Lloyd
Martin Carroll	William H. McNeil
John W. Chambers	John Messenger
James Daily	Abraham Newman
John Dean	John Newman
Franklin Doaks	George Washington Potter
John Doyle	Thomas Rankin
John Foust	William Riggsby
Isaac Hatfield	William Seaburn
John H. Hummell	John Stollar
Isaiah Karrh	

Troop C

Captain William A. McCoy
1st Lieutenant Arthur S. Palmer

Sergeants

1st Sergeant Francis M. Work
Commissary Sergeant John H. Dicks
Quartermaster Sergeant Thomas Meredith

William K. Brown	George W. Jackson	James L. Jennings
Isaac Roberts	James H. Wilson	

Corporals

Frank T. Bartholomew	Richard Bousy	Edmond Guthrie
William Helmick	Henry Melrose	Thomas H. Marshall
Charles Reading		

Bugler Barnabas Dela Grange
Farrier Enoch Deem
Saddler Hannibal McClain

Privates

Jacob Arnot	James Montea
James Barry	Michael Murphy
Joseph S. Boone	Michael O'Hara
Henry Braden	George W. Phillips
Colby W. Brown	James R. Reader
Leonidas J. Brown	James A. Roach
Patrick Cain	Maloy W. Rock
William Cranston	George W. Rockhold
John Dinnethorn	Milton Smith
John Gaits	Hezekiah Tait
Martin M. Geer	Jacob Thompson
William T. Graham	Martin Van Buren Vernon
Thomas C. Haslow	William Verry
Jacob Henry	Henry A. A. Walker
Harry J. Holtz	Blackburn Weaver
Albert King	Melvin H. Weaver
George B. Law	Rufus E. Weaver
Thomas Little	William Weaver
Samuel J. Malone	Frederick Wolf
Thomas McCarty	William Worley

Troop D

Captain William C. Carmen
2nd Lieutenant Charles A. Armstrong

Sergeants

1st Sergeant Eugene Gallagher
Commissary Sergeant Ebenezer B. McMillen
Quartermaster Sergeant William H. Foulke

Harrison Allum	George V. Foreman	William Heskett
Clark Lynn	Lewis Phillips	

Corporals

Henry Moreland	John H. Reed	Thomas Schofield
Richard Stock	Charles L. Wilson	Godfrey C. Winzenreid

Bugler Charles Geissler
Blacksmith Henry Harris
Saddler Andrew Solden
Farrier Jacob Watson

Privates

Joseph P. Birdett	Edward Martin
Samuel Bricker	John McGilvey
Samuel Brooks	George McKee
James Brown	William D. McKirahan
Lewis Brown	James McMannis
Enos J. Brownfield	Augustus Merkle
Henry Conkel	William F. Miller
Samuel F. Conoway	James Newman
Adam Coss	William Pfaffenbach
George Dunley	Henry C. Rose
William Givans	Alexander Simmerall
Joseph Gow	Edward Simon
Jesse Hallowell	Edward Smallfoot
Uriah W. Halsted	Curtis B. Stedd
Jacob Hatcher	Thomas Todd
John Hatcher	John C. Winzenreid
Julius F. Hohman	Joseph Wiseman
James Kinslow	Samuel B. Woodmansee
John W. Klein	

Troop E

Captain William H. Harris
1st Lieutenant Newberry W. Wheeler
2nd Lieutenant Hiram Robinett

Sergeants

1st Sergeant Joseph Humphrey
Commissary Sergeant James D. Spencer
Quartermaster Sergeant Francis M. Brohard

Erastus H. Parker   Gideon D. Smith
Henderson M. Smith   James W. Wheeler

Corporals

Drury Badgley   John M. Buckley   John Guynn
John A. Michael   John D. Rapp   Frederick M. Satow
Joseph P. Warne   Edward Wilds

Blacksmith Simon C. Arnold
Saddler William M. Flinn
Farrier William M. Hanna
Bugler Jerome B. Huntington

Privates

George W. Alger   Francis Gilmore
William Bailey   Elmore Hardman
William Barrett   Pratt Humphrey
Thomas A. Black   Daniel Killingworth
James M. Boyer   David Killingworth
John D. Bracy   James Killingworth
Joseph L. Buckley   Claudius Maddox
Reason Burdett   John J. Mullen
William Henry Harrison Burdett   John M. Nottingham
James Sampson Carver   John W. Pennell
Alexander S. Coleman   Major Randolph
Charles Cook   Carl August Satow
John Coss   John W. Summerville
George A. Drennen   Samuel Wheeler
Washington Monroe Flinn

Troop F

1st Lieutenant Maxwell Carroll

Sergeants

1st Sergeant William Porter Wilken
Quartermaster Sergeant Garrett C. Selby

Stephen Malone Isaac W. Moore William Sanders

Corporals

Joseph Gabbert Benjamin F. Griffith
William M. Holton Mordecai K. Wilkinson

Farrier Samuel Brown
Saddler Robert P. Flesher

Privates

Joshua Beverlin Alexander Lydy
Daniel M. Bowden Thomas B. Lynch
William F. Brewer John McGhee
Frank H. Brown William T. Morrow
Hamilton Butcher William Newsome
Isaac Cunningham Charles P. Rose
Francis Garrety Joseph B. Smith
Henry J. Goff Edward Stanford
James Hughes Philip White
Daniel Jones Flavius K. Wilson
William F. Jones John T. Young

Troop G

Captain John A. Byers
1st Lieutenant William St. Clair
2nd Lieutenant Irwin C. Swentzel

Sergeants

1st Sergeant John McNaughton
Commissary Sergeant Thomas Markes
Quartermaster Sergeant Abel W. Rock

| Joseph Canterbury | Benjamin Hatfield | Joseph A. Lesage |
| Robert F. McCormick | Lewis H. Smith | |

Corporals

Judson Ferrell	William H. Hollenback	Joseph Lycan
James F. McCorkle	Burwell Newman	John Ray
Cornelius Shannon	John M. Underwood	

Saddler William G. Elkins
Blacksmith William Kennedy

Privates

James F. Adams	Lewis Hunter
Roland S. Bias	Patrick V. Justice
Christian S. Blake	John McCanles
Alexander W. Church	Abraham Miller
James D. Dunkle	Alexander Newman
Francis A. M. Dyer	James W. Poteete
James A. Furguson	Jacob Rau
Alexander Hoback	John R. Ready
John H. Holland	Harrison J. Shannon
John R. Howell	Jeremiah Stevenson

Troop H

Captain David Mequillet
1st Lieutenant James F. Poole
2nd Lieutenant Henry J. Leasure

Sergeants

1st Sergeant Francis M. Cunningham
Quartermaster Sergeant George C. Giles

Joseph E. Cramer James W. Poston
Rudolphus Robinson Elias M. Smith

Corporals

Henry Ebeckhousen   William Seabright   William Shaw
Enoch M. Sutton   Solomon Walker

Blacksmith Jacob Miller

Privates

John Archey Michael M. McMorris
Joseph Archey James Russell
John H. Brown Isaac C. Shaw
Abraham Coon Joseph Shaw
James D. Emery Victor Shaw
Jacob Handlin Harrison Skiles
Edward D. Harden Isaac Steward
Alexander Harlow William Whaley
Daniel Jobs Walter Williams
Robert Kelley Charles Winders
Augustus Kraft Augustus Zimmerman

Troop L

1st Lieutenant John Seltzer
2nd Lieutenant John J. McDonald

Sergeants

1st Sergeant Robert E. Mahood
Commissary Sergeant Thomas B. McConnell
Quartermaster Sergeant William McKinley

George Collins	John Estep, Sr.	James Gallaway
Patrick Monahan	John A. J. Palmer	James Ware

Corporals

Alexander McFarland	William W. Patterson	Jeremiah Pettit
Samuel F. Rose	Robert Slee	George Snider
John Brooks		

Blacksmith William Elliott

Privates

William Brice
James Burns
Jonathan Burns
John Churchman
Robert G. Dorsey
John Durbin
Francis Estep
John Estep, Jr.
Thomas Faulkner
Michael Gallagher
William G. Gill
William Glen
Henry Henchman
Henry Holman
James Hopkins
Joseph Huff
Abram Lepps
Shannon Lyons
George V. Massgrove
Floranas Matts
Thomas McDonough
George Moore
John Mushrush
Laban Osborn
John S. Rose
William Ruddick
John T. Stewart
Henry Swihart
James Thomas
David Van Sickle
Julius Weihi
William Wolf

Troop M

1st Lieutenant Shesh Bentley Howe
2nd Lieutenant Gottleib Wipf

Sergeants

1st Sergeant Lewis Haag

Henry Bachman
Frederick Starline

Charles Ernst
George Wehe

Corporals

John Beaschler	Charles Bretzler	William Faehnle
Dietrich Findling	William Leppert	Nicholas Reuter
Mathias Sauer	Martin Thoma	

Saddler Gottfried Luikert
Blacksmith George Scheck

Privates

Ignaz Assmann	John Konrad
Frederick Brians	Adolf Lausterer
George Brunner	Dissmass Leibfritz
Jacob Dischenger	Andrew Loubner
John Dornick	Thomas McGuire
Jacob Fick	Phillip Meyer
Adam Fischer	Albert Neutzling
Leonard Fischer	John Ohlinger
Henry Genheimer	Anthony Ostermann
Augustin Graber	George Pfarr
Frederick Haack	Gottleib Rausher
Caspar Happel	Frederick Robert
August Hauck	Andrew Schlarb
John Heinrich	George Schlegel
Mathias Heitger	Lewis Schmidt
Nicholas Heitger	George Schreiber
Martin Holzmuller	Conrad Seitz
Henry Joachim	Henry Strohmeyer
Charles Koehler	Gideon Weller
Henry Koehler	Englebert Zipperich

Troop N

1st Lieutenant Joseph H. Wilson
2nd Lieutenant Henry W. Clark

Sergeants

1st Sergeant Samuel B. Paxton
Quartermaster Sergeant William J. Hiles

Samuel B. Davis	Joseph Murray	David Wood

Corporals

Jesse Chamberlain	Moses Craig	William C. Davis
George C. Leughty	George Marshall	Robert F. Wilson

Blacksmith Calvin C. Hassen

Privates

Thomas Anderson	Jacob Kline
Reuben W. Carter	John C. Majors
Joseph S. Conrodd	Morrison A. Sample
George Crider	Cumberland G. Smith
Thomas Dawson	Jacob Staley
Peter Fry	Samuel O. Stevenson
Elisha H. Gifford	Joseph Swihart
Melvin C. Hull	William L. Wilderman
William Huston	Edward Wood
Cephas Kinney	

Appendix F

3rd Division, 2nd Brigade Staff Roster
June 30, 1863

Headquarters Staff

Brig. Gen. George Armstrong Custer	Commanding Brigade	
Surg. Samuel R. Wooster	Chief Surgeon	F&S 1 Michigan
Capt. Frederick W. Armstrong	Act. Asst. Inpector General	M-2 New York
Capt. George Augustus Drew	Act. Asst. Inspector General	G-6 Michigan
Capt. Robert F. Judson	Act. Asst. Inpector General	L-5 Michigan
1st Lt. Richard Baylis	Act. Asst. Adjutant General	F&S 5 Michigan
1st Lt. Duane Doty	Act. Asst. Adjutant General	F&S 7 Michigan
1st Lt. William H. Wheeler	Additional Aide-de-Camp	F&S 1 Michigan
2st Lt. William Colerick	Additional Aide-de-Camp	I-1 Michigan
2st Lt. Edward G. Granger	Additional Aide-de-Camp	C-5 Michigan
Sergeant Levant Hobbs	Orderly	C-5 Michigan
Sergeant Kellogg B. Martindale	Wagonmaster	B-7 Michigan
Corporal Philip Laboe	Foragemaster	C-5 Michigan
Corporal James D. Quick	Wagoner	E-7 Michigan
Private James M. Arnbor	Orderly	B-7 Michigan
Private Peter Martin Boehm	Bugler / Orderly	B-5 United States
Private James Burnett	Orderly	B-7 Michigan
Private Joseph Burson	Orderly	L-5 Michigan
Private Benjamin H. Butler	Orderly	M-1 Michigan
Private Norvill F. Churchill	Orderly	L-1 Michigan
Private Peter Coston	Orderly	M-5 Michigan
Private Henry G. Coulthard	Orderly	C-1 Michigan
Private Michael J. Fierstine	Orderly	H-7 Michigan
Private George L. Foster	Orderly	C-1 Michigan
Private Joseph Fought	Orderly	D-5 United States
Private Charles H. Goodrich	Orderly	M-5 Michigan
Private George L. Harrington	Orderly	L-6 Michigan
Private William Hastings	Orderly	I-7 Michigan
Private Edward Hawley	Wagoner	L-5 Michigan
Private Joseph N. Hunt	Postmaster	A-5 Michigan
Private William Johnson	Orderly	B-7 Michigan
Private George B. McIntyre	Orderly	B-7 Michigan
Private Charles H. Reilly	Orderly	H-1 Michigan
Private John G. Schaible	Orderly	F-6 Michigan
Private Charles Stephenson	Orderly	B-7 Michigan
Private Thomas True	Orderly	B-7 Michigan
Private Erastus E. Ward	Orderly	F-6 Michigan
Private Nodiah C. Ward	Orderly	D-5 Michigan
Private George White	Orderly	M-5 Michigan

Ambulance Corps Staff

1st Lt. Farnham Lyon	Acting Ambulance Officer	F&S 7 Michigan
Quartermaster Sergeant Elias Hall		B-5 Michigan
Sergeant James D. Roe		C-1 Michigan
Private Hiram Allen		C-7 Michigan
Private Thomas Anderson	Teamster	B-7 Michigan
Private George W. Boice		C-1 Michigan
Private Elijah H. Bruce		C-1 Michigan
Private Henry Cole		D-6 Michigan
Private Seviar Crevia		B-5 Michigan
Private Benjamin S. Dalrymple	Teamster	I-5 Michigan
Private Charles Dowman		E-5 Michigan
Private Milton Hodge		K-5 Michigan
Private Mason Ide	Teamster	C-7 Michigan
Private Joel Joslyn	Teamster	L-6 Michigan
Private Eli H. Kinear		C-5 Michigan
Private William A. Maslen		A-5 Michigan
Private George L. Monroe		A-5 Michigan
Private George W. Morse		K-5 Michigan
Private Robert B. Nevison		M-5 Michigan
Private David Perkins		H-7 Michigan
Private Charles Pettys		A-6 Michigan
Private Alvah B. Powelson	Wagoner	C-7 Michigan
Private Winchester R. Rice	Teamster	M-6 Michigan
Private David H. Seaman	Teamster	I-5 Michigan
Private Harvey H. Shepard	Teamster	I-6 Michigan
Private John T. Sprague		A-6 Michigan
Private Sylvester A. Stone		E-5 Michigan
Private Andrew J. Taylor		G-5 Michigan
Private Orson J. Wolcott		E-7 Michigan

Provost Marshal Staff

2nd Lt. George S. White	Acting Assistant Provost Marshal	K-5 Michigan
Sergeant John D. Cruice		F-7 Michigan
Corporal William H. Armstrong		F-7 Michigan
Corporal Henry Guio		F-7 Michigan
Corporal Oscar S. Ralph		F-7 Michigan
Private Clark H. Beardslee		F-7 Michigan
Private Jasper Braden		F-7 Michigan
Private Ashley A. Brown		A-5 Michigan
Private David Campbell		D-6 Michigan
Private Levi Cross		F-7 Michigan
Private Henry Dorman		F-7 Michigan
Private George Drury		I-5 Michigan
Private William Edwards		I-5 Michigan
Private John R. Grover		F-7 Michigan
Private Charles W. Higgins		D-5 Michigan
Private Joshua E. James		D-5 Michigan
Private Mortimer Phillips		F-7 Michigan
Private Marvin E. Whiting		D-5 Michigan

Quartermaster Staff

1st Lieutenant William O. North	Act. Assistant Quartermaster	K-5 Michigan
Sergeant Willard F. Rhoades	Quartermaster Sergeant	B-1 Michigan
Sergeant Charles O. Pratt		A-7 Michigan
Corporal James C. Morley	Blacksmith	I-7 Michigan
Private James Armstrong	Blacksmith	D-5 Michigan
Private Judson Beach		H-5 Michigan
Private Almon Bennett	Wagoner	D-1 Michigan
Private Benjamin Bingham		D-7 Michigan
Private William Black	Wagoner	G-1 Michigan
Private Isaac Brace		H-5 Michigan
Private Oscar H. Carus		H-5 Michigan
Private William Chapman	Teamster	L-5 Michigan
Private Alonzo B. Cleveland	Blacksmith	D-5 Michigan
Private George A. Davis	Teamster	D-1 Michigan
Private Thomas Densmore		H-5 Michigan
Private James Griffith		G-5 Michigan
Private George Herring	Teamster	D-7 Michigan
Private George W. Hoover	Teamster	C-1 Michigan
Private Ira C. Horton		A-6 Michigan

Private George S. Jeffords	Blacksmith	D-5 Michigan
Private John Kiley		H-5 Michigan
Private Samuel Lefever		D-7 Michigan
Private Justin B. Meeker	Farrier	I-7 Michigan
Private Charles Merryweather		B-5 Michigan
Private Edson Mintonye	Wagoner	K-1 Michigan
Private Samuel E. Munger	Wagoner	I-1 Michigan
Private Coleman C. Peck	Wagoner	M-1 Michigan
Private Ira M. Potter	Blacksmith	M-5 Michigan
Private Andrew Pray		D-7 Michigan
Private Esborn Quackenbush	Wagoner	B-1 Michigan
Private Thomas J. Richards	Wagoner	H-5 Michigan
Private Daniel Rummel	Wagoner	M-1 Michigan
Private Jerman Sutherland		A-5 Michigan
Private Ira M. Swartz	Wagoner	K-1 Michigan
Private John P. Van Horn		B-5 Michigan
Private Olney J. Worden	Wagoner	E-1 Michigan

Brigade Teamsters & Staff

Private George Baker		B-7 Michigan
Private Charles Beaver		I-5 Michigan
Private John Bennett		G-5 Michigan
Private Jacob E. Bullock		D-5 Michigan
Private Reuben Burdick		I-5 Michigan
Private James Collins		I-5 Michigan
Private David Cudworth	Cook	E-5 Michigan
Private Edwin J. Ewing		D-6 Michigan
Private Timothy Galligher		C-7 Michigan
Private David L. Gould		B-7 Michigan
Private George D. Kingsley		D-5 Michigan
Private Frederick Koster		H-7 Michigan
Private Columbus L. Luther		C-7 Michigan
Private Francis D. Martin		H-7 Michigan
Private Francis H. Mattison		L-6 Michigan
Private John McGregor	Cook	G-7 Michigan
Private Robert Morton		C-7 Michigan
Private Abram Reky		L-5 Michigan
Private James B. Rice		D-5 Michigan
Private Evans J. Robins		H-7 Michigan
Private Charles A. Smith		C-7 Michigan
Private Washington M. Smith		I-7 Michigan

Regimental Teamsters & Wagoners

Sergeant John Mitchell	Wagonmaster	D-7 Michigan
Corporal Freeman Nevers	Teamster	H-7 Michigan
Private Ambrose Allen	Teamster	H-7 Michigan
Private Peter F. Bower	Teamster	D-6 Michigan
Private Charles Brock	Teamster	C-5 Michigan
Private Justus Case	Teamster	M-6 Michigan
Private Hamilton Force	Teamster	D-5 Michigan
Private William Huntley	Teamster	E-5 Michigan
Private Charles E. Moses	Teamster	I-5 Michigan
Private Micajah S. Root	Teamster	D-5 Michigan
Private Eugene King Starkweather	Wagoner	D-5 Michigan

Troop Teamsters & Wagoners

Private Zacheus L. Armstrong	Wagoner	C-1 Michigan
Private James Auble	Teamster	A-6 Michigan
Private Enos S. Baldwin	Teamster	D-7 Michigan
Private Reuben Banfill	Wagoner	E-5 Michigan
Private Samuel Barton	Teamster	K-6 Michigan
Private Samuel D. Billings	Teamster	B-5 Michigan
Private Jeremiah Brayman	Teamster	C-6 Michigan
Private Archibald Campbell	Teamster	B-6 Michigan
Private Joseph Chapman	Teamster	K-5 Michigan
Private Lewis Conklin	Teamster	B-5 Michigan
Private Thomas Cunningham	Teamster	H-1 Michigan
Private Orren D. Curtis	Teamster	M-5 Michigan
Private William D. Davis	Teamster	A-7 Michigan
Private George Elliott	Wagoner	F-1 Michigan
Private Charles E. Emmons	Wagoner	H-6 Michigan
Private Hugh Findlater	Teamster	E-7 Michigan
Private Alexis Hill	Teamster	G-6 Michigan
Private Charles K. Holliday	Wagoner	K-5 Michigan
Private Francis Johnson	Wagoner	E-7 Michigan
Private Oscar E. Keeney	Wagoner	L-6 Michigan
Private Joseph B. Long	Teamster	H-6 Michigan
Private Merenus Meades	Teamster	M-6 Michigan
Private Patrick Mitchel	Teamster	G-5 Michigan
Private Hiram B. Morrison	Wagoner	C-6 Michigan
Private Wallace Nichols	Teamster	H-1 Michigan
Private John F. Patten	Teamster	K-5 Michigan
Private James W. Rathbun	Wagoner	D-6 Michigan
Private Francis Reid	Teamster	C-5 Michigan
Private Harvey L. Reynolds	Teamster	A-7 Michigan

Troop Teamsters & Wagoners *(continued)*

Private George Robertson	Teamster	F-6 Michigan
Private James A. Rose	Teamster	E-7 Michigan
Private Daniel Stewart	Wagoner	B-6 Michigan
Private Myron D. Sullivan	Teamster	H-7 Michigan
Private William H. Surline	Teamster	C-6 Michigan
Private William J. Tuffs	Teamster	B-6 Michigan
Private Charles P. Utley	Wagoner	A-6 Michigan
Private Norman Van Alstine	Teamster	G-7 Michigan
Private William H. Watkins	Teamster	M-5 Michigan
Private James H. Webster	Wagoner	C-5 Michigan
Private David B. Welch	Wagoner	E-6 Michigan
Private John C. West	Teamster	G-7 Michigan
Private Henry Williams	Teamster	D-7 Michigan
Private Eber B. Youngs	Teamster	E-7 Michigan

Hospital & Medical Department Staff

Private Samuel Clark	Attendent	I-5 Michigan
Private Harvey S. Curtiss	Attendent	M-6 Michigan
Private Henry J. Dean	Attendent	D-5 Michigan
Private John Draker	Teamster	C-1 Michigan
Private Merrick Henderson	Attendent	H-5 Michigan
Private Edwin Holloway	Attendent	H-5 Michigan
Private John Kittle	Attendent	H-5 Michigan
Private Levi Milendy	Attendent	A-6 Michigan
Private William M. Pringle	Nurse	I-6 Michigan
Private Jonathan H. Rice	Nurse	A-5 Michigan
Private James K. Smith	Attendent	M-6 Michigan
Private William H. Stone	Attendent	M-6 Michigan
Private Marshall Warner	Attendent	B-5 Michigan

1st Regiment, Michigan Volunteer Cavalry

11 Troops (A-B-C-E-F-G-H-I-K-L-M)
38 Officers & 596 Enlisted Men
June 30, 1863

Troop	Officer	NCO	B'smith	Bugler	Farrier	Saddler	Private
F & S	9	8	0	0	0	0	1
A	3	9	1	1	0	1	36
B	3	12	2	0	0	1	36
C	2	10	1	0	1	1	29
E	3	14	1	0	0	1	42
F	2	14	1	0	1	1	43
G	3	13	1	0	1	1	39
H	3	13	1	0	0	1	37
I	2	14	1	0	1	1	31
K	3	10	1	2	1	0	43
L	3	12	0	0	0	0	41
M	2	14	0	1	2	1	45
Totals	38	143	10	4	7	9	423

Field & Staff

Colonel Charles H. Town
Lieutenant Colonel Peter Stagg
Major Melvin Brewer
Major Angelo Paldi
Commissary Joseph L. Bullock
Quartermaster Thomas Ballard
Chaplain Jonathan Hudson
Assistant Surgeon Arthur K. St. Clair
Assistant Surgeon Amos K. Smith

Sergeant Major Dewitt C. Smith
Chief Trumpeter Milton Rice
Commissary Sergeant Francis E. Blake
Quartermaster Sergeant Chauncey T. Carrier
Saddler Sergeant Joseph H. Morrill
Veterinary Surgeon Jerome Bitely
Hospital Steward Henry Cox
Hospital Steward William Richard Sterling
Private Samuel D. Fuller (Surgeon's Orderly)

Troop A

Captain Charles H. Sprague
1st Lieutenant William H. Perkins
2nd Lieutenant Albert S. Emerson

Sergeants

1st Sergeant Michael Cochran
Commissary Sergeant Albert H. Rush
Quartermaster Sergeant Renzi Loud

Henry Post   George W. Robinson   Carroll L. Rood

Corporals

Jacob H. Hosner   Charles McCormick   Fayette I. Sheldon

Saddler John Armstrong
Bugler John F. Deyoe
Blacksmith Herman Krapf

Privates

James Anderson	Oscar Marsh
James Austin	George McClintock
Simeon B. Boorn	Jeduthan Predmore
John Brown	George Sanders
John L. Clark	William R. Spencer
William E. Clark	Henry C. Stanley
Edward Corselius	James W. Subb
David M. Daily	Harvey V. Taylor
Hubbard H. Dakin	Dewitt H. Teeple
Alonzo A. Daniels	Edwin Vanenacker
William Debeauclair	Joseph Warner
Benjamin C. Harrington	Philetus R. Weydemeyer
William A. Heath	John C. Wideroder
Henry Heinmiller	George Wietzel
Edwin A. Herrick	John Wiley
Jesse G. Hosner	Niles H. Winans
Peter Hubbell	Henry Woodhouse
Sira Huntley	Wilson M. Wright

Troop B

Captain William M. Hazlitt
1st Lieutenant James D. Robertson
2nd Lieutenant Andrew Jackson Pulver

Sergeants

1st Sergeant Chester C. Crooks
Commissary Sergeant John E. Fleming

Mitchell Belloir	George A. Ewing
Philip G. Gardner	William H. Ingersoll

Corporals

Lansing D. Collyer	Michael Consadine	George Gillett
Peter Hoffman	Michael W. Ryan	Henry I. Williams

Saddler Edward C. Anthony
Blacksmith Elias Hutchings
Blacksmith Joseph Scharbonaugh

Privates

Theron L. Armstrong	Benjamin O. Hutchings
William S. Arnold	Charles King
Silas S. Bachman	Henry Kramer
George R. Ball	Joseph Kunkel
William H. Benson	Charles C. Lamb
Harrison T. Bostwick	Alfred Lapelly
Jacob Bradley	William A. Lawson
Henry W. Brownell	Jeremiah Longdo
Joseph H. Brownell	Darius Manchester
Benjamin Cole	Charles L. Negus
Christopher C. Dubois	John O. O'Keefe
Fabian Dufrane	Ephraim H. Partridge
Eugene J. Dunbar	John Porter
Charles R. Eggleston	John Reed
William Fox	John Shadd
Louis Genereaux	Myron B. Skinner
Morey Harrington	John Ulch
William Hepley	Robert Van Orden

Troop C

Captain William R. Elliott
2nd Lieutenant Thomas Redfield

Sergeants

1st Sergeant William Clay Shaw
Commissary Sergeant Edward H. Russell
Quartermaster Sergeant Sanford D. Wiley
Stephen R. Spencer

Corporals

Leonard H. Griffin	William D. Jewell	Jesse O. Kinner
Henry Larnard, Jr.	Joseph M. Naracon	Oscar J. Smith

Farrier Thomas Davis
Saddler Frederick Fare
Blacksmith Lathrop Fuller

Privates

Stephen J. Armstrong	Dexter M. Macomber
George Atkins	William H. Michels
James Baku	Edwin M. Norwood
Henry L. Beckwith	Daniel B. Oathout
John W. Blauvelt	William H. Putnam
Charles Brennan	Charles F. Robinson
Harrison Briggs	Amasa Rogers
John Brown	Austin Stowe
John R. Clark	Walter M. Terrill
Henry V. Donnagan	Samuel H. Thomas
Jasper N. Elliott	William G. Thomas
E. M. Hitchcock	S. E. Vanderhoff
Andrew G. Holliday	John B. Vantickel
George L. Holmes	Henry Woodruff
Ezekiel Johnson	

Troop E

Captain Daniel Tyler Wells
1st Lieutenant George R. Maxwell
2nd Lieutenant Robert G. McKay

Sergeants

1st Sergeant Francis J. Hatten
Commissary Sergeant William H. Sweeny

Jeremiah H. Doyle	Henry Dubendorf	John R. Furmell
Thomas H. Sheperd	Truman H. Wheeler	

Corporals

Dexter Brown	Madison Decker	John Hamilton
James Hine	Philip Knapp	Michael Sheehy
	Edward J. Steward	

Saddler Ebenezer W. Beach
Blacksmith Joseph Haine

Privates

Charles A. Allen	James Graham	John Miller
Alva Beebe	George Hamilton	Reinhart Miller
Charles S. Bell	Orrin Hamp	George Moon
Zenas Birch	Henry Hanson	James O'Connor
Thomas Burton	Vessey Harris	Timothy O'Sullivan
John L. Campen	John Hoth	Lewis Peppinger
John W. Chappell	John Kies	Ansel M. Scoville
John Collier	Lewis Lamore	James M. Smith
Edward G. Crosby	Lewis Langenderfer	Jacob Steele
John B. Deeds	William J. Lovell	Henry Thompson
Oscar Dimmick	Henry Marshall	George Turner
William J. Everest	Peter McCardle	George W. Weller
Peter Fisher	Alonzo McNeil	Patrick Welsh
James N. Flint	Joseph Middleton	Ramsom W. Welton

Troop F

Captain Charles J. Snyder
2nd Lieutenant George H. Kilburn

Sergeants

1st Sergeant George H. Hutchins
Commissary Sergeant Charles P. Parker
Quartermaster Sergeant Jarius Silas Peterson

Ehphriam Allen
Joel D. Kenney

John S. Bovee
George C. Whitney

Corporals

Huburtus Blinn
Charles McArthur

George A. Cramton
William McCormack
Charles S. Mills

Newton I. Lathrop
Stephen W. Millichamp

Farrier Edwin Brown
Blacksmith Henry Gallinger
Saddler Sylvester Kelch

Privates

Harrison E. Barnum
Horace N. Basna
James E. Bird
Samuel Steward Bird
William D. Bird
John William Bland
Isaiah Butler
Francis M. Castle
Erin Cleveland
George W. Crampton
Samuel Dodd
Chandler H. Everest
Consider E. Flower
Almon Gage
Cyrenus Gallinger

Henry Graper
Elijah G. Gray
Lucius F. Handy
James Morgan
Horatio N. Jenks
Charles James Jennings
Sylvanus Lathrop
James W. Lutz
David Mapes
Robert McCrary
Samuel Mills
Almon Munsch
James Everard Needham
George S. Pool

Charles M. Pratt
Samuel W. Reynolds
William Wort Rice
George W. Smith
Elijah Stiles
James Henry Taylor
Andrew Jackson Thrasher
Octavus Townsend
William H. Trumbull
Charles E. Vaughn
Clement Waldron
James Wildey
Alva Wood
Royal Rufus Wood

Troop G

Captain George Washington Andrews
1st Lieutenant James S. McElheny
2nd Lieutenant Warner H. Pierson

Sergeants

1st Sergeant John H. Mosher
Commissary Sergeant William L. Rose
Quartermaster Sergeant Louis Reeve

James Bolton	Cyrus Phipps	James B. Tubbs

Corporals

Delos Adams	Marvin Bolton	Henry W. Carey
Seth Francis	Benjamin Giddings	Ronald McDonald
	Selah Pierce	

Farrier Alexander Brigham
Saddler Benjamin Mapes
Blacksmith Ira C. McLellan

Privates

Robert Bachman	Andrew Kerr
John A. Bordineau	Henry Kling
Perry S. Bowers	Abner Letts
Jacob Brigger	Archibald Lyons
William Cady	Alvah N. Marsh
Adelbert Chittenden	William McKinzie
James Clewitt	Charles Parkinson
John D. Coleman	Angelo Pascia
Montraville Daniels	Peter Schaunn
George D. Delameter	Carl D. Seivers
Daniel Dugan	John Sharp
Thomas Featum	Lorenzo D. Stevens
George Frick	Robert E. Stimson
John B. George	Milo A. Thomson
Capius M. Halverson	Barton S. Tibbits
Joseph M. Hathaway	John B. Wallace
Beldier P. Hill	Major Whealer
James Horton	Charles H. Wilber
James R. Hutton	Alvin Wood
George Karn	

Troop H

Captain Andrew W. Duggan
1st Lieutenant Amasa E. Matthews
2nd Lieutenant Hiram M. O'Dell

Sergeants

1st Sergeant William E. Waterman
Quartermaster Sergeant William O. Mallory

Jesse Clark
Peter Mashoie

William Farley
Timothy O. Sullivan

Corporals

James Furlong
William H. Phelps

Alexander Gordon
David Rich
Thomas Shannahan

Joseph B. McIlhargy
Alfred G. Ryder

Saddler Charles A. Bradford
Blacksmith William Simmons

Privates

William Adams
James Buckley
Henry O. Burr
William Butcher
Milan Canfield
Hiram Chadwick
John Chapiton
Benjamin J. Clark
Patrick Confrey
Franklin B. Daby
Charles Davis
George W. Dixon
Edward Eagle
Orlando P. Echler
Reuben Farewell
Oliver Helverson
Albert Hough
John Hynes
Joseph Kitchen

Charles Layman
Mathew McDermott
James McKinney
George Morris
Bernard Murray
Robert O'Donnell
John P. Phillips
Wilson Potter
Leonard Schnitzer
John Schuler
John Sheridan
Richard Solon
Patrick H. Sullivan
Orange Thomas
Paul Weitzel
Jasper Winchell
George B. Windover
John B. Wolfe

Troop I

Captain Herman E. Hascall
1st Lieutenant Elmer F. Decker

Sergeants

1st Sergeant Stephen H. Irwin
Commissary Sergeant Oscar A. Eastman

Charles M. Belcher	Abner Cross	Nahum Gilbert
Henry C. Munger	Wellington Wright	

Corporals

Marvin Auton	Augustus W. Bently	William S. Briggs
Horace P. Dunning	James Ferry	Lucius L. Judson
Henry Whitmore		

Farrier George Beadle
Saddler William J. Monteith
Blacksmith Samuel C. Sweeney

Privates

James Allen	Edward Nelson
George G. Bond	John Norton
Willard H. Briggs	William C. Richer
Charles L. Brignall	Edgar J. Rickard
William H. Brown	Michael Ryan
John Chambers	Henry O. Sawyer
Benjamin F. Collins	Thomas Schlosser
Henry J. Collins	Richmond L. Shaw
Enoch Cross	Horace S. Sheldon
George Hyman	Alfred Sherman
Thomas Jeffs	Riley Slater
Orlando Jones	Wheaton R. Smith
Adolph Keska	Christian Weid
Daniel B. McMaster	Henry White
Augustus H. Miller	Levi D. Zinn
Smith Munger	

Troop K

Captain William M. Brevoort
1st Lieutenant Thomas H. Stephenson
2nd Lieutenant Peter Karpp

Sergeants

1st Sergeant Israel R. Lockwood
Commissary Sergeant John J. McNaughton
Quartermaster Sergeant James Lawrence
Gabriel R. Goodell   Joseph L. Karpp

Corporals

| Edwin H. Babcock | Myron J. Brockway | Alexander H. Howe |
| Cyrus E. Littlefield | James McConnell | |

Bugler Charles W. Earnest
Bugler William A. Irwin
Blacksmith Reuben M. Reynolds
Farrier Chester Townsend

Privates

Jerome Allen	Henry C. Hendricks	George W. Pence
Elisha B. Anson	Horace Holcomb, Jr.	John Pixley
Wheeler Beckley	Robert W. Houston	Nathan C. Putnam
Albert Brockway	William Jackson	Michael Reynolds
Eli Campeau	John P. Johnson	Paschal Rowe
Elijah H. Cook	Benjamin Keller	William Sanborn
Leader Druillard	John King	John Schrockran
Henry Ducant	Jacob Lambert	Gustave Schwartz
Ira L. Fales	Gustavus Lange	Hezekiah Townsend
Bendal Fisher	Oliver Marcott	Andrew J. Trisket
John French	Theodore Mead	Garrett H. Van Vorhies
John Fulcher	George H. N. Miller	Charles Wait
Thomas C. Gould	Lewis Moat	James E. Webb
William Gravlin	Nicholas Partell	John M. Wheaton
Francis R. Hawley		

Troop L

Captain William C. Davies
1st Lieutenant Albert T. Jackson
2nd Lieutenant Henry L. Willetts

Sergeants

1st Sergeant John Rattray
Quartermaster Sergeant George Burke

Alphoso W. Chilson
Wallace W. Taylor

James B. Lyon
Colbert R. Watson

Corporals

| Reuben Burgess | John N. Deneen | Daniel Johnson |
| Harvey H. Rowley | William H. Rutherford | Daniel C. Smith |

Privates

James Alger
Delos A. Beals
Benjamin J. Butterfield
Burton H. Chapman
Edward E. Clark
Dwight Coykendall
Chyler B. Davis
Joseph Davis
William Henry Harrison Davis
George W. Edgerton
Joseph H. Edgerton
Zadock K. French
Adolph Gichan
Loren Gilbert
Caleb F. Hall
Lorenzo Hart
George Hopkins
Edward H. Ives
James E. Johnson
William H. Linton
Andrew J. Nicholson

Dennis O'Neal
Darius Reed
Seymour Reed
Henry E. Rowley
William Russell
Colby Short
Jacob M. Shumar
Charles Sitts
Lemuel Skellinger
Alonzo Smith
Hubbard Smith
Lewis F. Smith
Orson H. Van Kleek
Romain Van Kleek
Thomas H. Vandecar
Thomas Weightman
Philip Wilcox, Jr.
Horace Woodworth
Orrin Wrey
Harrison L. Wright

Troop M

Captain David W. Clemmer
2nd Lieutenant Richard N. Van Atter

Sergeants

1st Sergeant Charles Allen
Commissary Sergeant Henry B. Babcock

Paroon F. Bently	Lorenzo D. F. Poor
John H. Simmons	Joseph L. Tice

Corporals

Peter F. Baldwin	Francis Barclay	Theodore A. Barnum
Harrison H. Cole	Charles Meacham	James W. Randall
Albert Vincent	Charles C. Wilcox	

Farrier John N. Farncrook
Saddler Archibald McNeil
Bugler George W. Pierson
Farrier Abraham R. Sigerfoor

Privates

Philip Angle	Stephen A. Gregory	Harris Price
Cyrus A. Bateman	John Grush	Luman C. Roberts
William F. Becraft	Marcus W. Henry	John W. Robinson
John Bilderback	Leander W. Howell	Richard M. Robinson
Silas Bowen	Franklin Huff	Benjamin H. Rutter
Obediah M. Brown	Charles H. Johnson	John N. Shaw
Joseph L. Bullard	Jesse R. Johnson	Watson N. Shilling
Jerome J. Cable	John R. King	Joseph R. C. Simmons
Joseph Chatterson	Albert H. Lewis	George W. Srackengast
John C. Cleland	Edmund McAfee	Lewis Strahl
Albert H. Cook	Hiram McCrary	Seth S. Stults
Isaac A. Dewitt	Collins F. Miller	Myron C. Tice
Matthew Dopp	Cassius M. Norton	Joseph H. Watson
Charles Dwight	Darwin Olney	James P. Wiley, Jr.
Oscar Elliott	William M. Pettigrew	George W. Woolcott

5th Regiment, Michigan Volunteer Cavalry

10 Troops (A-B-D-E-F-G-H-I-K-M)
30 Officers & 633 Enlisted Men
June 30, 1863

Troop	Officer	NCO	B'smith	Bugler	Farrier	Saddler	Private
F & S	10	8	0	0	0	0	8
A	2	16	1	1	1	1	47
B	3	13	2	2	0	0	46
D	2	15	0	0	0	1	48
E	3	11	3	1	1	1	31
F	1	10	2	0	0	0	50
G	3	13	1	0	0	1	51
H	2	15	0	1	0	0	47
I	2	15	0	1	1	1	51
K	1	13	2	1	0	1	40
M	1	15	0	0	1	0	42
Totals	30	144	11	7	4	6	461

Field & Staff

Colonel Russell Alexander Alger
Lieutenant Colonel Ebenezer Gould
Major Noah Henry Ferry
Major Luther Stephen Trowbridge
Acting Adjutant Henry Starkey
Commissary Dallas Norvall
Quartermaster Daniel D. Thurber
Chaplain Oliver Taylor
Surgeon John P. Wilson
Assistant Surgeon Sylvester R. Morris

Sergeant Major Charles Y. Osborne
Chief Trumpeter John Allen
Commissary Sergeant Dwight B. Pendleton
Quartermaster Sergeant Oliver A. Whitney
Saddler Sergeant Alexander S. Smith
Acting Veterinary Surgeon Alanson Mathews
Hospital Steward Byron B. Beach
Hospital Steward John W. Southworth
Private Abner H. Burson (Colonel Alger's Orderly)
Private Adam Dell (Commissary Norvall's Orderly)
Private William H. Dunn (Major Trowbridge's Orderly)
Private George C. Granger (Major Gould's Orderly)
Private Robert J. Kelly (Foragemaster)
Private Sawyer J. Lockwood (Major Gould's Orderly)
Private Warren D. Macomber (Colonel Alger's Orderly)
Private George E. Munn (Major Ferry's Orderly)

Troop A

Captain Wellington W. Gray
1st Lieutenant Samuel Harris

Sergeants

1st Sergeant Phillip Mothersill
Commissary Sergeant Samuel N. Brownson
Quartermaster Sergeant Dighton Voorheis

Frank A. Barbour	Stephen Buzzell	John E. Norton
Richard H. Whitehead	Edwin W. Wood	

Corporals

Henry C. Beebe	Asa S. Crossman	Joseph Kimble
George M. Richmond	Lewis Y. Struble	Ephraim Van Berger
Alexander Wilber	John S. Wolverton	

Saddler John S. Bedell
Blacksmith Isaac Crawford
Farrier Benjamin F. Johnston
Bugler James Richmond

Privates

Hiram Ackerman	William H. Fall	David A. Pierce
Charles W. Austin	Romanzo Farrand	William Quick
George Baldwin	David G. Fisher	John T. Reid
Hamilton M. Bigelow	Lewis Fitch	John Reynolds
Jarvis N. Blakely	Elias Hutton	Isaac Robinson
James Boyd	Andrew T. Jackson	Solomon Russell
Edward W. Burrows	Henry R. Jones	Edwin J. Sharp
John R. Butterfield	Isaac N. Jones	Nelson Sharp
George H. Buzzell	Walter Jones	Lucian H. Spencer
Jesse Chapman	Frank Kendrick	James Sumner
Albert Churchill	John Laughlin	Theophilus Syan
John P. Churchill	Peter Lavalley	Phineas Tucker
James Connor	Cyrenius E. Lucas	Darius B. Wheeler
Aaron J. Crossman	George B. Marble	Jesse W. Whitmore
Miles R. C. Dexter	William McCauley	Ezra A. Wood
William Dopp	Andrew O'Brien	Fletcher Wood
Henry Eaton	Anthony O'Brien	Oscar C. Wood
Andrew Evans	Isaac Perkins	

Troop B

Captain David Oliphant
1st Lieutenant Myron Hickey
2nd Lieutenant Robert A. Haire

Sergeants

1st Sergeant Edwin B. Bigelow
Commissary Sergeant Daniel C. Howe

William Brennen	Edward T. Bulson
George W. Merwin	Alonzo M. Wolaver

Corporals

William G. Beckwith	Ezra D. Biggam	James M. Cook
Benjamin Curtis	William H. Pepper	Hansen H. Rogers
	Charles W. Sweet	

Blacksmith Eichard D. Ballard
Blacksmith William Boyle
Bugler James P. Burch
Bugler Charles R. Crimble

Privates

George S. Allison	Lewis Gardner	Alvah Reynolds
Horatio N. Allison	Benjamin F. Guiles	Alva Roe
Eugene Armstrong	Orren Guiles	Ephraim M. Rolf
Abraham Bishop	Frederick Harris	Charles J. Schultz
Charles Blenden	George W. Hood	William Simmons
William Bone	James I. Hubbard	Philo N. Smith
Abraham Briningstull	William L. Ingraham	Stephen Smith
Simeon L. Brink	George Kenzel	Marquis D. Sumner
Amos S. Burroughs	Wilber C. Lockwood	Eli Thayer
Levi B. Coons	Darius A. Markham	Charles Vanberg
Hamilton Courson	Warren A. Maxfield	James Weldon
Surinus L. Eastwood	Reuben H. McWethy	Patrick Weldon
Paul Ellsworth	Harrison L. Ostrander	John C. Wilman
William B. Finch	William Perry	Amon Wilson
Edward E. Frisbie	George P. Reed	Charles Yates
James E. Frisbie		

Troop D

Captain Eli K. Simonds
1st Lieutenant Thomas J. Dean

Sergeants

1st Sergeant Leander W. Ferguson
Commissary Sergeant James K. London
Quartermaster Sergeant George E. Smith

William C. Halleck   Norton C. Marshall   Stephen Rider
Louis K. Van Gieson   Henry M. White

Corporals

Lancaster Gorton   Hiram Lount   Bishop Miller
George W. Newman   William W. Smith   William D. Pennington
William Woodburn

Saddler William S. Stewart

Privates

Nelson A. Allen
Alfred C. Anderson
Arzel C. Blair
Jasper Brown
Reuben T. Brown
Henry Burnett
Abram Butterfield
Calvin B. Castele
Francis M. Clark
George Cox
William H. Davis
James M. Greer
John D. Gugith
James B. Hallick
Andrew C. Hank
Edward S. Hastings

Edward A. King
Adolph Larriven
John W. Ledyard
Philander Lewis
Nelson S. Lloyd
Charles S. Masters
William J. McCormick
John McVay
Charles H. W. Miller
Albert Nelson
Daniel H. Noyes
Charles W. O'Donnell
Daniel H. Palmer
James E. Quirk
John Radner
William B. Rane

Chauncey J. Rathburn
Enoch Sanborn
Levi Sanderson
Harding Smith
Josephus Smith
Benjamin Swan
Edward Trainor
John Trainor
Michael Trainor
John Van Houghton
Edwin A. Wheaton
Stephen C. Wheeler
John J. White
Henry D. Willis
Seymour Winans
John Wolcott

Troop E

Captain Edward Merwin Lee
1st Lieutenant William H. Rolls
2nd Lieutenant George R. Barse

Sergeants

1st Sergeant A. Judson Barber
Quartermaster Sergeant Ephraim Roberts

Charles A. Ballard   Charles A. Snover   William V. Stewart

Corporals

Horace S. Barse   Phillip H. Hill   William Henry Morgan
Freeman Perkins   Homer G. Sperry   Newton Wyman

Bugler Gilbert W. Chapman
Blacksmith Newton H. Hubbard
Blacksmith Elias North
Farrier Jacob T. B. Skillman
Saddler Jeremiah Wetherwax
Blacksmith Leonard Woods

Privates

Charles M. Abbott
John Benning
Henry Benton
Morris Bonney
Roswell Burby
Edward Chapman
Horace Chapman
Oscar Cook
George F. Cruppin
Alpheus G. Day
William Fesmer
George Hichler
Schuyler Jones
William Kilgore
Charles Martin
Henry McKinstry

Robert G. McNaught
Christopher B. Miller
Ezekiel Morse
Joseph Neshman
Ira A. Parks
Elisha Parrish
Anthony Phillips
Frederick A. Pond
John Roloff
Isaiah Smith
Benjamin H. Terry
Albert Thompson
Charles S. Warner
Lyman Williams
Hiram Winas

Troop F

Captain Abram C. Vanderburgh

Sergeants

1st Sergeant Henry Becker
Commissary Sergeant James Sprague
Quartermaster Sergeant Thomas F. Plunkett

John Barber	James Gibbs, Jr.	William H. Huston

Corporals

Henry Clark	James Duffey
George W. Gould	Archibald McCullum

Blacksmith Frank Baker
Blacksmith Alexander W. Clark

Privates

Halver Anderson	Zorester Green	Augustus C. Perry
Allen Baker	Reinholt Hengstler	John Peterson
William F. Barber	David S. Hinds	Peter Peterson
Adam Behm	Moses S. Hinds	Henry Reed
Alexander Bell	Griffin Howland	Alfred Ryther
Peter Bentson	Warren Jones	Carl Schenke
George H. Bickford	Charles Klunder, Jr.	Simon Sickman
Ezra Blakely	Henry Koster	Charles E. Smith
Thomas Byrnes	Jacob Koster	John H. Smith
Frederick Clark	Joseph Long	Nathan W. Smith
William Darcoe	August Lund	Thomas H. Smith
David Davis	John McNeil	Benjamin D. Storms
Frederick E. Deymond	James G. Medler	C. Adam Straub
David Dill	Anton Menges	Mathias Swenson
John Dill	David M. Merrifield	Charles Waitman
Henry Forsyth	John Munson	Theodore Watson
Adolph Friday	James O'Connell	Christian White
Henry Friday	Ole C. Oleson	Adam Wonderly
Johannes Gabrielson	John Orenburger	

Troop G

Captain William T. Magoffin
1st Lieutenant George W. Townsend
2md Lieutenant John Gunderman

Sergeants

1st Sergeant Charles J. Young
Commissary Sergeant Benjamin Hause
Quartermaster Sergeant William W. Humaston

Sylvester P. Bailey	John S. Bordon	Chauncy Morton

Corporals

Gabriel Anderson	Artemus H. Clark	Nelson S. Bartholomew
Aaron D. Lyon	Willet Reynolds	William E. Smith
Lyman Van Sickle		

Blacksmith Amos B. Lobdell
Saddler Jacob Ridenour

Privates

David F. Baird	Daniel Gunderman	John O'Neil
Henry S. Beebe	John Gunderman, Jr.	William S. Parker
Marcus Bentley	John K. Hammond	Pulaski Pierce
Martin Blackford	Myron F. Harris	Adam Russell
James A. Chapman	Noel Harris	Nathaniel Russell
Loren D. Chapman	Bethnel H. Hause	Charles H. Shepard
Chester B. Church	William J. Havens	William Sherriff
Samuel J. Coleman	John B. Hetchiler	Irwin M. Skinner
James Cronk	Henry Hofsmith	George H. Sowle
William A. Crowell	Wesley Howell	William H. Stanton
Nathaniel J. Debar	Oliver P. Ingersol	Albert H. Vredenburg
Joel K. Fairbanks	Thomas Johnson	Henry F. Warren
Daniel K. Ferguson	Almon Jolls	James H. Washington
Ward A. Field	Francis P. Kent	Martin Weaver
Levi Gibbs	Samuel B. McPherson	Miles D. Webster
George E. Godfrey	James P. Minard	Ethan A. Wright
Jacob Grubaugh	Albert S. Norris	George Young

Troop H

Captain Stephen P. Purdy
2nd Lieutenant George Drake

Sergeants

1st Sergeant Harrison Berdan

James L. Carhart	Walter Crawford	William J. Daly
William S. Horton	Aaron B. James	Samuel McCartney
James Ramsey		

Corporals

John Brown	Thomas J. Carter	Henry Larkin
Edwin J. Lathrop	Martin Middaugh	Edward H. Phillips
Calvin Pinckney		

Bugler Albert Merriman

Privates

Louis Abear	James L. Foote	Simon D. Platt
William Aldrich	William Franklin	Arthur Reed
Charles A. Avery	Henry Gies	Andrew Seiler
Joseph Barbo	George B. Griswold	Byron C. Shurtliff
Oliver H. Beach	Joseph Jessup	Joseph W. Smith
Franklin B. Bird	Philip Kennedy	Almerin Sprague
General M. Brown	Andrew J. Kinner	Henry C. Steben
William Brown	William Kinney	Robert G. Taggert
Zachariah J. Coffin	Philip Klein	Wayland Tenney
Peter Comas	John Luce	Calvin H. Tuller
Matthew Coughlin	Michael Lynn	Joseph J. Tuttle
George Cure	George Masten	Milton Van Tassel
George Donaldson	Louis Maupin	James Washington
Charles Donner	James McLain	William H. H. Watson
John Felt	Julian L. Morey	William Wolgar
Charles Fitz	Rayner H. Newton	

Troop I

Captain George N. Dutcher
2nd Lieutenant Charles H. Safford

Sergeants

1st Sergeant George W. Lonsbury
Commissary Sergeant Hannibal Hart
Quartermaster Sergeant Lawrence L. Crosby

Martin Baldwin	George W. Earl
William A. Piper	William C. Weeks

Corporals

Henry Avery	Irvin D. Batchelor	Herman Garvelink
Louis Hirner	John E. Murphy	William H. Rockwell
George H. Smith	William White	

Farrier Mortimer Andrews
Bugler Orlando R. Croff
Saddler Jacob E. Miner

Privates

Austin Andrews	Abial Emmons	Giles A. Piper
Samuel W. Atkins	Lafayette Fox	Myron A. Powell
Caleb Bennett	George N. Gardner	George Pullman
Henry G. Bliss	George Verner Goucher	Kasper Raab
Orris Buchanan	Smith Hammond	Jacob Rhinehart
E. J. Burlingham	Morgan B. Hawks	Raphael Ross
Darwin E. Calloway	George H. Hicks	Albert Rynick
Gabriel Cole	John Hill	Samuel Shaver
Moses Cole	George Hodgetts	George Shupert
Daniel E. Collier	George Kanouse	Anthony Slack
Thomas Collier	James Kitchen	Nathan Slater
Hendrick Cook	Morgan D. Lane	Charles Taylor
Henry Dalman	Harvey W. Mann	George W. Thompson
William Drury	Orlando C. Masson	Marcus C. Thompson
James Dyer	William McWilliams	Edward A. Warner
Robert Dyer	Franklin Miller	Homer Wasson
Russell Dyer	Gottlieb Miller	Henry Werner
Seth Dyer	William Newhoff	Henry Zoerman
Orletus P. Eaton	John Notting	

Troop K

Captain John E. Clark

Sergeants

1st Sergeant Emory L. Brewer
Commissary Sergeant Charles Brooke
Quartermaster Sergeant James E. Sumner

Joseph R.Chambers
Carlton H. Hawks

Andrew J. Eggleston
Erastus M. Stevens

Corporals

Henry D. Howes
Homer Moore

John F. Lusk
John T. Sinclair

Juriel W. Monroe
William M. Wheeler

Saddler Alva Brace
Bugler Murray W. Hess
Blacksmith Thomas Kerns
Blacksmith Reuben Seely

Privates

Darwin H. Babbitt
Andrew J. Beamis
John Buell
Frederick Corcelins
Cornelius Crowley
Stewart Curle
Nathan Davis
Jacob Fahnestock
William H. Gillett
Samuel R. Gregory
John Hanes
Erastus P. Hawks
Henry Berkimer
Curtis Higley
Noah W. Holcomb
Richard Hollis
James G. Howard
Oliver C. Lamkin
Abram Lewis
Frank J. Lewis

John B. Looker
Frederick Markley
James Newberry
Orville Ogden
William S. Pailthorpe
Daniel J. Randall
Edgar F. Randall
Edward F. Riggs
Lyman Riggs
Luther Roblee
Michael Ryan
Oscar Shattuck
Frederick Slander
Leo Thayer
George W. Thorp
James B. Warner
Milan S. Warren
Orlando F. Wilkinson
Allen I. Williams
Nelson Williams

Troop M

Captain Smith Hugh Hastings

Sergeants

1st Sergeant Madison W. Bibbins
Quartermaster Sergeant Squire E. Skeels

Amos Bingham	William H. Hunt	Zelotes H. Mather
Mortimer I. Shrontz	Howard A. Simons	

Corporals

John Adams	William Andrews	William H. Black
William Harkness	James S. Mills	John R. Morey
Ephraim Oviatt	Cyrus B. Shad	

Farrier Elijah Johnson

Privates

William A. Ball	Nesbut J. Nevel
Henry Barnes	Edward S. Ogden
Oren F. Barnes	Isaac C. Osborn
John Benedict	Samuel J. Osborn
William H. Briggs	Ezra Post
Levi Busley	John H. Pratt
Sylvester T. Chase	Polydore M. Reynolds
Henry Clark	Major W. Russell
Charles C. Craft	John A. Snyder
Charles Albert Ford	Hiram B. Studly
Henry M. Fox	Charles Thompson
James A. Furguson	Albert J. Tift
David Gibbins	Horace N. Tift
Arnold Goodman	Samuel K. Van der Karr
Edson E. Gould	William L. Van Giesen
Isham Grimes	Hiram Van Hyning
Edgar Harris	William L. Victory
Charles M. Hobbs	Jarius Watkins
Fernando A. Jones	Richard Watkins
John M. Little	Vincent Watkins
Calvin McCrary	Francis M. Wright

6th Regiment, Michigan Volunteer Cavalry

10 Troops (A-B-C-D-E-F-G-H-K-L)
33 Officers & 668 Enlisted Men
June 30, 1863

Troop	Officer	NCO	B'smith	Bugler	Farrier	Saddler	Private
F & S	8	6	0	0	0	0	3
A	2	13	1	2	0	1	59
B	2	14	0	2	1	1	44
C	3	13	1	2	0	1	48
D	3	15	0	2	2	0	49
E	3	16	0	1	1	0	59
F	3	14	0	2	1	0	49
G	2	16	0	2	2	0	45
H	2	11	0	1	2	0	43
K	2	9	1	1	0	1	48
L	3	14	1	1	0	0	47
Totals	33	141	4	16	9	4	494

Field & Staff

Colonel George Gray
Major Simeon B. Brown
Major Thaddeus Foote
Acting Major Peter A. Weber
Acting Adjutant Aaron Cane Jewett
Commissary Joel S. Shelden
Quartermaster Charles H. Patten
Assistant Surgeon David C. Spaulding

Sergeant Major Henry V. Hobart
Commissary Sergeant James H. Dudley
Quartermaster Sergeant Oliver N. Taylor
Veterinary Surgeon Orson N. Earle
Hospital Steward Edwin R. Cobb
Hospital Steward John G. Havens
Private Martin House (Orderly)
Private Miller M. McGraw (Orderly)
Private Thomas Rigby (Colonel Gray's Orderly)

Troop A

Captain Henry Elmer Thompson
2nd Lieutenant Stephen H. Ballard

Sergeants

1st Sergeant Thomas A. Edie
Commissary Sergeant James M. Page

David Collins	Birney Hoyt	Reuben W. Jewell
Richard E. Parshall	Darwin P. Swain	

Corporals

William M. Brigham	Leander Jewell	Abram D. Lobdell
Merritt C. Mosher	James M. Smith	Richard J. Swain

Blacksmith Earl W. Gardiner
Saddler Charles C. Krauss
Bugler William R. Radford
Bugler Martin Rens

Privates

James O. Berry	Peter Gooseman	Austin Pixley
Alexander Bevard	Henry D. Gross	Thomas Purple
Benjamin F. Coe	William Gross	Walter Rowe
Alexander H. Coon	John Hanna	John Sennett
James Crane	John Helsel	Thomas R. Shaw
Joseph Crane	John Holcomb	John Sked
Thomas A. Crotty	David L. Hyden	Vine Sked
John Cryderman	Abraham H. Johnson	David T. Sorrick
William Dalziel	Phillip Jordan	James Stark
George W. Dancer	Francis C. Kelley	Stephen T. Sweetman
James M. Davis	Aaron C. Magoon	Giles Townsend
Martin Davis	William McCall	James Walters
Isaac DeGraw	Joseph McCune	George J. Washburn
Charles H. Dean	Jonathan McFall	Emory Wheeler
George S. Dean	Samuel D. Mills	Lanson Wheeler
Joseph Douglass	Robert Minor	William W. White
Reuben B. Douglass	David A. Monroe	Silas Whitford
Jacob Duffy	Francis C. Morgan	William G. Whitworth
Andrew Flynn	Charles S. Palmer	Wilson Wood
James C. Gillmore	Count P. Phelps	

Troop B

1st Lieutenant Daniel H. Powers
2nd Lieutenant Charles E. Bolza

Sergeants

1st Sergeant George T. Patten
Commissary Sergeant Pliny Smith
Quartermaster Sergeant Nelson C. Thomas

Egbert S. Conklin	Edmund B. Dikeman	William E. Keyes
Elliott M. Norton	Harvey B. Potter	

Corporals

David G. Caywood	James E. Johnson	David E. McVeen
Allen D. Pease	John P. Platt	Edwin E. Whitney

Farrier James D. Gay
Bugler Calvin R. Glazier
Saddler Henry H. McCollister
Bugler John Newton

Privates

Newton Ackley	Gilbert D. Griffith	Edwin E. Robinson
Charles Batson	Frank Gross	Remus Rogers
Solon W. Baxter	Perley W. Johnson	Abram Rosel
Solon M. Bentley	Frederick S. Kettle	David Rust
Lewis Borman	James N. Lewis	Harvey K. Seeley
Ezra Brown	Lewis Marsac	George Sharp
Isaac R. Church	Alonzo R. Martin	Josiah T. Slighter
Prozene R. Clark	Thomas McGowan	Henry W. Stewart
Alva Colton	James H. Merrill	Oscar Stout
James M. Cronkright	Oakland W. Merryfield	Stephen L. Stow
Philip Cunningham	William Moss	Walter W. Wait
Smith Felton	Flavius J. Neal	Charles W. Watkins
Daniel Fuller	James R. Neal	Henry L. Welsh
Horace N. Gooch	Augustus Norton	William B. Whitney
William Green	Francis Pelton	

Troop C

Captain Wesley Armstrong
1st Lieutenant Edward Potter
2nd Lieutenant William Creevy

Sergeants

1st Sergeant Charles W. Cox
Quartermaster Sergeant Mortimer Rappelye
James W. Pettys   Frederick Platt   Josiah Reynolds

Corporals

Alexander H. Cook	Albert B. Dimond	Godolphin Dodge
David Gibson	Harrison Loop	Alexander McDonald
Neal C. McEachern	Harvey Tucker	

Farrier William Baird
Blacksmith Shubal Dutton
Bugler John Fitzgerald
Bugler Simon Miller

Privates

Isaac Anderson	George W. Hill	John Proctor
Edwin A. Austin	James P. Hubbell	Allen Rice
John Barcume	Amos Huffman	Charles E. Roney
John William Barlow	Joseph Kilbourn	Frank Rosbury
David Blair	Gustavus Langdonburg	John Rosbury
Francis J. Blanchard	Jacob Layer	Samuel Ryckman
George Chambers	Alfred Levington	Charles O. Smith
William Chambers	John D. Lutwyche	John Smith
William W. Daniels	Sidney Marr	Simon Smith
John Demay	Henry Mathews	James Spencer
Frederick Diem	Alexander McClure	John Stover
John Dingman	Nathan McClure	William Sweet
William G. Dixon	Darius P. McGuirk	Oliver N. Tower
Oliver E. Durant	Perry Oaks	Jacob W. Watson
Thomas A. Edmonson	Charles Peck	Frederick Williams
Michael Gibbons	James M. Preston	John Yax

Troop D

Captain David G. Royce
1st Lieutenant Seymour Shipman
2nd Lieutenant Horace B. Rogers

Sergeants

1st Sergeant Henry M. Billings
Commissary Sergeant Jared L. Cook
Quartermaster Sergeant George W. Barbour

Augustus C. Fox	Alonzo L. Furgason
Luther C. Kanouse	Charles Simpson

Corporals

George W. Botsford	William H. Daily	Horace Hart
Rufus Hitchcock	Carlos Rider	John W. Soule
George Telling	James Ward	

Farrier Henry A. Norton
Bugler William A. Olds
Farrier George K. Tucker
Bugler Andrew J. Williams

Privates

George W. Aldrich	Levi F. Jones	John H. Randall
Jacob H. Alliton	Edwin Judd	Allen W. Rhoades
Augustus M. Barnes	John Judd	Hiram Rix, Jr.
Ezra D. Barnes	William H. Kendall	William H. Rust
Lyman Blodgett	Henry G. Lewis	Samuel B. Scammon
George A. Bugbee	Charles Lovesey	Jacob Sciler
George B. Chandler	William Lowe	Samuel Scripture
Henry Cole	William H. Mitchel	Joseph Shafer
Gilbert H. Dutcher	Dexter L. Monger	William H. Shaft
Alva F. Ewing	Thomas Murray	Samuel Sherburne
John H. Gifford	Edwin Nichols	Willis Shinner
James Gordon	Albert Otis	John G. Snook
Nathan H. Green	Martin Otis	Eugene K. Tyler
Hartford M. Harding	William H. Piper	John T. Van Dyke
Ira C. Harding	Abram Polley	Dennis C. Welch
George Hopkins	Amos Platt	Lewis E. Wright
Charles E. Huff		

Troop E

Captain James Harvey Kidd
1st Lieutenant Edward L. Craw
2nd Lieutenant Angelo E. Tower

Sergeants

1st Sergeant Levant W. Barnhart
Commissary Sergeant Jacob O. Probasco
Quartermaster Sergeant James L. Manning

Marvin E. Avery	Solon H. Finney	John J. Hammel
Schuyler Triphagen	William Willett	

Corporals

James W. Brown	Memly Cronkite	Orren W. Daniels
Isaac R. Hart	George J. Henry	Elias Hogle
Amos W. Stevens	Charles W. Wyman	

Bugler John A. Gates
Farrier George M. Osborn

Privates

William Almy	Edward R. Halleck	George W. Rall
John S. Axtell	Henry M. Harrison	Orlando V. R. Showerman
Lester A. Berry	Luther Hart	James O. Sliter
George Brown	Robert Hempstead	Samuel J. Smith
Hemens Brown	Eli Holliday	Josiah R. Stevens
Seth Brown	George E. Holliday	David Stowell
Marion Case	Warren Hopkins	Jesse Stuart
William H. Compton	Louis Kepfort	Josiah R. Thompson
Edward H. Cook	Seeright C. Koutz	William Toynton
James H. Corwin	Archibald Lambertson	Albert Truax
John Cryderman	Martin Lerg	John Tunks
Ameron Decker	Solomon Mangus	Oliver L. Van Tassel
Thomas Dickenson	George W. Marchant	John Van Wagner
Rinehart Dikeman	Gershom W. Mattoon	Sidney Van Wagner
Daniel Draper	Timothy J. Mosher	Byron A. Vosburgh
Benjamin C. Eaton	Moses C. Nestell	Erastus J. Wall
Marvin A. Filkins	Edwin Olds	Israel Wall
Francis N. Friend	Jedediah D. Osborn	Lewis H. Yeoman
George J. Goodale	Albert M. Parker	Almon Yerrington
Ira M. Green	Walter E. Pratt	

Troop F

Captain William Hyser
1st Lieutenant Donald George Lovell
2nd Lieutenant George Washington Crawford

Sergeants

Acting 1st Sergeant Hanford E. Cobb
Commissary Sergeant Frank Konkle
Quartermaster Sergeant John T. Gould

Latham H. Averill   Hobart H. Chipman   Cornelius Van Liew

Corporals

Truman J. Bacon   John S. Farnill   George Frazer
John Livingston   Monroe Livingston   Edwin A. Morris
Isaac C. Stanton   George Trager

Bugler Amos Konkle
Bugler Orville G. Welles
Farrier Frank Whitney

Privates

James B. Arms	Andrew J. Fluent	Robert W. Parkinson
Oliver S. Bilson	George S. Gordon	David B. Phillips
Thomas C. Borden	John Grant	Amos Post
George Briggs	Harkness Green	Francis M. Proper
James A. Brooks	Reuben Gross	Henry E. Rector
Charles O. Butler	Samuel Hughes	Francis D. Richardson
Benjamin T. Carpenter	William S. Jacobs	Benjamin Ronig
Ezra N. Chaffee	Hezekiah Lacey	George A. Russell
Joseph H. Chandler	George Lawrence, Jr.	George W. Sanders
Joshua P. Clark	William F. Lutz	Daniel Smith
James Cornell	Jeremiah McDonald	Asa T. Spicer
James M. Crammer	Finley McPherson	Ira Stout
Gardner Cranston	Robert W. Miller	Edgar E. Warner
Francis M. Crawford	James Mizner	George H. Welles
John A. Cushing	Walter Mizner	William H. Welles
Phillip Dohm	Henry Muma	Chauncey G. Wood
Morton English		

Troop G

1st Lieutenant William Hull
2nd Lieutenant Charles E. Storrs

Sergeants

1st Sergeant John C. Molloy
Commissary Sergeant John B. Kay
Quartermaster Sergeant Morton Gregory

James Balls	Sears E. Galusha	George B. W. Ingersoll
William Smith, Jr.	Daniel J. Wyker	

Corporals

George D. Clark	George Dutcher	Albert A. Frain
William M. Linsley	Franklin Morton	James N. Smith
Henry Sprague	Orange Williams	

Farrier Andrew B. Culp
Bugler William F. Johnston
Farrier Jacob Pettitt
Bugler John C. Taylor

Privates

John Allen	Avery D. French	Merritt O. Miller
Artemus W. Angell	Charles Glosser	Jesse Monroe
Thomas B. Armstrong	John E. Graham	John H. Moon
Samuel B. Blumberg	Samuel Graham	William W. Neff
David Camp	Jacob A. Heist	Silas S. Newton
Francis Carter	Saril Hill	Abraham Ott
Francis Clark	Seth B. Hinckley	Peter J. Putnam
John Cowell	Henry Hirst	Samuel J. Southworth
William Curliss	Henry Hopkinson	Almond N. Stevens
Albert F. Davis	Andrew D. Jackson	Nelson W. Stiles
Isaac Denniston	Delos Johnson	James Vanderhoof
John Dennison	Nelson A. Madden	James Vincent
Allen Dryer	James McDaniels	Joel Vincent
Seth Dutcher	Peter McLean	William F. Williams
Leming J. Eckler	Lafayette Miller	Christian Wotenburg

Troop H

Captain Henry L. Wise
2nd Lieutenant James W. Kellogg

Sergeants

1st Sergeant Albert T. Henshaw

Samuel Bryant	Jeremiah J. Martin	Burnett Ripley
Jeptha C. Rosenkrans		John J. Stage

Corporals

James S. Andrus	Chauncey B. Fields	Angus J. McClellan
John Post	Charles N. Taylor	

Farrier John Nellins
Bugler Cassius M. Wise
Farrier Jeremiah H. Workman

Privates

William Annis	Joseph Simmens
Isaac E. Auble	Barnabas Smith
Robert Bell	Charles J. Smith
William M. Brockway	John H. Smith
George Bryant	Orrin Smith
Dennis Buckley	Horace B. Smoke
Charles Budnow	Ezra Spaulding
George W. Fay	Orlean Spaulding
Emera W. Fish	Seth Streeter
Philip W. Gibe	Marquis D. Teeple
Nicholas F. Hartford	Perry Teeple
Charles Hayes	Neal Walters
Charles Joles	Henry F. Wheaton
Joseph Lewis	Peter Wild
James Lind	Charles Williams
John Madison	John Winters
Charles F. Myers	John S. Wisner
Amos Palmer	Harvey H. Wolvern
John W. Parish	Lewis D. Wolvern
Chauncey O. Powell	Abraham Wood
Argalos M. Rosenkrans	William L. Yale
James W. Sharp	

Troop K

Captain Harrison N. Throop
2nd Lieutenant Cortez P. Pendill

Sergeants

Lorenz D. Cobb
Parley H. Rice

John C. Dillon
Benjamin F. Stevens

William H. Jewell

Corporals

Matthew Baird
Milo O. West

Presley W. Hoskinson

Selden E. Norton

Blacksmith Jeremiah D. Barabough
Bugler John J. Cobb
Saddler Russell K. Stanton

Privates

Jacob Albertson
David Baird
Stephen Barnum
Lewis Blackman
William E. Bolton
David Brown
William H. Brown
George H. Brownell
Wesley Austin Clark
Emerson Courtright
John H. Dennis
Marquis Dowd
Charles Ennis
Varsal P. Fales
Joseph Fishburn
Harry Fletcher
Justus German
Erwin E. Harmon
Adelan Hart
Frederick Hart
James H. Hulet
Elisha Inman
John Irwin
Jacob Kahler

Thomas Jefferson Kelly
Ira Kelsey
Dewit C. Kenion
Jeremiah Kilmer
Wells T. Latourette
Franklin R. Lewis
Hiram McCartney
Edwin Meads
John A. Miller
Mason Norton
Myron Paull
George M. Payne
Elisha Skillman
Jonathan W. Smith
Justin A. Smith
Eber A. Stanley
Lewis F. Vester
Elijah H. Wade
Elijah C. Wagoner
Henry A. Ward
David Way, Jr.
Cyrus S. Welch
Lycurgus J. Wheeler
Dana S. Wilson

Troop L

Captain Philip G. Cory
1st Lieutenant James Mathers
2nd Lieutenant Elliott F. Covill

Sergeants

1st Sergeant George W. Simonds
Quartermaster Sergeant Osmer F. Cole

Albert Cash	William Hall	William Ramsdell
Theophilus T. Whitcomb		George H. Wightman

Corporals

George M. Belding	Angelo W. Chadsey	Thomas Havens
Robert P. James	Loren G. Parsons	Silas Peters
William B. Peters		

Bugler William Canavan
Bugler Chester N. Eldred
Blacksmith Joseph Harrison

Privates

Semulous Adams	Flavius J. Harrison	Miles H. Seeley
Martin V. Adams	Spencer Harrison	John H. Sheldon
James A. Aldrich	James S. Henshaw	Holland Simmons
Martin V. Austin	Champlin Keeney	Seth W. Simmons
William H. Batt	John L. Main	John Spillane
Samuel Bloom	Charles Marsh	David Stokes
Albert Chase	Jared Morton	Lorenzo D. Sweet
Hiram Church	Sidney Murray	Henry Thompson
Augustus Derbey	Charles Oliver	George H. Van Force
John H. Dickey	John W. Piper	Francis O. Vandersluice
Benjamin F. Earl	Ransom Piper	Jesse D. Webster
Allen Evans	Charles E. Ramsdell	Lafayette Wheeler
Thomas J. Ford	Newton Ransom	William H. Whitcomb
Augustus Giddings	James Ray	Evelyn Whitmore
John C. Gore	Adumea A. Russell	George T. Woodmansee
William Gore	Loomis W. Russell	

7th Regiment, Michigan Volunteer Cavalry

10 Troops (A-B-C-D-E-F-G-H-I-K)
27 Officers & 447 Enlisted Men
June 30, 1863

Troop	Officer	NCO	B'smith	Bugler	Farrier	Saddler	Private
F & S	7	9	0	0	0	0	10
A	2	9	0	1	1	1	38
B	1	12	1	1	0	0	38
C	2	13	2	2	0	1	38
D	3	13	1	2	1	1	47
E	2	10	1	0	1	1	32
F	2	11	0	0	1	0	19
G	2	12	1	0	0	0	26
H	3	12	0	0	0	0	16
I	1	12	1	0	0	0	19
K	2	6	0	1	0	0	23
Totals	27	119	7	7	4	4	306

Field & Staff

Colonel William D'Alton Mann
Lieutenant Colonel Allyne Cushing Litchfield
Major John S. Huston
Major George K. Newcombe
Acting Adjutant George G. Briggs
Commissary James W. Bentley
Assistant Surgeon George R. Richards

Sergeant Major James B. Loomis
Commissary Sergeant Henry De Graff
Quartermaster Sergeant Daniel McNaughton
Saddler Sergeant Hilbert S. Beldon
Veterinary Surgeon Squire W. Wheeler
Sergeant Lucius F. Carver (Adjutant Briggs' Clerk)
Sergeant Edward S. Lang (Foragemaster)
Hospital Steward Marion A. Shafer
Hospital Steward George A. Smith
Private Martin Ahearn (Orderly)
Private Carlton Llewellyn Cornell (Orderly)
Private Stephen A. Crane (Orderly)
Private Peter C. De Graff (Postmaster)
Private Phillip Dillingham (Color Guard)
Private Eli Druyor (Color Guard)
Private John Lloyd (Orderly)
Private Charles S. Marsh (Orderly)
Private Silas J. Robinson (Orderly)
Private Walter Smith (Colonel Mann's Orderly)

Troop A

Captain Alexander Walker
2nd Lieutenant Franklin P. Nichols

Sergeants

1st Sergeant Charles M. Holton
Commissary Sergeant Erastus B. Crocker
Quartermaster Sergeant Edwin D. Cooke

William G. Graham Edwin R. Havens William H. O'Brien

Corporals

Henry L. Anthony Edwin Dumphrey Charles Wilcox

Saddler John Heinck
Bugler Noel Matchett
Farrier George W. Vosburgh

Privates

Henry Allen
James Barber
Rufus Beers
Nelson Bennett
Charles W. Bonnell
Edward J. Brickell
Alonzo Brininstool
Horace R. Brownell
Albert E. Caines
Chester Calvin
Frank Chapman
Chester C. Chappell
James F. Edwards
Horace H. C. Ewing
Putnam M. Fish
John K. Fisher
Edward H. Harvey
Giles B. Hataway
Charles Hollis

Peter Horsch
Freeman W. Howe
Oscar I. Hunt
William H. H. Knight
John W. Luke
Charles Malcomb
Alexander McNeil
Edgar A. Nye
Allen C. Park
Charles Gilbert Perrine
Sidney S. Pierce
Asa S. Reams
Joseph Springer
John H. Stead
Ray T. Streeter
Pitts J. Walling
Nelson Walters
Marquis D. Wheeler
George A. Worthen

Troop B

1st Lieutenant Elliott Gray

Sergeants

1st Sergeant Riley A. Gregg
Commissary Sergeant George E. Smith
Quartermaster Sergeant William W. Brown

Evan Hendershott   William J. Laird

Corporals

Ansel V. Badger	James Haskin	Nathan V. Lovell
Albert McClouth	Myron H. Perkins	William A. Stearns
Egbert Underhill		

Bugler James Barney
Blacksmith William McCaughen

Privates

Steven Austin	Ebenezer B. Jakeway
George Birdsey	Nathaniel Jones
August Boskey	Hiram J. Larue
David Burk	Hiram J. Larue
John J. Burrows	Edward Long
William Campbell	David McConnell
William Carouth	William McKinney
Newton Caville	William Millson
Jacob Cheout	John Orford
Nathan Childs	Edwin J. Phillips
James E. Converse	Daniel Reno
Jerome Gessler	Henry C. Russell
William Gleason	Jason N. Russell
George W. Hartsell	Peter S. Smalley
William Haskins	Willard D. Springer
William Hawthorn	Robert Thompson
George H. Heddon	Adelbert H. Weston
Isaac Hess	Joseph F. Whittaker
Hamilton Hicks	Abram Williams

Troop C

Captain Daniel H. Darling
1st Lieutenant George W. McCormick

Sergeants

1st Sergeant Caleb Griffith
Quartermaster Sergeant Morris M. Bliss
Color Sergeant Benjamin Church

Elliott A. Cook
Joseph Payne

Morris Kelliher
David B. Rose

Corporals

Hiram Bentley
Walter L. Honsinger

John H. Cook William
Gilbert B. Murrow

Glover Gage
William Van Voorhees

Bugler Stephen Claygo
Blacksmith Isaac Hanninger
Bugler John Schimmerhorn
Blacksmith Alanson Thayer
Saddler Philander Tozer

Privates

Henry Austen
Martin Barnhart
Benjamin Bidwell
William J. Cameron
Silas D. Case
William H. Darby
Francis M. Dutton
Roswell R. Farnsworth
Benjamin F. Fredenburg
Jerome Gass
Bartholomew Griffin
Peter Gross
Francis E. Hays
John Hill
Preston Honsinger
William Hoover
William W. Hunter
Henry James
Edward L. Levitt

Andrew C. McFarland
James McFarland
George Menthon
Jacob Lorenzo Miller
George W. Parmalee
Joseph Parmalee
Oliver H. Perry
Thomas Ryan
Nelson B. Sherman
Charles Smith
James C. Smith
Joshua Theret
John Thompson
John Tozer
Charles A. Voorhies
William Wallenwine
Michael Waters
Thomas H. Way
John N. Wilson

Troop D

Captain George A. Armstrong
1st Lieutenant John Quincey Adams Sessions
2nd Lieutenant Edwin Knight

Sergeants

Commissary Sergeant Daniel W. Dunnett

Henry D. Benham
George Ferris

Otis W. Carpenter
Henry F. Thomas

Corporals

Hiram J. Covey
Wallace McArthur
George E. Van Ness

Charles H. Holmes
John L. Milbourn
Isaac Wilcox

Martin Karcher
George A. Powers

Blacksmith Levant C. DeWolf
Bugler Charles Hance
Farrier Joel L. Migrants
Saddler Eliseph A. Preston
Bugler Joseph W. Reed

Privates

William H. Adams
Frederick Bush
Peter Compau
Ephraim Degraw
Ralph L. Disbrow
George W. Dobson
Franklin R. Donaldson
William F. Drier
Daniel Eldrich
Clark Esmond
Albert Fordham
John M. Fordham
Joseph S. Gibbs
George W. Gilbert
Lewis S. Goshorn
James A. Grant

Henry Haines
Daniel L. Hale
George I. Hale
Hobert P. Hartland
Joseph N. Hawkins
Levi M. Hill
Russell Hodges
Orlando D. Jackson
David Jones
Jehiel Karcher
Michael Keenan
Adelbert Kent
Charles F. Kinney
George I. Mason
John L. McNally
William H. Migrants

Frank Milbourn
William Milbourn
Joseph Moreau
Salem E. Pettibone
Orange Pickett
William H. Pollard
Peter B. Polmateer
William Price
Chauncy Reynolds
Abram Smoke
Benjamin Sprague
Henry Thompson
David Turner
David Vroorman
William H. Wait

Troop E

Captain Wellington Willits
1st Lieutenant John A. Clark

Sergeants

1st Sergeant William H. Fisher

John Burnham	Henry Canfield	Hamilton A. Gates
Rufus J. Neal	Daniel O. Vaughn	

Corporals

Francis P. Bates	Franklin B. Clark
Walden W. Raymond	Luther F. Todd

Blacksmith Isaac N. Clark
Farrier Arthur Kemp
Saddler Thomas S. Smith

Privates

William H. Arsnoe	James Lowell
Eli Berleson	Christopher J. McClain
James L. Chrysler	Harmon Nay
Charles Cliff	Orville Parmenter
Amherst H. Dickinson	Richard Phillips
Milton M. Dillon	James B. Robinson
Samuel Eberly	Albert O. Simonds
Charles O. Finch	William Smith
Robert Finch	Joseph Stanford
Thomas Finney	Jacob Story
John Guthrie	John Thomas
Eugene Harkness	John F. Van Orden
Horace Hopkins	Richard Whalen
Barnum B. House	Lewis Wilber
Michael Keating	James Willett
Vincent King	Rees Williams

Troop F

1st Lieutenant James L. Carpenter
2nd Lieutenant Winchester T. Dodge

Sergeants

1st Sergeant Harlan B. Cochran
Commissary Sergeant Isaac Van Vleet
Quartermaster Sergeant Andrew N. Buck

Charles E. Miner
Harmon Smith

Irving Rose
Henry J. Wright

Corporals

James Livingston
Almon W. Warner

William Phelps
Charles P. White

Farrier Porter Brown

Privates

George N. Austin
Harlan Bedell
James T. Bedell
Moses Bedell
John Bitley
Charles Dopp
Nelson Gavely
George A. Godsmark
Benson Gray
Robert Hoag

Robert S. Klac
George W. Lundy
Thomas S. Mercer
Jacob Paule
Frank Prescott
William H. Scott
William Tracey
Royal S. Wilson
Warren J. Wolcott

Troop G

Captain Bradley Martin Thompson
1st Lieutenant Joseph J. Newman

Sergeants

1st Sergeant Lewis Carson
Commissary Sergeant Butler S. Tubbs
Quartermaster Sergeant Leonard L. How

John S. Gates   George S. Phillips   Irvin Wellman

Corporals

William C. Barden   Francis H. Cunningham   Martin R. Delameter
Peter Filben   Alanson J. McCarn   Nathaniel Whiting

Blacksmith William W. Bartholomew

Privates

Zephamiah Ackley
Irving W. Bennett
Alfred W. Churchill
Nehemiah L. Courter
Ira Dutton
James Elder
Owen Filben
Amos Finch
Randall Hart
Samuel Hascall
Adam Heckman
George Henderson
Phelix Henon

John Huxley
James Isham
Juman H. Johnson
James P. Kimball
Lewis Mathison
Thomas Mottley
Jacob Rhodes
Luther D. Sheldon
Freeman Spear
James Town
Andrew J. Wagoner
Henry Wetherbee
Benjamin Wilds

Troop H

Captain Richard Douglass
1st Lieutenant David Sargeant
2nd Lieutenant John J. Hicks

Sergeants

1st Sergeant William H. Nichols
Quartermaster Sergeant John Lepper

Luke R. Haughey	Alfred Kemp	William Mesick
Samuel Post	Edwin C. Talcott	

Corporals

Edward Earl	Edward Lockwood	William H. McClary
Edward Mowry	Wilson Pace	

Privates

Henry Andrus	George Perry
James Cornell	Henry M. Reasner
Isaiah Crone	William H. Richards
James W. Deyo	Henry D. Samples
Josiah B. Firman	Perry W. Smith
William Fisher	John Stewart
Bradley Knapp	Irvin Teneyck
Charles S. Mason	Florence J. Welch

Troop I

2nd Lieutenant William E. Harrington

Sergeants

1st Sergeant John B. Masten
Quartermaster Sergeant Andrew Westcott

Alexander Laird	Stephen McCleary
Arthur D. Nolan	Henry Swoords

Corporals

William Butcher	James Jackson	Griffin Powers
Thomas Pulling	William Russel	Squire Williams

Blacksmith Zenus Parsons

Privates

John Bell	Stephen L. Mosher
Reuben Bennett	George W. Popple
James Carney	Jesse Roberts
John Cupples	William H. Rogers
James Etheridge	William S. Ryan
Robert Hasty	Asa Sprague
Charles C. Henderson	Leman A. Sweezy
Willard J. Keith	Alphonso Wakefield
George McGinnis	Charles Wiley
John W. Monaghan	

Troop K

Captain Heman N. Moore
2nd Lieutenant Hiram J. Ingersoll

Sergeants

1st Sergeant Isaac W. Lucas
Commissary Sergeant Hassan A. Buck
Quartermaster Sergeant Fitch M. Searle
James Campbell   Oscar W. Crofford

Corporal

Jacob R. Downer

Bugler Daniel Murphy

Privates

John K. Afton
Daniel H. Baker
Acil Champlin
Jonas Clark
Edgar M. Conley
Daniel Dann
William Duzenbury
Morris England
Alvin Evans
George S. Harris
John Andrew Jackson Henderson
Eber E. Ingledue

Daniel Kreps
Ogden B. Laverty
Merritt Lewis
Narvy Powers
Jacob Ruger
Eli Smith
John Tompkins
David Tracey
Philip Tubbs
William A. Wright
Chauncy Youngs

Appendix G

Confederate Staffs

June 30, 1863

Stuart's Division

Major General James Ewell Brown Stuart – Commanding
Major Norman R. Fitzhugh – Quartermaster
Major W. J. Johnson – Chief Commissary
Major Henry B. McClellan – Assistant Adjutant General
Major Andrew Reid Venable – Assistant Adjutant General
Surgeon Tacott Eliason – Chief Surgeon
Captain William Willis Blackford – Chief Engineer
Captain J. L. Clarke – Aide-de-Camp
Captain John Esten Cooke – Chief of Ordnance
Captain J. M. Hanger – Assistant Quartermaster
1st Lieutenant Chiswell Dabney – Aide-de-Camp
Lieutenant Theodore S. Garnett – Aide-de-Camp

Acting Sergeant S. A. Nelson – Orderly (Company B, 4th Virginia)
Private E. D. Cole – Orderly (Company H, 15th Virginia)
Private Frank H. Deane – Orderly (Company E, 4th Virginia)
Private A. H. Ellis – Orderly (Company H, 13th Virginia)
Private Robert W. Goode – Orderly (Company G, 1st Virginia)
Private William P. Jones – Orderly (Company E, 9th Virginia)
Private W. T. Thompson – Orderly (Company G, 13th Virginia)
Private Benjamin F. Weller – Orderly (Company E, 1st Virginia)
Private George N. Woodbridge – Orderly (Company E, 4th Virginia)

Hampton's Brigade

Brigadier General Wade Hampton – Commanding
Surgeon Benjamin Walter Taylor – Chief Surgeon
Captain Theodore C. Barker – Assistant Adjutant General
Lieutenant Wade Hampton. Jr. – Aide-de-Camp
Lieutenant William Preston Hampton – Aide-de-Camp

Fitzhugh Lee's Brigade

Brigadier General Fitzhugh Lee – Commanding
Surgeon J. B. Fontaine – Chief Surgeon
Captain J. D. Ferguson – Assistant Adjutant General
Captain James Breckinridge (2nd Virginia)
Captain C. T. Litchfield (1st Virginia)
Captain Julius G. Tucker – Aide-de-Camp (Company E, 10th Virginia)
1st Lieutenant Henry C. Lee – Aide-de-Camp
Lieutenant Charles Minnegerode – Aide-de-Camp

Chambliss's Brigade

Colonel John Randolph Chambliss, Jr. – Commanding
Major Albert Gallatin Dade – Commissary of Subsistence
Lieutenant Walter B. Chambliss – Aide-de-Camp
Lieutenant Junius B. Jones – Aide-de-Camp

Appendix H

3rd Division Soldiers Detached
&
Serving in Other Commands

June 30, 1863

Captain

Harvey H. Vinton	M-6 Michigan	Absent Sick – Rockville, Md.

1st Lieutenants

Manning D. Birge	A-6 Michigan	Absent Sick – Washington, D. C.
Frederick A. Copeland	M-5 Michigan	Assustant Commissary of Subsistence– Gen. J. Copeland – Washington, D. C.
Phineas G. White	K-6 Michigan	Acting Assistant Quartermaster – Gen. J. Copeland – Washington, D. C.

2nd Lieutenant

Elias Stone	M-6 Michigan	Absent Sick – Rockville, Md.

Sergeants

George P. Barnes, Sr.	A-1 Ohio	Orderly – Arlington, Va.
Charles A. Phelps	G-5 New York	Scout

Corporals

Henry E. Davis	E-5 Michigan	Orderly – Gen. Alexander Hays – 3rd Division, II Corps
John J. Johnston	C-1 Ohio	Orderly – Gen. Alexander Hays – 3rd Division, II Corps
William R. Noble	E-5 Michigan	Orderly – Gen. Julius Stahel – Fairfax, Va.

Privates

Emory Abby	K-6 Michigan	Orderly – Gen. Joseph Copeland – Washington, D. C.
Elijah L. Bates	E-5 Michigan	Orderly – Gen. Alexander Hays – 3rd Division, II Corps

Privates *(continued)*

Jacob Bayhaw	C-1 Ohio	Orderly – Gen. Alexander Hays – 3rd Division, II Corps
George R. Beard	G-5 Michigan	Orderly – Gen. Julius Stahel – Fairfax, Va.
Jesse M. Bloomer	A-1 Ohio	Orderly – Arlington, Va.
Christian Briesh	K-5 Michigan	Orderly – Gen. Joseph Copeland – Washington, D. C.
Henry Brunner	M-1 W.Virginia	Orderly – Col. Percy Wyndham
Thomas Burroughs	G-1 Vermont	Orderly – Gen. John Slough – Alexandria, Va.
William H. Carpenter	K-7 Michigan	Orderly – Gen. William French – Harpers Ferry, W. Va.
Edward Carroll	K-7 Michigan	Orderly – Capt. George Meade – Army of Potomac
Enoch W. Chappell	G-7 Michigan	Orderly – Gen. Samuel Crawford – 3rd Division, V Corps
William P. Cleaveland	A-1 Ohio	Orderly – Arlington, Va.
John Coln	I-7 Michigan	Orderly – War Department – Washington, D. C.
John B. Creary	A-1 Ohio	Orderly – War Department – Washington, D.C.
Ulrich L. Crocker	M-6 Michigan	Orderly – Gen. Joseph Copeland – Washington, D. C.
David Cummins	I-5 Michigan	Orderly – Gen. Joseph Copeland – Washington, D. C.
William A. Denton	E-5 Michigan	Orderly – Gen. Alexander Hays – 3rd Division, II Corps
John Dresel	C-1 Ohio	Nurse – Cumberland, Md.
Albert Eaton	E-5 Michigan	Orderly – Gen. Alexander Hays – 3rd Division, II Corps
Cornelius Gavin	I-5 Michigan	Orderly – Gen. Joseph Copeland – Washington, D. C.
William S. Gordon	A-1 Ohio	Orderly – War Department – Washington, D. C.
Plinney A. Graves	F-5 New York	Orderly – Gen. Gustavus DeRussey – Washington, D. C.
Jacob Haist	D-6 Michigan	Orderly – War Department – Washington, D. C.
Able Hanes	E-5 Michigan	Orderly – Gen. Alexander Hays – 3rd Division, II Corps
John Wesley Harrod	C-1 Ohio	Orderly – Gen. Samuel Heintzelman Washington, D. C.
Albert Hirst	C-1 Ohio	Orderly – Gen. John Abercrombie – Washington, D. C.
Abram Hoagland	F-7 Michigan	Orderly – Alexandria, Va.

Privates *(continued)*

Ambrose Jeffries	C-1 Ohio	Orderly – Gen. Alexander Hays – 3rd Division, II Corps
Charles H. Jessup	F-7 Michigan	Orderly – Alexandria, Va.
John Jordan	D-6 Michigan	Orderly – War Department – Washington, D. C.
John H. Keller	F-7 Michigan	Orderly – Arlington, Va.
Hezekiah C. Kirkham	E-5 Michigan	Orderly – Gen. James Blunt – Kansas
William R. McClure	G-1 W. Virginia	Orderly – Col. Charles Coster – 2 Division, 1 Brigade, XI Corps
Dewitt C. Meech	F-7 Michigan	Orderly – Arlington, Va.
Truman Osgood	D-6 Michigan	Orderly – War Department – Washington, D. C.
James C. Parsons	I-6 Michigan	Orderly – Gen. Joseph Copeland – Washington, D. C.
Henry L. Patterson	B-1 Vermont	Orderly – Gen. John Slough – Alexandria, Va.
James W. Pease	D-6 Michigan	Orderly – War Department – Washington, D. C.
John Peterman	C-1 Ohio	Orderly – Gen. Alexander Hays – 3rd Division, II Corps
Joseph Powers	K-7 Michigan	Orderly – Gen. William French – Harpers Ferry, W. Va.
Miles Riley	F-7 Michigan	Orderly – Arlington, Va.
Wyman A. Robinson	A-1 Vermont	Orderly – Gen. John Slough – Alexandria, Va.
Bryant Rudd	C-7 Michigan	Orderly – Gen. Samuel Crawford – 3rd Division, V Corps
David Sanborn	C-1 Vermont	Orderly – Gen Erastus Tyler – Baltimore, Md.
Henry Seymour	F-7 Michigan	Orderly – Arlington, Va.
Edward Simpson	D-6 Michigan	Orderly – War Department – Washington, D. C.
Clark H. Stewart	I-7 Michigan	Orderly – Arlington, Va.
Jonas L. Thornton	A-1 Ohio	Orderly – Gen. Alexander Hays – 3rd Division, II Corps
Henry C. Tidy	A-1 Ohio	Orderly – Arlington, Va.
Furman Upham	C-1 Ohio	Orderly – Gen Erastus Tyler – Baltimore, Md.
Ernest Von Daniels	C-7 Michigan	Orderly – Gen. Samuel Crawford – 3rd Division, V Corps
William Wilkinson	C-1 Ohio	Orderly – Gen. John Abercrombie – Washington, D. C.
Henry Willhauck	C-1 Ohio	Orderly – Gen. John Abercrombie – Washington, D. C.

5th Michigan Cavalry
(with wagon train)

Major Crawley P. Dake – Commanding
Private Peter B. Ives (Major Dake's Orderly)

Troop C

Captain Horace W. Dodge

Sergeants

1st Sergeant Frederick Nims
Commissary Sergeant John A. Gaylord
Quartermaster Sergeant Pharo Gray

Henry D. Gale	Elijah J. Goodell
Elliott Stedman	Egbert Webb

Corporals

William E. Alexander	Phillip Bisbie	Victor E. Comfle
Reuben K. Dockham	Matthew Gramlich	John E. Hobbs
William Kirchmaier	Joseph Miller	

Bugler Orange Berdan
Blacksmith George Folton
Saddler William R. Frasier
Blacksmith Abraham Masten

Privates

John Anderhall	Martin Goodell	Henry C. Palmer
David Baldwin	George W. Graham	William Plues
Charles N. Blackman	Richard Hodges	Augustine Revard
Lewis Boda	Andrew Johnston	Maro Robinson
Alexander Brown	George Johnston	John Ronan
William Carroll	Frederick Lafleur	Xavier Salgat
Godfrey Cauchee	John G. Lutz	William P. Snow
Andrew J. Cole	John J. Marker	Henry Snowball
Richard N. Collins	John D. Marten	Solomon Stegril
Augustus F. Corser	George W. Mason	William H. Stoddard
Francis Decker	Grice Mathewson	George P. Townsend
Lewis Derwin	John D. McIntyre	Oliver M. Warner
Samuel K. Essler	August Mish	Rollin S. Webb
John R. Folton	Henry E. Moore	William W. Whiting
George Geigrich		

Troop L

1st Lieutenant Benjamin Franklin Axtell
2nd Lieutenant Robert C. Wallace

Sergeants

1st Sergeant James Allen
Commissary Sergeant Joseph S. Davisson

David W. Fansher	Edwin H. Hawley	Daniel Miller
Albert Utley Noble	Albert H. Randall	

Corporals

Henry J. Brownell	Samuel E. Gustin	Alonzo Haskin
Sylvanus A. Morton	Thomas Phelan	Lewis E. Tripp

Saddler John Allen
Blacksmith William F. Barrows
Blacksmith Patrick Dugan
Blacksmith George H. Struble

Privates

Lewis Adam	Christopher P. Dormond	Christopher Maguire
Richard W. Armstrong	Charles Dunn	Egbert Mayo
Warren Armstrong	Samuel Earle	Hiram McKeel
Flavius Baldwin	Herbert Ege	John Mowry
Walter Bennett	William J. Epperson	Hiram W. Nourse
Watson Boyles	George Esch	Oliver H. Perry
Frank M. Brown	David Fineout	Michael Powers
Peter Burbank	George W. Fish	Floyd Rockwell
Milton S. Burson	Addison French	William Sloan
Samuel Case	George Gerould	Richard Townsend
John Castner	John G. Glover, Jr.	Garrett Van Bree
Richard Clifford	Freeman B. Hill	William Warren
Alfred R. Colton	Leander W. Kennedy	Zaphna Welton
Manlius Cross	James C. Kennicut	Henry S. Winks
John W. Cummins	Leonard Leland	George Wixsom
John E. Davis	George W. Lusk	John Wright
John Dixon		

Bibliography

Adjutant General's Office. *Official Army Register of the Volunteer Force of the United States Army for the Years 1861, '62, '63, '64, '65.* 8 volumes + Index. Gaithersburg, Md.: Ron R. Van Sickle Military Books, 1987.

Altshuler, Constance Wynn. *Cavalry Yellow & Infantry Blue: Army Officers in Arizona Between 1851 and 1886.* Arizona: Arizona Historical Society, 1991.

Anthony, William. *Anthony's History of the Battle of Hanover (York County, Pennsylvania) Tuesday, June 30, 1863.* Hanover, Pa.: William Anthony, 1945.

Balfour, Daniel T. *13th Virginia Cavalry.* Lynchburg, Va.: H. E. Howard, Inc., 1986.

Bates, Samuel P. *A History of Cumberland, Franklin and Adams Counties.* Chicago: Warner Beers & Co., 1886.

Bates, Samuel P. *History of Pennsylvania Volunteers, 1861-5.* 5 volumes. Harrisburg: B. Singerly, 1871.

Bates, Samuel P. *Martial Deeds of Pennsylvania.* Philadelphia: T. H. Davis & Co., 1876.

Beale, George W. *A Lieutenant of Cavalry in Lee's Army.* Boston: Gorham Press, 1918.

Beale, Richard L. T. *History of the Ninth Virginia Cavalry.* Richmond: B. F. Johnson Publishing Co., 1899.

Beaudry, Louis N. *War Journal of Louis N. Beaudry, Fifth New York Cavalry.* Jefferson, N.C.: McFarland & Co., Inc., 1996.

Benedict, G. G. *Vermont in the Civil War, 1861 - 1865.* 2 volumes. Burlington, Vt.: Free Press Association, 1889.

Bliss, George N. *Duffié and the Monument to His Memory.* Providence: privately printed, 1890.

Bliss, George N. *The First Rhode Island Cavalry at Middleburg, Va., June 17, 1863.* Providence: privately printed, 1911.

Boatner, Mark Mayo III. *The Civil War Dictionary.* New York: David McKay Company, Inc., 1959.

Borcke, Heros Von, and Justus Scheibert. *The Great Cavalry Battle of Brandy Station, 9 June 1863.* Winston-Salem, N.C.: Palaemon Press Ltd., 1976.

Boudrye, Louis N. *Historic Records of the Fifth New York Cavalry, First Ira Harris Guard.* Albany: S. R. Gray, 1865.

Brackett, Albert G. *History of the United States Cavalry.* New York: Harper & Brothers, 1865.

Burgess, Milton V. *David Gregg, Pennsylvania Cavalryman.* State College, Pa.: published by author, 1984.

Busey, John W. *The Last Full Measure: Burials in the Soldiers' National Cemetery at Gettysburg.* Hightstown, N.J.: Longstreet House, 1988.

Busey John W. *These Honored Dead: Union Casualties at Gettysburg.* Hightstown, N.J.: Longstreet House, 1988.

Busey, John W., and David G. Martin. *Regimental Strengths and Losses at Gettysburg.* Hightstown, N.J.: Longstreet House, 1994.

Carroll, John M. *Custer in the Civil War: His Unfinished Memoirs.* San Rafael, Calif.: Presidio Press, 1977.

Carter, William H. *From Yorktown to Santiago with the Sixth U.S. Cavalry.* Baltimore, Md.: Lord Baltimore Press, 1900.

Chamber of Commerce, Publisher. *Encounter at Hanover: Prelude to Gettysburg.* Hanover, Pa.: Hanover Chamber of Commerce, 1963.

Coco, Gregory A. *A Vast Sea of Misery: A History and Guide to the Union and Confederate Field Hospitals at Gettysburg, July 1 – November 20, 1863.* Gettysburg: Thomas Publications, 1988.

Coddington, Edwin B. *The Gettysburg Campaign, A Study in Command.* New York: Charles Scribner's Sons, 1968.

Coffin, Howard. *Full Duty: Vermonters in the Civil War.* Woodstock, Vt.: The Countryman Press, Inc., 1993.

Cullum, George W. *Biographical Register of the Officers and Graduates of the U.S. Military Academy, at West Point, N.Y.* 3 volumes. Boston: Houghton Mifflin & Company, 1891.

Curry, William L., compiler. *Four Years in the Saddle: History of the First Regiment Ohio Volunteer Cavalry.* Columbus, Ohio: 1898.

Davenport, Alfred. *Camp and Field: Life of the Fifth New York Volunteer Infantry.* New York: Dick & Fitzgerald, 1879.

Davis, Burke. *Jeb Stuart: The Last Cavalier.* New York: Bonanza Books, 1957.

Dellenbaugh, Frederick S. *George Armstrong Custer.* New York: Macmillan Company, 1917.

Denison, Frederic. *Sabres and Spurs: The First Regiment Rhode Island Cavalry in the Civil War, 1861-1865.* Central Falls, R.I.: First Rhode Island Cavalry Veteran Association, 1876.

Downey, Fairfax. *Clash of Cavalry: The Battle of Brandy Station.* New York: David McKay Company, Inc., 1959.

Driver, Robert J. Jr. *1st Virginia Cavalry.* Lynchburg, Va.: H. E. Howard, Inc., 1991.

Driver, Robert J., Jr. *5th Virginia Cavalry.* Lynchburg, Va.: H. E. Howard, Inc., 1997.

Driver, Robert J., Jr. *13th Virginia Cavalry.* Lynchburg, Va.: H. E. Howard, Inc., 1992.

Driver, Robert J., Jr., and H. E. Howard. *2nd Virginia Cavalry.* Lynchburg, Va.: H. E. Howard, Inc., 1995.

Dyer, Frederick H. *A Compendium of the War of the Rebellion.* 3 volumes. New York: Yoseloff, 1959.

Fox, William F., editor. *New York at Gettysburg.* 3 volumes. Albany, N.Y.: J. B. Lyon Company, 1902.

Frassanito, William A. *The Gettysburg Bicentennial Album.* Gettysburg: The Gettysburg Bicentennial Committee, 1987.

Genco, James G. *Arming Michigan's Regiments, 1862 - 1864.* N.p., n.d.

Gillespie, Samuel L. ("Lovejoy"). *A History of Company A, First Ohio Cavalry, 1861-1865.* Washington Court House, Ohio: Press of Ohio State Register, 1898.

Glazier, Willard. *Three Years in the Federal Cavalry.* New York: R. H. Ferguson & Company, 1870.

Green, Charles O. *An Incident in the Battle of Middleburg, Va., June 17, 1863.* Providence: privately printed, 1911.

Hahn, Thomas F. *Towpath Guide to the C & O Canal, Section Two, Seneca to Harpers Ferry*. Shepherdstown, W.Va.: American Canal and Transportation Center, 1977.

Harris, Samuel. *Personal Reminiscences of Samuel Harris*. Chicago: Rogerson Press, 1897.

Heitman, Francis B. *Historical Register and Dictionary of the United States Army, from its Organization, September 29, 1789, to March 2, 1903*. 2 volumes. Washington, D.C.: Government Printing Office, 1903.

Huey, Pennock. *A True History of the Charge of the Eighth Pennsylvania Cavalry at Chancellorsville*. Philadelphia: Porter & Coates, 1885.

Hunt, Roger D., and Jack R. Brown. *Brevet Brigadier Generals in Blue*. Gaithersburg, Md.: Olde Soldier Books, 1990.

Isham, Asa B. *An Historical Sketch of the Seventh Regiment Michigan Volunteer Cavalry from Its Organization, in 1862, to Its Muster Out, in 1865*. New York: Town Topics Publishing, 1893.

Jackson, H. Nelson, compiler. *Dedication of the Statue to Brevet Major-General William Wells and the Officers and Men of the First Regiment Vermont Cavalry*. Privately printed, 1914.

Johnson, James R., and Alfred H. Bill. *Horsemen Blue and Gray*. New York: Oxford University Press, 1960.

Johnson, Robert U., and Clarence C. Buel, editors. *Battles and Leaders of the Civil War, Being for the Most Part Contributions by Union and Confederate Officers, Based Upon "The Century War Series."* 4 volumes. New York: Century Company, 1884-89.

Kidd, James H. *Personal Recollections of a Cavalryman*. Ionia, Mich.: Sentinel Printing, 1908.

Kinsley, D. A. *Favor the Bold*. 2 volumes. New York: Holt, Rinehart and Winston, 1967.

Krick, Robert K. *9th Virginia Cavalry*. Lynchburg, Va.: H. E. Howard, Inc., 1982.

Krick, Robert K. *Lee's Colonels: A Biographical Register of the Field Officers of the Army of Northern Virginia*. Dayton, Ohio: Morningside House, Inc., 1992.

Krick, Robert K. *The Gettysburg Death Roster: The Confederate Dead at Gettysburg.* Dayton: Morningside Press, 1985.

Ladd, David L., and Audrey J., editors. *The Bachelder Papers.* 3 volumes. Dayton, Ohio: Morningside House, Inc., 1994.

Lang, Theodore F. *Loyal West Virginia from 1861 to 1865.* Baltimore: The Deutsch Publishing Company, 1895.

Lee, William O., compiler. *Personal and Historical Sketches and Facial History of and by Members of the Seventh Regiment Michigan Volunteer Cavalry, 1862-1865.* Detroit: Ralston-Stroup Printing Company, 1904.

Longacre, Edward G. *The Cavalry at Gettysburg: A Tactical Study of Mounted Operations during the Civil War's Pivotal Campaign 9 June-14 July 1863.* Cranbury, N.J.: Associated University Press, 1986.

Longacre, Edward G. *Custer and His Wolverines: The Michigan Cavalry Brigade 1861 – 1865.* Conshohocken, Pa.: Combined Publishing, 1997.

Martin, Samuel J. *"Kill-Cavalry:" Sherman's Merchant of Terror.* Madison, N.J.: Fairleigh Dickinson University Press, 1996.

McClellan, Henry B. *The Life and Campaigns of Major General J. E. B. Stuart.* Boston: Houghton Mifflin & Co., 1885.

McClure, Alexander K. Compiler. *Annals of the War, Written by Leading Participants, North and South.* Philadelphia: 1879.

Meade, George Gordon. *With Meade at Gettysburg.* Philadelphia: John C. Winston Company, 1930.

Merington, Marguerite, editor. *The Custer Story: The Life and Intimate Letters of General George A. Custer and His Wife Elizabeth.* New York: Devin-Adair, 1950.

Meyer, Henry C. *Civil War Experiences Under Bayard, Gregg, Kilpatrick, Custer, Raulston, and Newberry, 1862, 1863, 1864.* New York: Knickerbocker Press, 1911.

Michigan at Gettysburg, July 1st, 2nd and 3rd, 1863. Detroit: Winn & Hammond, 1889.

Miller, Francis Trevelyan, editor. *The Photographic History of the Civil War.* 10 volumes. New York: The Review of Reviews Co., 1912.

Monaghan, Jay. *Custer: The Life of General George Armstrong Custer.* Boston: Little Brown Company, 1959.

Moore, James. *Kilpatrick and Our Cavalry.* New York: W. J. Widdleton, 1865.

Nanzig, Thomas P. *3rd Virginia Cavalry.* Lynchburg, Va.: H. E. Howard, Inc., 1989.

Nesbitt, Mark. *Saber and Scapegoat: J. E. B. Stuart and the Gettysburg Controversy.* Mechanicsburg, Pa.: Stackpole Books, 1994.

Nichols, James L. *General Fitzhugh Lee, A Biography.* Lynchburg, Va.: H. E. Howard, 1989.

Nicholson, John P. *Pennsylvania at Gettysburg: Ceremonies at the Dedication of the Monuments Erected by the Commonwealth of Pennsylvania to Major General George G. Meade, Major General Winfield S. Hancock, Major General John F. Reynolds and to Mark the Positions of the Pennsylvania Commands Engaged in the Battle,* 2 volumes. Harrisburg: Wm. Stanley Ray, State Printers, 1893.

O'Neill, Robert F., Jr. *The Cavalry Battles of Aldie, Middleburg and Upperville, June 10-27, 1863.* Lynchburg, Va.: H. E. Howard, Inc., 1993.

Phisterer, Frederick. *New York in the War of the Rebellion, 1861-1865.* 5 volumes. Albany: J. B. Lyon Company, 1912.

Powell, William H. *The Fifth Army Corps (Army of the Potomac), A Record of Operations During the Civil War in the United States of America, 1861-1865.* New York: G. P. Putnam's Sons, 1896.

Powell, William H., editor. *Officers of the Army and Navy (Volunteer) Who Served in the Civil War.* Philadelphia, 1893.

Preston, Noble D. *History of the Tenth Regiment of Cavalry, New York State Volunteers, August 1861, to August, 1865.* New York: D. Appleton & Company, 1892.

Price, George F. *Across the Continent with the Fifth Cavalry.* New York: Antiquarian Press Ltd., 1959.

Publication Committee of the Regimental Association, *History of the Eighteenth Regiment of Cavalry, Pennsylvania Volunteers (163d Regiment of the Line) 1862-1865.* New York: Wynkoop, Hallenbeck, Crawford, 1909.

Pyne, Henry R. *The History of the First New Jersey Cavalry: Sixteenth Regiment, New Jersey Volunteers.* Trenton: J. A. Beecher, 1871.

Raus, Edmund J., Jr. *A Generation on the March: The Union Army at Gettysburg.* Lynchburg, Va.: H. E. Howard, Inc., 1987.

Rea, Lilian, editor. *War Record and Personal Experiences of Walter Raleigh Robbins, from April 22, 1861, to August 4, 1865.* Chicago: privately printed, 1923.

Record of Service of Michigan Volunteers in the Civil War 1861 – 1865, First Michigan Cavalry. Kalamazoo: Ihling Bros. & Everard.

Record of Service of Michigan Volunteers in the Civil War 1861 – 1865, Fifth Michigan Cavalry. Kalamazoo: Ihling Bros. & Everard.

Record of Service of Michigan Volunteers in the Civil War 1861 – 1865, Sixth Michigan Cavalry. Kalamazoo: Ihling Bros. & Everard.

Record of Service of Michigan Volunteers in the Civil War 1861 – 1865, Seventh Michigan Cavalry. Kalamazoo: Ihling Bros. & Everard.

Reid, Whitelaw. Ohio in the War: Her Statesman, Generals and Soldiers. 2 volumes. Cincinnati: The Robert Clarke Company, 1895.

Rhodes, Charles D. *History of the Cavalry of the Army of the Potomac, Including that of the Army of Virginia (Pope's) and Also the History of the Operations of the Federal Cavalry in West Virginia During the War.* Kansas City, Mo.: Hudson-Kimberly Publishing Company, 1900.

Robertson, Jno., compiler. *Michigan in the War.* Lansing, Mich.: W. S. George & Co., 1880.

Rodenbough, Theophilus F. *From Everglade to Cañon with the Second Dragoons.* New York: D. Van Nostrand, 1875.

Rummel, George A. III. *72 Days at Gettysburg: Organization of the 10th Regiment, New York Volunteer Cavalry.* Shippensburg, Pa.: White Mane Publishing Company, 1997.

Schildt, John W. *Roads to Gettysburg.* Parsons, W.Va.: McClain Printing Company, 1978.

Sergent, Mary Elizabeth. *They Lie Forgotten.* Middletown, N.Y.: The Prior King Press, 1986.

Stackpole, Edward J. *From Cedar Mountain to Antietam, August-September, 1862.* Harrisburg: The Stackpole Company, 1959.

Starr, Stephen Z. *The Union Cavalry in the Civil War*. 3 volumes. Baton Rouge: Louisiana State University Press, 1979.

Stiles, Kenneth L. *4th Virginia Cavalry*. Lynchburg, Va.: H. E. Howard, Inc., 1985.

Stryker, William S., compiler. *Record of Officers and Men of New Jersey in the Civil War, 1861–1865*. 2 volumes. Trenton: John L. Murphy, 1876.

Tobie, Edward P. *History of the 1st Maine Cavalry, 1861 – 1865*. Boston: Press of Emery & Hughes, 1887.

Toombs, Samuel. *New Jersey Troops in the Gettysburg Campaign*. Orange, N.J.: The Evening Mail Publishing House, 1888.

Tousey, Thomas G. *Military History of Carlisle and Carlisle Barracks*. Richmond: The Dietz Press, 1939.

United States War Department. *The War of the Rebellion: A Compilation of the Official Records of the Union and Confederate Armies*. Volume 27, Parts 1-3. Washington, D.C.: Government Printing Office, 1889.

Urwin, Gregory J. W. *Custer Victorious: The Civil War Battles of General George Armstrong Custer*. Rutherford, N.J.: Fairleigh Dickinson University Press, 1983.

Warner, Ezra J. *Generals in Blue: Lives of the Union Commanders*. Baton Rouge: Louisiana State University Press, 1964.

Warner, Ezra J. *Confederate Generals in Gray: Lives of the Confederate Commanders*. Baton Rouge: Louisiana State University Press, 1959.

Wellman, Manly Wade. *Giant in Gray: A Biography of Wade Hampton of South Carolina*. Dayton, Ohio: Press of Morningside Bookshop, 1988.

Whittaker, Frederick. *A Complete Life of Gen. George A. Custer*. New York: Sheldon & Co., 1876.

Index

di Cesnola, Louis Palma, 22, 28-29, 36-38, 41, 103, 147

Dill House, 75-76

Dillsburg, Pa., 304-06, 312, 317, 319-20, 322, 336

Dimmick, Eugene Dumont, 171-72, 193n, 212-14, 239, 270, 297, 318

Dodge, Horace W., 228

Dougherty, James, 314, 324n

Douglass, Richard, 291

Dover, Pa., 302-04, 307, 319, 321

Drake, James Henry, 161, 185

Dresher, William, 205

Drew, George Augustus, 331-32

Drummond, Thomas, 24

Duffié, Alfred Napoleon Alexander, 22, 28-36, 41, 43, 50n-51n

Duggan, Andrew W., 350

Duttera, John, 197

E

Early, Jubal Anderson, 301-03, 322, 323n, 330, 336

Eckert, Henry C., 261

Eckert's Concert Hall, 265

Edson, Ptolemy, 265

Edwards Ferry, Md., 62-64, 68, 70, 91, 146

Edwards, Samuel William, 67

Eggleston, Beroth Bullard, 120

Elder, Samuel Sherer, 120, 169-70, 204, 224, 246, 255, 269-70, 274-75, 288-90, 321-22, 327, 363-64, 372, 374

Emmanuel Reformed Church, 4, 199, 299

Emmitsburg, Md., 77, 95, 109, 118, 122, 126, 128, 131-32, 141n

Estes, Llewellyn Garrish, 339-43

Evans, Peter Gustavus, 32

Ewell, Richard Stoddert, 6, 215, 297, 301, 307, 311-12, 322, 331, 333, 336-37, 372

Ewen, John, 308-09, 323n

F

Fairfax Court House, Va., 34-35, 43, 91, 102

Fairfield, Pa., 54

Falling Waters, Md., 281, 332, 348

Farley, Charles J., 268, 270, 292n

Farnsworth, Elon John, 24, 42, 53, 58-60, 62, 79n, 93, 103, 105, 107-11, 117-21, 132-34, 139-40, 168-69, 172, 181, 200, 202-05, 222-23, 227, 230, 235, 244, 246, 248, 250, 254-56, 259, 267-70, 272, 274, 290, 292n, 295, 298, 318, 320, 322, 325, 327, 331, 335, 341, 346, 363-64, 379-82

Farnsworth, John Franklin, 29, 43, 50n, 53, 59

Fauquier County, Va., 187

Felty, John , 345, 347-49, 355, 358-60, 363-68, 374-75

Ferebee, Dennis Dozier, 32

Finley, Henry Hamilton, 130

Fisher, George P., 156

Fisher's Hill, Battle of, 218n

Flickinger Foundry, 263, 265, 299

Flint River, Ga., 340

Folger, Abram, 251-53

Forney, Karl, 242, 244, 260, 268

Fort Washington, Pa., 102

Fought, Joseph, 60, 122, 357

Frederick County, Md., 6-7, 73, 78, 89, 92, 117, 123, 140

Frederick, Md., 7, 46, 59-60, 66, 71-78, 83, 85, 87-89, 91-94, 97, 99, 102-04, 107,